PYTHON FOR ACCOUNTING AND FINANCE

Python for Accounting and Finance: A Mind-Mapping Approach is an innovative textbook written for accounting and finance students and professionals with no prior coding experience. It introduces Python programming through a mind-mapping approach that presents complex concepts in a clear and structured way to support understanding and retention.

This book is organised into four parts: Python Basics, Data Analysis and Visualisation, Automation, and Machine Learning. It places programming within practical accounting and finance contexts so that learners can see the direct application of coding in their field. This textbook uses mind maps as a core instructional method. These visual diagrams show programming concepts and their connections, helping learners to understand, organise, and recall information, particularly those who learn through visual representation.

Enhanced with Google Colab notebooks, this book creates a highly supportive learning experience, equipping students of accounting and finance with essential programming skills for their speciality.

Michael Xin Guo is Senior Lecturer at the University of the West of Scotland and Senior Fellow of the Higher Education Academy.

PYTHON FOR ACCOUNTING AND FINANCE

A Mind-Mapping Approach

Michael Xin Guo

Routledge
Taylor & Francis Group
LONDON AND NEW YORK

Designed cover image: DrAfter123/Getty Images®

First published 2026
by Routledge
4 Park Square, Milton Park, Abingdon, Oxon OX14 4RN

and by Routledge
605 Third Avenue, New York, NY 10158

Routledge is an imprint of the Taylor & Francis Group, an informa business

British Library Cataloguing-in-Publication Data
A catalogue record for this book is available from the British Library

ISBN: 978-1-041-10814-6 (hbk)
ISBN: 978-1-041-10813-9 (pbk)
ISBN: 978-1-003-65696-8 (ebk)

DOI: 10.4324/9781003656968

Typeset in Optima
by codeMantra

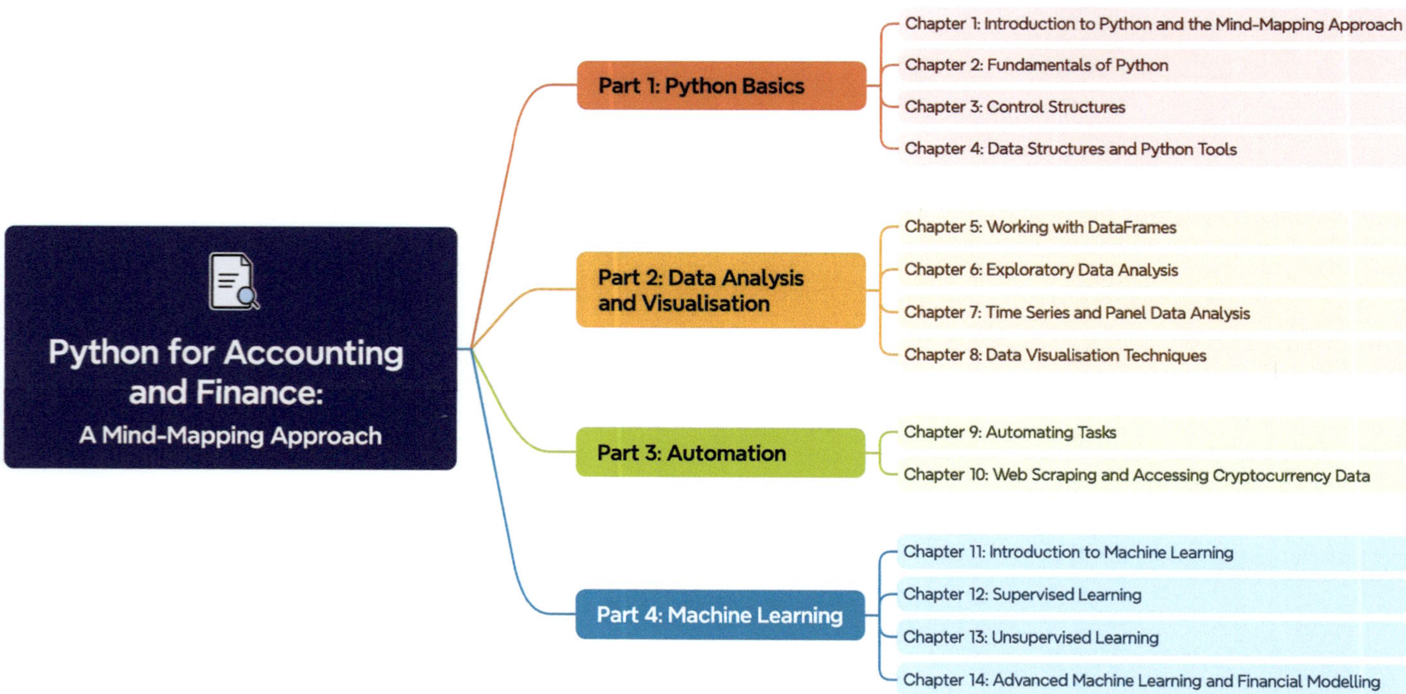

Python for Accounting and Finance:
A Mind-Mapping Approach
Part 1: Python Basics
Chapter 1: Introduction to Python and the Mind-Mapping Approach
Chapter 2: Fundamentals of Python
Chapter 3: Control Structures
Chapter 4: Data Structures and Python Tools
Part 2: Data Analysis and Visualisation
Chapter 5: Working with DataFrames
Chapter 6: Exploratory Data Analysis
Chapter 7: Time Series and Panel Data Analysis
Chapter 8: Data Visualisation Techniques
Part 3: Automation
Chapter 9: Automating Tasks
Chapter 10: Web Scraping and Accessing Cryptocurrency Data
Part 4: Machine Learning
Chapter 11: Introduction to Machine Learning
Chapter 12: Supervised Learning
Chapter 13: Unsupervised Learning
Chapter 14: Advanced Machine Learning and Financial Modelling

CONTENTS

FIGURES

CONTENTS

ACKNOWLEDGEMENTS

This book has benefitted from the use of the following tools:

Xmind: All mind maps in this textbook were created using Xmind. The software provided an effective method for organising and presenting ideas visually, contributing to the structure and clarity of the content.

Google Colab: Google Colab was used as the primary coding environment for developing and running Python examples in this textbook. Its cloud-based platform allowed code execution without local installation.

GitHub: All Python code examples and chapter quiz questions are hosted on GitHub. The platform enables reader access to the code and supports engagement with the material. GitHub Pages sites created by the author are used to demonstrate web scraping for educational purposes.

CoinGecko: Cryptocurrency price data used in this textbook were obtained via the CoinGecko API for educational illustration. The data are reproduced in accordance with CoinGecko's API Terms of Use.

The author gratefully acknowledges the support provided by these tools and platforms in the development of this textbook.

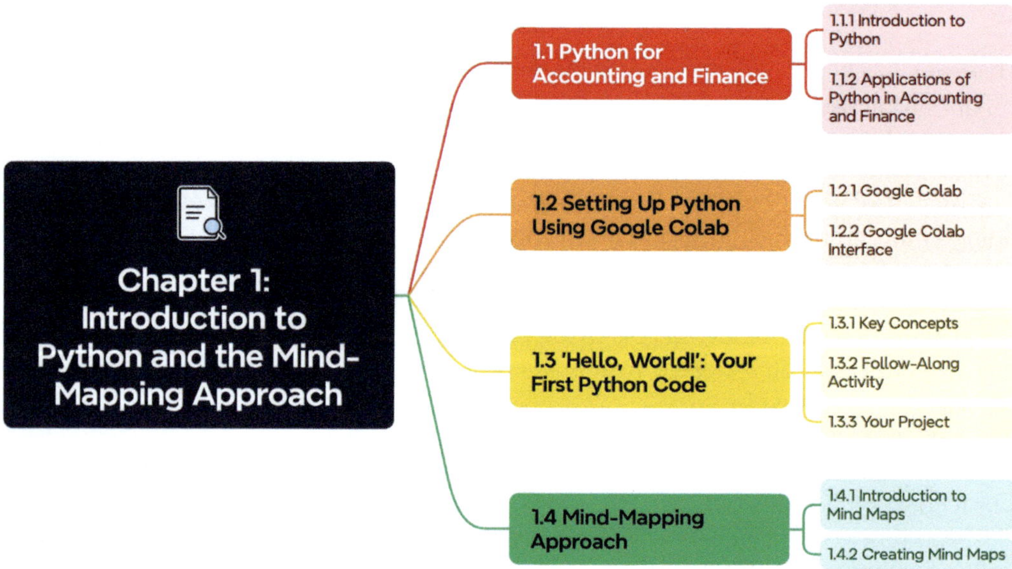

FIGURE 1.1 Structure of Chapter 1

1

INTRODUCTION TO PYTHON AND THE MIND-MAPPING APPROACH

This chapter introduces Python as a programming language used in accounting and finance. It explains how Python supports data analysis, automation, and machine learning. The chapter provides guidance on setting up a coding environment using Google Colab and writing a first Python program. It also presents mind mapping as a way to organise and make sense of programming concepts. By the end of the chapter, you will have written your first code in Python and developed a way to structure your learning through visual thinking (Figure 1.1).

Learning Objectives

By the end of this chapter, you will be able to

- Explain how Python supports data analysis, automation, and machine learning in accounting and finance.
- Set up a Google Colab notebook and run your first Python program.
- Construct a simple mind map to organise programming concepts and structure learning.

1.1 Python for Accounting and Finance

Python is a programming language used increasingly in accounting and finance. This section introduces Python and outlines its application across accounting and financial tasks.

1.1.1 Introduction to Python

Python was developed by Guido van Rossum and first released in 1991. The language is named after the British comedy group Monty Python's Flying Circus, reflecting Guido's interest in the show (Hunt, 2019) (see Figure 1.2).

DOI: 10.4324/9781003656968-1

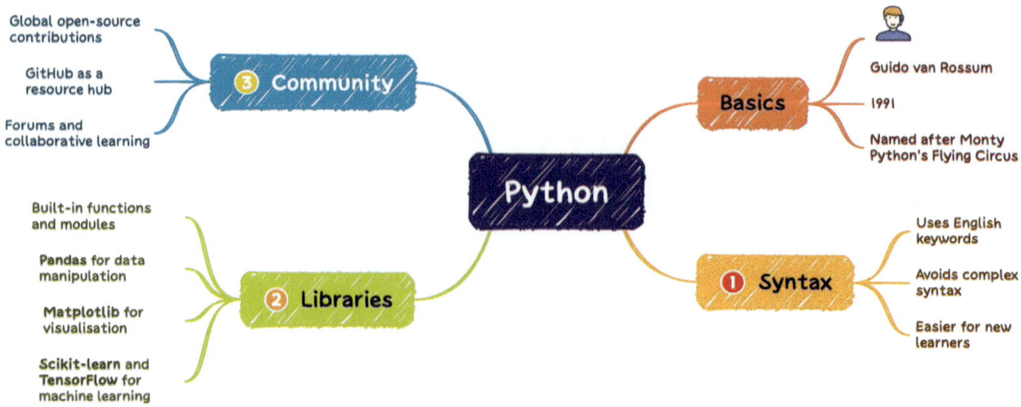

FIGURE 1.2 Python

Python has three key features:

- Python's syntax uses English keywords and avoids complex constructions found in other programming languages. The structure simplifies writing, interpretation, and correction of code. Python allows learners to focus on programming concepts and supports faster development.
- Python includes a standard library with built-in functions and modules that support various tasks. It is extended by an ecosystem of external libraries. Common libraries include Pandas for data manipulation, Matplotlib for data visualisation, and scikit-learn and TensorFlow for machine learning. These libraries enable users to apply existing functions without building them from scratch.
- Python has a global user community that provides tutorials, code, documentation, and solutions. Platforms such as GitHub host materials and support collaborative development. The community contributes to library maintenance, update distribution, and learner support through forums and discussion boards.

Over three decades, Python has developed from limited use into a programming language adopted across technology and business. Initial uptake occurred in academic and web development contexts, followed by expansion into sectors that manage large datasets and apply analytical methods, including accounting and finance. Researchers and practitioners use Python for data analysis, automation, and financial modelling.

1.1.2 Applications of Python in Accounting and Finance

Python has become increasingly important in accounting and finance due to its capabilities in data manipulation, automation, and predictive modelling.

- **Data Analysis and Visualisation:** Python manages and processes accounting and financial datasets. Tasks include data import, cleaning, handling missing values, sorting, and grouping. Exploratory data analysis involves summarisation and anomaly identification. Time series and panel data analysis using Python can identify trends, cycles, and seasonality. Visualisation uses libraries such as Matplotlib and Seaborn to generate and customise charts for presenting accounting and financial information.

- **Automation:** Python automates routine accounting and financial tasks such as data entry, calculation, and report generation. Python manages files and directories and handles errors. Automation applies to processes including invoice handling, data extraction from systems, and production of summary reports. Web scraping tools such as BeautifulSoup collect data from online sources. Application Programming Interfaces (APIs) provide access to real-time financial data and support integration into financial models.
- **Machine Learning:** Python supports machine learning workflows in accounting and finance. Supervised learning methods include linear regression, logistic regression, and random forests used for credit scoring and forecasting. Unsupervised learning methods such as clustering and isolation forest support segmentation and anomaly detection. Other applications include neural networks, algorithmic trading, and financial modelling.

These applications structure the textbook into four parts: Python basics (Chapters 1–4), data analysis and visualisation (Chapters 5–8), automation (Chapters 9–11), and machine learning (Chapters 12–15). Each part presents concepts and methods through examples and exercises based on accounting and finance (see Figure 1.3).

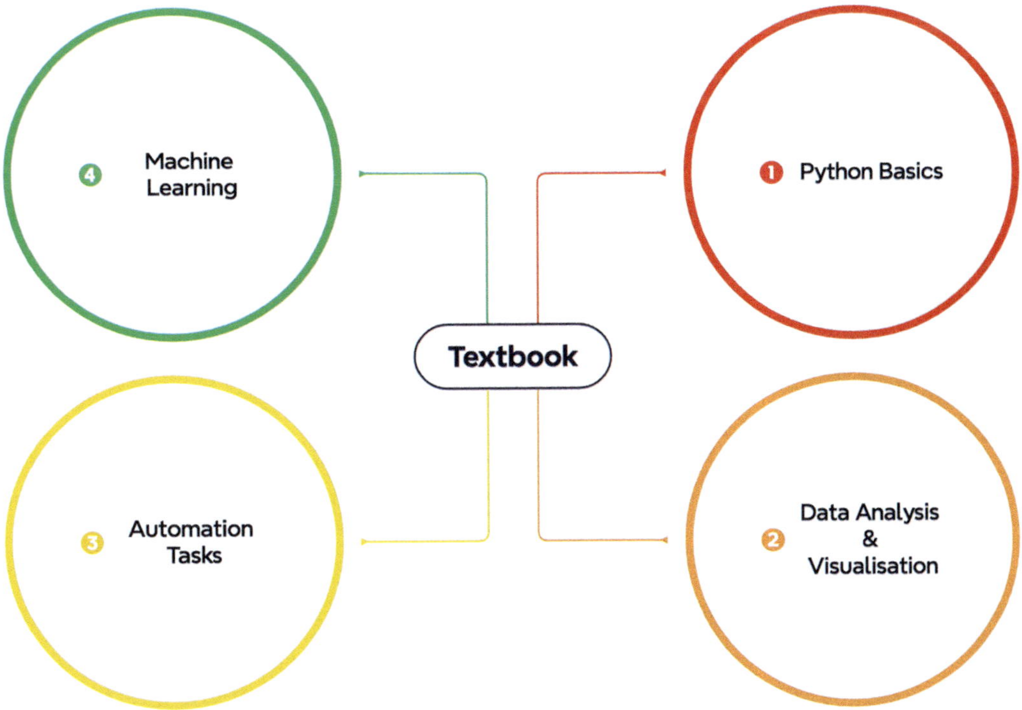

FIGURE 1.3 Textbook

1.2 Setting Up Python Using Google Colab

Google Colaboratory (Colab) is a free, cloud-based Python environment provided by Google. It allows users to write, run, and share Python code without installing software on a local machine. This section introduces Google Colab as the coding environment used in this textbook and also guides you through writing your first line of code (see Figure 1.4).

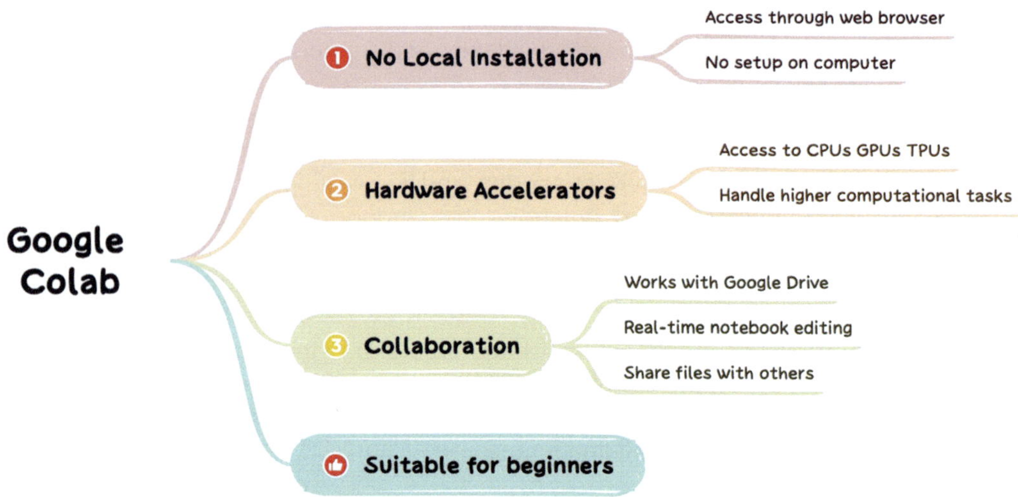

FIGURE 1.4 Google Colab

1.2.1 Google Colab

This textbook uses Google Colab as the primary coding environment. While other environments for Python are available, many require local installation and setup, which may create a barrier for new learners. Google Colab has been selected for three main reasons:

- No Local Installation: Users can access Google Colab through a web browser. No local setup is needed.
- Access to Hardware Accelerators: Google Colab may provide access to central processing units, graphics processing units, and tensor processing units, subject to availability and usage limits. These resources support code that requires greater computational power, such as machine learning tasks.
- Collaboration: Google Colab integrates with Google Drive, allowing file sharing and real-time collaborative coding. Multiple users can edit the same notebook at the same time.

Important Consideration: Data Protection in Future Projects

Google Colab is used for learning Python in this textbook. For future projects involving sensitive, personal, or business data, use a **local coding environment** instead. Local tools run on your own computer and reduce the risk of storing data on external servers. This approach supports compliance with data protection regulations.

Data Protection Tips for Learners

- **Do not upload** any files that include private, personal, or business information to online notebooks such as Google Colab.
- **Do not type** passwords or Application Programming Interface keys directly into your code.

1.2.2 Google Colab Interface

Google Colab interface has three main parts: the menu bar, file browser, and notebook cells (see Figure 1.5).

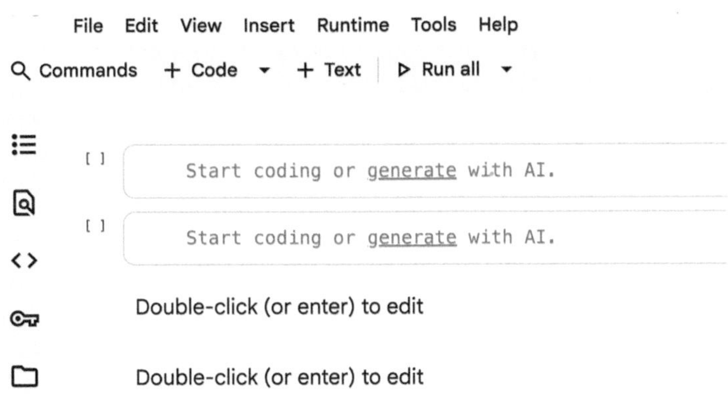

FIGURE 1.5 Google Colab Interface

Menu Bar: The menu bar is at the top. It includes

- File: Create, upload, save, download, and share Google Colab notebooks.
- Edit: Change content within cells.
- View: Adjust the interface layout.
- Insert: Add new code or text cells.
- Runtime: Control code execution.
- Tools: Change settings and features.
- Help: Get help and find documentation.

File Browser: On the left side, icons help manage files and settings:

- The folder icon opens the file browser.
- You can upload files or access files stored in Google Drive.

Notebook Cells: The notebook is made up of cells. There are two types:

- Code cells: Write Python code here. Click where it says 'Start coding or generate with AI' (see Figure 1.5) to begin. When the code runs, the result appears below the cell.
- Text cells: Write notes or explanations here. Click where it says 'Double-click (or enter) to edit' (see Figure 1.5) to begin.

1.3 'Hello, World!': Your First Python Code

1.3.1 Key Concepts

'Hello, World!' is often the first step in learning Python. The task is to write a short program that displays the phrase Hello, World! This is to confirm that the coding environment is functioning.

1.3.2 Follow-Along Activity

Step 1: Go to the Google Colab Website

Let's open a web browser. Type https://colab.research.google.com into the address bar and press Enter.

If we are not already signed in, we need to enter a Google email address and password. Google Colab requires a Google account to create and save notebooks.

Step 2: Create a New Notebook

On the Colab welcome page, let's click the 'New Notebook' button at the bottom-right corner. A new notebook will open in a new tab with a default name, such as Untitled0.ipynb.

Step 3: Rename the Notebook

Let's click the notebook name at the top-left of the page. Type a new name, for example 1.3_hello_world.ipynb, then press Enter.

Step 4: Write and Run the Code

Let's type the following code in the code cell:

```
print("Hello, World!")
```

Let's click the play ▶ icon to the left of the cell to run it. The output will appear below the cell (see Figure 1.6):

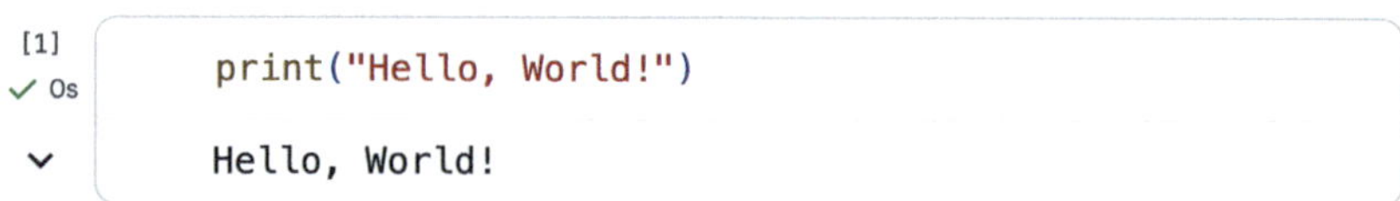

FIGURE 1.6 Hello World! Output

Explanation

- print("Hello, World!"): uses the print() function to display the message "Hello, World!" as output.
  - The print() function sends text or values to the screen.

Troubleshooting

- Syntax Error: Ensure that the print statement includes brackets and quotation marks exactly as shown: print("Hello, World!"). Missing brackets or quotation marks will cause errors.

Step 5: Save the Work

Let's click File, then Save. The notebook will be saved to Google Drive.

This follow-along activity is shown in Figure 1.7 *Hello World*.

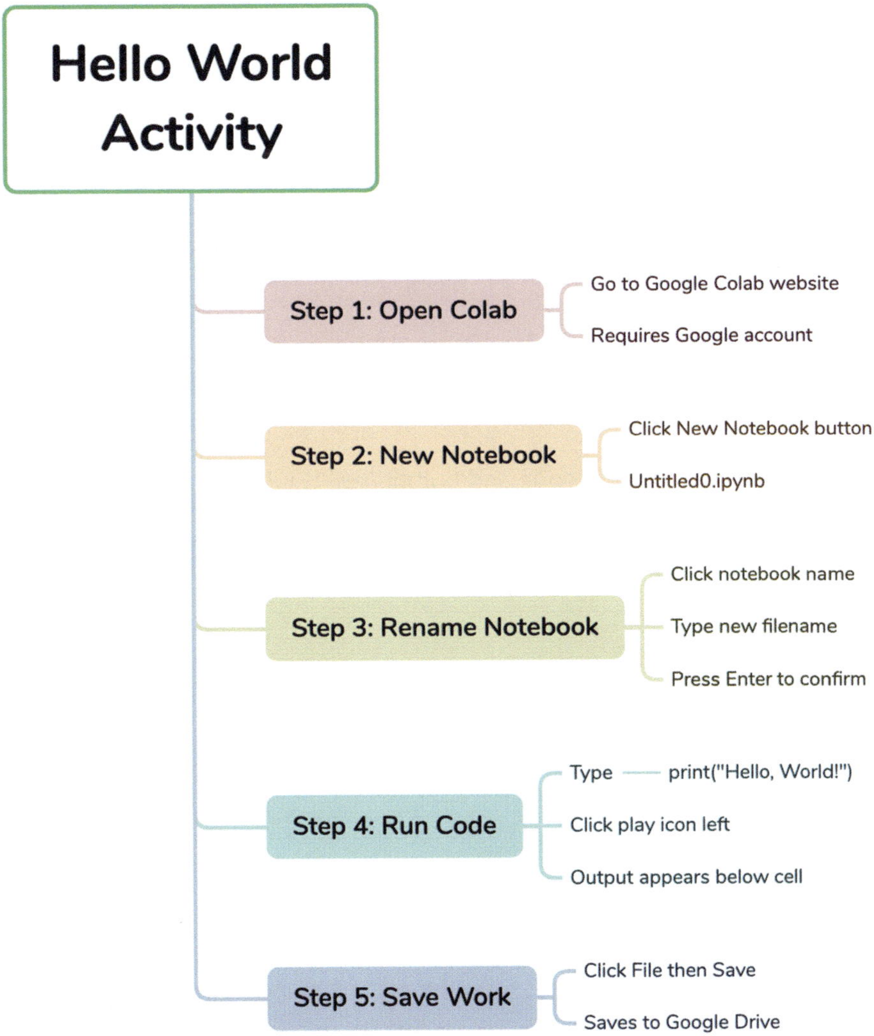

FIGURE 1.7 Hello World Activity

1.3.3 Your Project

You have printed Hello, World!. Now extend this by creating a welcome message for students beginning a course on Python in Accounting and Finance.

1.3.3.1 Task

Write a Python program that prints two lines:

```
Welcome
Welcome to Python for Accounting and Finance
```

Instructions and Example Code

1. Open your existing notebook (1.3_hello_world.ipynb) in Google Colab.
2. In a new code cell, type the following Python code.
3. Click the play icon to run the code.
4. Check that both lines appear in the output below the cell.

```
print("Welcome")
print("Welcome to Python for Accounting and Finance")
```

1.3.3.2 Expected Output

```
Welcome
Welcome to Python for Accounting and Finance
```

Scan the QR code to access the code and output (see 1.3_*hello_world.ipynb*).

https://github.com/DrMichaelGuo/PFAAFAMMA

1.4 Mind-Mapping Approach

This section introduces the mind-mapping approach used throughout the textbook. It explains how mind maps can support structured thinking and learning in Python for accounting and finance.

1.4.1 Introduction to Mind Maps

Mind mapping, developed by Tony Buzan, reflects how the brain processes information by branching ideas from a central concept. According to Buzan and Buzan (1993), mind

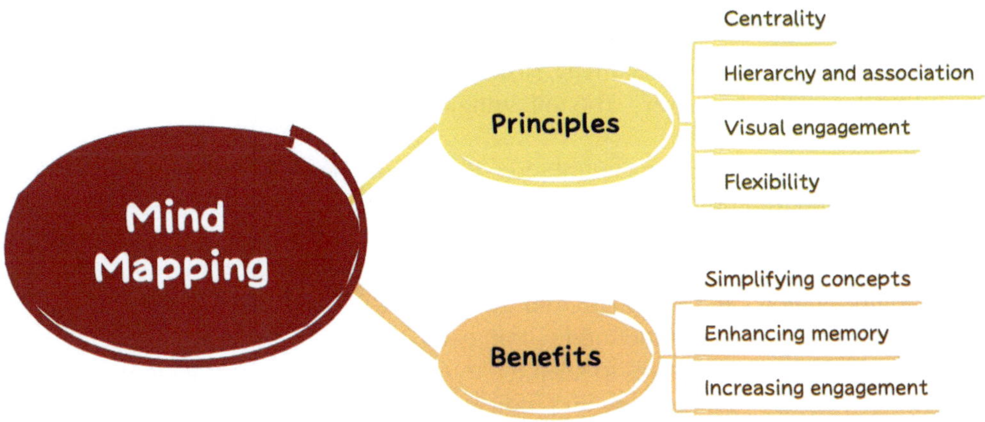

FIGURE 1.8 Mind Mapping

mapping 'harnesses the full range of cortical skills – word, image, number, logic, rhythm, colour and spatial awareness – in a single, uniquely powerful technique ... [and] gives you the freedom to roam the infinite expanse of your brain' (p.84) (see Figure 1.8).

Mind mapping has four principles. These principles help learners organise, relate, and review ideas more effectively.

- Centrality: Each mind map begins with a central concept. In this chapter, for example this might be 'Structure of Chapter 1' (see Figure 1.1) or a topic such as 'Python' (see Figure 1.2). The central idea acts as the starting point from which related ideas branch.
- Hierarchy and Association: Concepts in a mind map follow a hierarchy. Main branches cover key themes such as 'Principles' and 'Benefits' in Figure 1.8 Mind Mapping. These then expand into secondary or tertiary branches. The structure helps users understand how broad topics break down into subtopics.
- Visual Engagement: Mind maps incorporate colour, images, and symbols to support visual learning and memory. These visual elements help users organise and recall information effectively.
- Flexibility: Mind maps change as understanding develops. As students explore Python, they can create their maps by adding or rearranging content. This process supports reflection and strengthens subject knowledge.

The mind-mapping approach offers three key benefits. These benefits relate directly to how students manage, retain, and apply information.

- Simplifying Complex Concepts: Programming concepts can be abstract. Mind maps help structure content, making syntax and logic easier to understand.
- Enhancing Memory retention: Mind maps present related ideas visually, which helps students store and retrieve information.
- Increasing Student Engagement: By creating mind maps, students participate actively in the learning process. This approach also helps instructors guide students in reasoning, problem-solving, and critical thinking.

1.4.2 Creating Mind Maps

Creating a mind map involves creativity, structure, and logic. Mind maps can be drawn by hand or produced using software. The following steps outline the process (see Figure 1.9).

- The first step is to identify the central idea. This should be a concept or topic that forms the focus of the mind map.
- Next, add major branches. These represent the key components of the central idea. Each branch should reflect a main area of content or process related to the topic.
- Each major branch can then be broken down into sub-branches. These add detail and show how information is structured within each area.
- Use keywords or short phrases to keep the mind map concise. Visual elements such as icons may help support memory and indicate connections.
- The branches and sub-branches should be organised and connected to the central idea. The structure helps to show the relationships between elements.
- Finally, review the completed mind map for clarity and coverage. Revise the map as understanding of the topic develops, adding or adjusting content as needed.

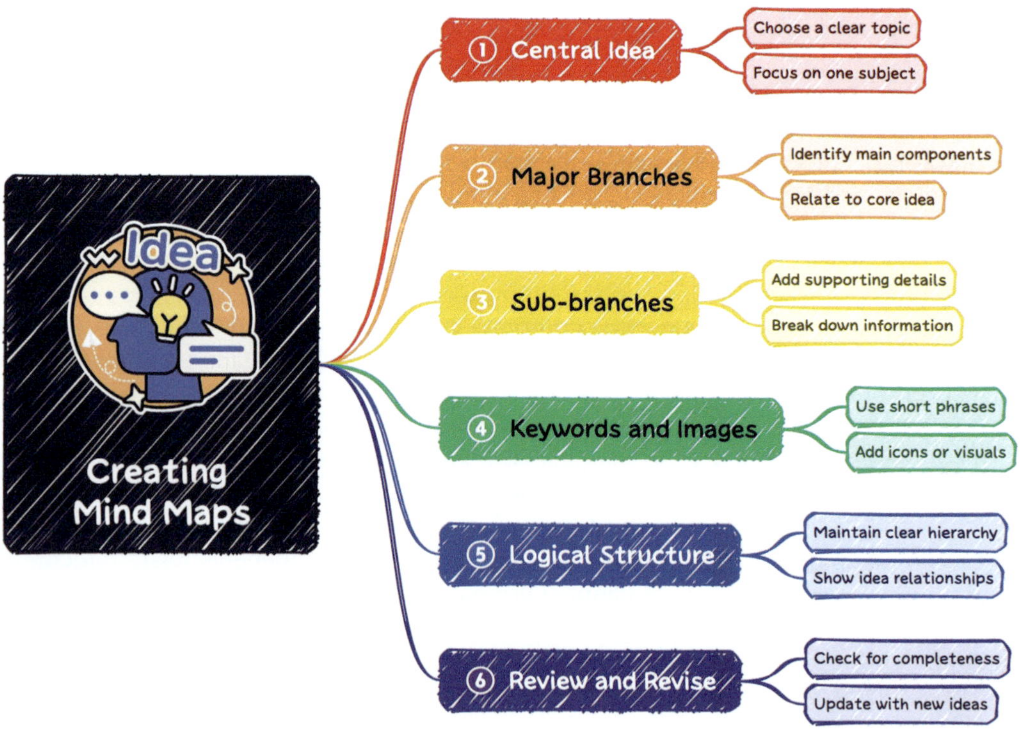

FIGURE 1.9 Creating Mind Maps

Summary of Chapter 1: Introduction to Python and the Mind-Mapping Approach

In this chapter, we have covered the following concepts:

Python for Accounting and Finance

- Python is used in accounting and finance for data analysis, automation, and machine learning.
- Key applications include financial reporting, risk modelling, audit analytics, and algorithmic trading.
- Python is accessible to learners and professionals due to its simple syntax, extensive libraries, and strong community support.

Setting Up the Coding Environment – Google Colab

- Google Colab is a cloud-based platform that enables coding without local installation.
- Google Colab Notebooks can be shared, edited, and stored online.
- Local environments may be more suitable for sensitive or confidential data.

Writing Your First Python Code

- The first program uses print("Hello, World!") to confirm that the environment is functioning.
- The print() function displays output on the screen.

Mind-Mapping Approach

- Mind mapping is a visual method for organising and linking ideas.
- A mind map starts with a central idea, followed by main branches and sub-branches.
- This textbook applies mind mapping to structure programming content.

Benefits of the Mind-Mapping Approach

- Breaks down complex programming topics into smaller, manageable parts.
- Supports memory retention and understanding.
- Promotes active learning and concept organisation.

Quiz Questions

Scan the QR code below to access the quiz questions for this chapter (see 1.md).

https://github.com/DrMichaelGuo/QuizPFAAFAMMA

References

Buzan, T. and Buzan, B. (1993) *The mind map book: How to use radiant thinking to maximise your brain's untapped potential*. Dutton: Published by Penguin Group.

Hunt, J. (2019) *A beginner's guide to Python 3 programming*. Cham: Springer.

Further Reading and Resources

Google (2025) *Google Colab introduction*. Available at: https://colab.research.google.com/notebooks/intro.ipynb (Accessed 9 July 2025).

Python Software Foundation (2025) *Python 3 documentation*. Available at: https://docs.python.org/3/ (Accessed 9 July 2025).

XMind (2025) *XMind mind map gallery*. Available at: https://xmind.app/share/?ref=com (Accessed 9 July 2025).

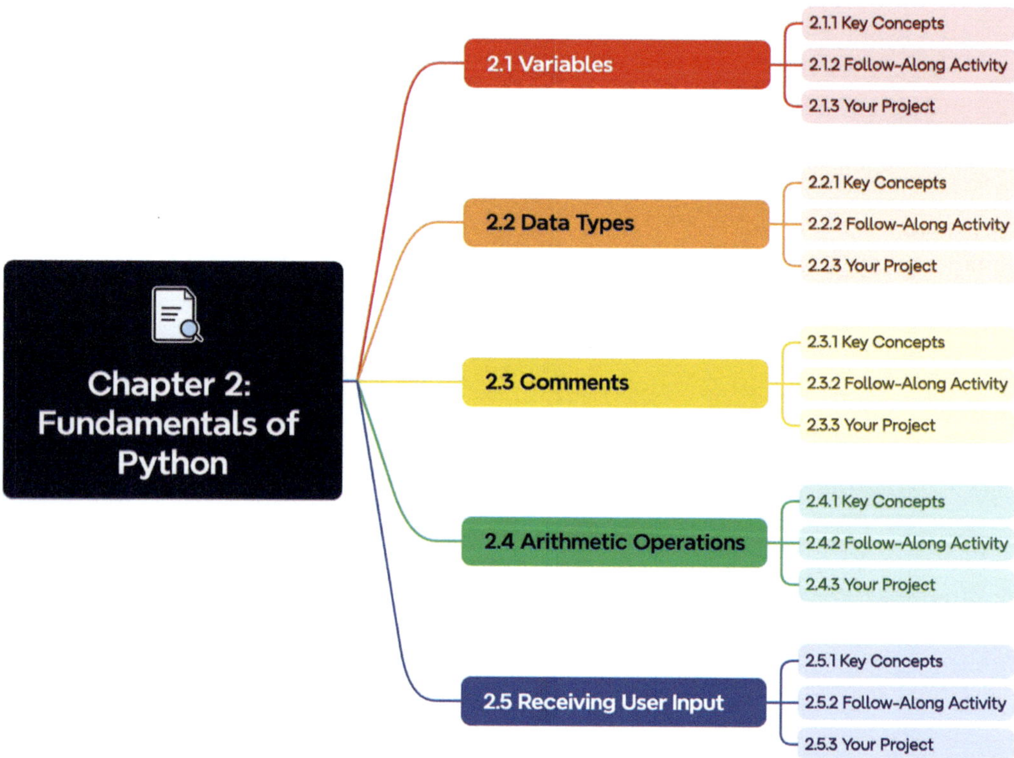

FIGURE 2.1 Structure of Chapter 2

2

FUNDAMENTALS OF PYTHON

This chapter introduces fundamental concepts in Python including variables, data types, comments, arithmetic operations, and user input. Each section combines explanation, guided activity, and project-based tasks to support learning through examples. The chapter presents Python fundamentals through accounting and finance applications (Figure 2.1).

Learning Objectives

By the end of this chapter, you will be able to

- Define and use variables to store and manage accounting and financial data.
- Identify and apply data types, including integer, float, string, and Boolean.
- Write single-line and multi-line comments to document Python code.
- Perform basic arithmetic operations to support accounting and financial calculations.
- Capture user input, convert data types, and produce formatted output for reporting purposes.

2.1 Variables

Variables are used in Python to store and manage information. This section introduces variables and explains how variables can be used to manage accounting and financial information (see Figure 2.2).

2.1.1 Key Concepts

2.1.1.1 Variable

A variable is a container that holds a value. In Python, a variable is created by assigning a value to a name.

```
sales = 2500
```

DOI: 10.4324/9781003656968-2

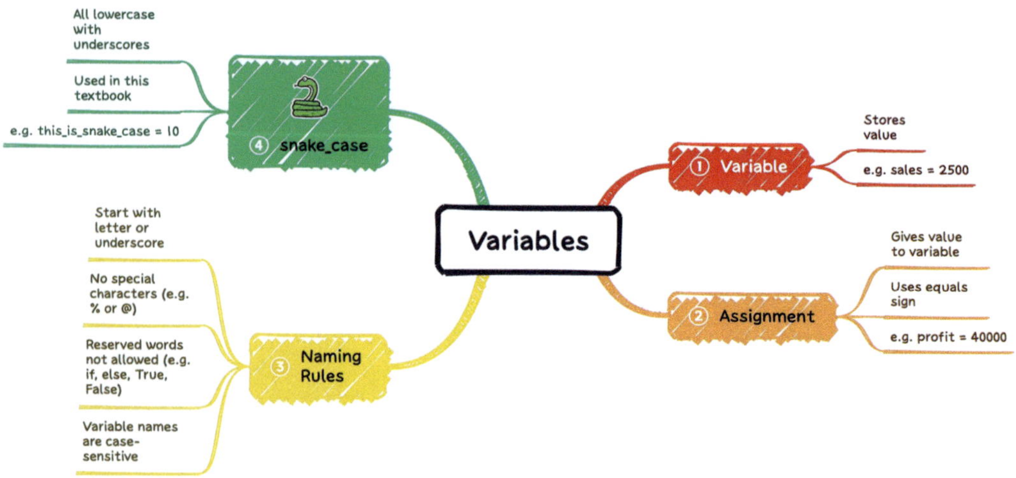

FIGURE 2.2 Variables

2.1.1.2 Assignment

Assignment is the process of giving a value to a variable. In Python, it uses the = sign.

```
revenue = 150000
profit = 40000
```

This means that revenue holds the value 150000 and profit holds 40000.

2.1.1.3 Variable Naming Conventions

To keep code readable and consistent,

- Variable names must start with a letter (a-z, A-Z) or underscore (_).
- After the first character, letters, digits, and underscores are allowed (e.g. q2_sales or income_2025). Variable names cannot begin with a digit.
- Avoid special characters such as % or @.
- Avoid using Python's reserved keywords (e.g. if, else, True, False).
- Variables are case-sensitive: revenue and Revenue are two different variables.

2.1.1.4 Snake Case Convention

This book uses snake_case for naming variables. This means using lowercase letters and underscores (_) between words:

```
this_is_snake_case = 10
cost_of_goods_sold = 5000
```

2.1.2 *Follow-Along Activity*

Step 1: Defining and Printing Variables

Let's define and use variables to manage financial information. In the code cell in the Google Colab notebook, type the following:

```
revenue = 150000
expenses = 85000
print(revenue)
print(expenses)
```

Explanation

- revenue = 150000: creates a variable named revenue and assigns it the value 150000. Do not include commas or currency symbols, as Python treats them as invalid characters in numbers.
- expenses = 85000: creates a variable named expenses and assigns it the value 85000.
- print(revenue): displays the value stored in the revenue variable.
- print(expenses): displays the value stored in the expenses variable.

Output: Run the code by clicking the play icon to the left of the cell. The output will appear below the cell:

```
150000
85000
```

Step 2: Updating and Printing Revised Variables

Let's assume that revenue increases due to a sales boost. Update the revenue variable and print the new value. Add a new code cell in the notebook and type the following:

```
revenue = 170000
print(revenue)
print(expenses)
```

Output: Run the code by clicking the play icon to the left of the cell. The output will appear below the cell:

```
170000
85000
```

Explanation

- revenue = 170000: assigns a new value 170000 to the existing revenue variable. This replaces the previous value of 150000.
- print(revenue): displays the updated value of revenue.
- print(expenses): displays the current value of expenses, which has not changed.

2.1.3 *Your Project*

2.1.3.1 *Tasks*

You are creating a new Google Colab notebook.

- In the first code cell, define variables for assets (£200000) and liabilities (£120000). Then, print assets and liabilities. Do not include commas or currency symbols in the code.
- In the second code cell, update assets to £210000 and then print both assets and liabilities again.

2.1.3.2 *Example Code*

```
assets = 200000
liabilities = 120000
print(assets)
print(liabilities)
```

```
assets = 210000
print(assets)
print(liabilities)
```

Scan the QR code to access the Python code and output (see 2.1.ipynb).

https://github.com/DrMichaelGuo/PFAAFAMMA

2.2 Data Types

Data types define the kind of data a variable can hold. This section introduces data types used in accounting and finance, including integer, float, string, and Boolean (see Figure 2.3).

2.2.1 *Key Concepts*

2.2.1.1 *Integer (int)*

An integer is a whole number without a decimal. It can be positive, negative, or zero.

```
profit = 25000
loss = -7000
net_balance = 0
```

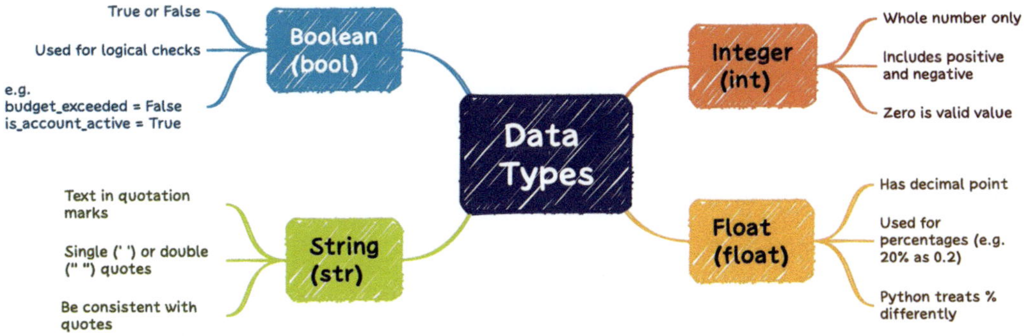

FIGURE 2.3 Data Types

2.2.1.2 Float (float)

A float is a number that includes a decimal point.

```
revenue = 152340.75
interest_rate = 0.045
vat_rate = 0.2
```

In interest_rate and vat_rate, percentages are written as decimal values. For example, 4.5% is written as 0.045, and 20% as 0.2. In Python, the % symbol represents the modulus operator, which returns the remainder after division.

2.2.1.3 String (str)

A string holds text. Strings in Python must be enclosed in matching quotation marks, either single (' ') or double (" "). Use one style consistently.

```
client_name = "ABC Consulting Ltd"
account_type = "Current Assets"
currency = 'GBP'
```

2.2.1.4 Boolean (bool)

A Boolean holds one of two values: True or False. Booleans are used to show logical conditions, such as whether a budget has been exceeded or whether an account is active.

```
budget_exceeded = False
is_account_active = True
```

In this example, each variable holds a Boolean value. budget_exceeded is set to False, meaning the budget has not been exceeded. is_account_active is True, meaning the account is active.

2.2.2 Follow-Along Activity

Step 1: Integer and Float Variables

Let's define variables for revenue and the number of transactions using a float and an integer. Then, print these variables.

```
revenue = 150000.75
transaction_count = 320
print("Revenue:", revenue)
print("Transaction Count:", transaction_count)
```

Output:

```
Revenue: 150000.75
Transaction Count: 320
```

Explanation

- revenue = 150000.75: assigns a float value to the variable revenue.
- transaction_count = 320: assigns an integer value to the variable transaction_count.
- print("Revenue:", revenue): prints the string "Revenue:", followed by the value stored in the variable revenue.
- print("Transaction Count:", transaction_count): prints the string "Transaction Count:", followed by the value of transaction_count.
- In both lines of print() code, the comma separates the string and the variable passed to the print() function.

Step 2: Strings for Report Descriptions

Let's add a description for the financial report using a string.

```
report_title = "Quarterly Financial Report"
print(report_title)
```

Output:

```
Quarterly Financial Report
```

Explanation

- report_title = "Quarterly Financial Report": assigns the string "Quarterly Financial Report" to the variable report_title.
- print(report_title): displays the value stored in report_title.

Step 3: Booleans and Decision Making

Let's create a Boolean variable to indicate whether a target has been reached and assign it the value True. Then, print the variable.

```
is_target_reached = True
print("Target Reached:", is_target_reached)
```

Output:

```
Target Reached: True
```

Explanation

- is_target_reached = True: assigns the Boolean value True to the variable is_target_reached.
- The print() function displays the text "Target Reached:" followed by the value of is_target_reached.

2.2.3 Your Project

2.2.3.1 Tasks

You are preparing a monthly finance report by defining and printing the following variables:

- total_expenses as a float: 85000.55
- employee_count as an integer: 50
- report_name as a string: "Monthly Expense Report"
- under_budget as a Boolean: True

2.2.3.2 Example Code

```
total_expenses = 85000.55
employee_count = 50
report_name = "Monthly Expense Report"
under_budget = True

print("Total Expenses:", total_expenses)
print("Employee Count:", employee_count)
print("Report Name:", report_name)
print("Under Budget:", under_budget)
```

Scan the QR code to access the code and output (see 2.2.ipynb).

https://github.com/DrMichaelGuo/PFAAFAMMA

2.3 Comments

Comments are used to clarify code by explaining what parts of the code do or why certain decisions are made. They support understanding of the structure and purpose of the code. This section introduces two types of comments in Python: single-line and multi-line comments (see Figure 2.4).

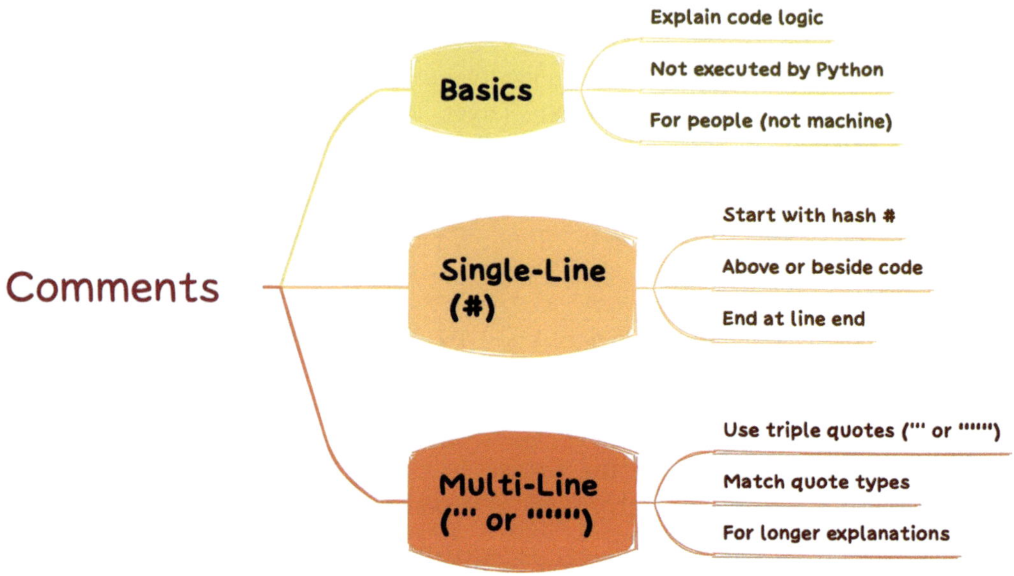

FIGURE 2.4 Comments

2.3.1 Key Concepts

2.3.1.1 Comments

Comments improve code readability by explaining the logic, assumptions, or steps in a calculation. They are not executed by Python and are ignored during the runtime of the program.

For beginners, comments support learning by serving as reminders and dividing the code into sections. Python code provides instructions for machines, while comments provide explanations for people.

2.3.1.2 Single-Line Comments (#)

Single-line comments begin with the hash symbol (#) and continue to the end of the line. They can be placed above or beside the relevant line of code. Python ignores these comments during execution.

```
# Monthly sales revenue in GBP
sales_revenue = 25000
```

```
sales_revenue = 25000  # Monthly sales revenue in GBP
```

2.3.1.3 Multi-Line Comments

Multi-line comments are used for longer explanations. They are enclosed in triple quotes (''' or """). The type of quotes used must match at the beginning and end. For example, if the comment begins with triple single quotes, it must end with triple single quotes. If it begins with triple double quotes, it must end with triple double quotes.

```
'''
This script calculates VAT:
- Standard rate is 20%
- VAT is applied to taxable revenue
'''
```

```
"""
This script prepares a payroll summary:
- Monthly salary is £3000
- Deductions include tax and pension contributions
"""
```

Note: Python treats the text inside triple quotes as a string. When the string is not assigned to a variable, Python ignores it during execution. This makes triple quotes useful for writing notes or explanations across several lines.

2.3.2 Follow-Along Activity

Step 1: Single-Line Comments above the Code

Let's write a single-line comment placed above the code:

```
# Total number of invoices issued
invoice_count = 120
print(invoice_count)
```

Output:

```
120
```

Explanation

- The first line is a comment. It begins with # and explains what the next line of code does. It is not executed by Python.
- invoice_count = 120: creates a variable named invoice_count and assigns it the integer value 120.
- print(invoice_count): uses the print() function to display the value of invoice_count.

Step 2: Single-Line Comments beside the Code

Let's write a single-line comment beside the code:

```
active_clients = 35          # Number of active clients
print(active_clients)
```

Output

```
35
```

Explanation

- The first line creates a variable named active_clients and assigns it the integer value 35. A single-line comment appears on the same line after the code. It begins with # and explains the purpose of the variable. Python ignores the comment during execution.
- print(active_clients): uses the print() function to display the value of active_clients.

Step 3: A Multi-line Comment

Let's write a multi-line comment above the code.

```
'''
This section defines the basic details for the financial report:
- Title of the report
- Department preparing the report
- Reporting period is assumed to be annual
'''

report_title = "Annual Financial Summary"
department = "Finance"
reporting_period = "Annual"

print(report_title)
print(department)
print(reporting_period)
```

Output:

```
Annual Financial Summary
Finance
Annual
```

Explanation

- Everything between the triple single quotes is a comment. Python ignores it during execution.

2.3.3 *Your Project*

2.3.3.1 *Tasks*

You are writing a Python code that creates a monthly sales report. The code should define variables for key details, include comments to explain each variable, and use print() statements to display the information.

1. Multi-Line Comment: Begin with a multi-line comment that explains the purpose of the code: 'This code creates a monthly sales report. It defines report details and displays each detail'. Use triple single quotes.
2. Define Variables: Create the following variables and place a single-line comment above each variable to explain its meaning:
   - monthly_sales with the value 75000 (monthly sales in GBP)
   - invoice_count with the value 150 (number of invoices issued this month)
   - employee_count with the value 20 (number of employees in the sales department)
   - report_status with the value "Complete" (status of the sales report)
   - data_verified with the Boolean value True (verification status of the data)
3. Print Variables: Use the print() function to display each variable. Include a single-line comment beside each print() statement to explain what is being displayed (e.g. display monthly sales).

2.3.3.2 *Example Code*

```
'''
This code creates a monthly sales report.
It defines report details and displays each detail.
'''

# Monthly sales in GBP
monthly_sales = 75000

# Number of invoices issued this month
invoice_count = 150

# Number of employees in the sales department
employee_count = 20

# Status of the sales report
report_status = "Complete"

# Verification status of the data
data_verified = True

print("Monthly Sales:", monthly_sales)     # Display monthly sales
print("Invoice Count:", invoice_count)     # Display invoice count
print("Employee Count:", employee_count)   # Display employee count
print("Report Status:", report_status)     # Display report status
print("Data Verified:", data_verified)     # Display verification status
```

Scan the QR code to access the code and output (see 2.3.ipynb).

https://github.com/DrMichaelGuo/PFAAFAMMA

2.4 Arithmetic Operations

This section introduces arithmetic operations in Python used in the context of accounting and finance. The operations include addition, subtraction, multiplication, division, and exponentiation (see Figure 2.5).

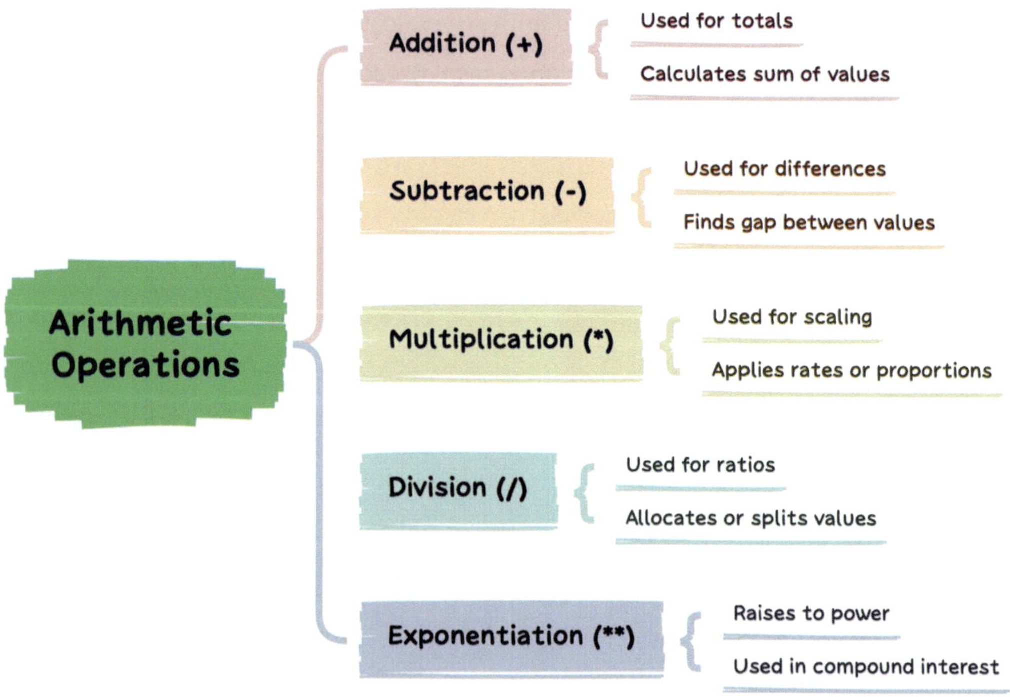

FIGURE 2.5 Arithmetic Operations

2.4.1 Key Concepts

2.4.1.1 Addition (+)

Addition is used to calculate total amounts or sums.

```
a = 1 + 2 # a = 3
expenses = 10000 + 2000 # expenses = 12000
```

2.4.1.2 Subtraction (–)

Subtraction is used to calculate differences between values.

```
b = 5 - 2   # b = 3
profit = 1200 - 800   # profit = 400
```

2.4.1.3 Multiplication (*)

Multiplication is used for scaling amounts or applying rates.

```
c = 4 * 3 # c = 12
interest = 1000 * 0.05  # interest = 50
```

2.4.1.4 Division (/)

Division is used to allocate amounts or calculate ratios.

```
d = 10 / 2  # d = 5
average_cost = 500 / 5  # average_cost = 100
```

2.4.1.5 Exponentiation (**)

Exponentiation is used to raise a number to a power, such as compound interest.

```
e = 2 ** 3  # e = 8
compound_interest = 1000 * (1.05 ** 2) # compound_interest = 1102.5
```

2.4.2 Follow-Along Activity

Step 1: Addition

Let's add revenue from two product lines.

```
# Revenue from two product lines
revenue_product1 = 50000
revenue_product2 = 75000

# Total revenue calculation
total_revenue = revenue_product1 + revenue_product2
print(total_revenue)
```

Output

```
125000
```

Explanation

- revenue_product1 = 50000: assigns the value 50000 to revenue_product1.
- revenue_product2 = 75000: assigns the value 75000 to revenue_product2.
- total_revenue = revenue_product1 + revenue_product2: adds these two values and stores the result in total_revenue.
- print(total_revenue): prints the value of total_revenue.

Step 2: Subtraction

Let's subtract expenses from revenue to calculate net income.

```
# Revenue and expenses
revenue = 100000
expenses = 60000

# Net income calculation
net_income = revenue - expenses
print("Net Income:", net_income)
```

Output

```
Net Income: 40000
```

Explanation

- revenue = 100000: assigns the value 100000 to revenue.
- expenses = 60000: assigns the value 60000 to expenses.
- net_income = revenue - expenses: subtracts expenses from revenue and stores the result in net_income.
- print("Net Income:", net_income): displays the text "Net Income:" followed by the value of net_income.

Step 3: Multiplication

Let's use multiplication to calculate interest earned on a principal amount.

```
# Principal amount and interest rate
principal = 10000  # (£)
interest_rate = 0.05  # 5% annual interest rate

# Interest calculation
interest = principal * interest_rate
print("Interest:", interest)
```

Output

```
Interest: 500.0
```

Explanation

- The output is 500.0 because any arithmetic operation that involves a float returns a float result, even if the result is a whole number. In this case, 10000 is an integer and 0.05 is a float. When Python performs the calculation 10000 * 0.05, it returns the result as a float: 500.0 (with one decimal place), even though the mathematical answer is 500.

Step 4: Division

Let's calculate the profit margin using division.

```
# Net income and revenue
net_income = 40000
revenue = 100000

# Profit margin calculation
profit_margin = (net_income / revenue) * 100
print("Profit Margin (%):", profit_margin)
```

Output:

```
Profit Margin (%): 40.0
```

Explanation

- The output is 40.0 because any arithmetic operation involving a float will result in a float output, even if the result is a whole number. In this case, both net_income and revenue are integers. When Python performs the calculation 40000/100000, it returns 0.4 as a float. Multiplying 0.4 by 100 gives 40.0, which is also a float.

Step 5: Exponentiation

Let's calculate compound interest over multiple periods.

```
# Compound interest calculation over 2 years
principal = 1000
rate = 0.05  # 5%
periods = 2

# Future value calculation
future_value = principal * (1 + rate) ** periods
print("Future Value:", future_value)
```

Output:

```
Future Value: 1102.5
```

Explanation

- principal = 1000: assigns the initial amount of 1000 to principal.
- rate = 0.05: assigns the interest rate 5%, expressed as a decimal, to rate.
- periods = 2: assigns the number of years to periods.
- future_value = principal * (1 + rate) ** periods: calculates the compound interest using the formula principal * (1 + rate) ** periods. This raises (1 + rate) to the power of periods and multiplies the result by principal.
- print("Future Value:", future_value): displays the value of future_value.

2.4.3 *Your Project*

2.4.3.1 *Tasks*

You are analysing a company's quarterly performance.

Define These Variables

- sales_q1 = 30000
- sales_q2 = 45000
- total_expenses = 45000
- tax_rate = 0.20 (representing 20%)

Perform the Following Operations

1. Calculate total_sales by adding sales_q1 and sales_q2.
2. Calculate gross_income by subtracting total_expenses from total_sales.
3. Calculate tax_amount by multiplying gross_income by tax_rate.
4. Calculate profit_margin as (gross_income / total_sales) * 100.
5. Estimate projected_sales after 2 years at an annual growth rate of 5% using exponentiation.

2.4.3.2 *Example Code*

```
# Define input values for the analysis
sales_q1 = 30000                    # Sales in Quarter 1 (£)
sales_q2 = 45000                    # Sales in Quarter 2 (£)
total_expenses = 45000              # Total expenses for the period (£)
tax_rate = 0.20                     # Tax rate (20%) represented as a decimal

# 1: Calculate total sales from both quarters
total_sales = sales_q1 + sales_q2
print("Total Sales:", total_sales)

# 2: Calculate gross income by subtracting expenses from total sales
gross_income = total_sales - total_expenses
print("Gross Income:", gross_income)

# 3: Calculate tax amount by multiplying gross income by tax rate
tax_amount = gross_income * tax_rate
print("Tax Amount:", tax_amount)
```

```
# 4: Calculate profit margin (gross income ÷ total sales × 100)
profit_margin = (gross_income / total_sales) * 100
print("Profit Margin (%):", profit_margin)

# 5: Estimate projected sales after 2 years of 5% annual growth
using exponentiation
annual_growth_rate = 0.05      # 5% annual growth rate
years = 2                      # Compounded over 2 years

projected_sales = total_sales * (1 + annual_growth_rate) ** years
print("Projected Sales (After 2 Years):", projected_sales)
```

Scan the QR code to access the code and output (see 2.4.ipynb).

https://github.com/DrMichaelGuo/PFAAFAMMA

2.5 Receiving User Input

Receiving user input allows interaction between the user and the program. This section explains how to capture input using Python's input() function, convert input into appropriate data types for calculations, and format output using f-strings (see Figure 2.6).

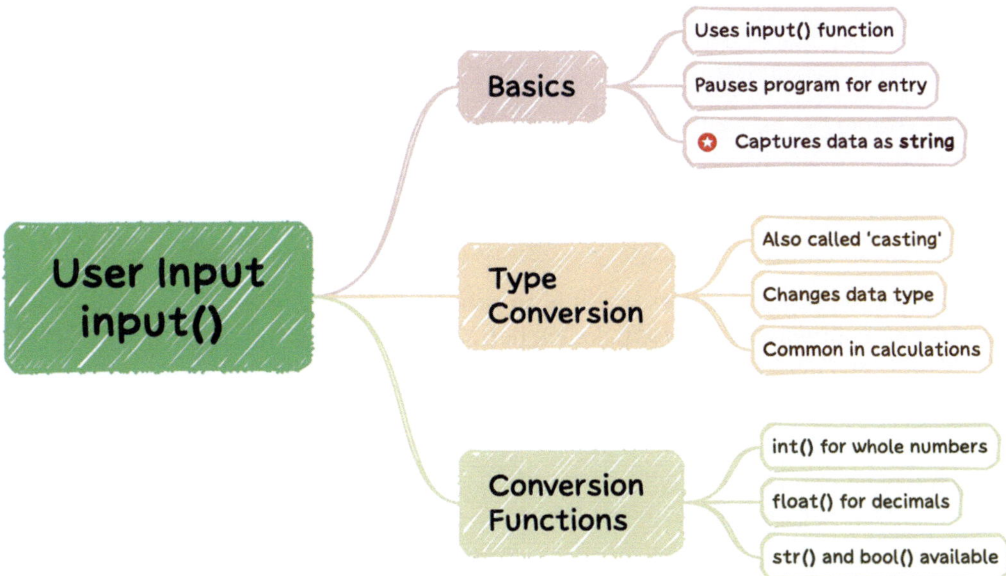

FIGURE 2.6 User Input

2.5.1 *Key Concepts*

2.5.1.1 User Input: input()

The input() function allows users to enter data during program execution. When the function runs, it displays a prompt and pauses the program until the user provides input and presses Enter. For example,

```
amount = input()
```

The input is captured as a string. For example, if the user enters 500, Python stores it as "500" (as a string). To use this value in calculations, "500" must be converted to a numeric type using a type conversion function.

2.5.1.2 Type Conversion (Casting)

Type conversion, or casting, changes a value from one data type to another. Python provides the following functions:

- int(): converts a value to an integer.
- float(): converts a value to a float.
- str(): converts a value to a string.
- bool(): converts a value to a Boolean.

In accounting and finance, int() and float() are often used to convert user input for use in calculations.

```
amount = int(amount)
```

```
amount = float(amount)
```

2.5.1.3 F-string

An f-string is used to format output by embedding expressions or variables within a string.

```
f"text: {value:.2f}"
```

The f before the string indicates that it is an f-string. Curly braces { } are used to include variables or expressions. The format specifier :.2f ensures that the numeric value is displayed with two decimal places (see Figure 2.7).

2.5.2 *Follow-Along Activity*

Step 1: Using input() to Capture a User Name

Let's use the input() function to collect a name from the user and display it on the screen.

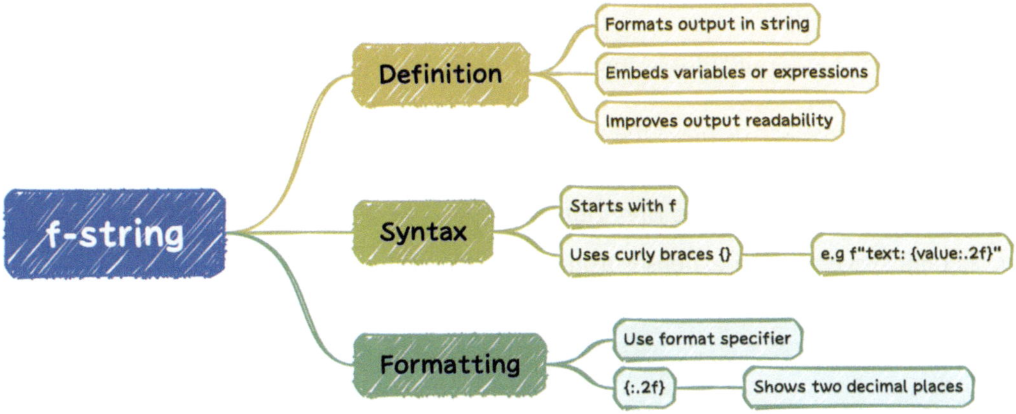

FIGURE 2.7 f-String

```
user_name = input()
print(user_name)
```

When the code runs, it waits for input.

If the user enters Muhammad and presses Enter,

```
Muhammad
```

Output

```
Muhammad
```

Explanation

- user_name = input(): captures the user's input and stores it in the variable user_name.
- print(user_name): displays the value stored in user_name.

To give the user more instruction, let's add a prompt inside the input() function:

```
user_name_2 = input("Please input your name: ")
print(user_name_2)
```

When the code runs, it displays a prompt and waits for user input.

If the user enters Olivia and presses Enter,

```
Please input your name: Olivia
```

Output

```
Olivia
```

Explanation

- user_name_2 = input("Please input your name: "): displays the prompt and captures the user's input.
- print(user_name_2): displays the value stored in user_name_2.

Step 2: Using input() to Capture Financial Data

Let's collect revenue and expenses from the user and display the user input.

```
revenue = input("Enter the company's revenue (£): ")
expenses = input("Enter the company's expenses (£): ")

print("Raw Revenue:", revenue)
print("Raw Expenses:", expenses)
```

When the code runs, it displays prompts and waits for user input. If the user enters 4000 for revenue and 2000 for expenses, the output will be

```
Enter the company's revenue (£): 4000
Enter the company's expenses (£): 2000
Raw Revenue: 4000
Raw Expenses: 2000
```

Explanation

- revenue = input("Enter the company's revenue (£): "): captures user input for revenue.
- expenses = input("Enter the company's expenses (£): "): captures user input for expenses.
- print("Raw Revenue:", revenue): displays the value stored in revenue.
- print("Raw Expenses:", expenses): displays the value stored in expenses.

Note: Both 4000 and 2000 are strings because the input() function always returns text. The values cannot be used for calculations.

Step 3: Converting Input to Floats for Calculations

Let's convert the input values from strings to floats and perform a calculation.

```
revenue = float(revenue)
expenses = float(expenses)

print(revenue)
print(expenses)

net_income = revenue - expenses
print("Net Income (£):", net_income)
```

Output:

```
4000.0
2000.0
Net Income (£): 2000.0
```

Explanation

- revenue = float(revenue): converts the string value in revenue to a float.
- expenses = float(expenses): converts the string value in expenses to a float.
- print(revenue): displays the value of revenue as a float.
- print(expenses): displays the value of expenses as a float.
- net_income = revenue - expenses: subtracts expenses from revenue and stores the result in net_income.
- print("Net Income (£):", net_income): displays the value of net_income.

Note: Python displays the number 4000 as 4000.0 to show that it is stored as a float. The output shows a net income of 2000.0 for the same reason.

Step 4: Improving the Output Using f-string

Let's format the output using an f-string.

```
print(f"Calculated Net Income (£): {net_income:.2f}")
```

Output

```
Calculated Net Income (£): 2000.00
```

Explanation

- f"Calculated Net Income (£): {net_income:.2f}": formats the output using an f-string.
  - The f before the quotation marks indicates that this is a formatted string (f-string).
  - Inside the string, {net_income:.2f} is a placeholder that tells Python to insert the value of the variable net_income at that position in the string.
  - The colon : begins the formatting instruction.
  - .2f specifies that the value should be formatted as a floating-point number with two digits after the decimal point.
  - In this case, as net_income is 2000.0, Python formats it as 2000.00 to show two decimal places.

2.5.3 Your Project

2.5.3.1 Tasks

You are creating a financial calculator for clients to determine profit margin.

- Prompt the user to enter their total sales and total costs.
- Convert the inputs to floats.
- Calculate gross profit as: gross_profit = total_sales - total_costs.
- Calculate the profit margin as: profit_margin = (gross_profit / total_sales) * 100.
- Display the gross profit and profit margin, each rounded to two decimal places.

2.5.3.2 Example Code

```
# Step 1: Capture user input for total sales and total costs
# input() prompts the user and stores the values as strings
total_sales = input("Enter total sales (£): ")
total_costs = input("Enter total costs (£): ")

# Step 2: Convert inputs to floats
# Convert the string inputs to float for numeric calculation
total_sales = float(total_sales)
total_costs = float(total_costs)

# Step 3: Calculate gross profit
# Gross profit is the difference between total sales and total costs
gross_profit = total_sales - total_costs

# Step 4: Calculate profit margin
# Profit margin is calculated as a percentage of total sales
# Formula: (Gross Profit / Total Sales) * 100
profit_margin = (gross_profit / total_sales) * 100

# Step 5: Display the results with formatting
# Use f-strings to display the results rounded to two decimal places
print(f"Gross Profit (£): {gross_profit:.2f}")
print(f"Profit Margin (%): {profit_margin:.2f}")
```

Scan the QR code to access the code and output (see 2.5.ipynb).

https://github.com/DrMichaelGuo/PFAAFAMMA

Summary of Chapter 2: Fundamentals of Python

In this chapter, we have covered the following concepts:

Variables

- Variables store and manage data in a Python program.
- Values are assigned using the equals sign (=).
- Variable names are case-sensitive.
- Use the snake_case naming convention for consistency.

Data Types

- Integer (int): whole numbers, e.g. profit = 25000
- Float (float): decimal numbers, e.g. interest_rate = 0.05
- String (str): text enclosed in quotes, e.g. "Annual Report"
- Boolean (bool): logical values True or False, e.g. is_active = True

Comments

- Single-line comments: begin with #, used for brief explanations.
- Multi-line comments: enclosed in triple quotes (''' or """), for longer notes.
- Comments support understanding of code structure and calculation.

Arithmetic Operations

- Addition (+): combines values, e.g. total_revenue = sales1 + sales2.
- Subtraction (–): computes difference, e.g. net_income = revenue – expenses.
- Multiplication (*): applies scaling, e.g. interest = principal * rate.
- Division (/): calculates ratios, e.g. profit_margin = net_income / revenue.
- Exponentiation (**): raises numbers to powers, e.g. future_value = principal * (1 + rate)**years.

User Input and Output

- Use the input() function to collect data from users.
- Input is received as a string and must be converted using int() or float() to perform accounting and finance calculations.
- Use f-strings for formatted output, e.g. f"Profit: £{net_income:.2f}".

Quiz Questions

Scan the QR code below to access the quiz questions for this chapter (see 2.md).

https://github.com/DrMichaelGuo/QuizPFAAFAMMA

Further Reading and Resource

Python Software Foundation (2025) *The Python Tutorial*. https://docs.python.org/3/tutorial/index.html (Accessed 3 November 2025).

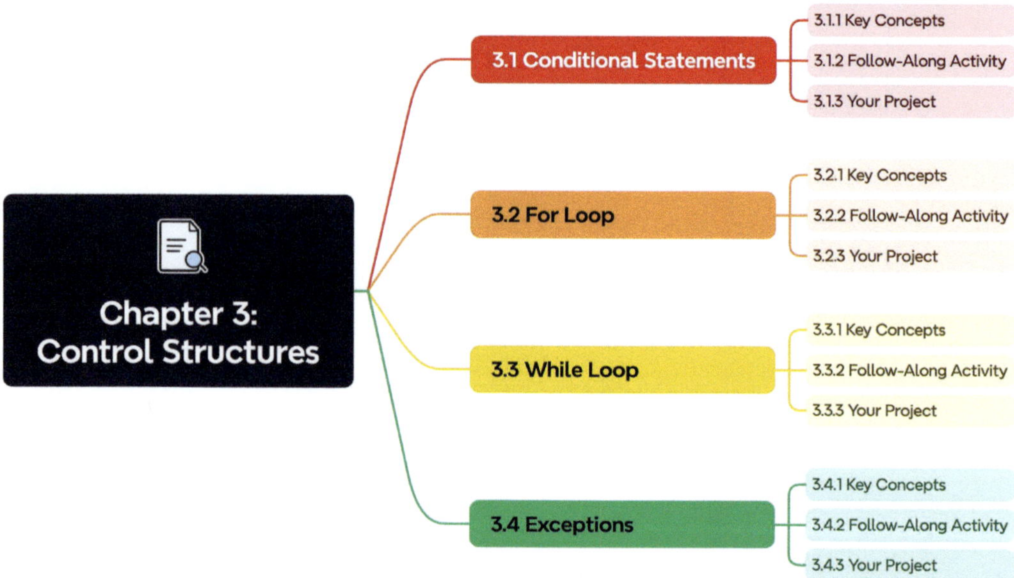

FIGURE 3.1 Structure of Chapter 3

3

CONTROL STRUCTURES

This chapter introduces key control structures in Python: conditional statements, loops, and exception handling. These structures enable decision-making and automation in financial programming. Through accounting and finance examples, the chapter shows how to write programs that respond to data, repeat tasks, and manage errors (Figure 3.1).

Learning Objectives

By the end of this chapter, you will be able to

- Use if, elif, and else statements to make decisions based on financial data.
- Apply for and while loops to automate repeated accounting calculations.
- Use try and except blocks to manage input and calculation errors.

3.1 Conditional Statements

Conditional statements enable a program to select actions based on conditions. This section introduces key conditional statements in Python – if, elif, and else – and explains the use of comparison operators (see Figure 3.2).

3.1.1 Key Concepts

3.1.1.1 Conditional Statements

A conditional statement allows a program to run a block of code only when a condition is met. In Python, conditions are usually comparisons that result in either True or False.

In an accounting context, a condition might be used to determine whether to issue a bonus by checking if the profit exceeds a certain threshold. For example, if the profit is above £10,000, a bonus is awarded. These decisions are written in code using if, elif, and else.

DOI: 10.4324/9781003656968-3

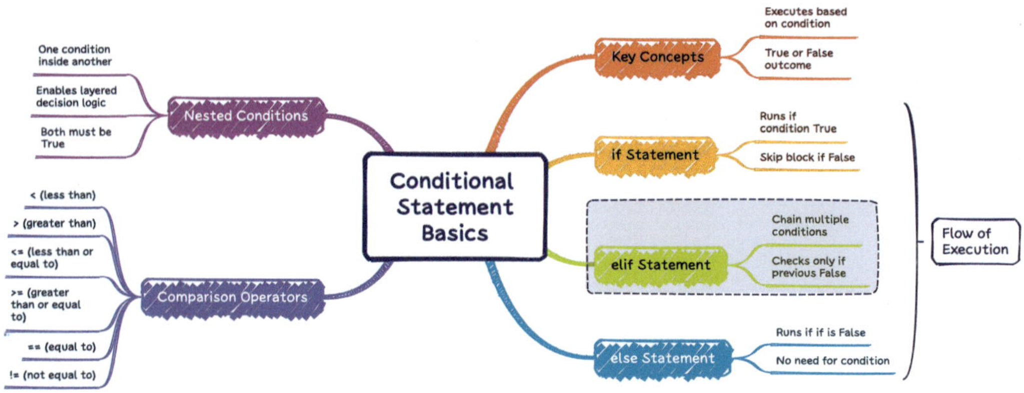

FIGURE 3.2 Conditional Statement Basics

3.1.1.2 if Statement

The if statement runs a block of code only if a condition is True. For example,

```
if profit > 10000:
    print("Bonus awarded")
```

Here, profit > 10000 is evaluated. If the result is True, the code block (print("Bonus awarded")) runs. If it is False, Python skips the code block. Note the colon (:) at the end of the if line. This tells Python that an indented code block follows.

Note: When writing numbers in Python code, do not include commas in large numbers (e.g. write 10000 instead of 10,000).

3.1.1.3 else Statement

To run an alternative code block when the if condition is not met, use else:

```
if profit > 10000:
    print("Bonus awarded")
else:
    print("No bonus")
```

Here, Python checks whether profit > 10000. If the condition is True, it runs the first block (print("Bonus awarded")). If the condition is False, it runs the else block (print("No bonus")).

3.1.1.4 elif Statement

The elif statement (short for 'else if') lets you chain multiple conditions:

```
if profit > 10000:
    print("High bonus")
elif profit > 5000:
```

```
    print("Moderate bonus")
else:
    print("No bonus")
```

Python checks the conditions in order. If profit > 10000 is True, it runs the first block (print("High bonus")). If not, it checks profit > 5000. If that is True, it runs the second block (print("Moderate bonus")). If both are False, it runs the else block (print("No bonus")).

3.1.1.5 *Comparison Operators*

Conditions often compare values using comparison operators:

- < (less than)
- > (greater than)
- <= (less than or equal to)
- >= (greater than or equal to)
- == (equal to)
- != (not equal to)

Examples

- profit < 5000 checks whether profit is less than 5000.
- revenue == expenses checks whether revenue equals expenses.
- tax_rate != 0.20 checks whether tax_rate is not 0.20.

3.1.1.6 *Nested Conditions*

Nested conditions are conditional statements placed within other conditional blocks. For example,

```
if revenue > 10000:
    if expenses < 5000:
        print("Excellent performance")
```

Here, Python first checks whether revenue > 10000. If True, Python then checks the nested condition if expenses < 5000. If that second condition is also True, Python runs the code block (print("Excellent performance")). If either condition is False, Python does not print anything.

In addition to the basic concepts above, the format of conditional statements is also important for Python to run code correctly. This includes the use of colons and indentation (see Figure 3.3).

3.1.1.7 *Colon (:)*

A colon (:) is required at the end of a line that introduces a conditional statement such as if, elif, or else. The colon signals that an indented block of code follows. Without it, Python does not recognise the beginning of the block and raises a syntax error.

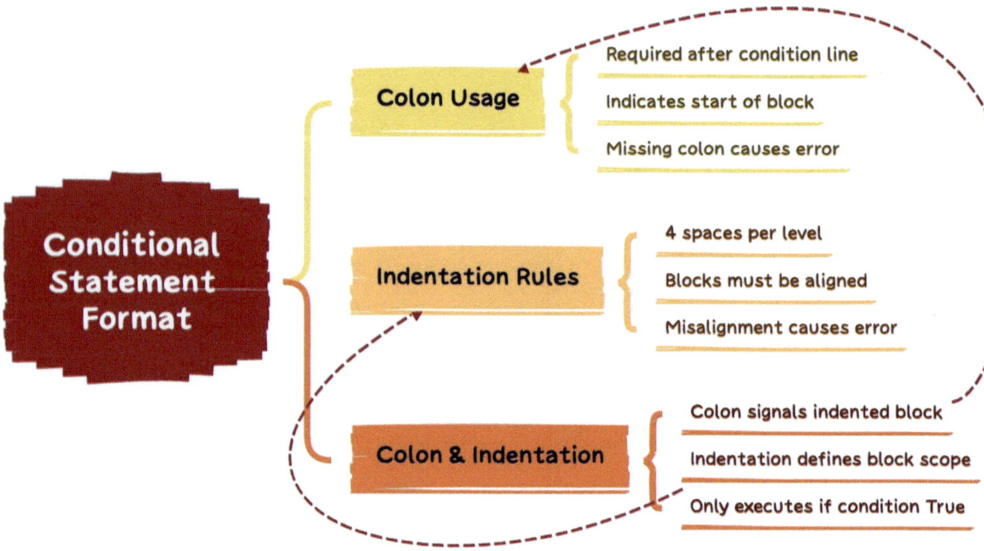

FIGURE 3.3 Conditional Statement Format

Correct example:

```
if profit > 0:
    print("Profitable")
    print("Keep it up")
```

Here, the colon after (if profit > 0) signals that the two indented print() statements belong to the if block.

Incorrect example:

```
if profit > 0
    print("Profitable")
    print("Keep it up")
```

Here, the if statement is missing a colon (:) at the end of the line. As a result, Python does not recognise this as a complete control structure and raises an error:

```
SyntaxError: expected ':'
```

3.1.1.8 Indentation

Indentation defines the structure of code blocks. The standard in Python is to use four spaces for each level of indentation. All lines within the same block must be aligned consistently. Inconsistent indentation results in an error.

Correct example:

```
profit = 7000

if profit > 10000:
    print("High profit")
elif profit > 5000:
    print("Moderate profit")
else:
    print("Low profit")
```

Here, each print() statement is indented by four spaces and is grouped under the corresponding condition.

Incorrect example:

```
profit = 7000

if profit > 10000:
    print("High profit")
     print("Profit is higher than expected.")
elif profit > 5000:
  print("Moderate profit")
  print("Profit is moderate.")
else:
    print("Low profit")
```

Here, the second print statement under the if block has five spaces instead of four. The two print statements under the elif block use only two spaces. These inconsistencies in indentation will raise an error when the code runs. Python requires that all lines within a block share the same indentation level (normally four spaces).

In Python, the colon and indentation collectively define the structure of conditional statements. A colon at the end of a line signals that an indented block of code follows. Indentation then groups the statements within that block. If the condition is True, Python runs all indented lines under that condition. If the condition is False, Python skips the block.

3.1.2 Follow-Along Activity

Step 1: Categorising Expenses

Let's classify expenses as "Low" if they are up to £100, "Medium" if they are over £100 and up to £500 (inclusive), and "High" if they are above £500. Let's type in the following code:

```
expense = 250

if expense <= 100:
    category = "Low"
```

```
elif expense <= 500:
    category = "Medium"
else:
    category = "High"

print(category)
```

Output

```
Medium
```

Explanation

- expense = 250: assigns the value 250 to the variable expense.
- Python then checks each condition in turn.
    - First, it evaluates expense <= 100. Since 250 <= 100 is False, Python moves to the next condition.
    - It then evaluates expense <= 500. Since 250 is within that range, this condition is True, and the category is set to "Medium".
    - Python skips the else block.
- print(category): prints the value of category, which is "Medium".
- Pay attention to the format of conditional statements.
    - A colon (:) must follow each if, elif, and else statement to indicate the start of the code block.
    - Each conditional code block requires consistent indentation (i.e. 4 spaces).

Step 2: Two-Category Check

Let's categorise an expense as either "Above Budget" or "Within Budget". Only two conditions are needed, so an elif is not required.

```
budget = 1000
expense = 900

if expense > budget:
    category = "Above Budget"
else:
    category = "Within Budget"

print("The expense category is:", category)
```

Output

```
The expense category is: Within Budget
```

Explanation

- budget = 1000: assigns the value 1000 to the variable budget.
- expense = 900: assigns the value 900 to the variable expense.
- The variable budget is set to 1000, and expense is set to 900.
- The condition if expense > budget checks whether 900 is greater than 1000. As this condition is false, the code in the else block runs and sets category to "Within Budget".
- print("The expense category is:", category): prints the result.

Step 3: Four-Category Check

Let's divide transactions into four groups: "Low", "Medium", "High", and "Very High". As there are four categories, an additional elif condition is needed.

```
transaction_amount = 750

if transaction_amount <= 100:
    category = "Low"
elif transaction_amount <= 500:
    category = "Medium"
elif transaction_amount <= 1000:
    category = "High"
else:
    category = "Very High"

print("The transaction category is:", category)
```

Output

```
The transaction category is: High
```

Explanation

- transaction_amount = 750: assigns the value 750 to the variable transaction_amount.
- Python then checks each condition in turn.
  - The first if condition checks whether transaction_amount <= 100. Since 750 <= 100 is false, Python moves to the next condition.
  - The second elif checks whether 750 <= 500. This is false, as 750 is not less than or equal to 500. Python moves to the next condition.
  - The third elif checks whether transaction_amount <= 1000. This is true because 750 is greater than 500 and less than or equal to 1000. As a result, the category is set to "High".
  - The else block is skipped because the third condition is true.
- print("The transaction category is:", category): prints the result.

3.1.3 *Your Project*

3.1.3.1 Task

You are writing Python code to assign an income category based on user input. Use the following thresholds:

- Low Income: up to £25,000 (inclusive)
- Middle Income: over £25,000 and up to £60,000 (inclusive)
- High Income: above £60,000

Note: When writing numbers in Python code, do not include commas in large numbers (e.g. write 25000 instead of 25,000).

Instructions

1. Prompt the user to enter an annual income value.
2. Use if, elif, and else statements to assign the appropriate category.
3. Display both the income and the assigned category.

Hints

- Use the input() statement to capture user input (see Chapter 2, Section 2.5).
- Place colons (:) at the end of each if, elif, and else line.
- Indent each code block by four spaces.
- Test your code using values such as 20000, 45000, and 75000. Enter plain numbers only (no commas or symbols), as commas or currency signs will cause an input error.

3.1.3.2 Example Code

```
# Step 1: Get the income value from the user
income_input = input("Enter the client's annual income (£): ")
income = float(income_input)  # Convert the input to a float for han-
dling decimals

# Step 2: Apply conditional statements for categorisation
if income <= 25000:
    category = "Low Income"
elif income <= 60000:
    category = "Middle Income"
else:
    category = "High Income"

# Step 3: Display the result
print(f"Income: £{income:,.2f} – Category: {category}")
```

Scan the QR code to access the code and output (see 3.1.ipynb).

https://github.com/DrMichaelGuo/PFAAFAMMA

3.2 For Loop

There are two types of loops in Python: for and while. A for loop executes the same action repeatedly for a specific number of times. A while loop continues to execute as long as a given condition remains true. This section introduces the for loop and demonstrates its use in accounting and finance (see Figure 3.4).

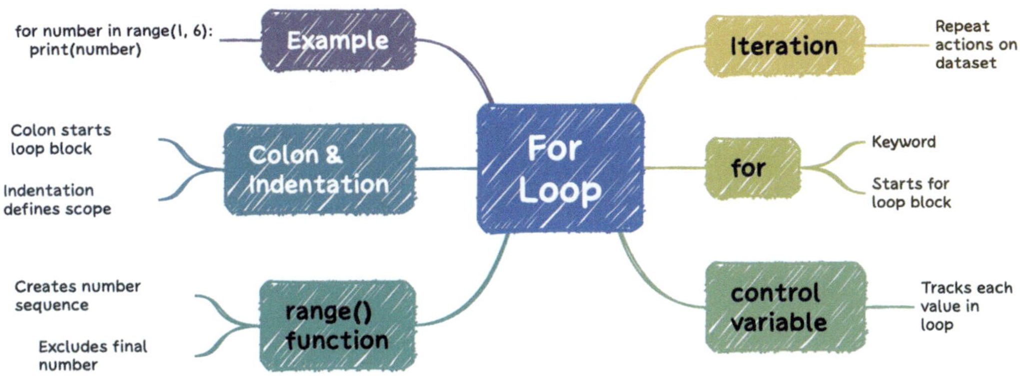

FIGURE 3.4 For Loop

3.2.1 Key Concepts

3.2.1.1 Iteration

Iteration is the process of repeating actions on each item in a dataset. For example, the following for loop repeats an action several times:

```
for number in range(1, 6):
    print(number)
```

3.2.1.2 *for*

In this example, for tells Python to begin a for loop. for is a keyword in Python. A keyword has a fixed meaning and cannot be used for other purposes, such as naming variables.

3.2.1.3 *Loop Control Variable*

A loop control variable records each step in a for loop. In the example, number is the control variable. It takes on each value in the specified range, one at a time.

3.2.1.4 *range() Function*

The range() function creates a sequence of numbers. It defines how many times a loop runs. In the example, range(1, 6) generates the values 1, 2, 3, 4, and 5. The loop starts at 1 and stops before 6. (The second value in range(start, stop) is excluded from the sequence.)

3.2.1.5 *Colon and Indentation*

As with conditional statements, a colon (:) is required at the end of the for statement to indicate the beginning of the loop block. Indentation shows which statements belong to the loop. Without correct indentation, the code will not run or will produce errors. In the example, the print(number) statement is indented, so it is executed each time the loop runs. Statements outside the indented block are not part of the loop.

3.2.2 *Follow-Along Activity*

Step 1: Basic Example

Let's consider the following for loop:

```
for a in range(1, 4):
    print(a)
```

Output

```
1
2
3
```

Explanation

- range(1, 4) generates a sequence of integers starting from 1 and ending before 4. The numbers generated are 1, 2, 3.
- The for loop selects each number in the sequence (1, 2, 3) one at a time and assigns it to the variable a.
- For each number in the sequence, Python prints the value of a on the screen.

Step-by-Step Execution

- First iteration: a = 1, prints 1.
- Second iteration: a = 2, prints 2.
- Third iteration: a = 3, prints 3.
- After this, the loop stops, as there are no more numbers in the range.

Note: Use a colon (:) at the end of the for loop line. Indent the loop body with 4 spaces.

Step 2: Compound Interest Calculation

Let's use a for loop to calculate compound interest on an investment over 3 years:

```
principal = 10000
rate = 0.05
years = 3

for year in range(1, years + 1):
    principal = principal * (1 + rate)
    print(f"Year {year}: £{principal:.2f}")
```

Output:

```
Year 1: £10500.00
Year 2: £11025.00
Year 3: £11576.25
```

Explanation

- principal = 10000: assigns the initial investment amount (£10,000) to the variable principal.
- rate = 0.05: assigns the annual interest rate (5%) to the variable rate.
- years = 3: assigns the investment period (3 years) to the variable years.
- for year in range(1, years + 1): starts a for loop that repeats the calculation for each year.
  - Since years = 3, the range becomes range(1, 4), producing 1, 2, and 3.
- principal = principal * (1 + rate): updates the value of principal each year using the compound interest formula.
  - Each year, the value of principal is updated by multiplying it by (1 + rate). This means the interest is added to the investment, and the result becomes the new principal for the next year. The calculation includes interest on both the original amount and any previously added interest.
- print(f"Year {year}: £{principal:.2f}"): prints the result for each year.
  - This line uses an f-string to include variable values inside a string. {year} shows the current year number. {principal:.2f} formats the investment amount to two decimal places.

Try it yourself: What happens if you calculate compound interest for 10 years? Change years = 3 to years = 10.

3.2.3 *Your Project*

3.2.3.1 *Task*

Your company has purchased an asset with an initial cost of £15,000. The residual value (the estimated value at the end of its useful life) is £3,000. The useful life of the asset is 6 years. The straight-line depreciation method is used.

Use a for loop to calculate and display the asset's value at the end of each year.

Suggested Steps

- Define variables.
- Calculate annual depreciation. This is the difference between the initial cost and the residual value, divided by the number of useful life years.
- Set up a for loop to track depreciation over time.
- Calculate the asset's value at the end of each year.
- Print the results.

Reminder

- Use a colon (:) at the end of the for loop line.
- Use indentation for the loop body.
- Use f-strings ({}) to format the output.
- Round the value to two decimal places using :.2f.

3.2.3.2 *Example Code*

```
# Define input values
initial_cost = 15000
residual_value = 3000
useful_life_years = 6

# Calculate annual depreciation
annual_depreciation = (initial_cost - residual_value) /
useful_life_years

# Loop through each year and calculate the depreciated value
for year in range(1, useful_life_years + 1):
    asset_value = initial_cost - (annual_depreciation * year)
    print(f"Year {year}: £{asset_value:.2f}")
```

Scan the QR code to access the code and output (see 3.2.ipynb).

https://github.com/DrMichaelGuo/PFAAFAMMA

3.3 While Loop

A while loop is a control structure that repeats a block of code as long as a given condition remains true. It can be used to automate repetitive tasks in accounting and finance. This section introduces the key concepts and common uses of while loops (see Figure 3.5).

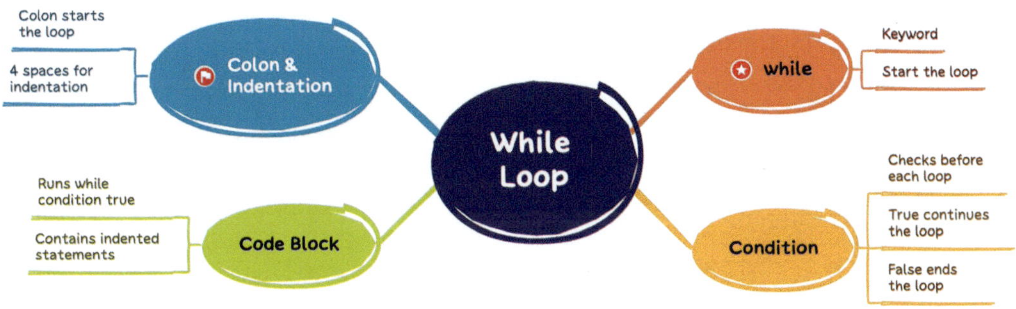

FIGURE 3.5 While Loop

3.3.1 Key Concepts

3.3.1.1 While Loop

A while loop runs code as long as a condition remains True. For example,

```
while <condition>:
    <code block>
```

3.3.1.2 While

The keyword while starts a conditional loop in Python.

3.3.1.3 Condition

The condition determines whether the loop continues. If the condition is True, Python runs the code block. When the condition becomes False, the loop stops.

3.3.1.4 Code Block

The code block contains statements that run while the condition is True.

3.3.1.5 Colon and Indentation

As with if statements and for loops, a colon (:) marks the start of the loop. Correct indentation (4 spaces) defines which statements belong to the loop. Incorrect indentation results in an error.

3.3.2 Follow-Along Activity

Step 1: Basic Example

Let's count and print the numbers 1 to 3 using a while loop.

```
number = 1

while number <= 3
    print(number)
    number = number + 1
```

Output

```
1
2
3
```

Explanation

- number = 1: assigns the value 1 to the variable number.
- while number <= 3: starts the loop. The loop runs while the condition (number <= 3) is True.
- If the condition is True, Python prints the current value of number and then increases it by 1 (number = number + 1).
    - number = number + 1: updates the value of number. Without it, the loop would not stop and would become an infinite loop.
- Python then checks the condition again. If number is still less than or equal to 3, the loop continues.
- When number becomes 4, the condition is False, and the loop ends.

Step-by-Step Execution

- First iteration: number = 1, prints 1, updates to 2.
- Second iteration: number = 2, prints 2, updates to 3.
- Third iteration: number = 3, prints 3, updates to 4.
- Once number becomes 4, the loop condition is False, loop ends.

Step 2: Example in an Accounting Context

Let's calculate how many years it takes to reach a savings target using compound interest.

```
balance = 5000
target = 10000
interest_rate = 0.05
years = 0

while balance < target:
    balance = balance + (balance * interest_rate)
    years = years + 1
    print(f"Year {years}: Balance is £{balance:.2f}")

print("It will take", years, "years to reach the target balance of
£10,000.")
```

Output

```
Year 1: Balance is £5250.00
Year 2: Balance is £5512.50
Year 3: Balance is £5788.12
Year 4: Balance is £6077.53
Year 5: Balance is £6381.41
Year 6: Balance is £6700.48
Year 7: Balance is £7035.50
Year 8: Balance is £7387.28
Year 9: Balance is £7756.64
Year 10: Balance is £8144.47
Year 11: Balance is £8551.70
Year 12: Balance is £8979.28
Year 13: Balance is £9428.25
Year 14: Balance is £9899.66
Year 15: Balance is £10394.64
It will take 15 years to reach the target balance of £10,000.
```

Explanation

- balance = 5000: assigns the initial investment amount (£5,000) to the variable balance.
- target = 10000: assigns the savings goal (£10,000) to the variable target.
- interest_rate = 0.05: assigns the annual interest rate (5%) to the variable.
- years = 0: assigns zero to the variable years to start the counter.

- while balance < target: runs the loop while the balance is less than the target. When the balance reaches or exceeds the target, the loop ends.
- balance = balance + (balance * interest_rate): calculates the annual interest and adds it to the current balance.
- years = years + 1: increases the year counter each time the loop runs. This tracks how many years it takes to reach the target.
- print(f"Year {years}: Balance is £{balance:.2f}"): shows the balance at the end of each year.
- print("It will take", years, "years to reach the target balance of £10,000."): displays the result. It is not indented, so it runs only once, after the loop ends.

Try it yourself: Change the starting balance, target amount, or interest rate to observe how each variable affects the number of years needed to reach the savings target.

3.3.3 *Your Project*

3.3.3.1 *Task*

You are creating a while loop to simulate a debt repayment. Use the following information to calculate how many months it will take to fully repay the debt.

- Initial Balance: £3,000
- Monthly Payment: £500
- Monthly Interest Rate: 10.5%

Suggested Steps:

- Create variables for balance, monthly_payment, monthly_interest_rate, and set months = 0.
- Use a while loop to apply interest and subtract the monthly payment.
- Print the remaining balance at the end of each month.
- After the loop ends, print the total number of months required to repay the debt.

3.3.3.2 *Example Code*

```
# Set initial balance, interest rate, and monthly payment
balance = 3000                     # Starting balance
monthly_interest_rate = 0.105      # 10.5% monthly interest
monthly_payment = 500              # Fixed monthly payment
months = 0                         # Counter for the number of months

# Calculate balance each month until fully paid off
while balance > 0:
    balance = balance + (balance * monthly_interest_rate)
    balance = balance - monthly_payment
    months = months + 1
    print(f"Month {months}: Balance = {balance:.2f}")

print(f"Debt paid off in {months} months.")
```

3.3.3.3 *Extra: Alternative Approach Using Break*

There are different ways to complete the task above. One method is to use the break statement. Understanding alternative approaches helps build programming competence.

```
balance = 3000
monthly_interest_rate = 0.105
monthly_payment = 500
months = 0

# Calculate balance each month until fully paid off
while True:
    balance = balance + (balance * monthly_interest_rate)
    balance = balance - monthly_payment
    months = months + 1
    print(f"Month {months}: Balance = {balance:.2f}")

    if balance <= 0:
        break

print(f"Debt paid off in {months} months.")
```

Explanation

- while True: starts a loop that continues until stopped with a break statement.
- balance = balance + (balance * monthly_interest_rate): adds interest to the current balance.
- balance = balance - monthly_payment: subtracts the monthly payment from the balance.
- months = months + 1: increases the month counter by 1.
- print(f"Month {months}: Balance = {balance:.2f}"): displays the current month and balance, rounded to two decimal places.
- if balance <= 0: checks if the balance is zero or less.
- break: exits the loop if the condition balance <= 0 is met. The break statement is used to exit a loop when a specific condition is met.

3.3.3.4 *Extra: += and -= Operators*

In Python, the += and -= operators provide shorthand for updating variable values. For example,

```
months += 1
```

is equivalent to

```
months = months + 1
```

This line (months += 1) increments the months counter by 1.

The same applies to balance calculations:

```
balance += balance * monthly_interest_rate
```

is equivalent to

```
balance = balance + (balance * monthly_interest_rate)
```

```
balance -= monthly_payment
```

is equivalent to

```
balance = balance - monthly_payment
```

The above code can be rewritten using these operators as follows:

```
balance = 3000
monthly_interest_rate = 0.105
monthly_payment = 500
months = 0

while True:
    balance += balance * monthly_interest_rate  # += Operators
    balance -= monthly_payment                  # -= Operators
    months += 1                                 # += Operators
    print(f"Month {months}: Balance = {balance:.2f}")

    if balance <= 0
        break

print(f"Debt paid off in {months} months.")
```

Recognising these operators can help simplify code and improve readability.

Scan the QR code to access the Python code and output (see 3.3.ipynb).

https://github.com/DrMichaelGuo/PFAAFAMMA

3.4 Exceptions

Real-world data are often incomplete or inconsistent. Code must therefore handle missing values, unexpected data types, and invalid operations such as division by zero. Python provides an approach for managing such issues through exceptions. This section explains how to handle exceptions using try and except with examples from accounting and finance (see Figure 3.6).

3.4.1 *Key Concepts*

3.4.1.1 *Exception*

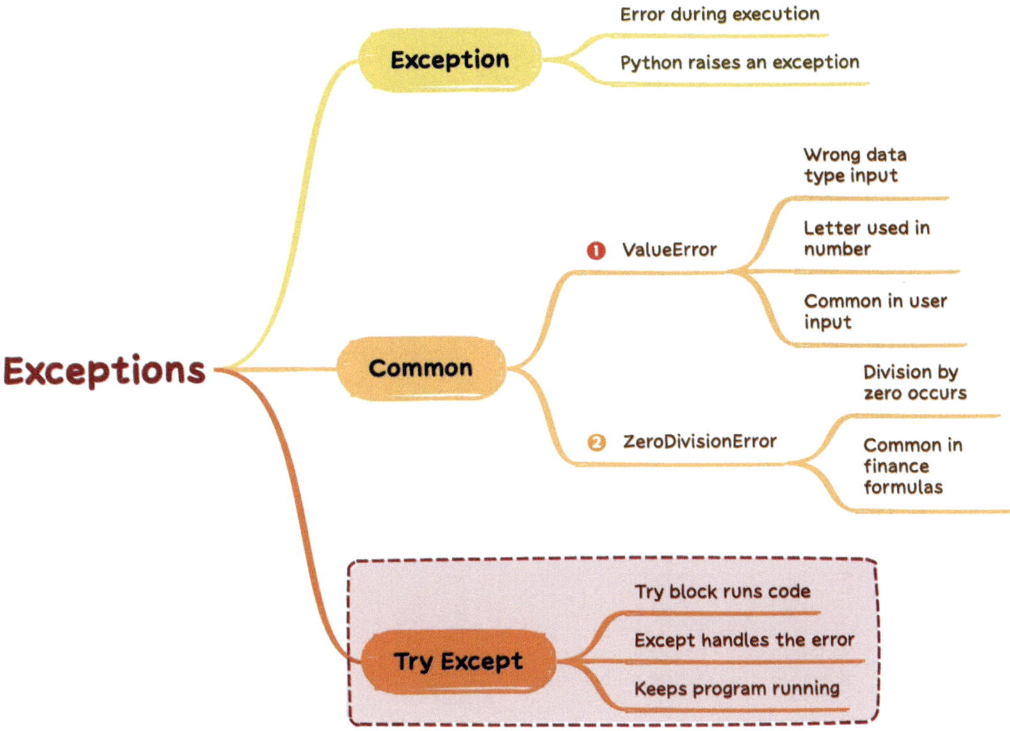

FIGURE 3.6 Exceptions

An exception is an error that occurs during program execution. When Python encounters such an error, it interrupts the normal flow of the program and raises an exception. Although the term error is used in general discussion, *exception* is the technical term in Python for a condition that can be identified and handled in the code.

Consider the following code:

```
x = 10 / 0
```

Output

```
ZeroDivisionError: division by zero
```

In this example, Python raises a ZeroDivisionError since the expression attempts to divide a number by zero. The program stops and displays an error message.

Two common exceptions in accounting and finance are ValueError and ZeroDivisionError.

3.4.1.2 *ValueError*

A ValueError occurs when the type or content of the data is invalid. For example,

```
amount = int("1OOO")
```

Output

```
ValueError: invalid literal for int() with base 10: '1OOO'
```

This error occurs because the string contains the letter 'O' instead of the digit zero. This type of error may appear when user input or imported data include typing or formatting issues.

3.4.1.3 *ZeroDivisionError*

A ZeroDivisionError occurs when a number is divided by zero. This can happen in financial calculations. For example,

```
net_profit = 5000
total_assets = 0
return_on_assets = net_profit / total_assets
```

Output

```
ZeroDivisionError: division by zero
```

This error occurs because the denominator (total assets) is zero.

3.4.1.4 *try-except Block*

A try-except block allows the program to handle exceptions and continue running. It catches and manages errors that would otherwise stop the program.

```
try:
    revenue = int("abc")
except ValueError:
    print("Invalid input: expected a number.")
```

Explanation

- try: tells Python to try running a block of code. This is where you write the code that might cause an error.
- except: tells Python what to do if an error happens while running the try block.

In this case, Python tries to run int("abc"). Since abc is not a number, a ValueError happens. Instead of stopping the program, Python runs the except block and prints

```
Invalid input: expected a number.
```

3.4.2 *Follow-Along Activity*

Step 1: Code without Error Handling

Let's begin with the following code:

```
equity_input = input("Enter equity (£): ")
debt_input   = input("Enter debt   (£): ")

equity = float(equity_input)
debt   = float(debt_input)

ratio = debt / equity
print(f"Debt-to-Equity Ratio: {ratio:.2f}")
```

This code calculates the debt-to-equity ratio based on user input. The code does not include error handling.

Step 2: Division by Zero Error (ZeroDivisionError)

Let's run the code from Step 1. If we enter zero for equity and 20000 for debt, Python stops and raises an exception because division by zero is not allowed:

```
Enter equity (£): 0
Enter debt   (£): 20000

-----------------------------------------------------------------------
-----
ZeroDivisionError                         Traceback (most recent call
last)
<ipython-input-3-5cd3b2f24cd3> in <cell line: 0>()
      6 debt   = float(debt_input)
      7
----> 8 ratio = debt / equity
      9 print(f"Debt-to-Equity Ratio: {ratio:.2f}")

ZeroDivisionError: float division by zero
```

Step 3: Non-Numeric Input Error (ValueError)

Let's rerun the code. This time, enter the letter a for equity and % for debt. Python crashes and raises an exception again because the input contains letters or symbols:

Output

```
Enter equity (£): a
Enter debt   (£): %
---------------------------------------------------------------------------
ValueError                                Traceback (most recent call
last)
<ipython-input-10-f0ff1e35a68d> in <cell line: 0>()
      3 debt_input    = input("Enter debt   (£): ")
      4
----> 5 equity = float(equity_input)
      6 debt   = float(debt_input)
      7

ValueError: could not convert string to float: 'a'
```

This error occurs because Python cannot convert the string 'a' into a float. The same applies to any symbol or letter that is not a valid number.

Step 4: Adding Basic Error Handling Using Try and Except

Let's rewrite the code using a try-except block to handle user input errors. This prevents the program from crashing when an error occurs.

```
equity_input = input("Enter equity (£): ")
debt_input   = input("Enter debt   (£): ")

try:
    equity = float(equity_input)
    debt   = float(debt_input)
    ratio  = debt / equity
    print(f"Debt-to-Equity Ratio: {ratio:.2f}")

except ZeroDivisionError:
    print("Error: equity is zero - ratio cannot be calculated.")

except ValueError:
    print("Error: please enter numbers only.")
```

Example Output 1 (if we input 0 for equity and 20000 for debt):

```
Enter equity (£): 0
Enter debt   (£): 20000
Error: equity is zero - ratio cannot be calculated.
```

Example Output 2 (if we input a for equity and % for debt):

```
Enter equity (£): a
Enter debt   (£): %
Error: please enter numbers only.
```

Explanation

- The try block attempts to convert the input values and perform the division. If an error occurs,
    - except ZeroDivisionError: handles cases where equity is zero.
    - except ValueError: handles cases where input cannot be converted to a float.
- In both cases, Python does not crash. Instead, the program displays a clear error message and continues to run.

3.4.3 Your Project

3.4.3.1 Task

You are writing Python code to calculate Return on Equity (ROE). The code should

- Ask the user for Net Profit and Shareholders' Equity.
- Convert both inputs to numbers.
- Calculate the ROE using the formula: net_profit / shareholders_equity.
- Use try-except blocks to handle two possible errors:
    - Shareholders' equity entered as zero.
    - Input not recognised as a number.
- Print either the ROE (to two decimal places) or a clear error message.
- Ensure that the code does not stop or crash, regardless of the input.

3.4.3.2 Example Code

```
# Return on Equity (ROE) calculator with basic error handling

# Prompt the user to enter Net Profit and Shareholders' Equity
net_profit_input            = input("Enter Net Profit (£): ")
shareholders_equity_input = input("Enter Shareholders' Equity (£): ")

try:
    # Convert input values from strings to floats
    # May raise ValueError if the input is not a number
    net_profit          = float(net_profit_input)
    shareholders_equity = float(shareholders_equity_input)

    # Calculate ROE
    # May raise ZeroDivisionError if shareholders' equity is zero
    roe = net_profit / shareholders_equity
```

```
    # Display the calculated ROE, formatted to two decimal places
    print(f"Return on Equity: {roe:.2f}")

# Handle the case where shareholders' equity is zero to prevent
division by zero
except ZeroDivisionError:
    print("Error: shareholders' equity is zero - ROE cannot be
calculated.")

# Handle the case where input values are not valid numbers
except ValueError:
    print("Error: please enter numbers only.")
```

Scan the QR code to access the Python code and output (see 3.4.ipynb). You will also see other exception types.

https://github.com/DrMichaelGuo/PFAAFAMMA

Summary of Chapter 3: Control Structures

In this chapter, we have covered the following concepts:

Conditional Statements (if, elif, else)

- if: executes a block of code if a condition is True.
- elif: checks another condition if the previous one was False.
- else: executes when all previous conditions are False.
- Use case: categorising income, expenses, or transactions based on thresholds or types.

Comparison Operators

- Used in conditional statements to compare values
    - > greater than
    - < less than
    - >= greater than or equal to
    - <= less than or equal to
    - == equal to
    - != not equal to
    - Use case: budget comparisons, tax band classification, and threshold checks.

Indentation and Colons

- Python uses indentation (4 spaces) to define blocks of code.
- Colons (:) are required after control structures like if, elif, else, for, and while.
- Common errors: missing colons or incorrect indentation lead to syntax errors.

Nested Conditions

- Placing one conditional inside another.
- Allows for complex decision-making.

For Loops

- Repeat code a specific number of times.
- Syntax: for i in range(5):
- Uses range() to define how many times to repeat.
- Use case: calculating compound interest or systematic depreciation.

While Loops

- Repeats code while a condition remains True.
- Must include a condition update to prevent infinite loops.
- Use case: savings accumulation and loan repayment tracking.

Exception Handling (Try and Except)

- Prevents program failure by handling errors during execution.
- Use case: managing invalid inputs, divide-by-zero errors, or unexpected data in financial tools.

Quiz Questions

Scan the QR code below to access the quiz questions for this chapter (see 3.md).

https://github.com/DrMichaelGuo/QuizPFAAFAMMA

Further Reading and Resource

Python Software Foundation (n.d.) *Python official tutorial – Control flow*. Available at: https://docs.python.org/3/tutorial/controlflow.html (Accessed 13 July 2025).

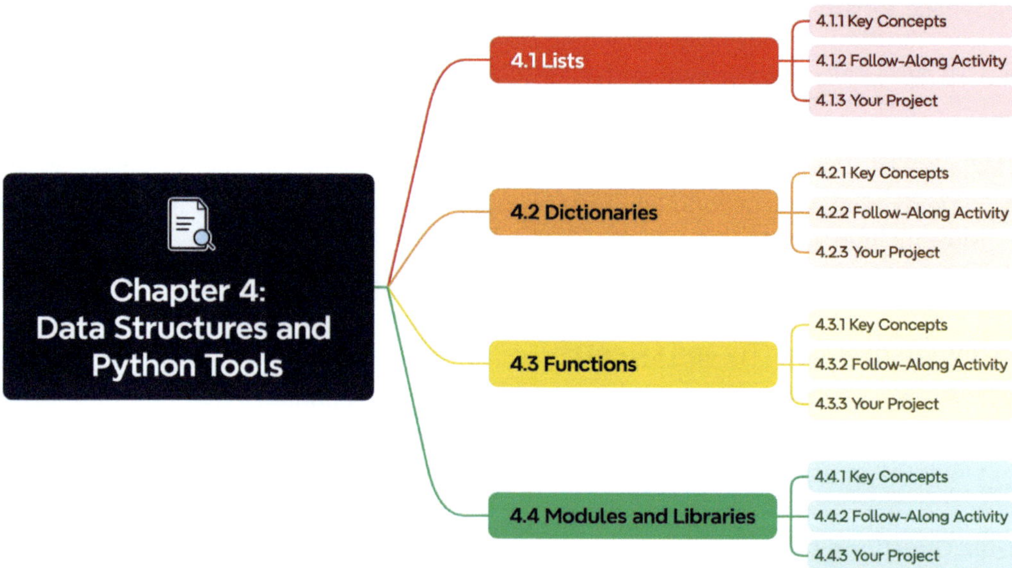

FIGURE 4.1 Structure of Chapter 4

4

DATA STRUCTURES AND PYTHON TOOLS

This chapter introduces core Python data structures and tools used to organise and analyse financial data. It explains how to use lists and dictionaries to store and process accounting information, how to define and reuse functions for financial calculations, and how to apply Python modules and libraries to automate data analysis tasks. Each topic includes examples, guided activities, and practical tasks based on accounting and finance applications (Figure 4.1).

Learning Objectives

By the end of this chapter, you will be able to

- Use lists and dictionaries to organise and process financial data in Python.
- Define and call functions to automate accounting and finance calculations.
- Import and apply Python modules and libraries.

4.1 Lists

Python lists group related values within a single variable. This section explains how to use lists to organise and change financial data. It includes indexing, slicing, and commonly used list functions in accounting and finance (see Figure 4.2).

4.1.1 Key Concepts

4.1.1.1 List

A list is an ordered collection of items enclosed within square brackets [ ]. Lists are mutable, meaning their contents can be changed. For example

```
monthly_revenues = [120, 150, 140, 130, 160, 145, 155, 148, 149,
152, 158, 162]
```

DOI: 10.4324/9781003656968-4

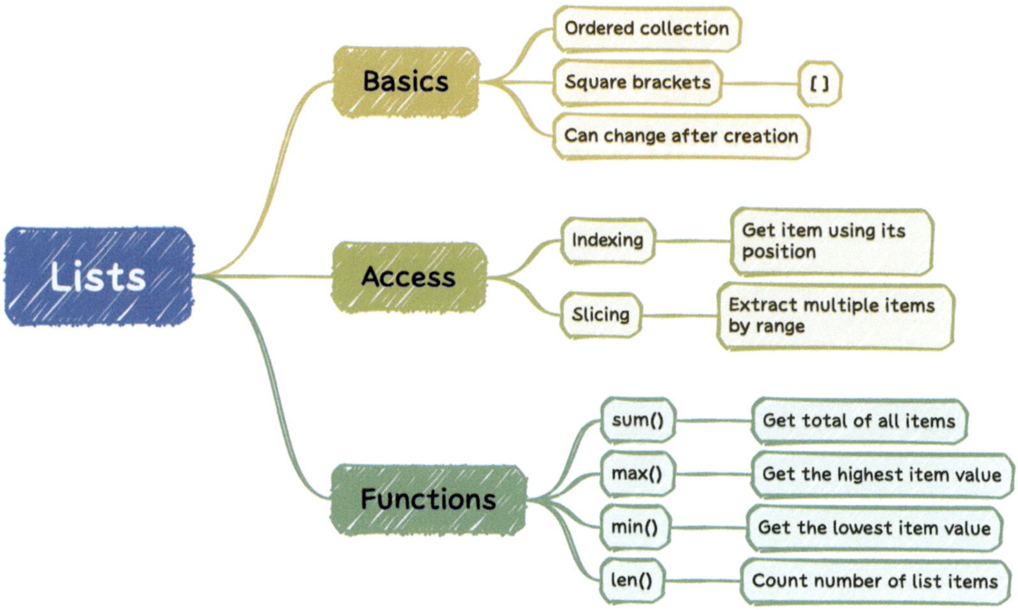

FIGURE 4.2 Lists

The variable monthly_revenues holds 12 revenue figures (in thousands of pounds).

4.1.1.2 Indexing

Indexing retrieves a single element by its position in the list.

4.1.1.3 Slicing

Slicing extracts a range of elements from a list.

4.1.1.4 Functions

The functions below are commonly used in accounting and finance:

- sum(): returns the total of all values.
- max(): returns the highest value.
- min(): returns the lowest value.
- len(): returns the number of items in the list.

4.1.2 Follow-Along Activity

Step 1: Create a List

Let's create and print a list of monthly revenues (in thousands of pounds) for a company.

```
monthly_revenues = [120, 150, 140, 130, 160, 145, 155, 148, 149,
152, 158, 162]

print(monthly_revenues)
```

Output

```
[120, 150, 140, 130, 160, 145, 155, 148, 149, 152, 158, 162]
```

Explanation

- The first line assigns a list of 12 numerical values to the variable monthly_revenues.
  - Each value represents the revenue for 1 month, measured in thousands of pounds. The values are stored in calendar order, with the first value (120) representing January, the second (150) representing February, and so on through to December.
- print(monthly_revenues): prints the contents of the list.

Step 2: Indexing

Let's retrieve the revenue data for January.

```
january_revenue = monthly_revenues[0]
print(january_revenue)
```

Output

```
120
```

Explanation

- In Python, list positions start at zero. This means the first item in the list is at index 0, the second item is at index 1, the third at index 2, and so on. In this code, index 0 refers to January, index 1 to February, and so forth.
- january_revenue = monthly_revenues[0]: assigns the first item in the list to the variable january_revenue.
- print(january_revenue): prints the value assigned to the variable.

Step 3: Slicing

Let's extract revenue data for the first and second quarters.

```
q1_revenues = monthly_revenues[0:3]
q2_revenues = monthly_revenues[3:6]

print("Q1:", q1_revenues)
print("Q2:", q2_revenues)
```

Output

```
[120, 150, 140]
[130, 160, 145]
```

Explanation

- Slicing uses the format list[start:stop]. It returns values from the index start up to, but not including, the index stop.
    - monthly_revenues[0:3]: returns items at index 0, 1, and 2 (January to March).
    - monthly_revenues[3:6]: returns the items at index 3, 4, and 5 (April to June).
- q1_revenues = monthly_revenues[0:3]: assigns the first quarter's data to q1_revenues.
- q2_revenues = monthly_revenues[3:6]: assigns the second quarter's data to q2_revenues.
- print("Q1:", q1_revenues): prints the values for Quarter 1.
- print("Q2:", q2_revenues): prints the values for Quarter 2.

Step 4: List Functions

Let's use built-in functions to summarise the revenue data. A built-in function is provided by Python and can be used without any additional setup.

```
total_revenue = sum(monthly_revenues)
max_revenue = max(monthly_revenues)
min_revenue = min(monthly_revenues)
num_months = len(monthly_revenues)

print("Total revenue (£000):", total_revenue)
print("Highest month (£000):", max_revenue)
print("Lowest month (£000):", min_revenue)
print("Number of months:", num_months)
```

Output

```
Total revenue (£000): 1769
Highest month (£000): 162
Lowest month (£000): 120
Number of months: 12
```

Explanation

- total_revenue = sum(monthly_revenues): calculates the total of all revenue values in the list and assigns the result to total_revenue.
- max_revenue = max(monthly_revenues): identifies the highest revenue value in the list and assigns it to max_revenue.
- min_revenue = min(monthly_revenues): identifies the lowest revenue value in the list and assigns it to min_revenue.
- num_months = len(monthly_revenues): counts the number of items in the list and assigns the result to num_months.
- Each print statement prints the corresponding value.

4.1.3 Your Project

4.1.3.1 Tasks

You are creating a to store quarterly financial data (in thousands of pounds). Positive values indicate profit; negative values indicate loss.

Data for the four quarters: 4500, –1200, 3700, 800.

Complete the following tasks:

- Create a list variable and assign the financial data to it.
- Use indexing to retrieve the value for the first quarter.
- Use slicing to extract data for the first half-year.
- Use the functions sum(), max(), min(), and len() to calculate the total, highest, lowest, and count of values in the list.

4.1.3.2 Example Code

```
# Quarterly financial data (positive values = profit, negative values
= loss)
quarterly_data = [4500, -1200, 3700, 800]

# Retrieve the value for the first quarter (Q1)
q1 = quarterly_data[0]
print("Q1:", q1)

# Extract the first half-year (Q1 and Q2) using slicing
h1 = quarterly_data[0:2]
print("First half-year:", h1)

# Calculate the total profit/loss across all quarters
total = sum(quarterly_data)

# Identify the highest value in the data
highest = max(quarterly_data)

# Identify the lowest value in the data
lowest = min(quarterly_data)

# Count the number of items in the list
count = len(quarterly_data)

# Display the results
print("Sum  (£000):", total)
print("Max  (£000):", highest)
print("Min  (£000):", lowest)
print("Items      :", count)
```

4.1.3.3 Extra Challenge: Categorise Profit and Loss

Continue from the above project. Write a for loop to go through the quarterly_data list. For each amount, check whether it represents profit or loss. Use a conditional statement to allocate the amount to either total_profit or total_loss. After the loop ends, display both totals.

4.1.3.4 Example Code

```
# Quarterly financial data (positive values = profit, negative values
= loss)
quarterly_data = [4500, -1200, 3700, 800]

# Initialise totals for profit and loss
total_profit = 0
total_loss = 0

# Iterate through the data and allocate values to profit or loss
for amount in quarterly_data:
    if amount > 0:
        total_profit += amount  # Add to profit
    else:
        total_loss += amount    # Add to loss

# Display the results
print("Total Profit:", total_profit)
print("Total Loss:", total_loss)
```

Scan the QR code to access the code and output (see 4.1.ipynb). You will also see other list functions.

https://github.com/DrMichaelGuo/PFAAFAMMA

4.2 Dictionaries

A dictionary is a data structure for storing key–value pairs. The dictionary works like an index in a handbook, where each keyword (the key) points to the page number (the value). This section explains how to create and use dictionaries for accounting and finance tasks in Python (see Figure 4.3).

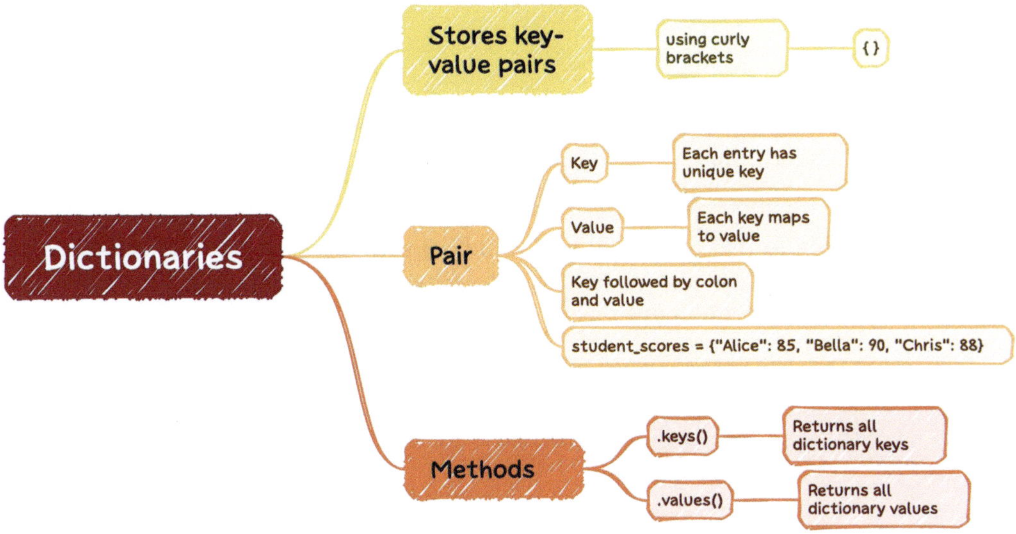

FIGURE 4.3 Dictionaries

4.2.1 Key Concepts

4.2.1.1 Dictionary

A dictionary is a collection of key–value pairs enclosed inside curly brackets { }.

```
student_scores = {"Alice": 85, "Bella": 90, "Chris": 88}
```

4.2.1.2 Key

A key identifies each entry in a dictionary. Each key must be unique. In the example above, 'Alice', 'Bella', and 'Chris' are the keys.

4.2.1.3 Value

Value is the data linked to that key. In the example above, 85, 90, and 88 are the values linked to the keys.

4.2.1.4 Key-Value Pair

Each item in a dictionary is a key followed by a colon :, then its value.

4.2.1.5 Dictionary Methods

Python includes methods to work with dictionaries. Examples include:

- .keys(): returns all the keys in the dictionary.
- .values(): returns all the values in the dictionary.

4.2.2 *Follow-Along Activity*

Step 1: Create a Dictionary

Let's create a dictionary to store a company's quarterly revenue data.

```
revenue_data = {"Q1": 25000, "Q2": 27000, "Q3": 30000, "Q4": 32000}
```

This is a condensed format, where all key–value pairs are written in a single line.

The same dictionary can also be written in an expanded format, where each key–value pair is placed on a separate line:

```
revenue_data = {
"Q1": 25000,
"Q2": 27000,
"Q3": 30000,
"Q4": 32000
}
```

Explanation

- The condensed format is suitable for short dictionaries.
- The expanded format improves readability when the dictionary contains more data or when the data structure becomes complex.

Step 2: Access Values by Key

Let's retrieve the revenue for a specific quarter using its key.

```
q1_revenue = revenue_data["Q1"]
print(q1_revenue)
q3_revenue = revenue_data["Q3"]
print(q3_revenue)
```

Output

```
25000
30000
```

Explanation

- Use square brackets [ ] with a key to access the corresponding value. "Q1" returns 25000, and "Q3" returns 30000.

Step 3: Add and Update Entries

Let's add a new entry and update an existing entry in the dictionary.

```
revenue_data["Q5"] = 34000  # Adds a new quarter
revenue_data["Q4"] = 33000  # Updates the revenue for Q4
print(revenue_data)
```

Output:

```
{'Q1': 25000, 'Q2': 27000, 'Q3': 30000, 'Q4': 33000, 'Q5': 34000}
```

Explanation

- revenue_data["Q5"] = 34000: adds a new key "Q5" with the value 34000. Note: "Q5" is included here only to demonstrate how to add new entries to a dictionary. In real financial data, there are four quarters in a year.
- revenue_data["Q4"] = 33000: updates the value for the existing key "Q4" from 32000 to 33000.
- print(revenue_data): displays the updated dictionary.

Step 4: keys() and values() Methods

Let's use .keys() to get a list of all the keys (quarters) and use .values() to get all the values.

```
quarters = revenue_data.keys()
revenues = revenue_data.values()
print(quarters)
print(revenues)
```

Output

```
dict_keys(['Q1', 'Q2', 'Q3', 'Q4', 'Q5'])
dict_values([25000, 27000, 30000, 33000, 34000])
```

Explanation

- .keys(): returns all the keys in the dictionary as a dict_keys object.
- .values(): returns all the values as a dict_values object.

Extra: The output shows special objects called dict_keys and dict_values. They are not normal lists, but they behave like lists in many situations, especially in loops.

4.2.3 Your Project

4.2.3.1 Tasks

You are writing Python code to manage a company's financial data, including revenue of 100000, expenses of 75000, and assets of 500000.

Complete the following steps:

- Define a dictionary to hold the financial data.
- Retrieve revenue and expenses from the dictionary.
- Calculate profit by subtracting expenses from revenue, and add profit to the dictionary.
- Add a new key 'taxes' to the dictionary with a value of 15000.
- Use .keys() to display all keys in the dictionary.
- Use .values() to display all values in the dictionary.
- Print the entire dictionary.

4.2.3.2 Example Code

```
# Define a dictionary to store the company's financial data
financial_data = {
"revenue": 100000,
"expenses": 75000,
"assets": 500000
}

# Extract revenue and expenses from the dictionary
revenue = financial_data["revenue"]
expenses = financial_data["expenses"]

# Calculate profit
profit = revenue - expenses

# Add profit to the dictionary
financial_data["profit"] = profit

# Add a new entry for taxes
financial_data["taxes"] = 15000

# Display all keys in the dictionary
print(financial_data.keys())

# Display all values in the dictionary
print(financial_data.values())

# Display the entire dictionary
print(financial_data)
```

Scan the QR code to access the code and output (see 4.2.ipynb). You will also see other dictionary functions.

https://github.com/DrMichaelGuo/PFAAFAMMA

4.3 Functions

Functions support the creation and reuse of a block of code. This section explains how to define functions and shows their use in accounting and finance (see Figure 4.4).

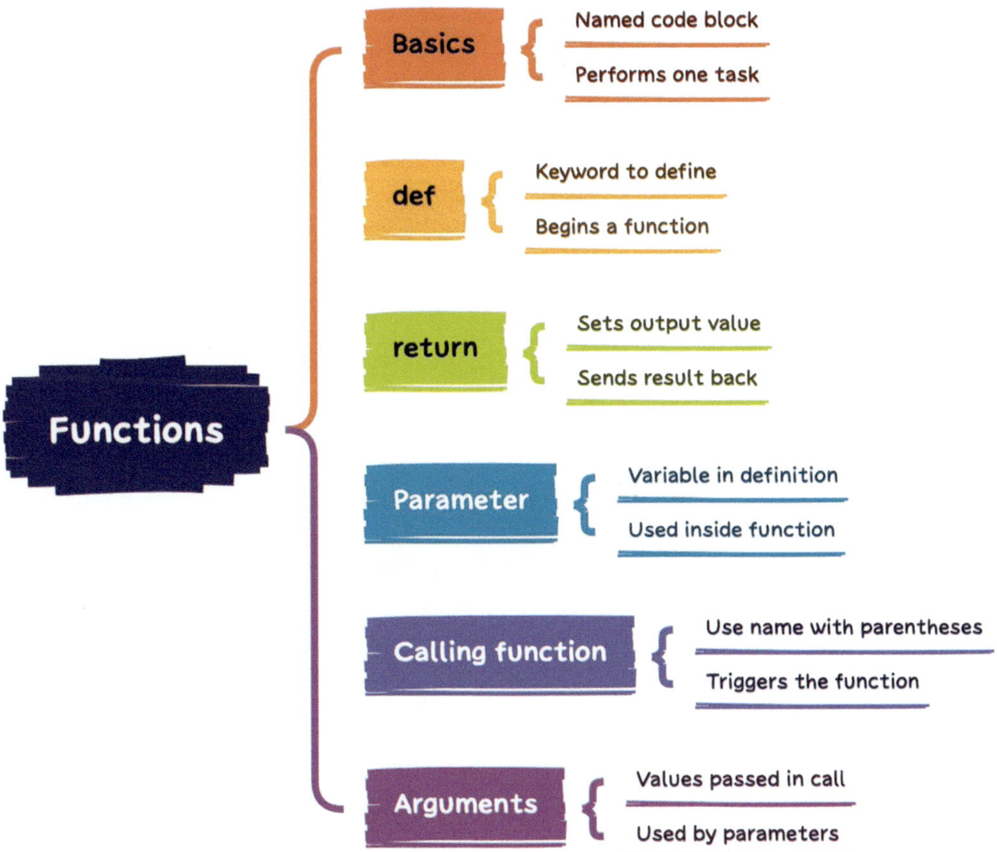

FIGURE 4.4 Functions

4.3.1 Key Concepts

4.3.1.1 Function

A function is a named block of code that carries out one specific task. For example,

```
def add(a, b):
    return a + b
```

4.3.1.2 def

The keyword def is short for define. It tells Python to create a function. In the example, add is the name of the function.

4.3.1.3 return

The keyword return sets the value that the function will output. In the example, return a + b outputs the sum of a and b.

4.3.1.4 Parameter

A parameter is a variable listed in the function definition. In the example, a and b are parameters.

4.3.1.5 Calling a Function

To use a function, write its name followed by parentheses. For example,

```
total = add(7, 3)       # call add function
print(total)
```

4.3.1.6 Arguments

An argument is the value given to the function when it is called. In the example, 7 and 3 are arguments.

Functions make code reusable. Once defined, a function can be called whenever that task is needed.

4.3.2 Follow-Along Activity

Step 1: Define a Function

Let's define a function to calculate return on investment (ROI):

```
def calculate_roi(net_profit, cost_of_investment):
    roi = (net_profit / cost_of_investment) * 100
    return roi
```

Explanation

- def calculate_roi(net_profit, cost_of_investment): defines a function named calculate_roi. The variables net_profit and cost_of_investment are the parameters of the function.
- roi = (net_profit / cost_of_investment) * 100: calculates ROI by dividing net_profit by cost_of_investment and multiplying by 100.
- return roi: sends the result of the function back to the part of the program that called the function.

Note: Use a colon at the end of the function definition line. Indent all lines inside the function body using four spaces.

Step 2: Call the Function

Let's call the function with a net profit of 20,000 and a cost of investment of 50,000 to calculate ROI:

```
result = calculate_roi(20000, 50000)
print("ROI is:", result, "%")
```

Output:

```
ROI is: 40.0 %
```

Explanation

- The function calculate_roi is called with two arguments: 20000 (net profit) and 50000 (cost of investment).
- The function calculates the ROI and returns the result.
- print("ROI is:", result, "%"): prints the result.

Step 3: Reuse the Function

Let's reuse the same function to calculate ROI for different values, for example a net profit of 30000 and a cost of investment of 40000:

```
result = calculate_roi(30000, 40000)
print("ROI is:", result, "%")
```

Output:

```
ROI is: 75.0 %
```

Explanation

- The same function is used with different input values. The formula remains unchanged. Only the arguments are updated.

4.3.3 *Your Project*

4.3.3.1 *Task 1*

Write Python code to calculate net profit margin.

- Use the example in the 'Follow-Along Activity' as a guide.
- Define a function net_profit_margin that calculates the net profit margin. The net profit margin is the difference between revenue and expenses divided by revenue.
- Call the function with revenue of 50,000 and expenses of 35,000. Print the result.

4.3.3.2 *Example Code*

```
def net_profit_margin(revenue, expenses):
    """Calculate Net Profit Margin as a percentage of revenue."""
    net_profit = revenue - expenses
    margin = (net_profit / revenue) * 100
    return margin

result = net_profit_margin(50000, 35000)
print("Net Profit Margin is:", result, "%")
```

4.3.3.3 *Task 2*

Continuing from Task 1.

- Reuse the net_profit_margin function.
- Allow users to enter revenue and expenses.
- Calculate the Net Profit Margin and round the result to two decimal places.

4.3.3.4 *Example Code*

```
revenue = float(input("Enter revenue: "))
expenses = float(input("Enter expenses: "))
result = net_profit_margin(revenue, expenses)
print(f"Net Profit Margin is: {result:.2f}%")
```

4.3.3.5 *Task 3*

Continue from Task 1.

- Reuse the net_profit_margin function to calculate the net profit margin for each quarter using the quarterly data provided below.
- Use a loop to go through the data.
- Round the result to two decimal places.

4.3.3.6 *Quarterly Data for Revenue and Expenses*

```
'''
Quarterly data for revenue and expenses:
The list quarterly_data contains four dictionaries, one for each
quarter (Q1, Q2, Q3, Q4).
Each dictionary includes:
- "quarter": the name of the quarter.
- "revenue": the revenue for that quarter.
- "expenses": the expenses for that quarter.
'''
quarterly_data = [
    {"quarter": "Q1", "revenue": 50_000, "expenses": 30_000},
    {"quarter": "Q2", "revenue": 60_000, "expenses": 35_000},
    {"quarter": "Q3", "revenue": 70_000, "expenses": 40_000},
    {"quarter": "Q4", "revenue": 55_000, "expenses": 33_000}
]
```

Note:
In Python, you can use underscores for large numbers to make them easier to read. For example, 50_000 means fifty thousand. The underscore does not affect the value; Python treats 50_000 and 50000 as the same number.

4.3.3.7 *Example Code*

```
# Quarterly data for revenue and expenses
quarterly_data = [
    {"quarter": "Q1", "revenue": 50_000, "expenses": 30_000},
    {"quarter": "Q2", "revenue": 60_000, "expenses": 35_000},
    {"quarter": "Q3", "revenue": 70_000, "expenses": 40_000},
    {"quarter": "Q4", "revenue": 55_000, "expenses": 33_000}
]

# Calculate Net Profit Margin for each quarter and print the results
for data in quarterly_data:
    revenue = data["revenue"]
    expenses = data["expenses"]
    quarter = data["quarter"]
    result = net_profit_margin(revenue, expenses)
    print(f"{quarter}: Revenue = £{revenue}, Expenses = £{expenses},
Net Profit Margin = {result:.2f}%")
```

Scan the QR code to access the code and output (see 4.3.ipynb).

https://github.com/DrMichaelGuo/PFAAFAMMA

4.4 Modules and Libraries

Modules and libraries are collections of code developed by others to perform specific tasks. Instead of writing all code from the beginning, you can use existing code that has already been tested and maintained. This section explains how to import modules and libraries, using the random module as an example (see Figure 4.5)

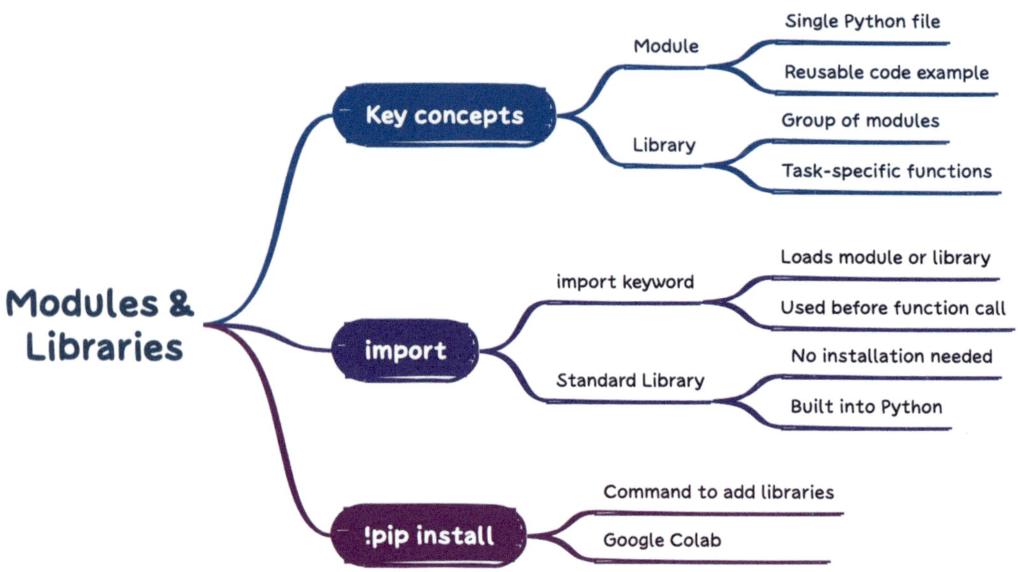

FIGURE 4.5 Modules and Libraries

4.4.1 Key Concepts

4.4.1.1 Module

A module is a single Python file that contains reusable code. Examples include:

- the math module for mathematical operations.
- the random module for random number generation.

4.4.1.2 Library

A package groups related modules together. We often use the broader term library to refer to third-party packages. Examples include:

- the pandas library for data manipulation.
- the Matplotlib library for data visualisation.

These libraries are often used in accounting and finance for data processing, analysis, and visualisation.

4.4.1.3 import

The keyword import is used to load modules and libraries into a Python program. For example,

```
import math
result = math.sqrt(16)
print(result)          # outputs: 4.0
```

Explanation

- import math: loads the math module.
- math.sqrt(16): calls the sqrt() function from the math module. The function returns the square root of 16.
- The result is stored in the variable result and printed using print(result).
- The math module is part of the Python Standard Library. There is no need to install the module.

4.4.1.4 !pip install – Installing External Libraries

Google Colab includes many common libraries such as pandas and Matplotlib. However, some libraries may not be pre-installed. The command !pip install is used to install additional libraries in Google Colab. (Note: Use !pip install only in Google Colab. In other coding environments or a terminal, run the command without the exclamation mark.)

For example, to install the pypdf library, use the following command:

```
!pip install pypdf
```

Once installed, the library can be imported and used:

```
import pypdf
```

pypdf is a Python library for working with PDF files.

4.4.2 Follow-Along Activity

The random module provides functions for generating random numbers and selecting random items.

Step 1: Import the Module

Let's import the random module.

```
import random     # keyword - import
```

Explanation

- import random: brings all the functions from the random module into the Google Colab notebook. The functions can then be used in the following steps.

Step 2: Accessing Documentation

Let's view the available functions in the random module using the help() function:

```
help(random)
```

Explanation

- The help() function displays Python's built-in documentation for the specified module. In this example, help(random) displays the documentation for the random module.

Output: The output includes the module name, a description, and a list of available functions. To save space, only the following four functions are shown here:

- random.randint(a, b): returns a random integer between a and b (inclusive).
- random.uniform(a, b): returns a random floating point number between a and b.
- random.choice(seq): returns a random element from a sequence such as a list.
- random.sample(seq, k): returns a list of k unique random elements from a sequence.

Step 3: Generate a Random Integer Using random.randint()

Let's generate a random integer between 1 and 10 using random.randint().

```
random_number = random.randint(1, 10)
print(random_number)
```

Output

```
8
```

Explanation

- In random.randint, the dot (.) is used to access the randint function from the random module.
- random.randint(a, b): returns a random integer between a and b, including both endpoints. In this example, random.randint(1, 10) generates a random integer between 1 and 10, including both 1 and 10.
- The output is 8 in this run, but the result could be any integer between 1 and 10.
- The result is stored in the variable random_number and displayed using print(random_number).
- The value will vary each time the code runs.

Step 4: Generate a Random Float Using random.uniform()

Let's generate a random float with two decimal places between 1.0 and 10.0 using random.uniform().

```
random_number_2 = random.uniform(1.0, 10.0)
print(f"{random_number_2:.2f}")
```

Output

```
4.92
```

Explanation

- random.uniform(a, b) returns a random float between a and b. In this example, random.uniform(1.0, 10.0) generates a random float between 1.0 and 10.0.
- The output is 4.92 in this run, but the result could be any float between 1.0 and 10.0.
- The result is stored in the variable random_number_2.
- print(f"{random_number_2:.2f}"): prints the result to two decimal places.
- The value will vary each time the code runs.

Step 5: Select a Random Item from a Sequence Using random.choice()

Let's select a random item from a list using random.choice().

```
options = ['buy', 'sell', 'hold']
selected_option = random.choice(options)
print("Selected option:", selected_option)
```

Output:

```
Selected option: buy
```

Explanation

- options = ['buy', 'sell', 'hold']: creates a list called options that contains three string elements: "buy', 'sell', and 'hold'.
- random.choice(options): selects one item from the list.
- The selected item is buy in this run, but the result could be any item from the list.
- print("Selected option:", selected_option): displays the results.

Step 6: Generate Lottery Numbers Using random.sample()

Let's generate six lottery numbers between 1 and 59 using random.sample().

```
winning_numbers = random.sample(range(1, 60), 6)
print("Winning lottery numbers:", winning_numbers)
```

Output

```
Winning lottery numbers: [50, 51, 10, 17, 33, 45]
```

Explanation

- random.sample(seq, k): selects k unique random elements from the sequence.
  - In this example, random.sample(range(1, 60), 6) selects six unique numbers from 1 to 59.
  - range(1, 60): creates a sequence from 1 to 59. The stop value 60 is not included.
- The selected numbers are 50, 51, 10, 17, 33, and 45 in this run, but the result could be any set of six unique numbers within the range.
- print("Winning lottery numbers:", winning_numbers): prints the selected numbers.

4.4.3 Your Project

4.4.3.1 Task 1

Write Python code to randomly select ten invoice numbers from a population of 200 invoices in audit testing.

- Import the random library.
- Use the random.sample() function to select ten unique invoice numbers from a range of 1 to 200, created using the range() function.
- Print the selected invoice numbers.

4.4.3.2 Example Code

```
import random # Import the random module

# Select 10 unique invoice numbers from 1 to 200
selected_invoices = random.sample(range(1, 201), 10)

# Print the selected invoice numbers
print(selected_invoices)
```

4.4.3.3 Task 2

Write Python code to generate five random addition questions. Each question involves adding two numbers between 1 and 20.

- Import the random module.
- Use a for loop to create five questions.
- Use random.randint() to generate two random numbers between 1 and 20 for each question.
- Print the questions using f-string.

4.4.3.4 Example Code

```
import random  # Import the random module

# Use a for loop to generate five questions
for i in range(1, 6):
    # Generate the first random number between 1 and 20
    num1 = random.randint(1, 20)

    # Generate the second random number between 1 and 20
    num2 = random.randint(1, 20)

    # Print the addition question using an f-string
    print(f"Question {i}: {num1} + {num2} = ")
```

Scan the QR code to access the code and output (see 4.4.ipynb). You will also find information on locating modules and libraries, different ways to import them, and guidance on installing libraries in different coding environments.

https://github.com/DrMichaelGuo/PFAAFAMMA

Summary of Chapter 4: Data Structures and Python Tools

In this chapter, we have covered the following concepts:

Lists

- A list is an ordered, mutable collection enclosed in square brackets [ ].
- Indexing retrieves elements by position, starting from 0.
- Slicing extracts a range of elements using list[start:stop].
- Common functions include sum(), max(), min(), and len().

Dictionaries

- A dictionary stores key–value pairs inside curly brackets { }.
- Keys must be unique and are used to retrieve values.
- Values can be numbers, strings, or other data types.
- Add or update entries using dict[key] = value.
- .keys() returns all keys; .values() returns all values.

Functions

- A function is a named block of code defined using def.
- Functions use parameters to receive input and return to send back a result.
- Functions support repeated calculations.
- Use functions to structure and automate accounting and finance tasks.

Modules and Libraries

- A module is a file of reusable Python code.
- A library is a group of related modules.
- Use import to load modules or libraries.
- The random module supports simulations and random sampling.
- Use !pip install in Google Colab to install third-party libraries when needed.

Quiz Questions

Scan the QR code below to access the quiz questions for this chapter (see 4.md).

https://github.com/DrMichaelGuo/QuizPFAAFAMMA

Further Reading and Resources

Python Software Foundation (2025) *Python official documentation – data structures*. Available at: https://docs.python.org/3/tutorial/datastructures.html (Accessed 2 November 2025).

Python Software Foundation (2025) *Python official docs – functions*. Available at: https://docs.python.org/3/tutorial/controlflow.html#defining-functions (Accessed 2 November 2025).

Python Software Foundation (2025) *Python module index (standard library)*. Available at: https://docs.python.org/3/py-modindex.html (Accessed 2 November 2025).

Python Package Index (n.d.) *PyPI – the Python package index*. Available at: https://pypi.org (Accessed 19 July 2025).

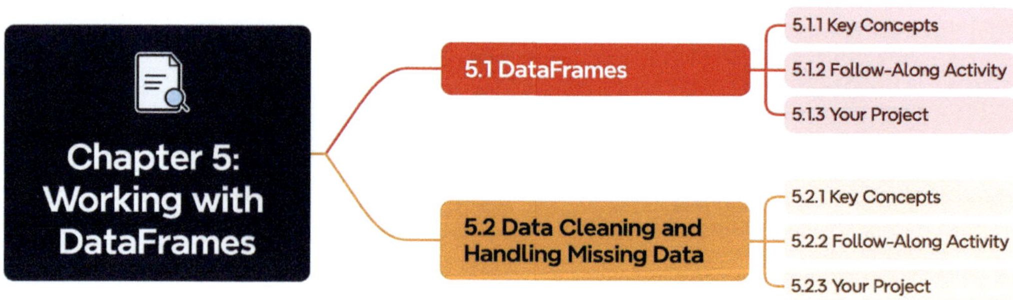

FIGURE 5.1 Structure of Chapter 5

5

WORKING WITH DATAFRAMES

This chapter introduces DataFrames, a core data structure in the pandas library, and shows how to use them to manage and analyse financial data. You will learn how to create, view, and modify tabular data. The chapter also explains how to identify and handle missing values using removal and imputation. Activities and tasks use examples drawn from accounting and finance to support the application of these techniques (Figure 5.1).

Learning Objectives

By the end of this chapter, you will be able to

- Create and modify pandas DataFrames to organise and analyse accounting and financial data.
- Identify and handle missing values using removal and imputation.

5.1 DataFrames

A DataFrame is a basic structure used for data analysis in Python. It is provided by the pandas library, which supports data manipulation and analysis. This section explains how to create and use DataFrames using pandas to organise and manage data (see Figure 5.2).

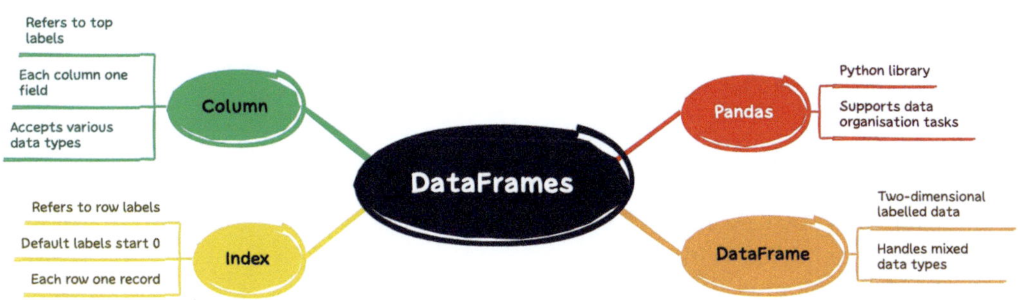

FIGURE 5.2 DataFrames

DOI: 10.4324/9781003656968-5

5.1.1 Key Concepts

5.1.1.1 Pandas

Pandas is a Python library for working with data organised in a fixed structure, such as rows and columns. It supports operations including reading and writing files, filtering data, and calculating summary statistics.

5.1.1.2 DataFrame

A DataFrame is a two-dimensional labelled data structure with rows and columns. It can contain different data types, such as integers, floats, strings, or Booleans. For example, a small greengrocer can organise stock data using a DataFrame:

```
      Product  Quantity  Price
0       Apple        50   0.60
1      Banana        30   0.40
2      Orange        20   0.50
3       Mango        15   1.20
4       Grape        40   0.80
5        Pear        25   0.55
6   Pineapple        10   1.50
7       Peach        18   0.90
8        Kiwi        12   0.75
9  Watermelon         5   3.00
```

5.1.1.3 Index

The index refers to the labels for the rows. By default, pandas assigns numeric labels starting from 0. In the example, the rows are numbered 0 to 9. Each row represents one record (one type of fruit in stock).

5.1.1.4 Column

Columns are the labels across the top of the DataFrame. These labels can be integers, floats, strings, or Booleans. In the example, the column labels are Product, Quantity, and Price. Each column holds the values for one field across all records.

5.1.1.5 Basic Operations

Basic operations with DataFrames include:

- Creating a DataFrame
- Displaying a DataFrame
- Accessing data by row index
- Accessing data by column name
- Adding new columns
- Filtering data based on conditions

5.1.2 Follow-Along Activity

This activity introduces basic operations with a DataFrame by using a small dataset of client transactions (see Figure 5.3).

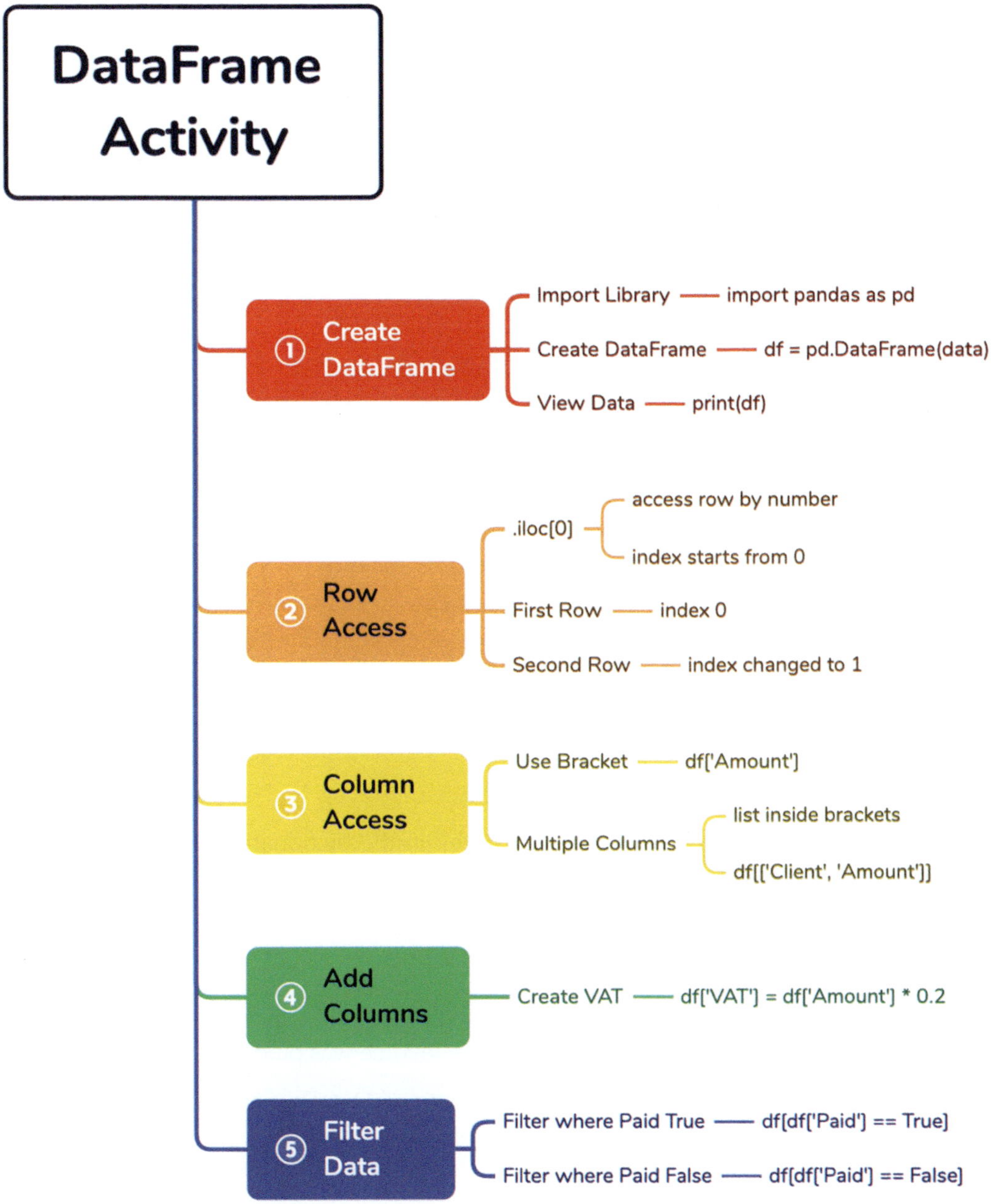

FIGURE 5.3 DataFrame Activity

Step 1: Creating a DataFrame

Let's begin by importing the pandas library.

```
import pandas as pd
```

Explanation

- import pandas: tells Python to load the pandas library so that its functions can be used.
- as: assigns an alias to the library.
- pd: the alias used in place of pandas when calling functions.

Next, create a DataFrame using pandas with a small dataset of client transactions.

```
data = {
    'Date': ['2025-01-10', '2025-01-11', '2025-01-12', '2025-01-13'],
    'Invoice_No': [101, 102, 103, 104],
    'Client': ['ABC Ltd', 'XYZ Ltd', 'LMN Ltd', 'ABC Ltd'],
    'Amount': [500, 1200, 700, 300],
    'Paid': [True, False, True, False]
}

df = pd.DataFrame(data)
print(df)
```

Output

```
        Date  Invoice_No   Client  Amount   Paid
0  2025-01-10         101  ABC Ltd     500   True
1  2025-01-11         102  XYZ Ltd    1200  False
2  2025-01-12         103  LMN Ltd     700   True
3  2025-01-13         104  ABC Ltd     300  False
```

Explanation

- A dictionary named data is created. Each key in the dictionary represents a column name, and each value is a list of data for that column:
  - 'Date': transaction date.
  - 'Invoice_No': invoice number.
  - 'Client': client name.
  - 'Amount': invoiced amount.
  - 'Paid': Boolean value showing whether the invoice was paid (True) or not (False).
- df = pd.DataFrame(data): passes the dictionary to pd.DataFrame(data) to create a DataFrame named df.
- print(df): prints the DataFrame as a table with rows and columns.

Step 2: Access Data by Row Index

Let's access a specific row by index using iloc[ ]:

```
print(df.iloc[0])
```

Output

```
Date            2025-01-10
Invoice_No             101
Client             ABC Ltd
Amount                 500
Paid                  True
Name: 0, dtype: object
```

Explanation

- df.iloc[0]: selects the row at index position 0 from the DataFrame.
    - In Python, indexing starts from 0. The first row is at index 0, the second row is at index 1, and so on.
    - iloc stands for integer location. It selects rows and columns based on their numerical index positions.
- The output lists each column name and its value for the selected row.
    - Name: 0: indicates the index of the selected row.
    - dtype: object refers to the data type of the output. In pandas, object usually refers to string (text) data or mixed types.

Let's access the second transaction, replacing 0 with 1 in iloc[ ].

```
print(df.iloc[1])
```

Output

```
Date            2025-01-11
Invoice_No             102
Client             XYZ Ltd
Amount                1200
Paid                 False
Name: 1, dtype: object
```

Step 3: Access Data by Column Name

Let's access a specific column:

```
print(df['Amount'])
```

Output

```
0     500
1    1200
2     700
3     300
Name: Amount, dtype: int64
```

Explanation

- df['Amount']: selects the 'Amount' column from the DataFrame.
  - To access one column, use a single pair of square brackets.
- The output shows the values in that column along with their row index.
  - Name: Amount: indicates the column name.
  - dtype: int64: shows the data type of the column. int64 represents 64-bit signed integers used for whole numbers.

Let's access two columns:

```
print(df[['Client', 'Amount']])
```

Output

```
   Client   Amount
0  ABC Ltd     500
1  XYZ Ltd    1200
2  LMN Ltd     700
3  ABC Ltd     300
```

Explanation

- df[['Client', 'Amount']]: selects both the 'Client' and 'Amount' columns.
  - To access multiple columns, provide a list of column names using square brackets.
  - In this case, the inner brackets define the list and the outer brackets select that list from the DataFrame.

Step 4: Add New Columns

Let's create a column called 'VAT' that calculates VAT at 20% on the 'Amount' column:

```
df['VAT'] = df['Amount'] * 0.2
print(df)
```

Output

```
         Date  Invoice_No    Client  Amount   Paid    VAT
0  2025-01-10         101   ABC Ltd     500   True  100.0
1  2025-01-11         102   XYZ Ltd    1200  False  240.0
2  2025-01-12         103   LMN Ltd     700   True  140.0
3  2025-01-13         104   ABC Ltd     300  False   60.0
```

Explanation

- df['VAT'] = df['Amount'] * 0.2: creates a new column named 'VAT' by multiplying each value in the 'Amount' column by 0.2, which represents 20%.
    - The new 'VAT' column is added to the DataFrame. Each row contains the VAT calculated from the corresponding value in the 'Amount' column.
- print(df): prints the updated DataFrame, which includes the new 'VAT' column.

Step 5: Filter Data

Let's filter the DataFrame to show only paid invoices:

```
paid_invoices = df[df['Paid'] == True]
print(paid_invoices)
```

Output

```
         Date  Invoice_No    Client  Amount  Paid    VAT
0  2025-01-10         101   ABC Ltd     500  True  100.0
2  2025-01-12         103   LMN Ltd     700  True  140.0
```

Explanation

- df['Paid'] == True: checks each value in the 'Paid' column and returns True where the invoice has been paid.
- df[df['Paid'] == True]: filters the DataFrame to select only the rows where the 'Paid' column is True.
- The result is stored in the variable paid_invoices.
- print(paid_invoices): prints the filtered DataFrame, showing only the paid invoices.

Let's filter the DataFrame to show only unpaid invoices:

```
unpaid_invoices = df[df['Paid'] == False]
print("Unpaid invoices:")
print(unpaid_invoices)
```

Output

```
Unpaid invoices:
        Date  Invoice_No   Client  Amount   Paid    VAT
1  2025-01-11         102  XYZ Ltd    1200  False  240.0
3  2025-01-13         104  ABC Ltd     300  False   60.0
```

Explanation

- df['Paid'] == False: checks each value in the 'Paid' column and returns True where the invoice has not been paid.
- df[df['Paid'] == False]: filters the DataFrame to select only the rows where the 'Paid' column is False.
- The result is stored in the variable unpaid_invoices.
- print(unpaid_invoices): prints the filtered DataFrame, showing only the unpaid invoices.

5.1.3 *Your Project*

5.1.3.1 Tasks

Use the code examples above as a guide to work with the dataset below, which represents the expenses of a small business.

Data

```
data = {
    'Date': ['2025-01-01', '2025-01-03', '2025-01-05', '2025-01-07'],
    'Expense_ID': [1, 2, 3, 4],
   'Category': ['Office Supplies', 'Utilities', 'Travel', 'Office Supplies'],
    'Amount': [150.75, 300.50, 450.00, 120.25],
    'Approved': [True, False, True, False]
}
```

Write Python code to

- Import pandas and load the dataset into a DataFrame. Print the data. Use pd.DataFrame().
- Access the first rows to retrieve relevant data. Use iloc[ ].
- Access the 'Category' column to retrieve relevant data.
- Calculate a special tax for each expense (10% of the amount) and add it as a new column.
- Filter the dataset to identify unapproved expenses. Use the condition (df['Approved'] == False) to select rows where the 'Approved' column is False.

5.1.3.2 Example Code

```
import pandas as pd

# The data represents expenses for a small business.
data = {
    'Date': ['2025-01-01', '2025-01-03', '2025-01-05', '2025-01-07'],
    'Expense_ID': [1, 2, 3, 4],
   'Category': ['Office Supplies', 'Utilities', 'Travel', 'Office Supplies'],
    'Amount': [150.75, 300.50, 450.00, 120.25],
    'Approved': [True, False, True, False]
}

# Step 1: Load the Expense Dataset
df = pd.DataFrame(data)
print("Expense Dataset:")
print(df)

# Step 2: Access a Specific Row
print("Accessing row at index 0:")
print(df.iloc[0])

# Step 3: Access a Specific Column
print("Accessing 'Category' column:")
print(df['Category'])

# Step 4: Add a New Column (Tax at 10%)
df['Tax'] = df['Amount'] * 0.1
print("Data after adding Tax column:")
print(df)

# Step 5: Filter Data (Unapproved Expenses)
unapproved_expenses = df[df['Approved'] == False]
print("Unapproved expenses:")
print(unapproved_expenses)
```

Scan the QR code to access the Python code and output (see 5.1.ipynb).

https://github.com/DrMichaelGuo/PFAAFAMMA

5.2 Data Cleaning and Handling Missing Data

Data cleaning ensures accurate financial reporting and reliable analysis. This section explores how to identify and address missing values in pandas (see Figure 5.4).

FIGURE 5.4 Data Cleaning

5.2.1 Key Concepts

5.2.1.1 Data Cleaning

Data cleaning refers to the process of detecting and correcting inaccurate or incomplete records.

5.2.1.2 Missing Values

A missing value is a data point that is not recorded. Missing values are common in large financial datasets due to system errors, data entry issues, or incomplete records. In pandas, this is represented as NaN (Not a Number), None, or NaT (Not a Time).

- NaN is used for missing numerical values.
- None may appear in text columns and is usually treated as a missing value by pandas.
- NaT is used for missing datetime values.

5.2.1.3 Identifying Missing Values

Identifying missing values involves locating entries that are empty or marked as NaN.

In pandas, missing values can be detected using .isna().

5.2.1.4 Removing Missing Values

Removing missing values involves dropping rows or columns that contain empty entries. This approach is often used during preliminary data cleaning, especially when preparing financial summaries where incomplete data may affect results.

In pandas, rows or columns with missing values can be removed using .dropna().

5.2.1.5 Imputation

Imputation is the process of replacing missing values with substitutes. Common methods include using the mean, median, mode, or a fixed value.

5.2.2 Follow-Along Activity

This activity introduces techniques for identifying and handling missing values using a financial dataset (see Figure 5.5).

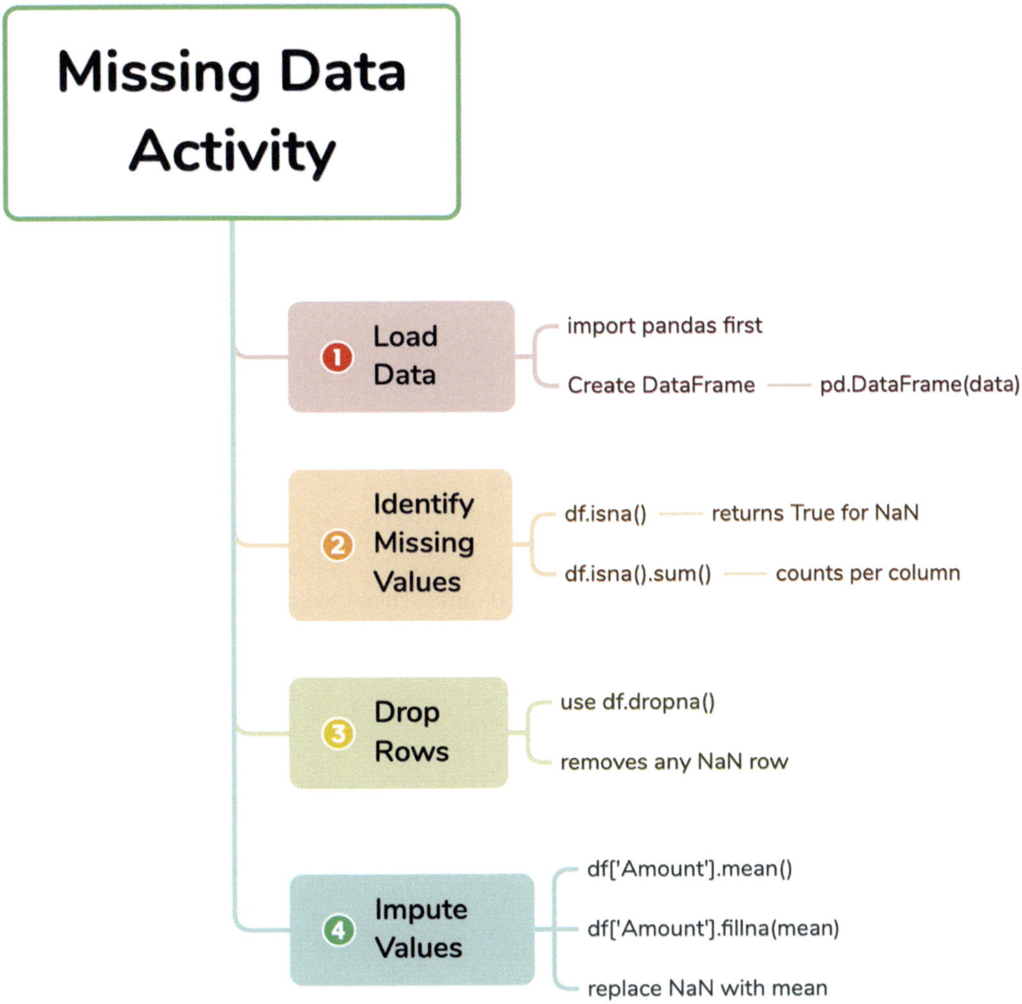

FIGURE 5.5 Missing Data Activity

Step 1: Loading Data with Missing Values

Let's use a small dataset of financial transactions where some entries are missing. The data is loaded into a pandas DataFrame.

```
import pandas as pd

# Sample financial data with missing values
data = {
    'Transaction ID': [1, 2, 3, 4, 5],
    'Client Name': ['Alice', 'Bob', None, 'David', 'Eve'],
    'Amount': [2000, None, 1500, 2500, None],
    'Category': ['Revenue', 'Expense', 'Revenue', None, 'Expense']
}

df = pd.DataFrame(data)
print(df)
```

Output:

```
   Transaction ID Client Name  Amount Category
0               1       Alice  2000.0  Revenue
1               2         Bob     NaN  Expense
2               3        None  1500.0  Revenue
3               4       David  2500.0     None
4               5         Eve     NaN  Expense
```

Explanation

- The data includes five transactions. Some entries are missing:
  - Client Name is missing in row 2 (index 2).
  - Amount is missing in rows 1 and 4 (indices 1 and 4).
  - Category is missing in row 3 (index 3).
- Missing entries appear as NaN in the DataFrame. These values must be identified and treated before analysis.

Step 2: Identifying Missing Values

Let's detect missing values using .isna().

```
print(df.isna())
```

Output

```
   Transaction ID  Client Name  Amount  Category
0           False        False   False     False
1           False        False    True     False
2           False         True   False     False
3           False        False   False      True
4           False        False    True     False
```

Explanation

- .isna(): returns True where a value is missing and False where a value is present.

Let's count the number of missing values in each column using .sum():

```
print(df.isna().sum())
```

Output

```
Transaction ID    0
Client Name       1
Amount            2
Category          1
```

Explanation

- .sum() adds the Boolean values returned by .isna().
- True is treated as 1 and False as 0.
- The result shows the number of missing entries in each column.

Step 3: Removing Missing Values

Let's remove rows with missing data using .dropna().

```
df_dropped = df.dropna()
print("After Dropping Missing Values:\n", df_dropped)
```

Output

```
After Dropping Missing Values:
   Transaction ID Client Name  Amount Category
0              1       Alice  2000.0  Revenue
```

Explanation

- df.dropna(): removes any row that contains at least one missing value. In this example, only the first row (index 0) contains no missing values and is retained. All other rows are removed.
- "After Dropping Missing Values:\n": describes the printed output.
- \n: inserts a line break so that the label and the DataFrame appear on separate lines.

Step 4: Imputation

Let's fill missing values by replacing them with a calculated value. In this step, we fill missing values in the Amount column using the mean of the available values.

```
mean_value = df['Amount'].mean()
df['Amount'] = df['Amount'].fillna(mean_value)
print("DataFrame after Imputing 'Amount' with Mean:\n", df)
```

Output

```
DataFrame after Imputing 'Amount' with Mean:
  Transaction ID Client Name  Amount Category
0              1       Alice  2000.0  Revenue
1              2         Bob  2000.0  Expense
2              3        None  1500.0  Revenue
3              4       David  2500.0     None
4              5         Eve  2000.0  Expense
```

Explanation

- df['Amount']: selects the Amount column from the DataFrame.
- .mean(): calculates the mean of the Amount column, ignoring missing values.
- .fillna(mean_value): replaces missing entries in the Amount column with the calculated mean (2000.0 in this case).
- The output shows that missing values in the Amount column have been filled.
    - Row 1 (index 1): the missing Amount is filled with 2000.0.
    - Row 4 (index 4): the missing Amount is filled with 2000.0.

5.2.3 Your Project

Write Python code to identify and handle missing data using the following financial transactions dataset:

```
data = {
    'Transaction ID': [101, 102, 103, 104, 105],
    'Client Name': ['Alice Ltd', 'Bob Corp', 'Cat Com', 'David & Co',
'Eve LLC'],
    'Invoice Amount': [5000, None, 3000, 7000, None],
    'Transaction Type': ['Sales', 'Purchase', 'Sales', 'Sales',
'Purchase'],
    'Payment Status': ['Paid', 'Unpaid', 'Paid', 'Paid', 'Unpaid'],
}
```

5.2.3.1 Tasks

Write Python code to complete the following:

- Load the dataset
    - Use pd.DataFrame() to load the data into a pandas DataFrame and display it.

- Identify missing values
  - Use .isna() to create a Boolean DataFrame showing True for missing values and False otherwise.
  - Use .sum() to count the number of missing values in each column.
- Handle missing values
  - Replace missing values in the Invoice Amount column with the mean of the available values in that column.

5.2.3.2 Example Code

```
import pandas as pd

# Load the Dataset into a pandas DataFrame and display it
data = {
    'Transaction ID': [101, 102, 103, 104, 105],
    'Client Name': ['Alice Ltd', 'Bob Corp', 'Cat Com', 'David & Co',
'Eve LLC'],
    'Invoice Amount': [5000, None, 3000, 7000, None],
    'Transaction Type': ['Sales', 'Purchase', 'Sales', 'Sales',
'Purchase'],
    'Payment Status': ['Paid', 'Unpaid', 'Paid', 'Paid', 'Unpaid'],
}

# Create DataFrame
df = pd.DataFrame(data)
print("Initial Dataset:\n", df)

# Identify Missing Values
print("\n Missing Values Per Column:\n", df.isna())

# Count missing values per column
print("\n Summary of Missing Values:\n", df.isna().sum())

# Handle Missing Values
# Replace missing values in the 'Invoice Amount' column with the
mean of the column
df['Invoice Amount'] = df['Invoice Amount'].fillna(df['Invoice
Amount'].mean())

print("\n DataFrame After Handling Missing Values:\n", df)
```

Scan the QR code to access the Python code and output (see 5.2.ipynb). You will also see other techniques for data cleaning in pandas.

https://github.com/DrMichaelGuo/PFAAFAMMA

Summary of Chapter 5: Working with DataFrames

In this chapter, we have covered the following concepts:

DataFrames

- A DataFrame stores data in rows and columns.
- DataFrame supports different data types, such as integers, floats, strings, and Booleans.

Creating DataFrames

- Create a DataFrame using pd.DataFrame() from a dictionary of lists.
- Use print() to view the DataFrame in tabular form.

Accessing Data

- Use .iloc[ ] to access rows by index position.
- Use df['Column'] to access a single column.
- Use df[['Column1', 'Column2']] to access multiple columns.
- Modify DataFrames.
- Add new columns by assigning calculations to a column name, e.g. df['VAT'] = df['Amount'] * 0.2.
- Update or overwrite existing columns as needed.

Filtering Data

- Use Boolean indexing to filter rows, e.g. df[df['Paid'] == True].
- Assign filtered results in a new DataFrame for further analysis.

Data Cleaning

- Identify missing values with .isna().
- Remove records with missing values using .dropna().
- Replace missing values with calculated values (e.g. mean) using .fillna() for imputation.

Quiz Questions

Scan the QR code below to access the quiz questions for this chapter (see 5.md).

https://github.com/DrMichaelGuo/QuizPFAAFAMMA

Further Reading and Resource

Pandas, no date. Pandas official documentation [online] Available at: https://pandas.pydata.org/docs/ (Accessed 23 July 2025).

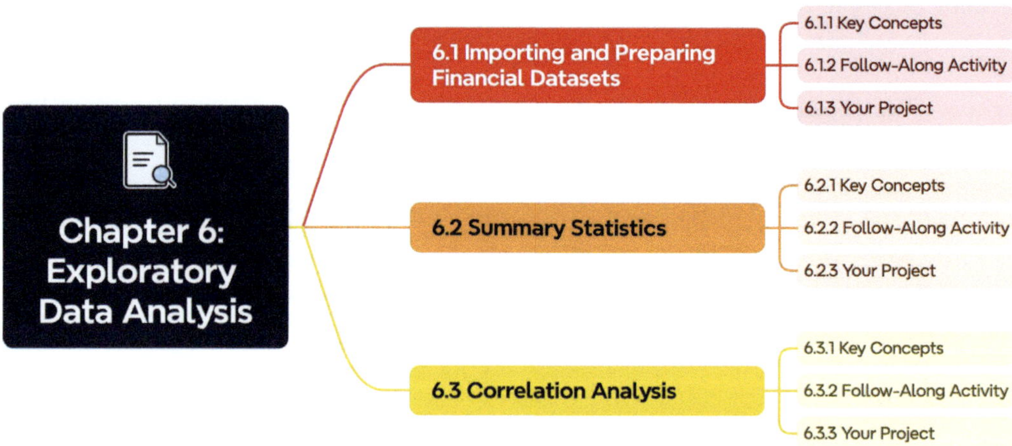

FIGURE 6.1 Structure of Chapter 6

6

EXPLORATORY DATA ANALYSIS

This chapter introduces techniques of exploratory data analysis (EDA) in Python for accounting and finance contexts. It explains how to import datasets from Excel and CSV files, clean and prepare data, and identify trends, anomalies, and relationships. Using coding examples and follow-along activities, the chapter covers summary statistics, data distribution, and correlation analysis to extract information from raw financial data (Figure 6.1).

Learning Objectives

By the end of this chapter, you will be able to

- Import, preview, and clean accounting and finance datasets using Python and pandas.
- Calculate and interpret summary statistics to describe accounting and finance data.
- Identify relationships between financial variables using correlation analysis.

6.1 Importing and Preparing Financial Datasets

Managing datasets in accounting and finance often involves working with CSV and Excel files. This section explains how to import these formats into Python and conduct basic data inspection as part of EDA (see Figure 6.2).

6.1.1 Key Concepts

6.1.1.1 CSV File (.csv)

A CSV (Comma-Separated Values) file is a plain text file in which each line represents a row of data, and values are separated by commas. It uses the .csv extension. CSV files can be opened in text editors or spreadsheet applications. As CSV files contain no formatting, they are smaller in size.

DOI: 10.4324/9781003656968-6

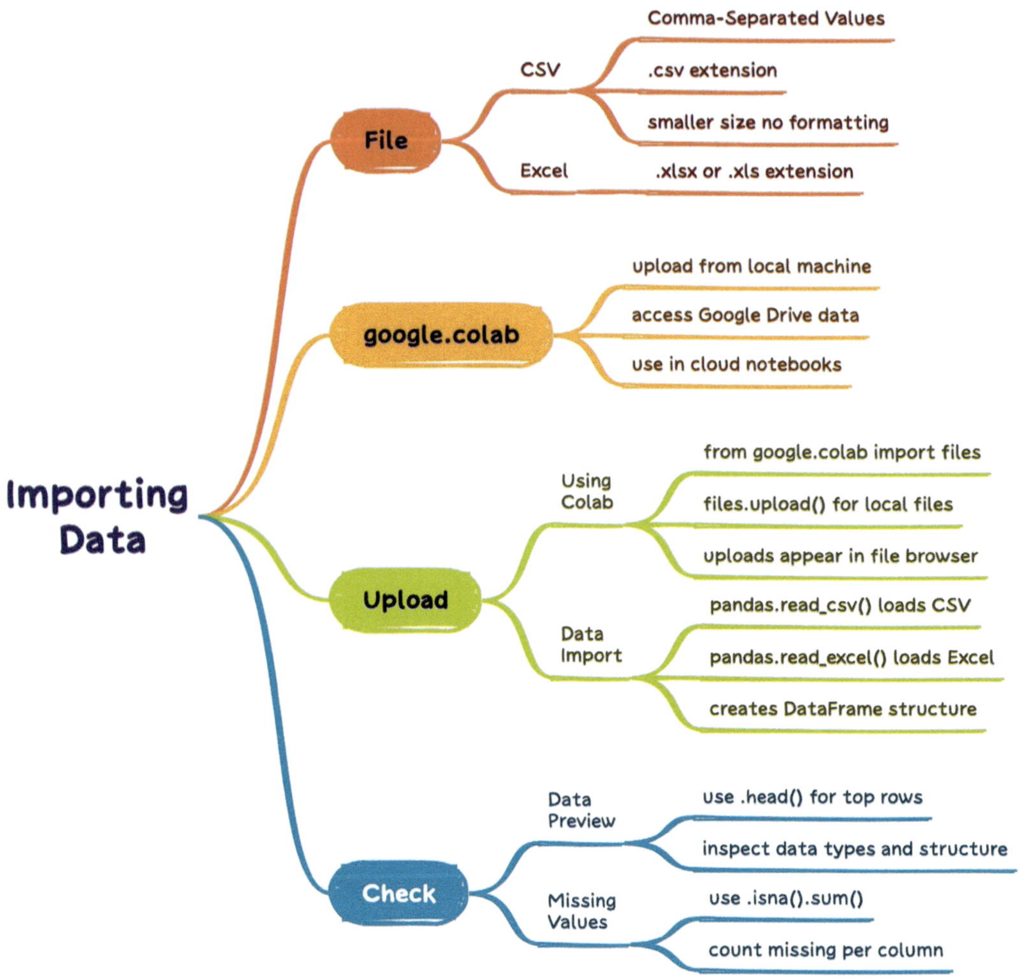

FIGURE 6.2 Importing Data

6.1.1.2 Excel File (.xlsx, .xls)

An Excel file is created using Microsoft Excel and uses the .xlsx or .xls extension. It can contain multiple sheets, cell formatting, and formulas. Python can read both .xlsx and .xls formats.

6.1.1.3 google.colab

google.colab is a module in the Google Colab environment. It includes functions for uploading files from a local machine, accessing Google Drive, and interacting with cloud-based notebooks.

6.1.1.4 Data Upload via Google Colab

To upload files from a local machine into Google Colab, use the files module:

```
from google.colab import files
uploaded = files.upload()
```

6.1.1.5 Data Import

Financial systems often export data in CSV or Excel formats. Use the following pandas functions to import data into Python:

- .read_csv(): reads a CSV file into a DataFrame.
- .read_excel(): reads an Excel file into a DataFrame.

6.1.1.6 Data Preview

A data preview helps verify that column names, data types, and row structure are correct before analysis:

- .head(): displays the first five rows of the DataFrame.

6.1.1.7 Check for Missing Values

It is important to check for missing values early in the analysis process.

- .isna().sum(): returns the number of missing values in each column.

6.1.2 Follow-Along Activity

This activity guides you through downloading, uploading, and inspecting a financial dataset using Google Colab and pandas (see Figure 6.3).

Step 1: Download the Dataset

This example uses the file 6_data.csv, available at:

https://github.com/DrMichaelGuo/PFAAFAMMA

To download,

- Open the link in a browser.
- Locate the file named 6_data.csv.
- Click on the file name to open the preview.
- In the top-right corner, click the three-dot icon (···).
- Select Download.
- The file will be saved to the computer's Downloads folder.

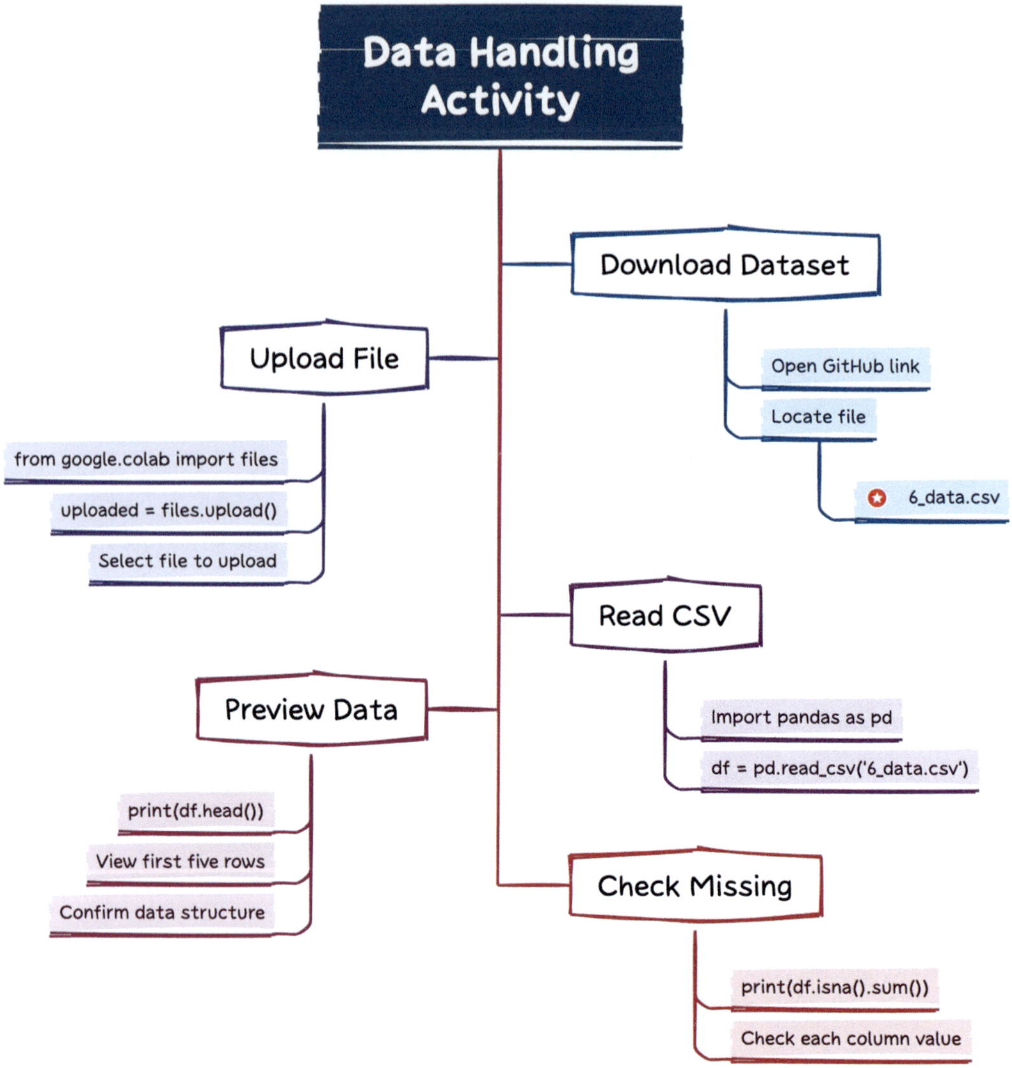

FIGURE 6.3 Data Handling Activity

Step 2: Upload the CSV File to Google Colab

Let's upload the CSV file into Google Colab using the following code:

```
from google.colab import files
uploaded = files.upload()
```

Output: When we run this code, a file selection dialogue will appear. Select 6_data.csv from the Downloads folder. After the upload completes, a confirmation message such as the following will appear:

```
6_data.csv(text/csv) - 1506 bytes, last modified: 30/04/2025 - 100% done
Saving 6_data.csv to 6_data.csv
```

Explanation

- from google.colab import files: imports the files module that supports file upload in Google Colab.
- files.upload(): opens a dialogue box to select and upload local files.
- uploaded = files.upload(): stores the uploaded file in the variable uploaded.

Step 3: Reading the CSV File into a DataFrame

Let's load the CSV file into pandas using the following code:

```
import pandas as pd
df = pd.read_csv('6_data.csv')
```

Output: This command does not produce visible output but stores the contents of the CSV file in a variable named df.

Explanation

- import pandas as pd: imports the pandas library with the alias pd.
- pd.read_csv('6_data.csv'): reads the contents of the CSV file and loads it into a pandas DataFrame. The DataFrame is stored in the variable df.

Step 4: Previewing the Data

Let's view the first few rows of the DataFrame.

```
print(df.head())
```

Output

```
   Quarter     Revenue   Expenses    Profit
0  2015-Q1  202483.57  160755.13  41728.44
1  2015-Q2  201763.13  152336.52  49426.61
2  2015-Q3  208177.46  164022.98  44154.48
3  2015-Q4  235814.63  183691.46  52123.18
4  2016-Q1  208829.23  150269.34  58559.89
```

Explanation

- df.head(): displays the first five rows of the DataFrame. This helps confirm that the file loaded correctly and shows the structure of the dataset.

Step 5: Checking for Missing Values

Let's check for missing values in the dataset.

```
print(df.isna().sum())
```

Output:

```
Quarter     0
Revenue     0
Expenses    0
Profit      0
dtype: int64
```

Explanation

- df.isna().sum(): returns the number of missing values in each column.
- In this example, all columns contain complete data, so no missing values require attention.

6.1.3 *Your Project*

This project uses an Excel file to practise uploading, importing, and inspecting financial data in Google Colab.

6.1.3.1 Task 1: Download the Excel File

This task uses the file 6_data.xlsx, available at:

https://github.com/DrMichaelGuo/PFAAFAMMA

To download,

- Open the link in a web browser.
- Locate the file named 6_data.xlsx
- Click the file name to open the file view page.
- In the top-right corner, click the three-dot icon (···).
- Select Download.
- The file will be saved to the Downloads folder on your computer.

6.1.3.2 Task 2: Upload the File to Google Colab

- Write Python code to upload the Excel file into the Google Colab environment.

6.1.3.3 *Task 3: Read the Excel File into a DataFrame*

- Type the following code into a Colab cell to read the Excel file:

```
import pandas as pd
df_xl = pd.read_excel('6_data.xlsx', sheet_name='Income_Statement')
```

6.1.3.4 *Task 4: Display the First Five Rows*

- Display the first five rows of the DataFrame.

6.1.3.5 *Task 5: Check for Missing Values*

- Check for missing values in each column.

6.1.3.6 *Example Code*

```
# Import the 'files' module from the 'google.colab' library
from google.colab import files

# Open a file upload dialogue and store the uploaded file(s) in the
'uploaded' dictionary
uploaded = files.upload()

# Import the pandas library and assign it the alias 'pd'
import pandas as pd

# Read data from the Excel file named '6_data.xlsx'
# Load the sheet named 'Income_Statement' into a pandas DataFrame
called 'df_xl'
df_xl = pd.read_excel('6_data.xlsx', sheet_name='Income_Statement')

# Display the first five rows of the Excel data
print(df_xl.head())

# Check for missing values in each column
print(df_xl.isna().sum())
```

Scan the QR code to access the code and output (see 6.1.ipynb).

https://github.com/DrMichaelGuo/PFAAFAMMA

6.2 Summary Statistics

Summary statistics provides an overview of the main features of a dataset. This section explains summary statistics in EDA, including central tendency, dispersion, and distribution shape (see Figure 6.4).

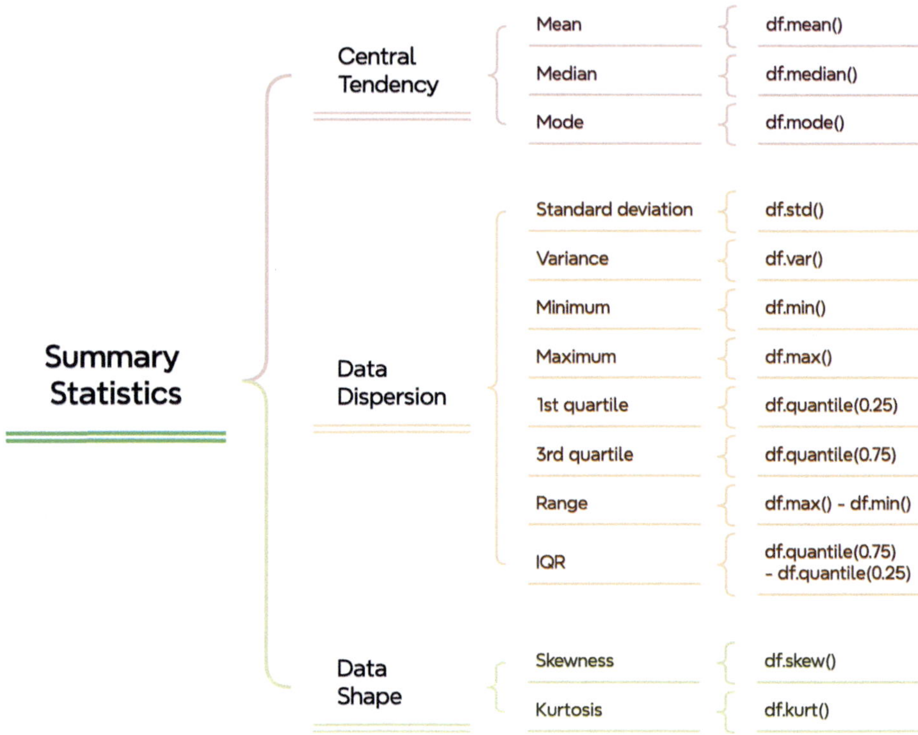

FIGURE 6.4 Summary Statistics

6.2.1 Key Concepts

6.2.1.1 Measures of Central Tendency

Central tendency refers to statistical measures that identify the centre or typical value of a dataset. The following functions are used to compute these measures:

- df.mean(): calculates the arithmetic mean of each column.
- df.median(): returns the median, or the middle value, when values in each column are sorted.
- df.mode(): returns the mode, or the most frequent value, in each column.

6.2.1.2 Measures of Dispersion

Dispersion refers to the variation or spread of values in a dataset. The following functions compute these measures:

- df.std(): calculates the standard deviation, which quantifies the average distance from the mean.
- df.var(): returns the variance, the square of the standard deviation.
- df.min(): returns the smallest value in each column.
- df.max(): returns the largest value in each column.
- df.quantile(0.25): returns the first quartile, the value below which 25% of the data fall.
- df.quantile(0.75): returns the third quartile, the value below which 75% of the data fall.
- df.max() - df.min(): calculates the range or the difference between the maximum and minimum values in a column.
- df.quantile(0.75) - df.quantile(0.25): calculates the interquartile range (IQR), which covers the middle 50% of the data.

6.2.1.3 Shape of the Distribution

Distribution refers to the pattern of values within a variable. The following functions provide information about its shape:

- df.skew(): measures skewness, which indicates the direction and extent of asymmetry in the distribution.
- df.kurt(): measures kurtosis, which denotes the concentration of values in the tails relative to a normal distribution.

6.2.2 Follow-Along Activity

This activity shows how to use summary statistics in EDA (see Figure 6.5). The activity uses the file 6_data.csv. See Section 6.1.2 for instructions on downloading the file.

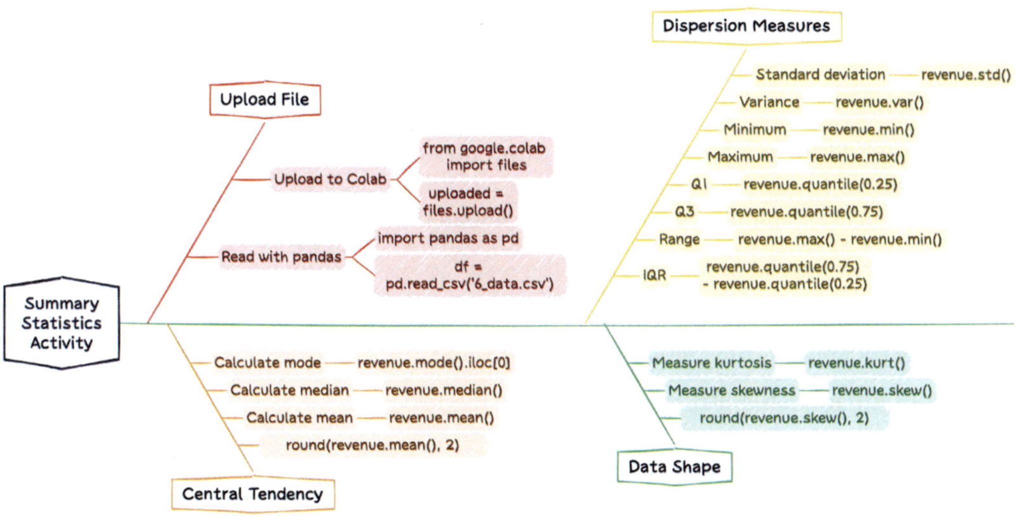

FIGURE 6.5 Summary Statistics Activity

Step 1: Upload and Read the CSV File

Let's use the following code to upload the CSV file to Google Colab and read it into a DataFrame.

```
from google.colab import files
uploaded = files.upload()

import pandas as pd
df = pd.read_csv('6_data.csv')
```

Explanation

- files.upload(): opens a dialogue for uploading files into the Google Colab environment.
- pd.read_csv(): reads the uploaded CSV file and stores the data in a DataFrame named df.

Step 2: Measure Central Tendency

The dataset includes four columns: Quarter, Revenue, Expenses, and Profit. Let's measure the central tendency for the Revenue column.

```
revenue = df['Revenue']

print("Mean:", round(revenue.mean(), 2))
print("Median:", round(revenue.median(), 2))
print("Mode:", round(revenue.mode().iloc[0], 2))
```

Output

```
Mean: 261656.77
Median: 261627.76
Mode: 201763.13
```

Explanation

- revenue = df['Revenue']: selects the Revenue column and assigns it to the variable revenue.
- revenue.mean(): calculates the arithmetic mean.
    - round(revenue.mean(), 2): rounds the result to two decimal places.
- revenue.median(): returns the middle value when sorted.
- revenue.mode(): returns the most frequent value.
    - .iloc[0] returns the first value if multiple modes exist.

Step 3: Measure Dispersion

Let's measure the spread of values in the Revenue column.

```
print("Standard Deviation:", round(revenue.std(), 2))
print("Variance:", round(revenue.var(), 2))
print("Minimum:", round(revenue.min(), 2))
print("Maximum:", round(revenue.max(), 2))
print("1st Quartile (Q1):", round(revenue.quantile(0.25), 2))
print("3rd Quartile (Q3):", round(revenue.quantile(0.75), 2))
print("Range (Max - Min):", round(revenue.max() - revenue.min(), 2))
print("Interquartile Range (Q3 - Q1):", round(revenue.quantile(0.75) -
revenue.quantile(0.25), 2))
```

Output

```
Standard Deviation: 39312.75
Variance: 1545492068.6
Minimum: 201763.13
Maximum: 354996.6
1st Quartile (Q1): 227943.16
3rd Quartile (Q3): 287478.15
Range (Max - Min): 153233.47
Interquartile Range (Q3 - Q1): 59534.98
```

Explanation

- revenue.std(): calculates the standard deviation.
  - round(revenue.std(), 2): rounds the result to two decimal places.
- revenue.var(): returns the variance.
- revenue.min(): returns the smallest value.
- revenue.max(): returns the largest value.
- revenue.quantile(0.25): returns the first quartile.
- revenue.quantile(0.75): returns the third quartile.
- The range is calculated by subtracting the minimum from the maximum.
- The IQR is calculated by subtracting the first quartile from the third quartile.

Step 4: Measure Shape of the Distribution

Let's measure the shape of the Revenue distribution.

```
print("Skewness:", round(revenue.skew(), 2))
print("Kurtosis:", round(revenue.kurt(), 2))
```

Output

```
Skewness: 0.38
Kurtosis: -0.61
```

Explanation

- revenue.skew(): measures skewness, the degree of asymmetry in the distribution.
  - round(revenue.skew(), 2): rounds the result to two decimal places.
  - A value of 0.38 suggests a slight positive skew, with a longer tail on the right.
- revenue.kurt(): measures kurtosis, the weight of the tails relative to a normal distribution.
  - A value of –0.61 indicates lighter tails and a flatter peak than a normal distribution.

6.2.3 Your Project

6.2.3.1 Tasks

Use the same file (6_data.csv) and write Python code to calculate summary statistics for the Expenses column. Use the functions listed below and round each result to two decimal places.

- Measures of Central Tendency
  - df.mean()
  - df.median()
  - df.mode()
- Measures of Dispersion
  - df.std()
  - df.var()
  - df.min()
  - df.max()
  - df.quantile(0.25)
  - df.quantile(0.75)
  - df.max() - df.min()
  - df.quantile(0.75) - df.quantile(0.25)
- Shape of the Distribution
  - df.skew()
  - df.kurt()

6.2.3.2 Example Code

```
# Upload CSV file
from google.colab import files
uploaded = files.upload()

# Read the data
import pandas as pd
df = pd.read_csv('6_data.csv')
```

```
# Select 'Expenses' column
expenses = df['Expenses']

# Central tendency
print("Mean:", round(expenses.mean(), 2))
print("Median:", round(expenses.median(), 2))
print("Mode:", round(expenses.mode().iloc[0], 2))

# Dispersion
print("Standard Deviation:", round(expenses.std(), 2))
print("Variance:", round(expenses.var(), 2))
print("Minimum:", round(expenses.min(), 2))
print("Maximum:", round(expenses.max(), 2))
print("1st Quartile:", round(expenses.quantile(0.25), 2))
print("3rd Quartile:", round(expenses.quantile(0.75), 2))
print("Range:", round(expenses.max() - expenses.min(), 2))
print("Interquartile Range:", round(expenses.quantile(0.75) -
expenses.quantile(0.25), 2))

# Shape of distribution
print("Skewness:", round(expenses.skew(), 2))
print("Kurtosis:", round(expenses.kurt(), 2))
```

Scan the QR code to access the code and output (see 6.2.ipynb).

https://github.com/DrMichaelGuo/PFAAFAMMA

6.3 Correlation Analysis

Understanding relationships between variables is a key step in EDA. This section introduces Pearson correlation using the .corr() function in pandas. The method measures the strength and direction of linear relationships between numerical variables (see Figure 6.6).

6.3.1 Key Concepts

6.3.1.1 Correlation

Correlation describes the extent to which two variables move together. When the value of one variable increases or decreases as the value of another changes, the variables are correlated.

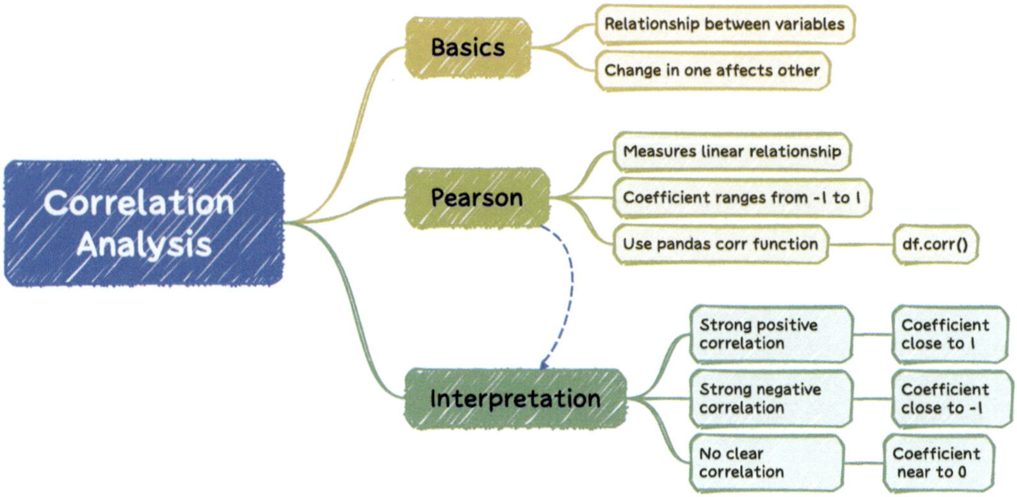

FIGURE 6.6 Correlation Analysis

6.3.1.2 Pearson Correlation Coefficient

The .corr() method in pandas calculates the Pearson correlation coefficient. This coefficient ranges from –1 to 1:

- A value near 1 indicates a strong positive correlation.
- A value near –1 indicates a strong negative correlation.
- A value near 0 indicates little or no linear correlation.

6.3.2 Follow-Along Activity

This activity shows how to calculate correlation coefficients (see Figure 6.7). The activity uses the file 6_data.csv. Refer to Section 6.1.2 for instructions on downloading the file.

Step 1: Upload and Read the CSV File

Let's begin by uploading and reading the CSV file into a pandas DataFrame.

```
from google.colab import files
uploaded = files.upload()

import pandas as pd
df = pd.read_csv('6_data.csv')
```

Explanation

- files.upload(): opens a file upload dialogue in Google Colab to allow selection and upload of 6_data.csv.
- pd.read_csv(): reads the uploaded CSV file and stores the data in a DataFrame named df.

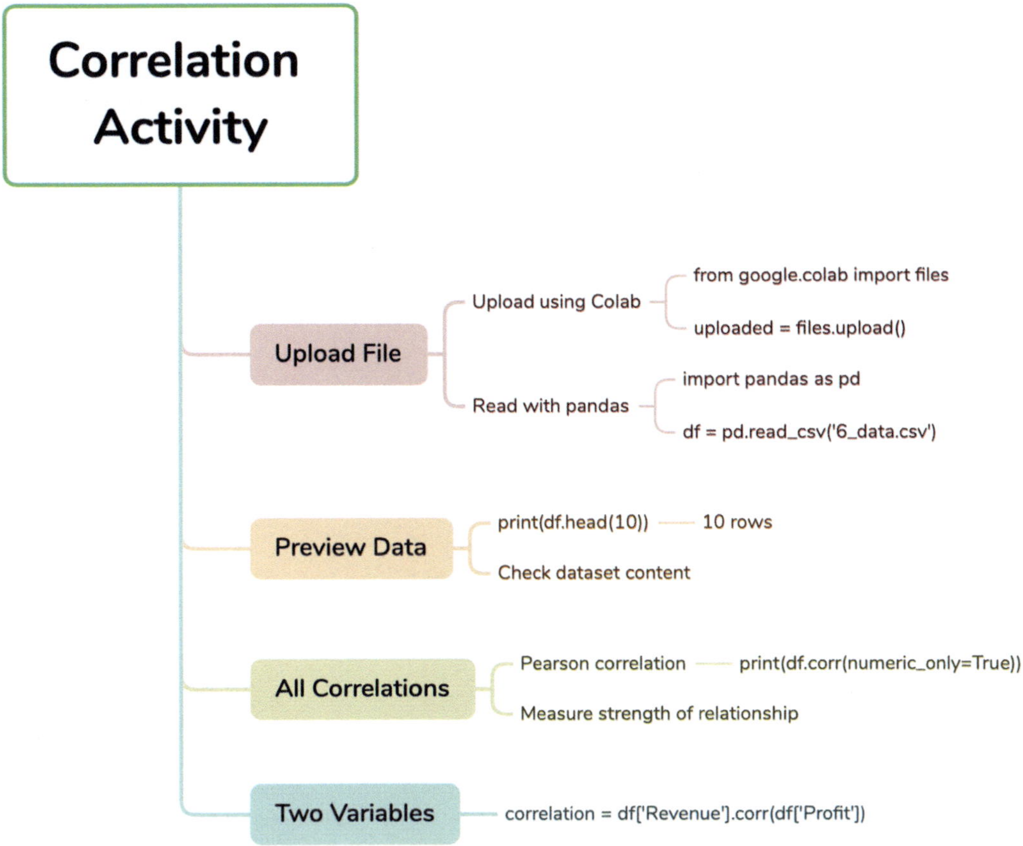

FIGURE 6.7 Correlation Activity

Step 2: Display First 10 Rows

Let's check the contents of the dataset by displaying the first 10 rows.

```
print(df.head(10))
```

Output

```
   Quarter    Revenue   Expenses    Profit
0  2015-Q1  202483.57  160755.13  41728.44
1  2015-Q2  201763.13  152336.52  49426.61
2  2015-Q3  208177.46  164022.98  44154.48
3  2015-Q4  235814.63  183691.46  52123.18
4  2016-Q1  208829.23  150269.34  58559.89
5  2016-Q2  211406.48  165821.93  45584.56
6  2016-Q3  223082.03  137797.44  85284.59
7  2016-Q4  243446.63  155610.25  87836.38
8  2017-Q1  218152.63  132864.87  85287.76
9  2017-Q2  225918.83  150250.95  75667.88
```

Explanation

- df.head(10): returns the first 10 rows of the DataFrame.
- The dataset contains quarterly financial data with columns for Revenue, Expenses, and Profit.

Step 3: Calculate Correlations

Let's calculate the correlation between all numeric columns using Pearson's method.

```
print("Pearson Correlation Matrix:")
print(df.corr(numeric_only=True))
```

Output

```
Pearson Correlation Matrix:
           Revenue  Expenses    Profit
Revenue   1.000000  0.854505  0.618631
Expenses  0.854505  1.000000  0.120506
Profit    0.618631  0.120506  1.000000
```

Explanation

- df.corr(numeric_only=True): calculates the Pearson correlation coefficients between all numeric columns.
  - numeric_only=True: ensures that only columns with numeric data types are included in the calculation.
- A value close to 1 or –1 indicates a strong correlation, while a value close to 0 indicates little or no linear relationship.

Step 4: Calculate the Correlation between Two Variables

Let's compute the correlation between Revenue and Profit.

```
correlation = df['Revenue'].corr(df['Profit'])
print("Correlation between Revenue and Profit:", round(correlation, 2))
```

Output

```
Correlation between Revenue and Profit: 0.62
```

Explanation

- df['Revenue'].corr(df['Profit']): calculates the Pearson correlation coefficient between the two columns.
  - round(correlation, 2): rounds the result to two decimal places.
- A value of 0.62 indicates a moderate positive relationship between Revenue and Profit.

6.3.3 *Your Project*

6.3.3.1 *Tasks*

Write Python code to conduct a correlation analysis using the Excel file 6_data.xlsx. Refer to Section 6.1.3 for instructions on downloading the Excel file.

Complete the following steps:

- Upload and read the file 6_data.xlsx.
- Load the sheet named Income_Statement into a DataFrame called df_excel using pandas. Refer to Section 6.1.3 for instructions on how to load a specific sheet from an Excel file.
- Display the first 10 rows of the dataset to review its structure.
- Use the .corr() method to generate a Pearson correlation matrix for all numeric columns in the DataFrame.
- Calculate the Pearson correlation between Revenue and Cost_of_Goods_Sold.

6.3.3.2 *Example Code*

```
# Upload the Excel file from your local machine
from google.colab import files
uploaded = files.upload()

# Import the pandas library for data handling
import pandas as pd

# Read the Excel file and select the sheet named 'Income_Statement'
df_excel = pd.read_excel('6_data.xlsx',
sheet_name='Income_Statement')

# Display the first 10 rows of the dataset to check the structure
print("Preview of dataset:")
print(df_excel.head(10))

# Calculate and display the Pearson correlation matrix for numeric
columns
print("Pearson Correlation Matrix:")
print(df_excel.corr(numeric_only=True))

# Calculate the Pearson correlation between Revenue and
Cost_of_Goods_Sold
correlation = df_excel['Revenue'].corr(df_excel['Cost_of_Goods_Sold'])
print("Correlation between Revenue and Cost_of_Goods_Sold:",
round(correlation, 2))
```

Scan the QR code to access the code and output (see 6.3.ipynb). You will also see other types of correlations and how to calculate them in Python.

https://github.com/DrMichaelGuo/PFAAFAMMA

Summary of Chapter 6: Exploratory Data Analysis

In this chapter, we have covered the following concepts:

Importing and Preparing Financial Datasets

- CSV files: Plain text format with CSV. Imported using .read_csv().
- Excel files: Spreadsheet files with extensions .xlsx or .xls. Imported using .read_excel().
- Google Colab: File uploads handled via google.colab.files.upload() for cloud-based analysis.
- Data preview: Use .head() to display the first few rows of a DataFrame.
- Missing values: Identify missing entries with .isna().sum().

Summary Statistics (Descriptive Statistics for Accounting and Finance Data)

- Central tendency:
  - .mean(): Calculates the average value.
  - .median(): Returns the middle value.
  - .mode(): Identifies the most frequent value.
- Dispersion:
  - .std(): computes standard deviation (spread around the mean).
  - .var(): calculates variance (square of standard deviation).
  - .min() and .max(): show minimum and maximum values.
  - .quantile(0.25) and .quantile(0.75): identify first and third quartiles.
  - Range: is calculated as maximum minus minimum.
  - IQR: is the difference between third and first quartiles.

Shape of Distribution

- .skew(): measures asymmetry in the data.
- .kurt(): assesses tail weight relative to a normal distribution.

Correlation Analysis

- Pearson correlation: measures linear relationships between variables using .corr().
- Coefficient values range from −1 (strong negative) to +1 (strong positive).
- Pairwise correlation: is calculated directly between two variables, e.g. df['Revenue'].corr(df['Profit']).

Quiz Questions

Scan the QR code below to access the quiz questions for this chapter (see 6.md).

https://github.com/DrMichaelGuo/QuizPFAAFAMMA

Further Reading and Resources

pandas development team (2025) *User guide*. pandas. https://pandas.pydata.org/docs/user_guide/index.html# (Accessed 24 July 2025).

Google (2025) *Welcome to Colab!* https://colab.research.google.com/ (Accessed 24 July 2025).

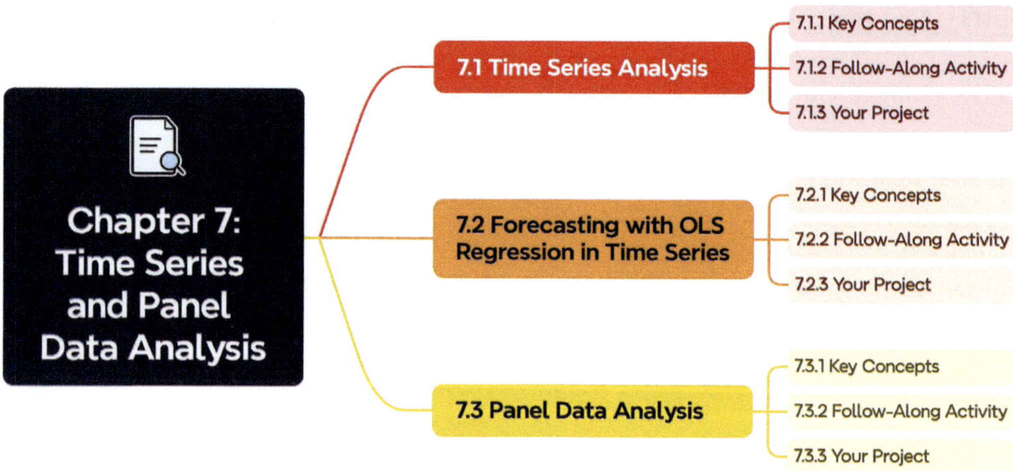

FIGURE 7.1 Structure of Chapter 7

7

TIME SERIES AND PANEL DATA ANALYSIS

This chapter introduces methods for analysing time-based and multi-entity financial data. It explains how to examine trends, seasonality, and cycles in time series data; apply resampling and rolling averages; and use ordinary least squares (OLS) regression for forecasting. It also covers panel data analysis by combining time series and cross-sectional data to evaluate financial performance across firms and over time. Through Python-based activities and structured projects, students will practise how to model, predict, and interpret financial patterns (Figure 7.1).

Learning Objectives

By the end of this chapter, you will be able to

- Use Python to analyse financial time series data by identifying trends, seasonality, and calculating rolling averages.
- Build and evaluate forecasting models with OLS regression.
- Apply fixed-effects and random-effects models to panel data to examine firm-level financial outcomes.

7.1 Time Series Analysis

Time series analysis is used in accounting and finance to examine data collected at regular time intervals. This section introduces basic methods for handling time series data using the pandas library (see Figure 7.2).

DOI: 10.4324/9781003656968-7

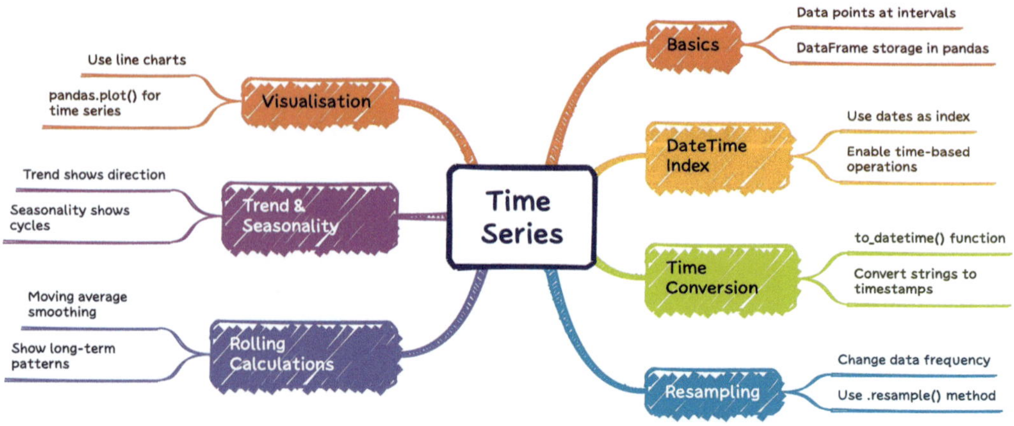

FIGURE 7.2 Time Series

7.1.1 Key Concepts

7.1.1.1 Time Series Analysis

A time series is a set of data points recorded at consistent time intervals. In Python, time series data is often stored in a pandas DataFrame. Time series analysis involves examining how values change over time to identify patterns and inform decisions.

7.1.1.2 DatetimeIndex

In pandas, a DatetimeIndex represents dates or times used as the index of a DataFrame. This enables operations such as resampling and rolling calculations. Applications include budgeting, cash flow forecasting, company valuation, and investment strategy evaluation.

7.1.1.3 Date and Time Conversion

The pandas.to_datetime() function is used to convert strings into datetime objects. For example, the string "2025-05-08" is converted into a timestamp. Setting the datetime column as the index enables time-based operations and prevents errors caused by treating dates as plain text.

7.1.1.4 Resampling

Resampling is the process of changing the observation frequency of time series data. For example, if data is collected monthly, it can be resampled to quarterly frequency. In Python, the .resample() method in pandas is used to perform resampling. For example, the frequency string 'QE' refers to quarter-end:

```
df.resample('QE').sum()
```

This command returns the sum of values for each quarter ending in March, June, September, and December.

7.1.1.5 *Rolling Window Calculations*

Rolling window calculations compute statistics over a defined window. For example, a 3-month moving average smooths short-term variations and shows longer-term patterns.

7.1.1.6 *Trend and Seasonality*

Time series data may contain long-term movement (trend) or regular cycles (seasonality). A trend shows a direction over time. Seasonality occurs at fixed intervals, such as annual changes in retail activity. Recognising these patterns supports forecasting and variance analysis in accounting and finance.

7.1.1.7 *Visualisation*

Line charts are commonly used to display time series data. Tools such as pandas.plot(), matplotlib, and seaborn help identify patterns and changes in the data over time.

7.1.2 Follow-Along Activity

This activity introduces time series analysis using a company's monthly revenue from 2021 to 2023 (see Figure 7.3). The dataset is available in the file 7.1.ipynb from the following site. Locate the dataset and copy the data into a Google Colab notebook.

https://github.com/DrMichaelGuo/PFAAFAMMA

```
data = {
    'Date': [
        '2021-01-01', '2021-02-01', '2021-03-01', '2021-04-01',
        '2021-05-01', '2021-06-01', '2021-07-01', '2021-08-01',
        '2021-09-01', '2021-10-01', '2021-11-01', '2021-12-01',
        '2022-01-01', '2022-02-01', '2022-03-01', '2022-04-01',
        '2022-05-01', '2022-06-01', '2022-07-01', '2022-08-01',
        '2022-09-01', '2022-10-01', '2022-11-01', '2022-12-01',
        '2023-01-01', '2023-02-01', '2023-03-01', '2023-04-01',
        '2023-05-01', '2023-06-01', '2023-07-01', '2023-08-01',
        '2023-09-01', '2023-10-01', '2023-11-01', '2023-12-01'
    ],
    'Revenue': [
        250000, 260000, 270000, 280000,
        290000, 300000, 310000, 320000,
        330000, 340000, 350000, 360000,
        270000, 280000, 290000, 300000,
        310000, 320000, 330000, 340000,
        350000, 360000, 370000, 380000,
        300000, 320000, 290000, 310000,
        305000, 330000, 340000, 360000,
        350000, 370000, 380000, 390000
    ]
}
```

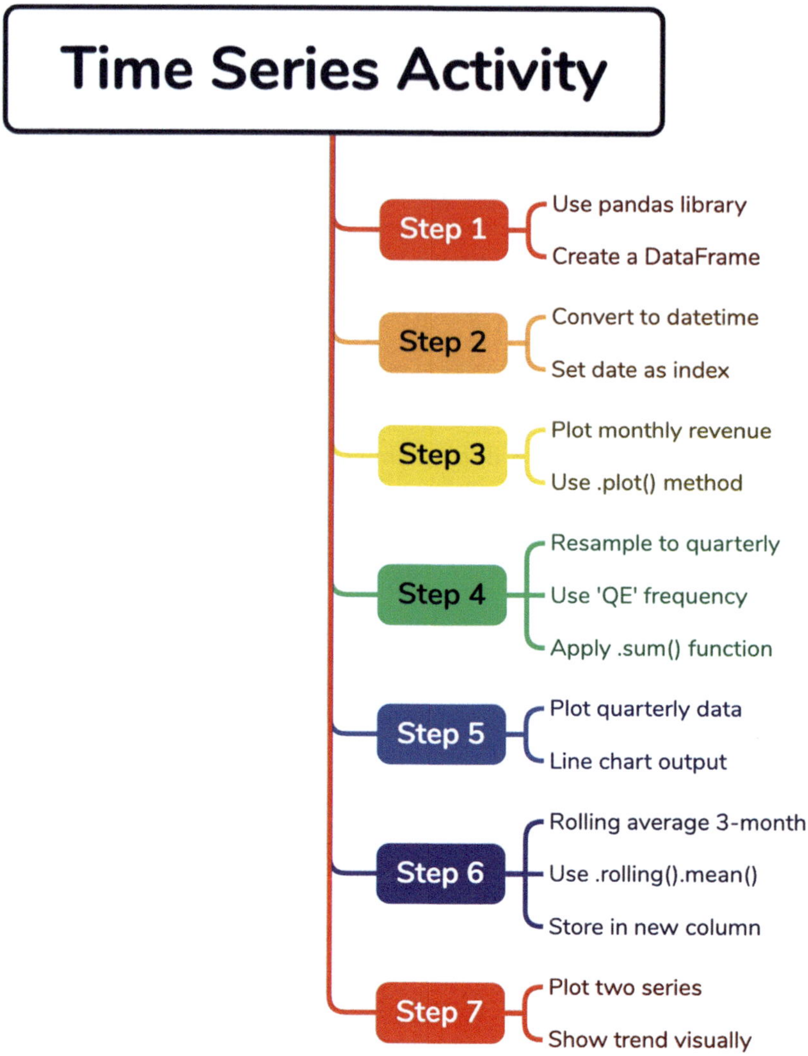

FIGURE 7.3 Time Series Activity

Step 1: Set Up the Data

Let's begin by creating a DataFrame from the dataset:

```
import pandas as pd

data = {
   'Date': [
       '2021-01-01', '2021-02-01', '2021-03-01', '2021-04-01',
       '2021-05-01', '2021-06-01', '2021-07-01', '2021-08-01',
       '2021-09-01', '2021-10-01', '2021-11-01', '2021-12-01',
       '2022-01-01', '2022-02-01', '2022-03-01', '2022-04-01',
```

```
        '2022-05-01', '2022-06-01', '2022-07-01', '2022-08-01',
        '2022-09-01', '2022-10-01', '2022-11-01', '2022-12-01',
        '2023-01-01', '2023-02-01', '2023-03-01', '2023-04-01',
        '2023-05-01', '2023-06-01', '2023-07-01', '2023-08-01',
        '2023-09-01', '2023-10-01', '2023-11-01', '2023-12-01'
    ],
    'Revenue': [
        250000, 260000, 270000, 280000,
        290000, 300000, 310000, 320000,
        330000, 340000, 350000, 360000,
        270000, 280000, 290000, 300000,
        310000, 320000, 330000, 340000,
        350000, 360000, 370000, 380000,
        300000, 320000, 290000, 310000,
        305000, 330000, 340000, 360000,
        350000, 370000, 380000, 390000
    ]
}
df = pd.DataFrame(data)
```

Explanation

- The dictionary data contains monthly revenue records from January 2021 to December 2023.
- df = pd.DataFrame(data): creates a DataFrame using the dictionary.

Step 2: Convert the Date and Set the Index

Let's convert the Date column to a datetime format and set it as the index.

```
df['Date'] = pd.to_datetime(df['Date'])
df.set_index('Date', inplace=True)
print(df.head())
```

Output

```
             Revenue
Date
2021-01-01    250000
2021-02-01    260000
2021-03-01    270000
2021-04-01    280000
2021-05-01    290000
```

Explanation

- pd.to_datetime(df['Date']): converts the values in the Date column from strings to datetime objects.
- df.set_index('Date', inplace=True): sets the Date column as the index and updates the DataFrame.

- inplace=True: means the DataFrame df is updated by setting the Date column as the index.
- print(df.head()): displays the first five rows of the DataFrame.

Step 3: Plot Monthly Revenue

Let's visualise the monthly revenue data.

```
df['Revenue'].plot(title="Monthly Revenue Over Time", grid=True)
```

Output: see Figure 7.4.

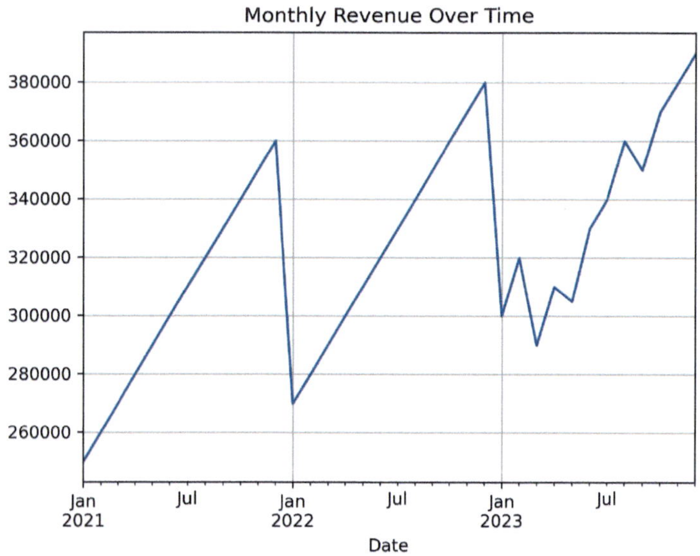

FIGURE 7.4 Monthly Revenue Over Time

Explanation

- df['Revenue']: selects the Revenue column from the DataFrame.
- .plot(...): creates a line plot of the revenue values over time.
- Title="Monthly Revenue Over Time": sets the title of the plot.
- Grid=True: adds a grid to assist with reading values.
- The plot shows an overall upward trend in monthly revenue, with short-term fluctuations.

Step 4: Resample the Data

Let's aggregate the revenue data to quarterly frequency.

```
quarterly_revenue = df['Revenue'].resample('QE').sum()
print(quarterly_revenue)
```

Output

```
Date
2021-03-31      780000
2021-06-30      870000
2021-09-30      960000
2021-12-31     1050000
2022-03-31      840000
2022-06-30      930000
2022-09-30     1020000
2022-12-31     1110000
2023-03-31      910000
2023-06-30      945000
2023-09-30     1050000
2023-12-31     1140000
Freq: QE-DEC, Name: Revenue, dtype: int64
```

Explanation

- .resample('QE'): groups data by quarter-end (31 March, 30 June, 30 September, 31 December).
- .sum(): calculates total revenue for each quarter.

Step 5: Plot Quarterly Revenue

Let's visualise the resampled quarterly data.

```
quarterly_revenue.plot(title='Quarterly Revenue', grid=True)
```

Output: see Figure 7.5.

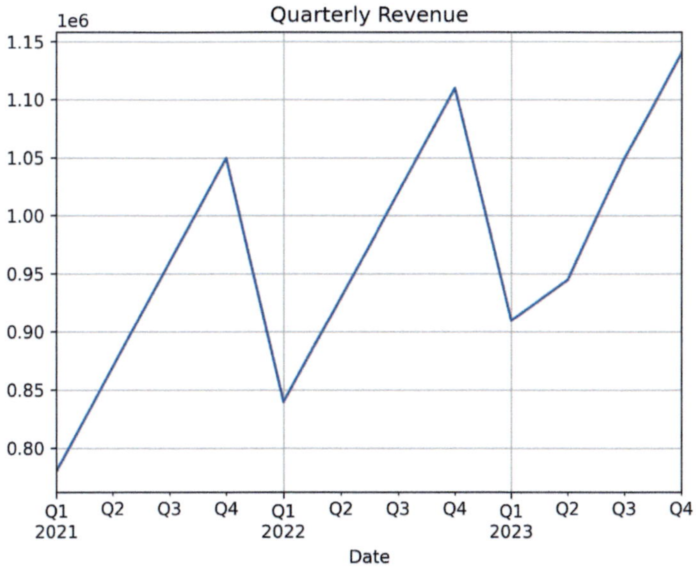

FIGURE 7.5 Quarterly Revenue

Explanation

- quarterly_revenue.plot(title='Quarterly Revenue', grid=True): creates a line plot of the quarterly revenue over time.
    - Title='Quarterly Revenue': sets the chart title.
    - grid=True: adds a grid to assist with reading values.

Step 6: Calculate a 3-Month Rolling Average

Let's calculate a rolling average over 3 months.

```
df['3_Month_Rolling_Avg'] = df['Revenue'].rolling(window=3).mean()
print(df.round(2))
```

Output

```
           Revenue  3_Month_Rolling_Avg
Date
2021-01-01   250000                  NaN
2021-02-01   260000                  NaN
2021-03-01   270000            260000.00
2021-04-01   280000            270000.00
2021-05-01   290000            280000.00
2021-06-01   300000            290000.00
2021-07-01   310000            300000.00
2021-08-01   320000            310000.00
2021-09-01   330000            320000.00
2021-10-01   340000            330000.00
2021-11-01   350000            340000.00
2021-12-01   360000            350000.00
2022-01-01   270000            326666.67
2022-02-01   280000            303333.33
2022-03-01   290000            280000.00
2022-04-01   300000            290000.00
2022-05-01   310000            300000.00
2022-06-01   320000            310000.00
2022-07-01   330000            320000.00
2022-08-01   340000            330000.00
2022-09-01   350000            340000.00
2022-10-01   360000            350000.00
2022-11-01   370000            360000.00
2022-12-01   380000            370000.00
2023-01-01   300000            350000.00
2023-02-01   320000            333333.33
2023-03-01   290000            303333.33
2023-04-01   310000            306666.67
2023-05-01   305000            301666.67
2023-06-01   330000            315000.00
2023-07-01   340000            325000.00
2023-08-01   360000            343333.33
```

```
2023-09-01    350000              350000.00
2023-10-01    370000              360000.00
2023-11-01    380000              366666.67
2023-12-01    390000              380000.00
```

Explanation

- df['Revenue'].rolling(window = 3): creates a rolling window of 3 consecutive months on the Revenue column.
  - .mean(): calculates the mean revenue within each 3-month window.
  - df['3_Month_Rolling_Avg']: stores the result in a new column named 3_Month_Rolling_Avg.
- df.round(2): rounds all numerical values in the DataFrame to two decimal places.

Step 7: Plot Revenue and Rolling Average

Let's plot both the original and the smoothed revenue values.

```
df[['Revenue', '3_Month_Rolling_Avg']].plot(title="Monthly Revenue
and 3-Month Rolling Average", grid=True)
```

Output: see Figure 7.6.

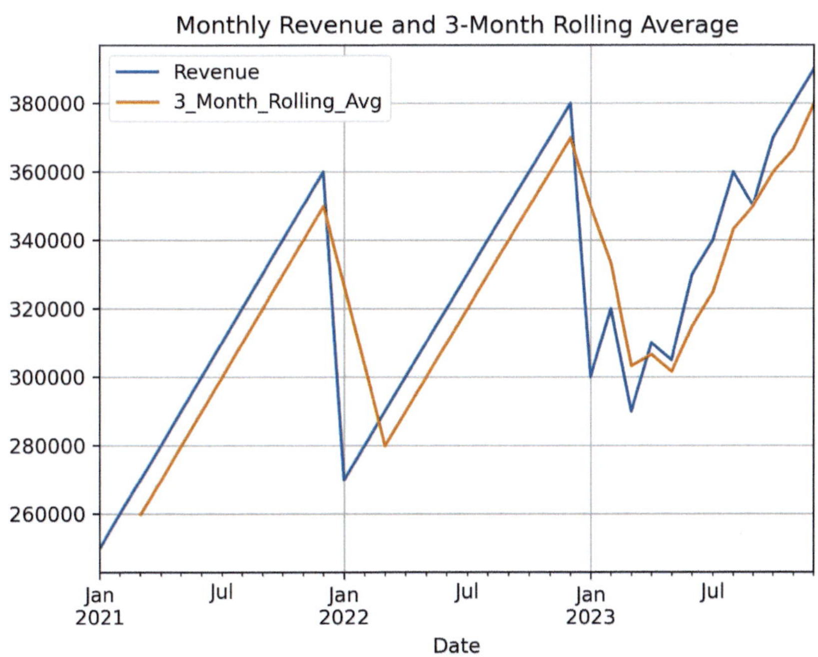

FIGURE 7.6 Monthly Revenue and 3-Month Rolling Average

Explanation

- This plot displays two lines:
    - Blue line: the original monthly revenue values.
    - Orange line: the 3-month rolling average.

7.1.3 Your Project

7.1.3.1 Tasks

Write Python code to apply time series analysis to a dataset of daily stock closing prices. Use the dataset provided in the 'Dataset for Your Project' section in the file 7.1.ipynb, available at the following link:

https://github.com/DrMichaelGuo/PFAAFAMMA

Copy the dataset into your Google Colab notebook.

```
data = {
    'Date': [
        '2023-01-01', '2023-01-02', '2023-01-03', '2023-01-04',
'2023-01-05',
        '2023-01-06', '2023-01-07', '2023-01-08', '2023-01-09',
'2023-01-10',
        '2023-01-11', '2023-01-12', '2023-01-13', '2023-01-14',
'2023-01-15',
        '2023-01-16', '2023-01-17', '2023-01-18', '2023-01-19',
'2023-01-20',
        '2023-01-21', '2023-01-22', '2023-01-23', '2023-01-24',
'2023-01-25',
        '2023-01-26', '2023-01-27', '2023-01-28', '2023-01-29',
'2023-01-30',
        '2023-01-31'
    ],
    'Closing Price': [
        150, 152, 148, 149, 151, 153, 154, 155, 157, 156,
        158, 160, 162, 161, 159, 158, 157, 156, 155, 153,
        154, 156, 157, 158, 159, 160, 162, 161, 160, 158,
        159
    ]
}
```

Note: The dataset includes daily closing prices for all calendar days in January 2023, including weekends. In practice, stock markets are closed on weekends and public holidays. This dataset is structured for demonstration purposes only.

Complete the following tasks:

- Load the data into a pandas DataFrame.
- Convert the Date column using pd.to_datetime and set it as the index.
- Plot the daily closing price.
- Resample the data to weekly frequency using .resample('W').mean().
- Plot the weekly average closing price.

- Calculate a 5-day rolling average.
- Plot both the daily closing price and the 5-day rolling average.

Complete each step in a separate Google Colab cell. This approach allows step-by-step execution, supports error checking, and displays the output of each step.

7.1.3.2 Example Code

```
# Step 1: Import pandas and create a DataFrame with the daily
closing price data

import pandas as pd

# Note: This dataset includes daily closing prices for every
calendar day in January 2023, including weekends.
# In practice, financial markets are usually closed on weekends and
holidays.
# This is a simplified example for demonstration purposes.

data = {
    'Date': [
        '2023-01-01', '2023-01-02', '2023-01-03', '2023-01-04',
'2023-01-05',
        '2023-01-06', '2023-01-07', '2023-01-08', '2023-01-09',
'2023-01-10',
        '2023-01-11', '2023-01-12', '2023-01-13', '2023-01-14',
'2023-01-15',
        '2023-01-16', '2023-01-17', '2023-01-18', '2023-01-19',
'2023-01-20',
        '2023-01-21', '2023-01-22', '2023-01-23', '2023-01-24',
'2023-01-25',
        '2023-01-26', '2023-01-27', '2023-01-28', '2023-01-29',
'2023-01-30',
        '2023-01-31'
    ],
    'Closing Price': [
        150, 152, 148, 149, 151, 153, 154, 155, 157, 156,
        158, 160, 162, 161, 159, 158, 157, 156, 155, 153,
        154, 156, 157, 158, 159, 160, 162, 161, 160, 158,
        159
    ]
}

# Create DataFrame
df = pd.DataFrame(data)
```

```
# Step 2: Convert the 'Date' column to datetime format and set it as
the index

df['Date'] = pd.to_datetime(df['Date'])  # Convert strings to
datetime objects
```

```
df.set_index('Date', inplace=True)        # Set the 'Date' column as
the index
```

```
# Step 3: Plot the daily closing price

import matplotlib.pyplot as plt
df['Closing Price'].plot(title="Daily Closing Price - January 2023",
grid=True)
```

```
# Step 4: Resample the data to weekly frequency and calculate
average closing price

weekly_closing = df['Closing Price'].resample('W').mean()  # Weekly
average
print(weekly_closing)  # Display the resampled data
```

```
# Step 5: Plot the weekly average closing prices

weekly_closing.plot(title='Weekly Average Closing Price', grid=True)
```

```
# Step 6: Calculate a 5-day rolling average to smooth short-term
variations

df['5_Day_Rolling_Avg'] = df['Closing Price'].rolling(window=5).mean()
print(df.round(2))  # Print the DataFrame with the new column,
rounded to 2 decimal places
```

```
# Step 7: Plot both the original closing price and the 5-day rolling
average

df[['Closing Price', '5_Day_Rolling_Avg']].plot(title="Daily Closing
Price and 5-Day Rolling Average", grid=True)
```

Scan the QR code to access the Python code and output (see 7.1.ipynb).

https://github.com/DrMichaelGuo/PFAAFAMMA

7.2 Forecasting with OLS Regression in Time Series

This section introduces how to use OLS regression to estimate future values in a time series. The analysis uses monthly revenue data and lagged variables to build a linear model (see Figure 7.7).

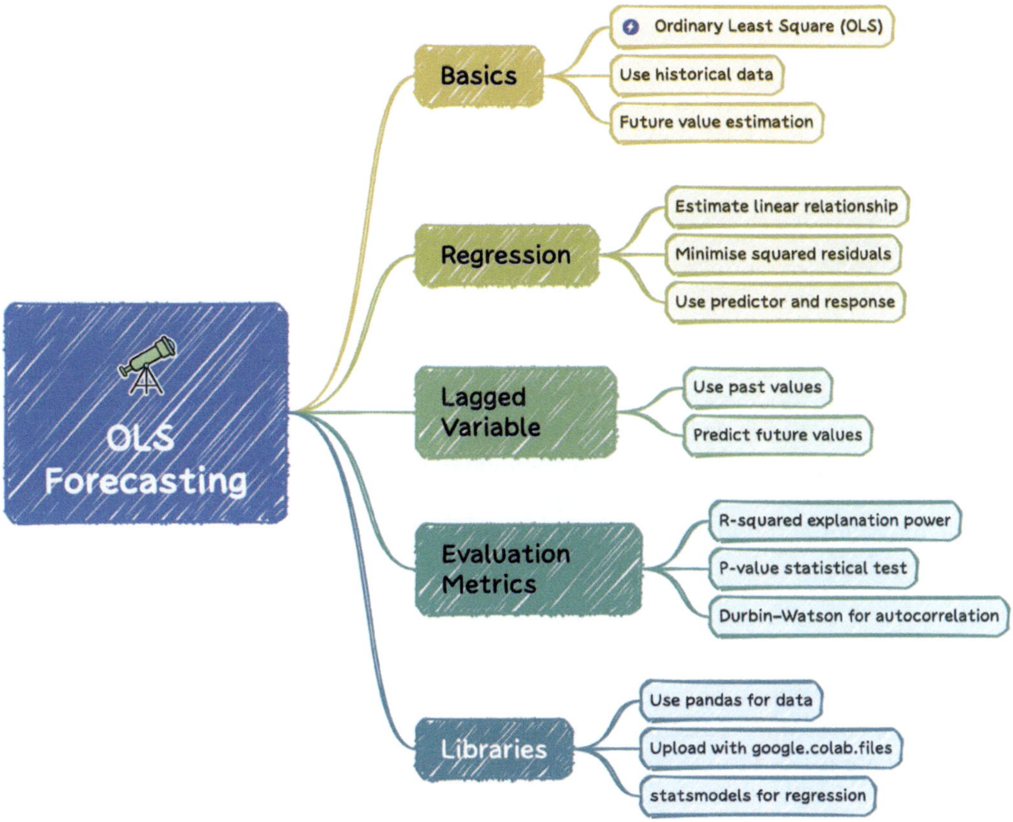

FIGURE 7.7 OLS Forecasting

7.2.1 Key Concepts

7.2.1.1 Forecasting

Forecasting uses historical data to estimate future values. It supports business decisions by projecting outcomes based on past patterns.

7.2.1.2 OLS Regression

OLS regression estimates the relationship between a dependent variable and one or more independent variables by minimising the sum of squared residuals. It generates a linear equation that explains variation in the dependent variable using information from the independent variables.

In OLS,

- The dependent variable (also called the response variable) is the outcome being explained or predicted.
- The independent variables (also called predictor variables) are the inputs used to explain or predict the dependent variable.

7.2.1.3 *Lagged Variable*

A lagged variable is a past value in a time series used as a predictor for the current or future value. In Python, lagged variables can be named with a suffix. For example,

- Revenue_Lag1: revenue from one time period earlier.
- Revenue_Lag2: revenue from two time periods earlier.

7.2.1.4 *Model Evaluation*

In OLS regression, model performance can be evaluated using statistics such as R-squared, p-values, and the Durbin–Watson statistic. R-squared measures the proportion of variance in the dependent variable explained by the model. P-values test whether the relationship between the predictors and the response is statistically significant. The Durbin–Watson statistic measures autocorrelation in the residuals and assesses whether the model errors are independent.

7.2.1.5 *Python Libraries*

This section uses three libraries: pandas is used to load, process, and manage tabular data; google.colab.files is used to upload files in the Google Colab environment; and statsmodels.api is used to fit statistical models, including OLS regression. These libraries are imported with the following code:

```
import pandas as pd
from google.colab import files
import statsmodels.api as sm
```

7.2.2 Follow-Along Activity

This activity uses the OLS method from the statsmodels library to construct a regression model to forecast values in a financial time series (see Figure 7.8). The dataset contains monthly revenue figures and is available as 7.2_data.csv at the following link:

https://github.com/DrMichaelGuo/PFAAFAMMA

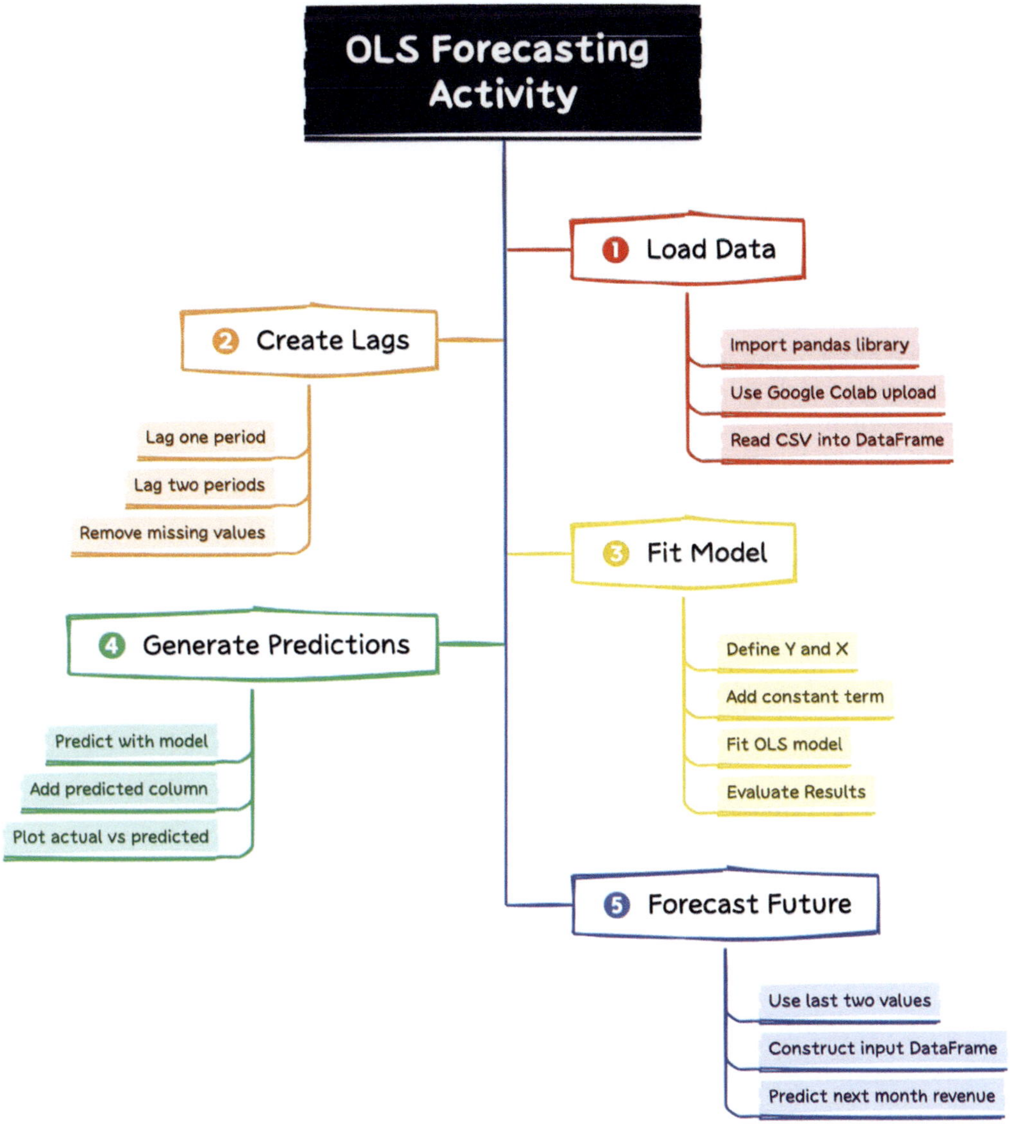

FIGURE 7.8 OLS Forecasting Activity

Step 1: Import Libraries and Load Dataset

Let's import the necessary libraries and load the dataset from a CSV file.

```
import pandas as pd
from google.colab import files
import statsmodels.api as sm

uploaded = files.upload()
df = pd.read_csv("7.2_data.csv")
print(df.head())
```

Output

```
         Date    Revenue
0  2020-01-31  204967.14
1  2020-02-29  201808.85
2  2020-03-31  212859.86
3  2020-04-30  224804.77
4  2020-05-31  210424.42
```

Explanation

- import pandas as pd: imports the pandas library.
- from google.colab import files: imports the files module to manage file uploads in Google Colab.
- import statsmodels.api as sm: imports the statsmodels library.
- uploaded = files.upload(): prompts the user to upload a file.
- df = pd.read_csv("7.2_data.csv"): reads the uploaded CSV file into a DataFrame.
- print(df.head()): displays the first five rows of the DataFrame.

Step 2: Create Lagged Revenue Variables

Let's create lagged versions of the revenue variable to use as predictors in the model.

```
df["Revenue_Lag1"] = df["Revenue"].shift(1)
df["Revenue_Lag2"] = df["Revenue"].shift(2)
df.dropna(inplace=True)
print(df.head())
```

Output

```
         Date    Revenue  Revenue_Lag1  Revenue_Lag2
2  2020-03-31  212859.86     201808.85     204967.14
3  2020-04-30  224804.77     212859.86     201808.85
4  2020-05-31  210424.42     224804.77     212859.86
5  2020-06-30  213616.08     210424.42     224804.77
6  2020-07-31  234941.06     213616.08     210424.42
```

Explanation

- df["Revenue_Lag1"] = df["Revenue"].shift(1): creates a new column where each value is the revenue from the previous time period.
    - shift(1): moves all values in the column down by one row, aligning the previous month's revenue with the current month.

- df["Revenue_Lag2"] = df["Revenue"].shift(2): creates another column where each value is the revenue from two time periods earlier.
  - shift(2): moves the values down by two rows, aligning revenue from 2 months ago with the current month.
- These lagged values are explanatory variables in the regression model. They allow the model to test whether past revenue values explain current revenue.
- df.dropna(inplace=True): removes all rows that contain missing values. Missing values appear in the first two rows as there is no enough earlier data to compute Revenue_Lag1 and Revenue_Lag2.
- print(df.head()): displays the first five rows of the updated DataFrame.
- The output starts from index 2 because rows 0 and 1 contain missing values in one or both lagged columns and are removed.

Step 3: Fit the OLS Model

Let's define the response and predictor variables and fit an OLS model.

```
Y = df["Revenue"]
X = df[["Revenue_Lag1", "Revenue_Lag2"]]
X = sm.add_constant(X)
model = sm.OLS(Y, X).fit()
print(model.summary())
```

Output

```
                            OLS Regression Results
==============================================================================
Dep. Variable:                Revenue   R-squared:                       0.930
Model:                            OLS   Adj. R-squared:                  0.926
Method:                 Least Squares   F-statistic:                     283.6
Date:                Sun, 27 Jul 2025   Prob (F-statistic):           1.70e-25
Time:                        10:52:28   Log-Likelihood:                -494.04
No. Observations:                  46   AIC:                             994.1
Df Residuals:                      43   BIC:                             999.6
Df Model:                           2
Covariance Type:            nonrobust
================================================================================
                   coef    std err          t      P>|t|      [0.025      0.975]
--------------------------------------------------------------------------------
const         7328.4180   1.14e+04      0.642      0.524   -1.57e+04    3.03e+04
Revenue_Lag1     0.5088      0.137      3.723      0.001       0.233       0.784
Revenue_Lag2     0.4823      0.137      3.514      0.001       0.205       0.759
==============================================================================
Omnibus:                        1.907   Durbin-Watson:                   2.299
Prob(Omnibus):                  0.385   Jarque-Bera (JB):                1.722
Skew:                           0.361   Prob(JB):                        0.423
Kurtosis:                       2.386   Cond. No.                     2.60e+06
==============================================================================
```

Explanation

- Y = df["Revenue"]: assigns the current revenue values to the response variable Y.
- X = df[["Revenue_Lag1", "Revenue_Lag2"]]: selects the two lagged variables as predictors.
- X = sm.add_constant(X): adds a constant term to the predictors to include an intercept in the model.
- model = sm.OLS(Y, X).fit(): fits the OLS model using Y and X.
- print(model.summary()): displays the regression results summary.

The model explains a large part of the variation in monthly revenue. The R-squared is 0.930. Both lagged revenue variables have statistically significant coefficients (p-values < 0.01), suggesting that revenue from 1 to 2 months earlier helps predict current revenue. The coefficients for Revenue_Lag1 and Revenue_Lag2 are 0.5088 and 0.4823, respectively. The Durbin–Watson statistic is 2.299, indicating no strong autocorrelation in the residuals.

Step 4: Generate Predictions

Let's use the model to generate in-sample predictions and plot the results.

```
df["Predicted_Revenue"] = model.predict(X)
ax = df[["Revenue", "Predicted_Revenue"]].plot(title="Actual vs
Predicted Revenue", grid=True)
ax.set_ylabel("Revenue (£)")
```

Output: see Figure 7.9.

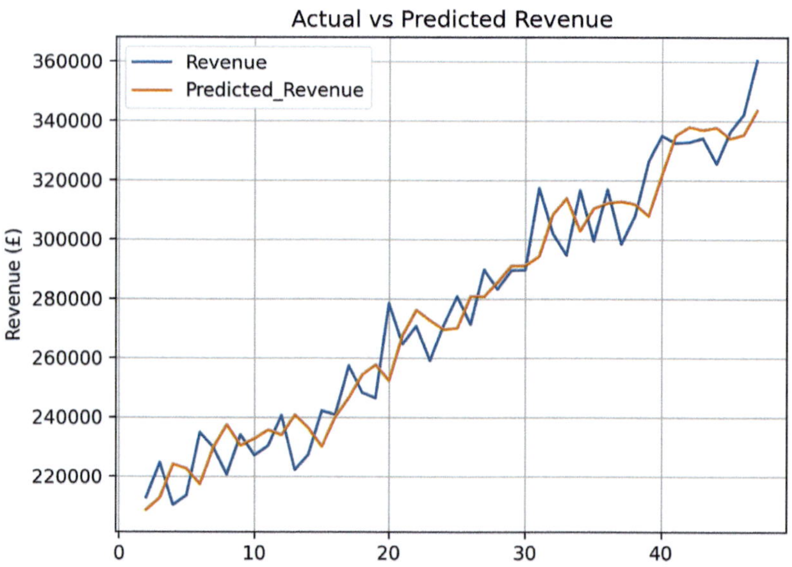

FIGURE 7.9 Actual vs Predicted Revenue

Explanation

- df["Predicted_Revenue"] = model.predict(X): calculates predicted revenue values and stores them in a new column.
- ax = df[["Revenue", "Predicted_Revenue"]].plot(...): plots actual and predicted revenue values.
- ax.set_ylabel("Revenue (£)"): labels the y-axis.

The line chart compares the actual revenue values with the predicted values from the regression model. The two lines follow a similar pattern, showing that the model captures the trend in the data. Both series increase over time, with some short-term variations. The predicted values are close to the actual values, although differences appear in some periods.

Step 5: Forecast Next Month's Revenue

Let's use the most recent lag values to forecast the revenue for the next month.

```
latest_lag1 = df["Revenue"].iloc[-1]
latest_lag2 = df["Revenue"].iloc[-2]
latest_data = pd.DataFrame({
    "const": [1],
    "Revenue_Lag1": [latest_lag1],
    "Revenue_Lag2": [latest_lag2]
})

forecast = model.predict(latest_data)
print(f"Forecasted revenue for next month: £{forecast.
values[0]:,.2f}")
```

Output

```
Forecasted revenue for next month: £356,509.72
```

Explanation

- latest_lag1 = df["Revenue"].iloc[-1]: retrieves the most recent revenue value.
- latest_lag2 = df["Revenue"].iloc[-2]: retrieves the second most recent revenue value.
- latest_data = pd.DataFrame(...): constructs a new DataFrame with the required input values for forecasting, including the constant term.
- forecast = model.predict(latest_data): applies the regression model to the new input data to obtain a forecast.
- print(...): displays the forecasted revenue for the next month.

The model predicts that revenue for the next month will be £356,509.72. This estimate is based on the most recent 2 months of revenue and the coefficients from the fitted regression model.

Note: The "const": [1] column represents the constant term (intercept) in the regression equation. It must be included because the model was fitted using sm.add_constant(X), which added a constant during estimation. When creating new input data for forecasting, the constant column must also be present so that the structure matches the fitted model. Both methods, adding a constant automatically with sm.add_constant() or defining "const": [1] manually, are equivalent provided they are used consistently.

Additional note: This is a one-step-ahead forecast that predicts the next period's value using the most recent observed data. To forecast multiple future periods, repeat the process by feeding each new predicted value back into the model as a lagged input for the following step.

7.2.3 Your Project

Write Python code to estimate and evaluate a forecasting model using OLS regression. The dataset file is named 7.2_your_project.csv and is available at the following link:

https://github.com/DrMichaelGuo/PFAAFAMMA

The dataset contains two columns:

- Date: weekly dates over a 30-week period.
- Units_Sold: number of units sold each week.

7.2.3.1 Tasks

- Import the required Python libraries.
- Upload and load the dataset from the CSV file.
- Create two lagged variables to represent the number of units sold in the previous 1 and 2 weeks (Units_Sold_Lag1 and Units_Sold_Lag2).
- Remove rows with missing lag values using df.dropna(inplace=True).
- Use the lagged variables to estimate an OLS regression model.
- Use the fitted model to generate in-sample predictions. Plot these predictions with the actual values to compare the model estimates against observed data. Display the model summary using model.summary().
- Use the most recent lagged values to forecast the number of units expected to be sold in the following week.

7.2.3.2 Example Code

```
# Import required libraries
import pandas as pd
from google.colab import files
import statsmodels.api as sm

# Upload and load the dataset
uploaded = files.upload()
df = pd.read_csv("7.2_your_project.csv")
print(df.head())
```

```
# Create lagged variables: sales from 1 and 2 weeks earlier
df["Units_Sold_Lag1"] = df["Units_Sold"].shift(1)
df["Units_Sold_Lag2"] = df["Units_Sold"].shift(2)

# Remove rows with missing lag values
df.dropna(inplace=True)
print(df.head())

# Define response and predictor variables
Y = df["Units_Sold"]
X = df[["Units_Sold_Lag1", "Units_Sold_Lag2"]]
X = sm.add_constant(X)  # Add constant (intercept) to the model

# Fit the OLS regression model
model = sm.OLS(Y, X).fit()
print(model.summary())

# Generate predictions for the in-sample period
df["Predicted_Units_Sold"] = model.predict(X)

# Plot actual vs predicted units sold
ax = df[["Units_Sold", "Predicted_Units_Sold"]].plot(
   title="Actual vs Predicted Units Sold", grid=True
)
ax.set_ylabel("Units Sold")

# Forecast units sold for the next week using the latest lagged values
latest_lag1 = df["Units_Sold"].iloc[-1]
latest_lag2 = df["Units_Sold"].iloc[-2]
latest_data = pd.DataFrame({
   "const": [1],
   "Units_Sold_Lag1": [latest_lag1],
   "Units_Sold_Lag2": [latest_lag2]
})

forecast = model.predict(latest_data)
print(f"Forecasted units sold for next week: {forecast.
values[0]:.0f}")
```

Scan the QR code to access the Python code and output (see 7.2.ipynb).

https://github.com/DrMichaelGuo/PFAAFAMMA

7.3 Panel Data Analysis

This section explains how to analyse panel data, which combines cross-sectional and time series observations, to explore financial relationships across multiple firms and periods. Panel data enables the identification of firm-specific effects and time-based trends using fixed-effects and random-effects models (see Figure 7.10).

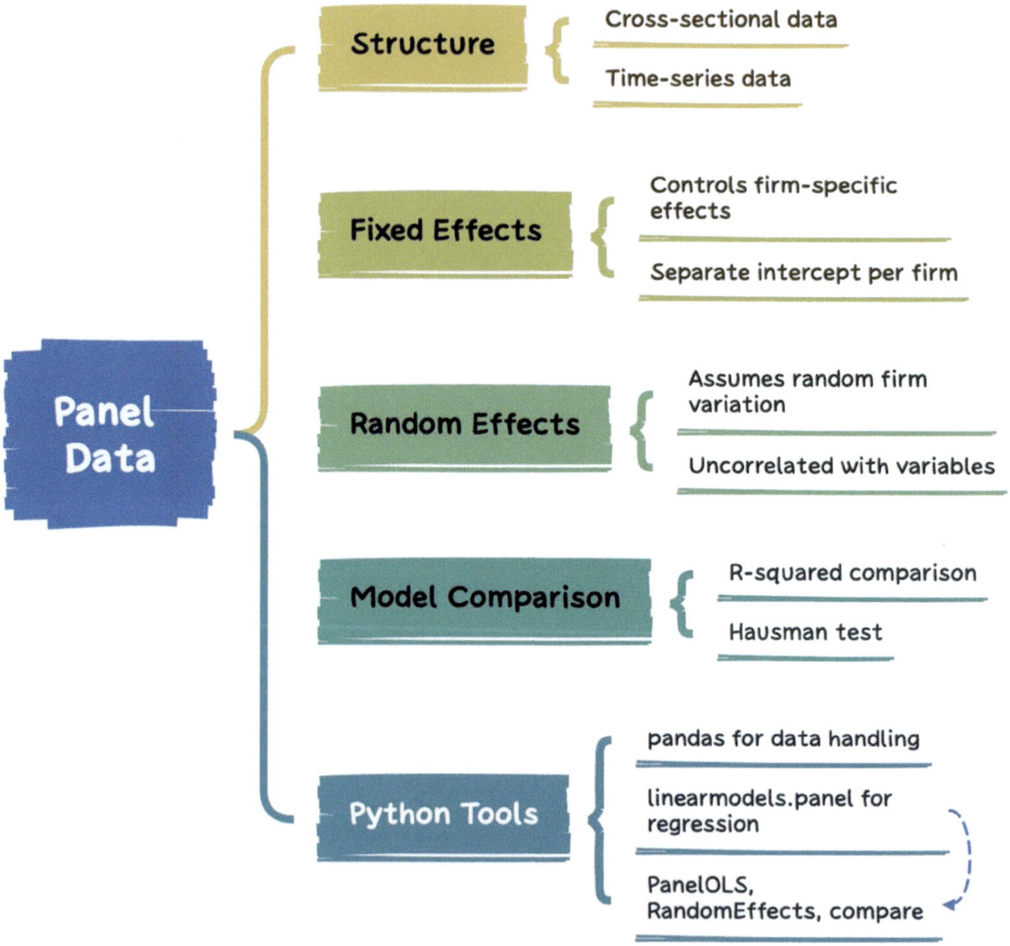

FIGURE 7.10 Panel Data

7.3.1 Key Concepts

7.3.1.1 Panel Data

Panel data combines cross-sectional data and time series data. Cross-sectional data refers to observations across different firms at a single point in time. Time series data refers to repeated observations of the same firm over several periods. Each row in a panel dataset represents a unique firm–time combination.

7.3.1.2 Fixed-Effects Model

Panel data analysis commonly uses two models: (i) fixed-effects and (ii) random-effects models. Both models aim to address unobserved differences across firms.

The fixed-effects model controls for firm-specific factors by estimating a separate intercept for each firm. The intercept reflects the average value of the dependent variable for a given firm when the independent variables are equal to zero. This approach removes the influence of time-invariant firm characteristics on the estimates.

7.3.1.3 Random-Effects Model

The random-effects model assumes that firm-specific variation is random and uncorrelated with the independent variables. It uses both within-firm and between-firm variations and provides more efficient estimates if the assumption of no correlation holds.

7.3.1.4 Model Comparison

Model performance is evaluated by comparing the estimated coefficients, significance levels, and R-squared values from the fixed-effects and random-effects models. The two models can be compared using a results comparison table and economic reasoning to decide which provides the more appropriate explanation of the data.

7.3.1.5 Python Libraries

This section uses two Python libraries: pandas is used for data manipulation and analysis, and linearmodels.panel estimates panel regression models. Fixed-effects models are estimated using PanelOLS, random-effects models using RandomEffects, and model comparisons using compare. These libraries are imported using the following code:

```
import pandas as pd
from linearmodels.panel import PanelOLS, RandomEffects, compare
```

7.3.2 Follow-Along Activity

This activity shows how to analyse panel data using fixed-effects and random-effects models. The analysis examines the relationship between advertising spend and revenue across three firms observed annually over 6 years (see Figure 7.11).

Step 1: Install Required Libraries

Let's install and import the necessary libraries.

```
!pip install -q linearmodels
import pandas as pd
from linearmodels.panel import PanelOLS, RandomEffects, compare
```

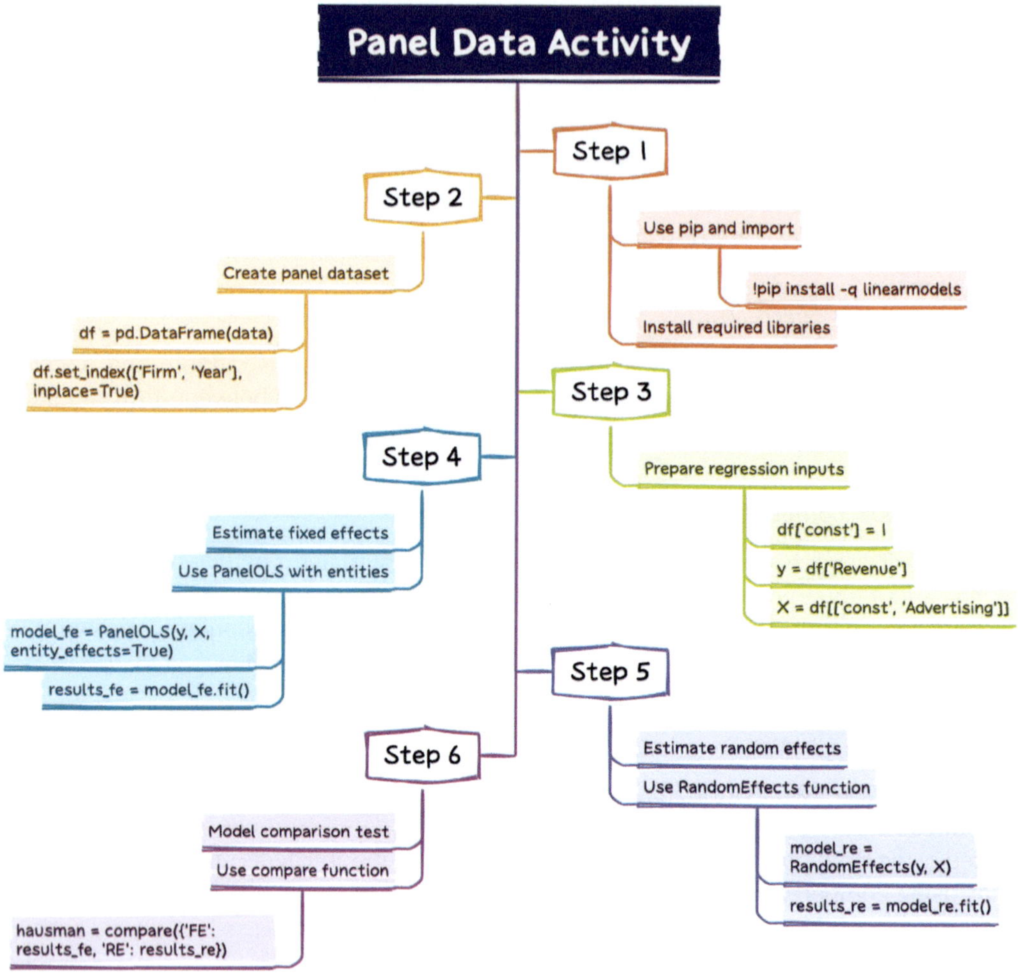

FIGURE 7.11 Panel Data Activity

Explanation

- !pip install -q linearmodels: installs the linearmodels library for panel data estimation. This step is required as the library is not included by default in Google Colab.
    - -q: enables a quiet mode to reduce installation output.
- import pandas as pd: imports the pandas library.
- from linearmodels.panel import PanelOLS, RandomEffects, compare: imports libraries to estimate fixed-effects and random-effects models, and a function to compare model results.

Step 2: Create Panel Dataset

Let's create a dataset with annual revenue and advertising spend for three firms from 2018 to 2023.

```
data = {
    'Firm': ['A']*6 + ['B']*6 + ['C']*6,
    'Year': [2018, 2019, 2020, 2021, 2022, 2023]*3,
    'Revenue': [210, 230, 250, 265, 280, 295,
                190, 200, 215, 225, 240, 260,
                180, 195, 210, 220, 235, 250],
    'Advertising': [20, 21, 22, 23, 24, 25,
                    15, 16, 17, 18, 19, 20,
                    10, 12, 14, 16, 18, 20]
}

df = pd.DataFrame(data)

df.set_index(['Firm', 'Year'], inplace=True)
print(df)
```

Output

```
Revenue  Advertising
Firm Year
A    2018       210          20
     2019       230          21
     2020       250          22
     2021       265          23
     2022       280          24
     2023       295          25
B    2018       190          15
     2019       200          16
     2020       215          17
     2021       225          18
     2022       240          19
     2023       260          20
C    2018       180          10
     2019       195          12
     2020       210          14
     2021       220          16
     2022       235          18
     2023       250          20
```

Explanation

- data = {...}: defines a dictionary with firm names, years, revenue, and advertising spend.
- df = pd.DataFrame(data): creates a DataFrame from the dictionary.
- df.set_index(['Firm', 'Year'], inplace=True): assigns a multi-level index to the DataFrame using 'Firm' and 'Year' as index levels. Each row is identified by a combination of firm and year. This structure supports panel data analysis by organising the dataset into cross-sectional units observed over time.
    - inplace=True: applies the change directly to the existing DataFrame instead of creating a new one.
- print(df): prints the DataFrame.

Step 3: Prepare Data for Panel Regression

Let's define the dependent and independent variables for model estimation.

```
df['const'] = 1
y = df['Revenue']
X = df[['const', 'Advertising']]
```

Explanation

- df['const'] = 1: adds a constant term to support intercept estimation.
    - The value 1 allows the model to estimate a single intercept for all observations.
- y = df['Revenue']: defines the dependent variable.
- X = df[['const', 'Advertising']]: defines the matrix of independent variables.

Step 4: Estimate Fixed-Effects Model

Let's fit a fixed-effects model.

```
model_fe = PanelOLS(y, X, entity_effects=True)
results_fe = model_fe.fit()
print(results_fe.summary)
```

Output

```
PanelOLS Estimation Summary
================================================================================
Dep. Variable:                Revenue   R-squared:                        0.8434
Estimator:                   PanelOLS   R-squared (Between):              0.4239
No. Observations:                  18   R-squared (Within):               0.8434
Date:                Fri, Jun 06 2025   R-squared (Overall):              0.7086
Time:                        08:13:35   Log-likelihood                   -67.095
Cov. Estimator:            Unadjusted
                                        F-statistic:                      75.405
Entities:                           3   P-value                           0.0000
Avg Obs:                       6.0000   Distribution:                    F(1,14)
Min Obs:                       6.0000
Max Obs:                       6.0000   F-statistic (robust):             75.405
                                        P-value                           0.0000
Time periods:                       6   Distribution:                    F(1,14)
Avg Obs:                       3.0000
Min Obs:                       3.0000
Max Obs:                       3.0000
```

```
                              Parameter Estimates
================================================================================
              Parameter  Std. Err.     T-stat    P-value    Lower CI    Upper CI
--------------------------------------------------------------------------------
const            53.333     20.585     2.5909     0.0214      9.1826      97.484
Advertising      9.6667     1.1132     8.6836     0.0000      7.2791      12.054
================================================================================
F-test for Poolability: 4.9868
P-value: 0.0232
Distribution: F(2,14)
Included effects: Entity
```

Explanation

- model_fe = PanelOLS(y, X, entity_effects=True): creates a fixed-effects model.
  - entity_effects=True: includes firm-specific intercepts to control for unobserved differences across firms. With entity_effects=True, the constant represents the common intercept, and each firm's intercept is estimated as a deviation from this value.
- results_fe = model_fe.fit(): estimates the model.
- print(results_fe.summary): prints estimation output.

The output shows that the fixed-effects model explains variation in revenue within firms (R-squared = 0.8434). The model is statistically significant (F-statistic = 75.405; P-value = 0.0000). Advertising has a positive and statistically significant effect on revenue (coefficient = 9.6667; P-value = 0.0000). The constant term is also statistically significant (coefficient = 53.333). The poolability test supports the use of firm-specific effects (P-value = 0.0232).

Note: In applied research, standard errors are often clustered by entity to account for correlation within firms. This can be done by adding cov_type='clustered', cluster_entity=True inside the .fit() function.

Step 5: Estimate Random-Effects Model

Let's fit a random-effects model that assumes firm-specific effects are uncorrelated with the explanatory variables.

```
model_re = RandomEffects(y, X)
results_re = model_re.fit()
print(results_re.summary)
```

Output:

```
RandomEffects Estimation Summary
================================================================================
Dep. Variable:                Revenue   R-squared:                        0.8130
Estimator:              RandomEffects   R-squared (Between):              0.8627
No. Observations:                  18   R-squared (Within):               0.7951
Date:                Fri, Jun 06 2025   R-squared (Overall):              0.8168
Time:                        08:13:36   Log-likelihood                   -71.459
Cov. Estimator:            Unadjusted
                                        F-statistic:                      69.543
Entities:                           3   P-value                           0.0000
Avg Obs:                       6.0000   Distribution:                    F(1,16)
Min Obs:                       6.0000
Max Obs:                       6.0000   F-statistic (robust):             69.543
                                        P-value                           0.0000
Time periods:                       6   Distribution:                    F(1,16)
Avg Obs:                       3.0000
Min Obs:                       3.0000
Max Obs:                       3.0000

                             Parameter Estimates
===============================================================================
             Parameter  Std. Err.     T-stat    P-value    Lower CI    Upper CI
-------------------------------------------------------------------------------
const           95.753     16.578     5.7759     0.0000      60.609      130.90
Advertising     7.3528     0.8817     8.3393     0.0000      5.4837      9.2220
===============================================================================
```

Explanation

- model_re = RandomEffects(y, X): creates a random-effects model object.
- results_re = model_re.fit(): fits the model.
- print(results_re.summary): prints the summary of results.

The output shows that the random-effects model explains variation in revenue (R-squared = 0.8130). The model is statistically significant (F-statistic = 69.543; P-value = 0.0000). Advertising has a positive and statistically significant effect on revenue (coefficient = 7.3528; P-value = 0.0000). The constant term is also statistically significant (coefficient = 95.753).

Step 6: Model Comparison Using Fixed-Effects and Random-Effects Models

Let's compare the fixed-effects and random-effects models using a results comparison table and economic reasoning.

```
hausman = compare({'FE': results_fe, 'RE': results_re})
print(hausman)
```

Output

```
Model Comparison
==========================================================
                                   FE                  RE
----------------------------------------------------------
Dep. Variable                 Revenue             Revenue
Estimator                    PanelOLS       RandomEffects
No. Observations                   18                  18
Cov. Est.                  Unadjusted          Unadjusted
R-squared                      0.8434              0.8130
R-Squared (Within)             0.8434              0.7951
R-Squared (Between)            0.4239              0.8627
R-Squared (Overall)            0.7086              0.8168
F-statistic                    75.405              69.543
P-value (F-stat)               0.0000              0.0000
=====================     ============     ===============
const                          53.333              95.753
                             (2.5909)            (5.7759)
Advertising                    9.6667              7.3528
                             (8.6836)            (8.3393)
====================== ============== =================
Effects                        Entity
----------------------------------------------------------
T-stats reported in parentheses
```

Explanation

- hausman = compare({'FE': results_fe, 'RE': results_re}): compares the fixed-effects model (results_fe) and the random-effects model (results_re) using a summary table.
- print(hausman): prints the comparison results.

The fixed-effects and random-effects models are compared using the compare() function. The fixed-effects model estimates a higher coefficient for Advertising (9.6667) than the random-effects model (7.3528), indicating a correlation between advertising and firm-specific factors. The fixed-effects model also reports a higher within R-squared (0.8434 vs 0.7951), suggesting greater explanatory power for variation within firms. Based on these results, the fixed-effects model is more appropriate for this dataset.

7.3.3 Your Project

You are a financial analyst writing a Python code to evaluate whether investment in research and development (R&D) is associated with profitability across five firms. You have access to a panel dataset that records annual R&D expenditure and profit figures for five firms over a 20-year period.

The dataset, 7.3_your_project_data.csv, is available at the following link: https://github.com/DrMichaelGuo/PFAAFAMMA

The dataset includes four columns:

- Firm: identifies five firms (Firm A to Firm E).
- Year: covers the period from 2004 to 2023.
- R&D_Spend: reports annual expenditure on research and development (in millions).
- Profit: reports annual profit (in millions).

Each row records one firm-year observation.

7.3.3.1 *Tasks*

Complete the following tasks:

- Install and import the required libraries, including the files module for uploading files in Google Colab.
- Upload the CSV file, load the dataset, and construct the panel data structure.
- Define the dependent and independent variables for regression.
- Estimate the fixed-effects model.
- Estimate the random-effects model.
- Compare the two models using a model comparison table.

7.3.3.2 *Example Code*

```
# Step 1: Install and import necessary modules
!pip install -q linearmodels
import pandas as pd
from linearmodels.panel import PanelOLS, RandomEffects, compare
from google.colab import files

# Step 2: Upload CSV, load dataset and prepare panel structure
uploaded = files.upload()
df = pd.read_csv('7.3_your_project_data.csv')
df.set_index(['Firm', 'Year'], inplace=True)  # Set hierarchical
index for panel data
print(df.head())

# Step 3: Prepare variables for regression
df['const'] = 1
y = df['Profit']
X = df[['const', 'R&D_Spend']]

# Step 4: Estimate fixed effects model
model_fe = PanelOLS(y, X, entity_effects=True)
results_fe = model_fe.fit()
print(results_fe.summary)

# Step 5: Estimate random effects model
model_re = RandomEffects(y, X)
```

```
results_re = model_re.fit()
print(results_re.summary)

# Step 6: Compare models using a model comparison table
hausman = compare({'FE': results_fe, 'RE': results_re})
print(hausman)
```

Scan the QR code to access the Python code and output (see 7.3.ipynb).

https://github.com/DrMichaelGuo/PFAAFAMMA

7.3.3.3 Summary of Chapter 7: Time Series and Panel Data Analysis

In this chapter, we have covered the following concepts:

Time Series Analysis

- Time series data: observations indexed by time, used for forecasting and analysing financial trends.
- DatetimeIndex: enables time-based operations such as resampling and rolling calculations.
- Resampling: changes data frequency (e.g. from monthly to quarterly) using .resample() with methods such as .sum() or .mean().
- Rolling averages: smooth short-term fluctuations using .rolling().mean().
- Trend and seasonality: identify long-term movement and periodic patterns in financial data.
- Visualisation: use .plot() to display patterns over time.

Forecasting with OLS Regression

- OLS: a regression method to model relationships between current and lagged financial values.
- Lagged variables: previous period values used to predict future outcomes.
- Model evaluation: measures performance using R-squared and p-values.
- Forecasting: predicts future values with fitted models based on recent lagged data.

Panel Data Analysis

- Panel data: combines time series and cross-sectional data (e.g. multiple firms over several years).

- Fixed-effects model: controls for unobservable, firm-specific factors by including separate intercepts for each entity.
- Random-effects model: assumes firm-specific effects are random and uncorrelated with independent variables.
- Hausman test: compares fixed and random effects to determine the more appropriate model.
- Python tools: use linearmodels.panel to estimate panel models, including PanelOLS and RandomEffects.

Quiz Questions

Scan the QR code below to access the quiz questions for this chapter (see 7.md).

https://github.com/DrMichaelGuo/QuizPFAAFAMMA

Further Reading and Resources

pandas (n.d.) *Time series/date functionality. pandas Documentation*. Retrieved July 25, 2025, from https://pandas.pydata.org/pandas-docs/stable/user_guide/timeseries.html

Seabold, S., and Perktold, J. (2010) 'Statsmodels: Econometric and statistical modeling with python', *SciPy*, 7(1), pp. 92–96.

Sheppard, K. (2021) *Linearmodels*. Retrieved July 25, 2025, from https://bashtage.github.io/linearmodels/

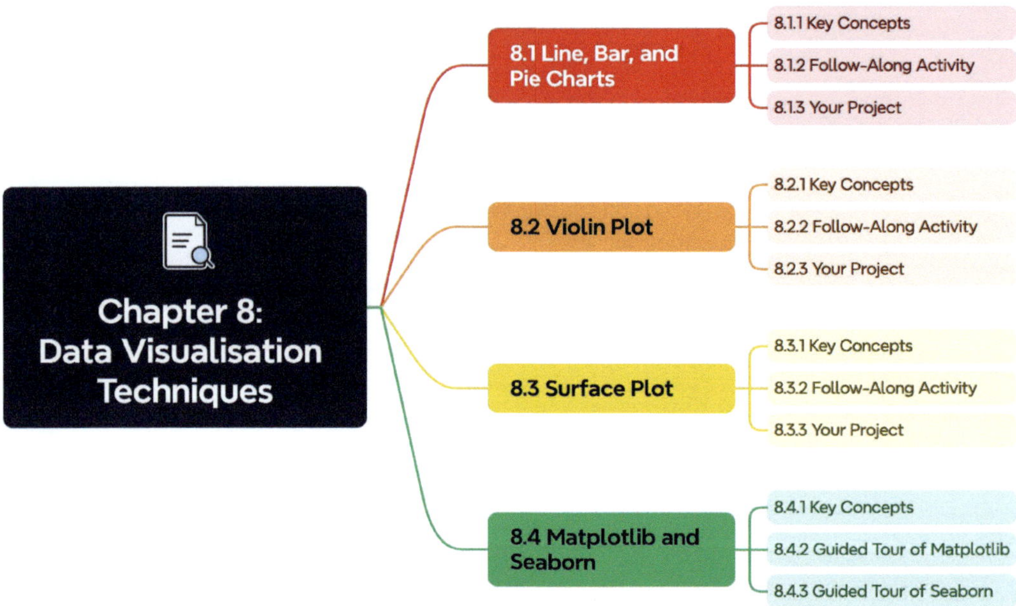

FIGURE 8.1 Structure of Chapter 8

8

DATA VISUALISATION TECHNIQUES

This chapter introduces visualisation techniques in Python to support data analysis in accounting and finance. It begins with line charts, bar charts, and pie charts using the Matplotlib library. It then presents violin plots and three-dimensional (3D) surface plots. The chapter ends with a comparison of Matplotlib and Seaborn and a walkthrough on how to create and modify visualisations (Figure 8.1).

Learning Objectives

By the end of this chapter, you will be able to

- Create and customise line, bar, and pie charts using Matplotlib.
- Build violin plots and interpret data distributions across groups.
- Produce 3D surface plots to explore relationships among variables.
- Use Matplotlib and Seaborn to present data.

8.1 Line, Bar, and Pie Charts

In accounting and finance, data visualisation helps with the understanding and presentation of numerical information. This section introduces line, bar, and pie charts using the Matplotlib library in Python (see Figure 8.2).

8.1.1 Key Concepts

8.1.1.1 Matplotlib

Matplotlib is a Python library used to create charts. The library includes tools for constructing a range of visual outputs from data.

DOI: 10.4324/9781003656968-8

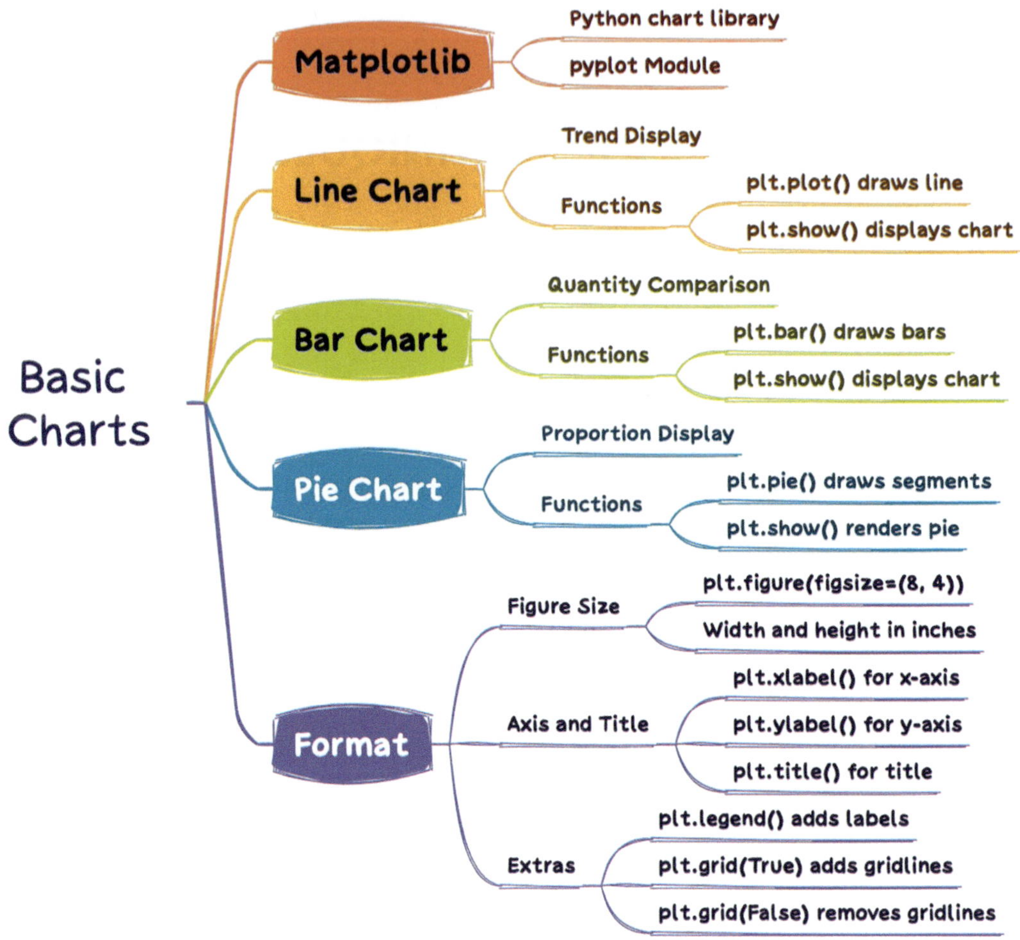

FIGURE 8.2 Basic Charts

8.1.1.2 matplotlib.pyplot

The pyplot module is a commonly used part of Matplotlib. It contains functions for creating various chart types. It is standard practice to import this module using the alias plt:

```
import matplotlib.pyplot as plt
```

8.1.1.3 Line Chart

A line chart is used to display trends over time, such as monthly sales or annual profit.
To create a line chart,

- plt.plot(): draws the line.
- plt.show(): displays the plot.

8.1.1.4 *Bar Chart*

A bar chart is used to compare quantities, such as revenue by department or profit by quarter.

To create a bar chart,

- plt.bar(): draws the bars.
- plt.show(): displays the plot.

8.1.1.5 *Pie Chart*

A pie chart shows proportions or percentage distributions, such as market share or budget allocation.

To create a pie chart,

- plt.pie(): draws the segments.
- plt.show(): displays the plot.

8.1.1.6 *Additional Formatting Functions*

Matplotlib provides functions to improve the clarity and structure of charts:

- Figure size: for example plt.figure(figsize=(8, 4)) sets the chart size.
  - The first value (8) sets the width in inches.
  - The second value (4) sets the height in inches.
  - These values can be adjusted to change the chart dimensions.
- Axis Labels and title
  - plt.xlabel() adds a label to the x-axis.
  - plt.ylabel() adds a label to the y-axis.
  - plt.title() adds a title to the chart.
- Legend:
  - plt.legend() provides labels for chart elements, such as multiple lines or bars.
- Gridlines:
  - plt.grid(True) adds gridlines.
  - plt.grid(False) removes gridlines.

8.1.2 *Follow-Along Activity*

This activity provides step-by-step instructions for creating basic charts in Python using the Matplotlib library (see Figure 8.3).

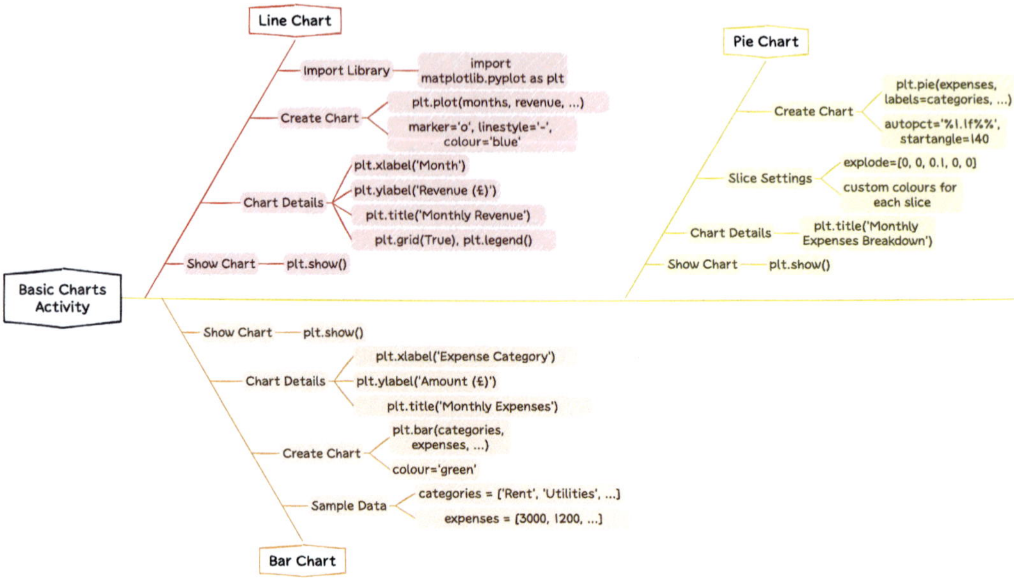

FIGURE 8.3 Basic Charts Activity

Step 1: Line Chart

Let's create a line chart to show monthly revenue.

First, import Matplotlib. Use the pyplot module from Matplotlib and import it using the alias plt.

```
import matplotlib.pyplot as plt
```

Next, let's create the chart using some sample data.

```
# Sample data for monthly revenue (in £)
months = ['Jan', 'Feb', 'Mar', 'Apr', 'May', 'Jun']
revenue = [10000, 12000, 9000, 15000, 13000, 17000]

# Creating a figure and plotting the line chart
plt.figure(figsize=(8, 4))
plt.plot(months, revenue, marker='o', linestyle='-', color='blue',
label='Revenue')

# Adding labels and title
plt.xlabel('Month')
plt.ylabel('Revenue (£)')
plt.title('Monthly Revenue')

# Adding a grid and legend for clarity
plt.grid(True)
plt.legend()

# Display the plot
plt.show()
```

Output: see Figure 8.4.

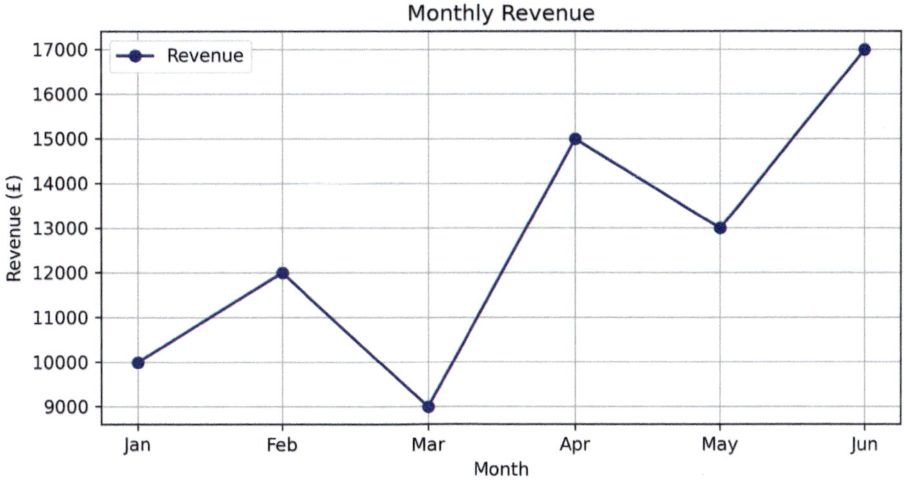

FIGURE 8.4 Monthly Revenue

Explanation

- plt.figure(figsize=(8, 4)): sets the chart size to 8 inches wide and 4 inches high.
- plt.plot(months, revenue, marker='o', linestyle='-', color='blue', label='Revenue'): draws the line using the revenue data.
    - months: the x-axis values represent each month.
    - revenue: the y-axis values represent revenue in pounds (£).
    - marker='o': adds circular markers on each data point.
    - linestyle='-': uses a solid line to connect the points.
    - color='blue': uses a blue line for visual clarity.
    - label='Revenue': assigns a label for the legend.
- plt.xlabel(), plt.ylabel(), and plt.title(): add axis labels and a title to the chart.
- plt.grid(True): adds gridlines.
- plt.legend(): displays the label.
- plt.show(): displays the chart.

Note: In this textbook, British English spelling is used in the writing (e.g. colour). However, in Python code, you must use the American spelling (e.g. color) to ensure the code runs correctly.

Step 2: Bar Chart

Let's create a bar chart to show different expense categories for a month.

```
# Sample data for monthly expenses (in £)
categories = ['Rent', 'Utilities', 'Salaries', 'Marketing',
'Miscellaneous']
expenses = [3000, 1200, 7000, 1500, 800]
```

```
# Creating the bar chart
plt.figure(figsize=(8, 4))
plt.bar(categories, expenses, color='green')

# Adding labels and title
plt.xlabel('Expense Category')
plt.ylabel('Amount (£)')
plt.title('Monthly Expenses')

# Display the plot
plt.show()
```

Output: see Figure 8.5.

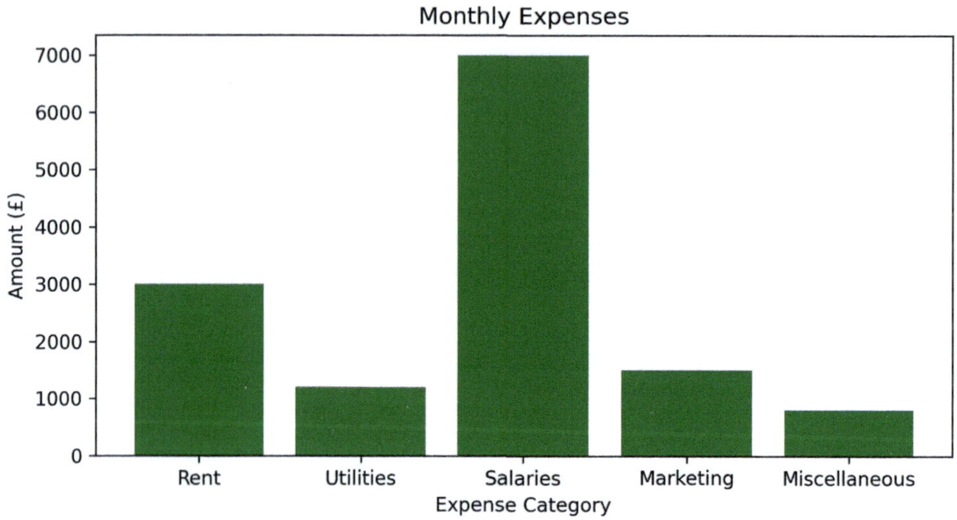

FIGURE 8.5 Monthly Expenses

Explanation

- plt.figure(figsize=(8, 4)): sets the chart size to 8 inches wide and 4 inches high.
- plt.bar(categories, expenses, color='green'): creates a vertical bar chart.
    - categories: the x-axis values represent each spending category.
    - expenses: the y-axis values show the amount spent in each category.
    - color='green': uses green bars.
- plt.xlabel() and plt.ylabel(): add labels to the x-axis and y-axis.
- plt.title(): adds a title.
- plt.show() displays the chart.

Step 3: Pie Chart

Let's create a pie chart to show the proportion of each expense category.

```
# Data: Expense categories and their corresponding amounts (£)
categories = ['Rent', 'Utilities', 'Salaries', 'Marketing',
'Miscellaneous']
expenses = [3000, 1200, 7000, 1500, 800]

# Create the pie chart
plt.figure(figsize=(7, 7))
plt.pie(
    expenses,
    labels=categories,
    autopct='%1.1f%%',
    startangle=140,
    colors=['lightblue', 'orange', 'lightgreen', 'red', 'purple'],
    explode=[0, 0, 0.1, 0, 0]  # Slightly separates the 'Salaries'
slice
)

# Add a title
plt.title('Monthly Expenses Breakdown')

# Display the pie chart
plt.show()
```

Output: see Figure 8.6.

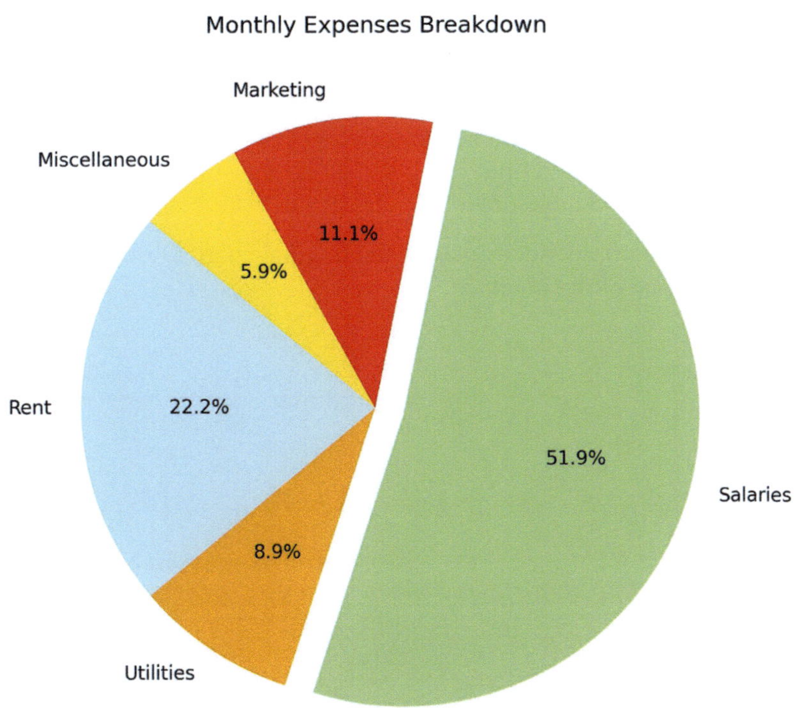

FIGURE 8.6 Monthly Expenses Breakdown

Explanation

- plt.figure(figsize=(7, 7)): sets the figure to a square shape, suitable for pie charts.
- plt.pie(expenses, labels=categories, autopct='%1.1f%%', startangle=140, colors=['lightblue', 'orange', 'lightgreen', 'red', 'purple'], explode=[0, 0, 0.1, 0, 0]): creates the pie chart.
    - expenses: defines the size of each slice.
    - labels=categories: adds labels to each slice.
    - Autopct='%1.1f%%': displays the percentage share of each slice, rounded to one decimal place.
    - startangle=140: rotates the chart for better layout.
    - colors=['lightblue', 'orange', 'lightgreen', 'red', 'purple']: uses custom colours for each slice.
    - explode=[0, 0, 0.1, 0, 0]: slightly separates the Salaries slice to highlight it.
- plt.title() adds a title.
- plt.show() displays the chart.

8.1.3 *Your Project*

Use the code from Section 8.1.2 to modify the size and style of the charts.

8.1.3.1 Task 1: Modifying the Line Chart

- Use the line chart code from Step 1 in Section 8.1.2.
- Resize the figure to 10 inches wide and 6 inches high.
- Update the plot() function with the following arguments to change the chart style:
    - Marker = 's' # square markers
    - linestyle = '--' # dashed line
    - color = 'green' # change color
- Run the code and compare the result with the original chart. Observe how the changes affect the appearance of the chart.

8.1.3.2 Example Code

```
import matplotlib.pyplot as plt

months = ['Jan', 'Feb', 'Mar', 'Apr', 'May', 'Jun']
revenue = [10000, 12000, 9000, 15000, 13000, 17000]

# Resize the figure to 10 inches wide and 6 inches high
plt.figure(figsize=(10, 6))

"""
Restyle the line chart by updating the plot() function with the
following arguments:
marker='s'          # square markers
```

```
linestyle='--'        # dashed line
color='green'        # change color
"""
plt.plot(months, revenue, marker='s', linestyle='--', color='green',
label='Revenue')

plt.xlabel('Month')
plt.ylabel('Revenue (£)')
plt.title('Monthly Revenue')
plt.grid(True)
plt.legend()
plt.show()
```

8.1.3.3 *Task 2: Modifying the Bar Chart*

- Use the bar chart code from Step 2 in Section 8.1.2.
- Switch to a horizontal layout by replacing plt.bar() with plt.barh().
- Change the bar colour to orange by setting: color='orange'.
- Run the code and compare the result with the original bar chart. Observe how the chart layout and orientation have changed.

8.1.3.4 *Example Code*

```
categories = ['Rent', 'Utilities', 'Salaries', 'Marketing',
'Miscellaneous']
expenses = [3000, 1200, 7000, 1500, 800]

plt.figure(figsize=(8, 4))

# Switch to a horizontal layout by replacing plt.bar() with plt.barh()
# Change the bar color to orange by setting: color='orange'
plt.barh(categories, expenses, color='orange')

plt.xlabel('Amount (£)')
plt.ylabel('Expense Category')
plt.title('Monthly Expenses (Horizontal Bar Chart)')

plt.show()
```

8.1.3.5 *Task 3: Modifying the Pie Chart*

- Use the pie chart code from Step 3 in Section 8.1.2.
- Rotate the chart by setting startangle=90 in the plt.pie() function.
- Change the exploded slice to highlight Rent instead of Salaries by setting: explode = [0.1, 0, 0, 0, 0].
- Run the code and compare the result with the original pie chart. Observe how the rotation and exploded slice affect the layout and focus of the chart.

8.1.3.6 Example Code

```
categories = ['Rent', 'Utilities', 'Salaries', 'Marketing',
'Miscellaneous']
expenses = [3000, 1200, 7000, 1500, 800]

plt.figure(figsize=(7, 7))

plt.pie(expenses,
        labels=categories,
        autopct='%1.1f%%',
        startangle=90, # Rotate the chart
        colors=['lightblue', 'orange', 'lightgreen', 'red', 'purple'],
        explode=[0.1, 0, 0, 0, 0]) # 10% gap on the first slice

plt.title('Monthly Expenses Breakdown')

plt.show()
```

Scan the QR code to access the Python code and output (see 8.1.ipynb).

https://github.com/DrMichaelGuo/PFAAFAMMA

8.2 Violin Plot

Matplotlib supports a wide range of chart types. This section introduces the violin plot. The NumPy module is used to generate data for demonstration purposes (see Figure 8.7).

FIGURE 8.7 Violin Plot

8.2.1 Key Concepts

8.2.1.1 NumPy

NumPy is a Python library used in data analysis. It includes functions for generating random numbers and performing mathematical operations. It is standard practice to import the library using the alias np.

```
import numpy as np
```

8.2.1.2 Violin Plot

A violin plot is a two-dimensional graph shaped like a violin. It shows how a numerical dataset is distributed across different groups. It presents the range of values, the frequency of those values, and the concentration or dispersion of the data.

8.2.2 Follow-Along Activity

This activity shows how to create a violin plot using sample data to compare monthly revenue across three departments (see Figure 8.8).

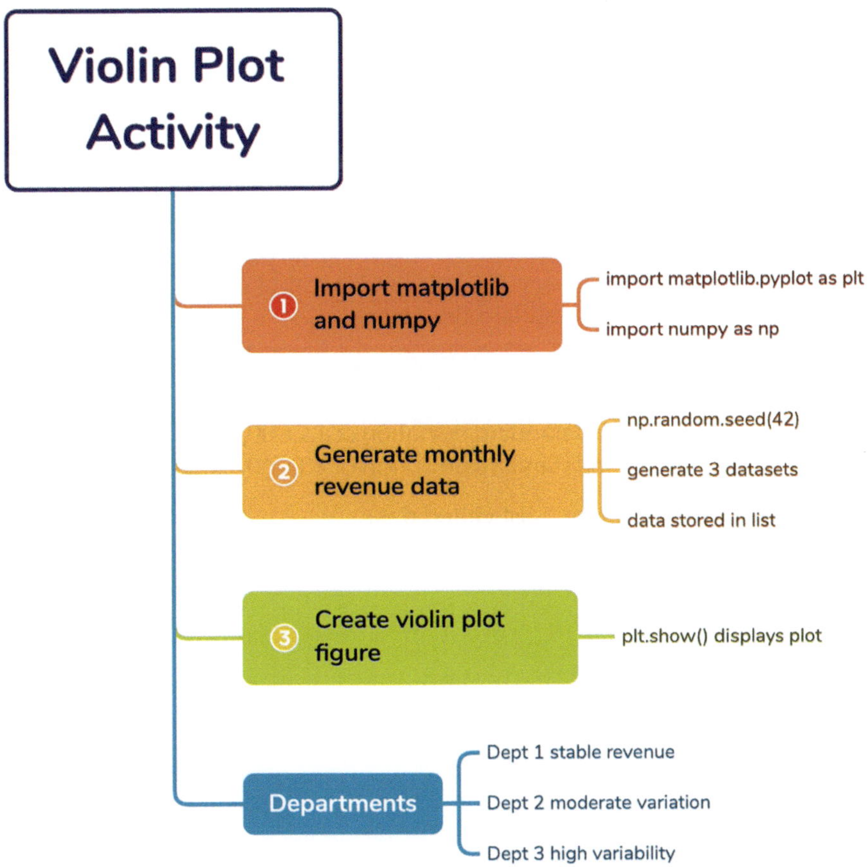

FIGURE 8.8 Violin Plot Activity

Step 1: Import Libraries

Let's import the Matplotlib and NumPy libraries.

```
import matplotlib.pyplot as plt
import numpy as np
```

Explanation

- matplotlib.pyplot (as plt) is used to create the violin plot.
- numpy (as np) is used to generate random numerical data.

Step 2: Generate Sample Data

Let's simulate monthly revenue (in thousands) for three departments using normal distributions.

```
np.random.seed(42)
data1 = np.random.normal(50, 10, 100)
data2 = np.random.normal(60, 15, 100)
data3 = np.random.normal(55, 20, 100)
data = [data1, data2, data3]
```

Explanation

- np.random.seed(42): sets the starting point for random number generation to ensure the same output each time the code runs. The number 42 is an arbitrary choice; any integer can be used. This makes the results reproducible, which is important for teaching and demonstration purposes.
- np.random.normal(mean, std_dev, n): generates n samples from a normal distribution with the specified mean and standard deviations.
    - data1: mean of monthly revenue of 50,000 and standard deviation of 10,000, simulated over 100 months.
    - data2: mean of 60,000 and standard deviation of 15,000, simulated over 100 months.
    - data3: mean of 55,000 and standard deviation of 20,000, simulated over 100 months.
- All three datasets are stored in a list called data.

Step 3: Create a Violin Plot

```
fig, ax = plt.subplots(figsize=(8, 6))
ax.violinplot(data, showmeans=True)
ax.set_title("Violin Plot of Monthly Revenue for 3 Departments")
ax.set_xlabel("Department")
ax.set_ylabel("Monthly Revenue (£'000s)")
ax.set_xticks([1, 2, 3])
ax.set_xticklabels(["Dept 1", "Dept 2", "Dept 3"])
plt.show()
```

Explanation

- fig, ax = plt.subplots(figsize=(8, 6)): creates a chart area 8 inches wide and 6 inches high.
- ax.violinplot(data, showmeans=True): creates the violin plots and includes a line showing the mean.
- set_title, set_xlabel, and set_ylabel: label the chart and axes.
- set_xticks and set_xticklabels: label the x-axis with the department names.
- plt.show(): displays the violin plot.

Output: see Figure 8.9.

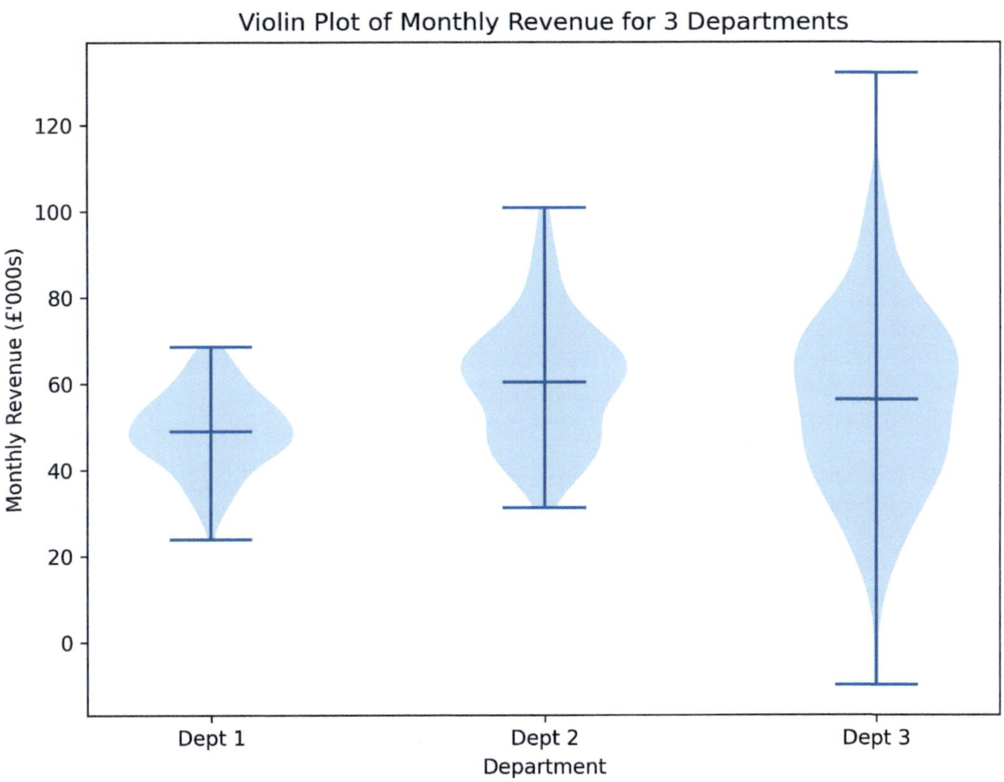

FIGURE 8.9 Violin Plot of Monthly Revenue

The plot shows how revenue is distributed for three departments.

- Dept 1: The narrow shape suggests values are clustered near the mean (lower variability).
- Dept 2: The wider shape indicates a greater variation across observations.
- Dept 3: The most spread-out shape shows a broad range of revenue values.

8.2.3 *Your Project*

Use the code from Section 8.2.2 to complete the tasks below. Modify the original code to extend the violin plot.

8.2.3.1 Tasks

- Add two more departments. Generate revenue data for two additional departments using the following code:

```
data4 = np.random.normal(45, 5, 100)
data5 = np.random.normal(65, 10, 100)
```

- Set the figure size to 10 inches wide by 6 inches high.
- Update the chart title and x-axis labels to reflect all five departments.

8.2.3.2 Example Code

```
import matplotlib.pyplot as plt
import numpy as np

# Task 1: Generate sample data for 5 departments (e.g., monthly
revenue in thousands)
np.random.seed(42)
data1 = np.random.normal(50, 10, 100)
data2 = np.random.normal(60, 15, 100)
data3 = np.random.normal(55, 20, 100)

# Task 1 continued: Add two more departments
data4 = np.random.normal(45, 5, 100)
data5 = np.random.normal(65, 10, 100)

# Combine all department data into a list
data = [data1, data2, data3, data4, data5]

# Create the violin plot and change the plot size
fig, ax = plt.subplots(figsize=(10, 6))
ax.violinplot(data, showmeans=True)

# Task 2: Update title
ax.set_title("Violin Plot of Monthly Revenue by 5 Departments")
ax.set_xlabel("Department")
ax.set_ylabel("Monthly Revenue (£'000s)")

# Update x-axis labels for 5 departments
ax.set_xticks([1, 2, 3, 4, 5])
ax.set_xticklabels(["Dept 1", "Dept 2", "Dept 3", "Dept 4", "Dept 5"])

plt.show()
```

Scan the QR code to access the Python code and output (see 8.2.ipynb).

https://github.com/DrMichaelGuo/PFAAFAMMA

8.3 Surface Plot

This section introduces surface plots, which are used to display 3D data. The example uses synthetic data to demonstrate how to create a 3D surface plot in Python (see Figure 8.10).

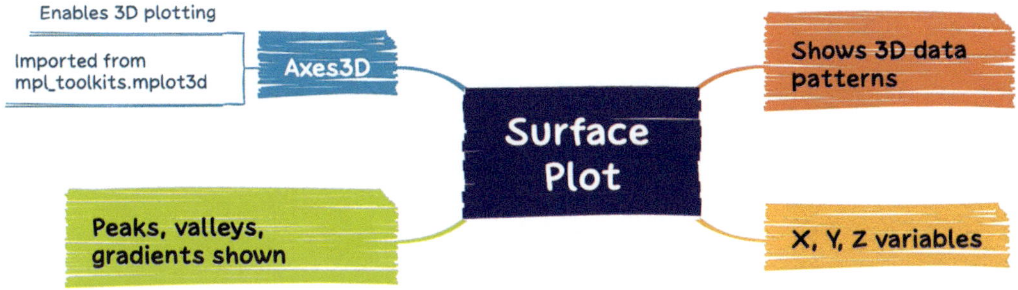

FIGURE 8.10 Surface Plot

8.3.1 Key Concepts

8.3.1.1 Surface Plot

A surface plot is a 3D chart that shows a surface defined by three variables:

- X-axis: first explanatory variable.
- Y-axis: second explanatory variable.
- Z-axis: response variable.

This chart shows how two input variables relate to a third variable. The resulting surface reveals patterns such as peaks, valleys, or gradients.

8.3.1.2 Axes3D

To create 3D plots in Matplotlib, it is necessary to use a module called Axes3D that supports three-dimensional visualisation. The module enables 3D plotting functionality in

Matplotlib. Without this, 3D plots will not display correctly. Axes3D is imported using the code:

```
from mpl_toolkits.mplot3d import Axes3D
```

8.3.2 Follow-Along Activity

This activity shows how to create a 3D surface plot using synthetic data to represent the relationship among pricing, sales volume, and profit (see Figure 8.11).

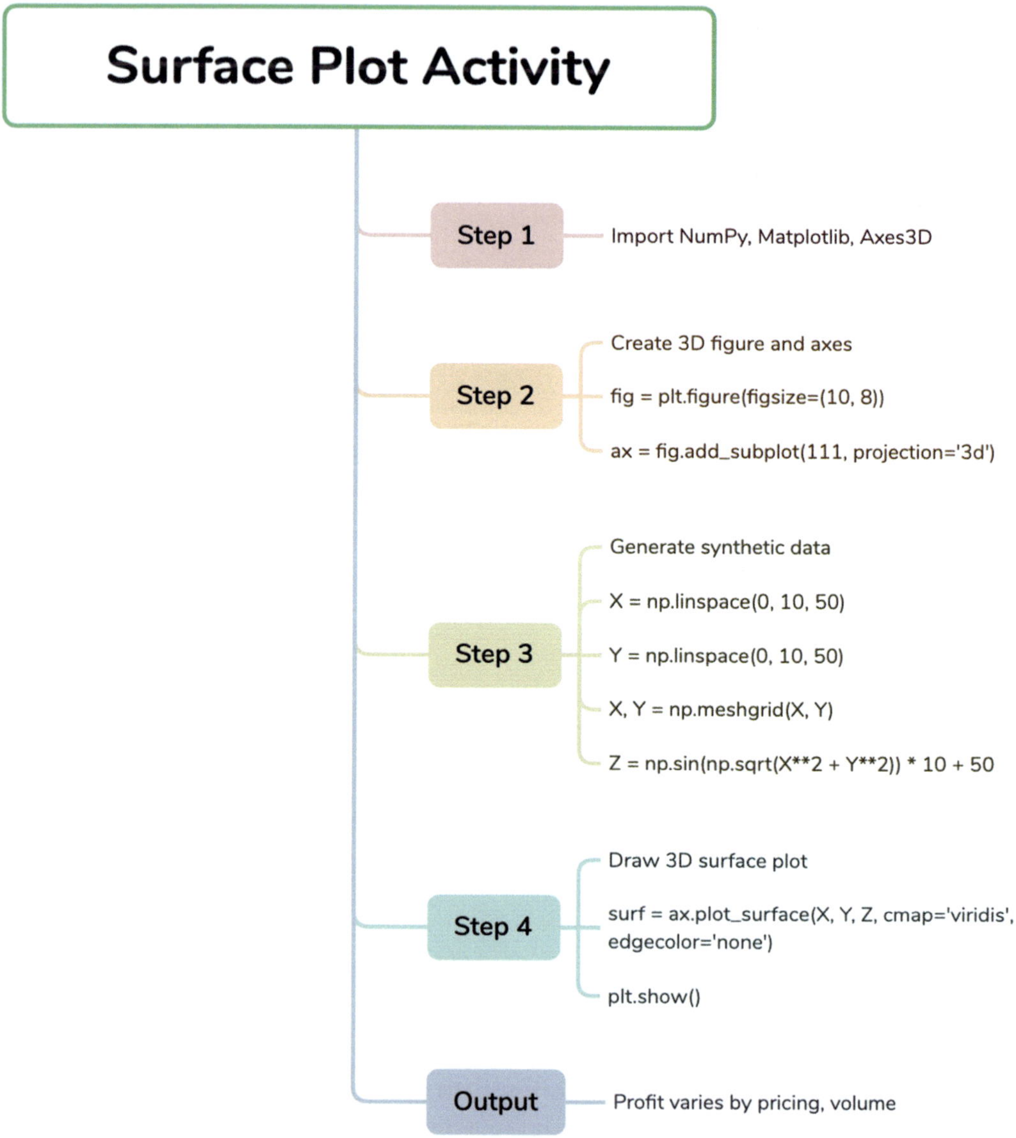

FIGURE 8.11 Surface Plot Activity

Note: When running this example, all four steps must be executed together in a single code cell. If the code is split into separate cells (e.g. Step 1 to Step 4 run individually), the 3D plot may not display because Matplotlib does not retain the figure between steps. Always run the complete code block from start to finish to generate the correct output.

Step 1: Import Libraries

Let's import the required libraries.

```
import numpy as np
import matplotlib.pyplot as plt
from mpl_toolkits.mplot3d import Axes3D
```

Explanation

- NumPy is imported as np for data generation.
- Matplotlib is imported as plt for plotting the surface plot.
- Axes3D is imported to enable 3D plotting functionality.

Step 2: Set Up the 3D Canvas

Let's set up the 3D Canvas (i.e. the plot area).

```
fig = plt.figure(figsize=(10, 8))
ax = fig.add_subplot(111, projection='3d')
```

Explanation

- fig = plt.figure(figsize=(10, 8)): sets the figure size to 10 inches wide by 8 inches high.
- add_subplot(111, projection='3d'): adds a 3D plot to the figure.
    - The value 111 is a code that defines a 1×1 grid layout and selects the first subplot.
    - Projection='3d': instructs Matplotlib to create a 3D plot.

Step 3: Generate Synthetic Data

Let's generate a dataset representing pricing, sales volume, and profit:

```
X = np.linspace(0, 10, 50)
Y = np.linspace(0, 10, 50)
X, Y = np.meshgrid(X, Y)
Z = np.sin(np.sqrt(X**2 + Y**2)) * 10 + 50
```

Explanation

- X = np.linspace(0, 10, 50): creates 50 values between 0 and 10 to represent pricing.
- Y = np.linspace(0, 10, 50): creates 50 values between 0 and 10 to represent sales volume.

- X, Y = np.meshgrid(X, Y): forms two 2D grids that cover all combinations of pricing and sales volume.
- Z = np.sin(np.sqrt(X**2 + Y**2)) * 10 + 50: uses a sample formula to calculate profit for each combination of pricing and sales volume. The result is stored in Z, which is used to draw the surface plot.

Step 4: Plot the Surface Plot

Let's use the generated data to draw the 3D surface plot.

```
surf = ax.plot_surface(X, Y, Z, cmap='viridis', edgecolor='none')
ax.set_title("Surface Plot: Profit Surface")
ax.set_xlabel("Pricing")
ax.set_ylabel("Sales Volume")
ax.set_zlabel("Profit")
fig.colorbar(surf, shrink=0.5, aspect=5)
plt.show()
```

Explanation

- surf = ax.plot_surface(X, Y, Z, cmap='viridis', edgecolor='none'): draws the surface using the values in X, Y, and Z.
    - cmap='viridis': adds colour to show different profit levels.
    - edgecolor='none': removes lines between the surface cells for a smoother appearance.
- ax.set_title("Surface Plot: Profit Surface"): sets the title.
- ax.set_xlabel("Pricing"): labels the x-axis as "Pricing".
- ax.set_ylabel("Sales Volume"): labels the y-axis as "Sales Volume".
- ax.set_zlabel("Profit"): labels the z-axis as "Profit".
- fig.colorbar(surf, shrink=0.5, aspect=5): adds a colour bar next to the plot to show how colours relate to profit values.
    - shrink=0.5: makes the colour bar smaller.
    - aspect=5 adjusts the shape of the colour bar.
- plt.show(): displays the plot.

Output: see Figure 8.12.

The 3D plot shows how profit changes with different combinations of price and sales volume.

- Increasing price or sales volume does not always increase profit.
- A low price with high sales volume may still produce low profit.
- A high price with low sales volume may result in fewer units sold and lower profit.
- Peaks on the surface show combinations of price and volume that produce higher profit.

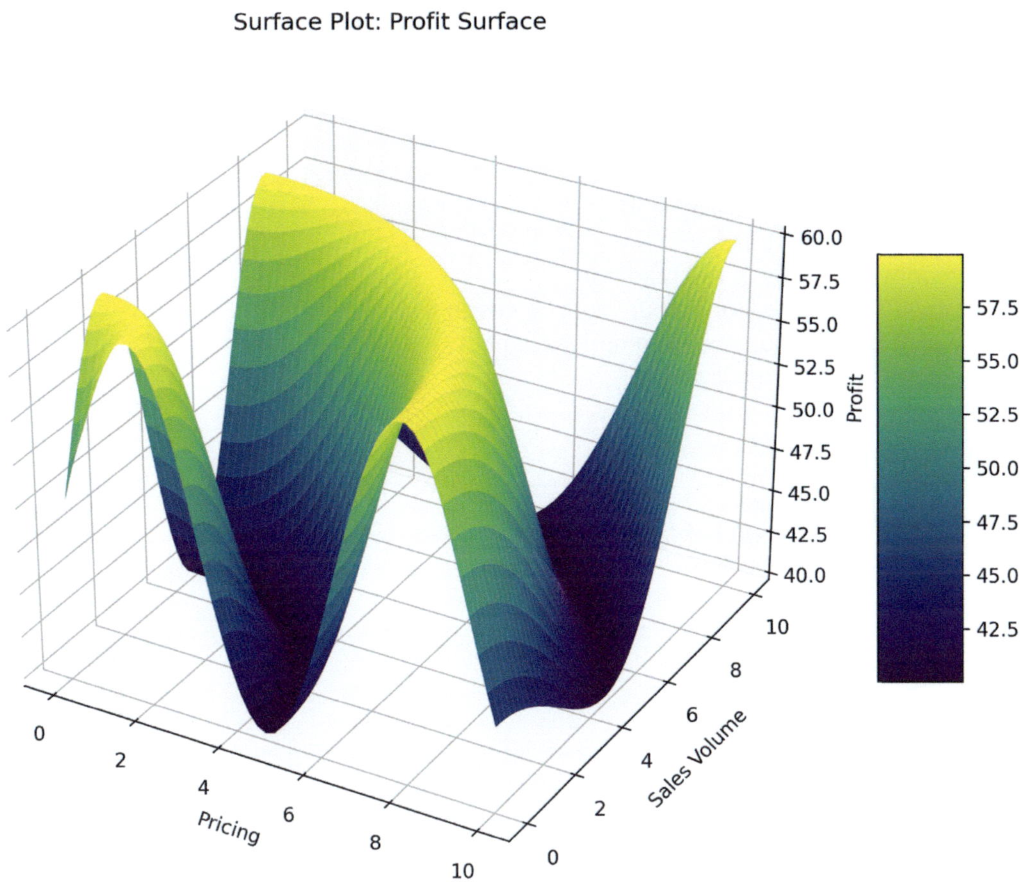

FIGURE 8.12 Surface Plot

8.3.3 Your Project

Use the code from Section 8.3.2 and modify it to complete the tasks below.

8.3.3.1 Tasks

- Update the X and Y ranges. Change the range of the X and Y variables to

```
X = np.linspace(-5, 5, 50)
Y = np.linspace(-5, 5, 50)
```

- Modify the surface plot to use a different colour map.

  Replace

```
surf = ax.plot_surface(X, Y, Z, cmap='viridis', edgecolor='none')
```

with

```
surf = ax.plot_surface(X, Y, Z, cmap='plasma', edgecolor='none')
```

- Explore alternative colour maps.
  - 'viridis': default in Matplotlib.
  - 'plasma': warm tones.
  - 'coolwarm': blue to red gradient.
  - 'cividis': designed for colour vision accessibility.
  - 'inferno': high contrast from dark to light.
  - 'terrain': earth-tone gradient.

8.3.3.2 Example Code

```
import numpy as np
import matplotlib.pyplot as plt
from mpl_toolkits.mplot3d import Axes3D

fig = plt.figure(figsize=(10, 8))
ax = fig.add_subplot(111, projection='3d')

X = np.linspace(-5, 5, 50)
Y = np.linspace(-5, 5, 50)
X, Y = np.meshgrid(X, Y)
Z = np.sin(np.sqrt(X**2 + Y**2)) * 10 + 50

# Plot the surface
surf = ax.plot_surface(X, Y, Z, cmap='plasma', edgecolor='none')
ax.set_title("Surface Plot: Profit Surface")
ax.set_xlabel("Pricing")
ax.set_ylabel("Sales Volume")
ax.set_zlabel("Profit")
fig.colorbar(surf, shrink=0.5, aspect=5)
plt.show()
```

Scan the QR code to access the Python code and output (see 8.3.ipynb).

https://github.com/DrMichaelGuo/PFAAFAMMA

8.4 Matplotlib and Seaborn

Matplotlib and Seaborn are two key plotting libraries in Python. This section provides an overview of both libraries and includes a guided activity to explore their features (see Figure 8.13).

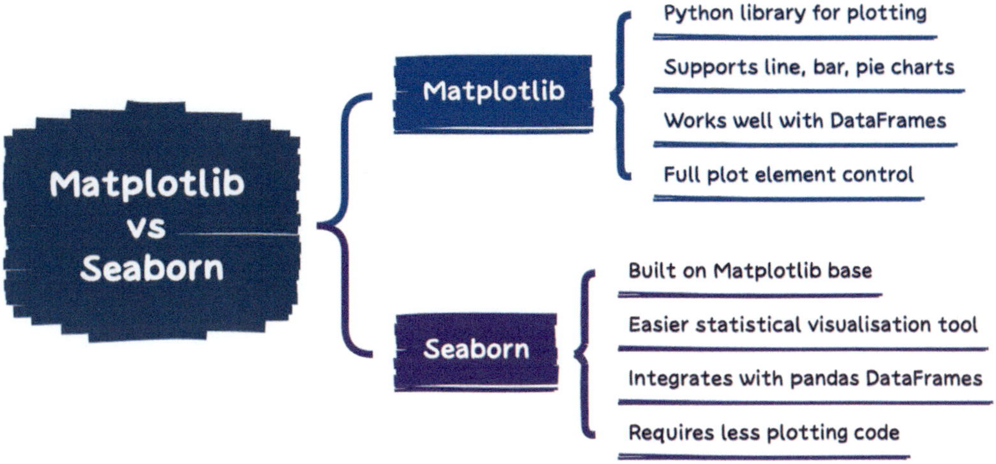

FIGURE 8.13 Matplotlib vs Seaborn

8.4.1 Key Concepts

8.4.1.1 Matplotlib

Matplotlib is a Python library for creating plots. Its module, matplotlib.pyplot, enables users to construct basic charts such as line, bar, and pie charts. Matplotlib integrates with pandas DataFrames and provides detailed control over plot elements.

Documentation and examples are available at:
https://matplotlib.org

8.4.1.2 Seaborn

Seaborn is another data visualisation library built on top of Matplotlib. It is designed to work with pandas DataFrames and simplifies the process of generating statistical graphics. Seaborn requires less code to produce structured plots.

Documentation and tutorials are available at:
https://seaborn.pydata.org

8.4.2 Guided Tour of Matplotlib

Step 1: Open the Gallery

- Visit the Matplotlib website: https://matplotlib.org
- Click Plot Types in the header to view the plot gallery.

Step 2: Scan the Plots

- Scroll through the thumbnails to view different plot types.
- Consider how each plot could be used in accounting and finance.

Step 3: Select a Plot

- Click on a plot that interests you.
- You will see a sample image and the Python code used to generate it.

Step 4: Copy and Run the Code

- Copy and paste the example code into your Google Colab notebook.
- Run the code.

Step 5: Modify the Plot

- Edit the data values to observe changes in the output.

8.4.3 Guided Tour of Seaborn

Step 1: Open the Gallery

- Visit the Seaborn website: https://seaborn.pydata.org
- Click Gallery in the header to view the plot gallery.

Step 2: Scan the Plots

- Scroll through the thumbnails to view different plot types.
- Consider how each plot could apply to accounting or finance.

Step 3: Select a Plot

- Click on a plot that interests you.
- You will see a sample image and the Python code used to create it.

Step 4: Copy and Run the Code

- Copy and paste the code into your Google Colab notebook.
- Run the code.

Step 5: Modify the Plot

- Adjust the data values to see how the plot changes.

Summary of Chapter 8: Data Visualisation Techniques

In this chapter, we have covered the following concepts:

Basic Charts

- Line Chart: shows trends over time using plt.plot().
- Bar Chart: compares values across categories using plt.bar() or plt.barh().
- Pie Chart: displays proportions of a whole using plt.pie().
- Formatting tools include plt.figure(), plt.xlabel(), plt.ylabel(), plt.title(), plt.legend(), and plt.grid().

Violin Plot

- Shows distribution across groups using ax.violinplot().
- Adds mean lines and axis labels.

3D Surface Plot

- Displays relationships among three variables using ax.plot_surface().
- Uses Axes3D from mpl_toolkits.mplot3d.

Matplotlib vs Seaborn

- Matplotlib: provides control over chart elements.
- Seaborn: supports statistical plotting with DataFrames.

Quiz Questions

Scan the QR code below to access the quiz questions for this chapter (see 8.md).

https://github.com/DrMichaelGuo/QuizPFAAFAMMA

Further Reading and Resources

Hunter, J., Dale, D., Firing, E., Droettboom, M., and the Matplotlib Development Team (2025) *User guide – Matplotlib documentation*. https://matplotlib.org/stable/users/index.html (Accessed 28 July 2025).

Waskom, M. (2025). *Seaborn: Statistical data visualization*. https://seaborn.pydata.org/ (Accessed 28 July 2025).

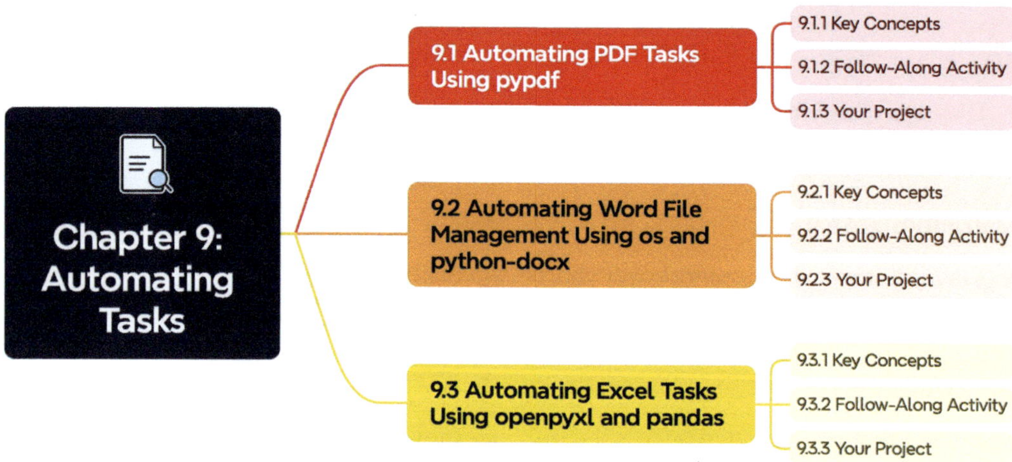

FIGURE 9.1 Structure of Chapter 9

9

AUTOMATING TASKS

This chapter introduces automation techniques using Python to manage repetitive tasks in accounting and finance. It covers how to process PDF invoices, handle Word documents, and analyse Excel spreadsheets using libraries such as pypdf, python-docx, pandas, and openpyxl. Through guided activities and project-based exercises, you will develop skills to automate workflows, increase output, and reduce manual errors in financial tasks (Figure 9.1).

Learning Objectives

By the end of this chapter, you will be able to

- Use pypdf to read, rotate, merge, and split PDF files.
- Generate, rename, and edit Word documents using the os module and python-docx.
- Read, summarise, and update Excel files using pandas and openpyxl to support financial reporting and data analysis.

9.1 Automating PDF Tasks Using pypdf

This section explains how to manipulate PDF documents in Python using the pypdf library. It covers reading, merging, splitting, and rotating PDF files. These functions support the automation of document handling in accounting and finance, especially when managing a large volume of PDF files (see Figure 9.2).

9.1.1 Key Concepts

9.1.1.1 PDF Automation

The portable document format (PDF) is widely used for invoices, financial statements, contracts, and reports. Automating tasks involving PDF files reduces manual processing and improves consistency and speed.

DOI: 10.4324/9781003656968-9

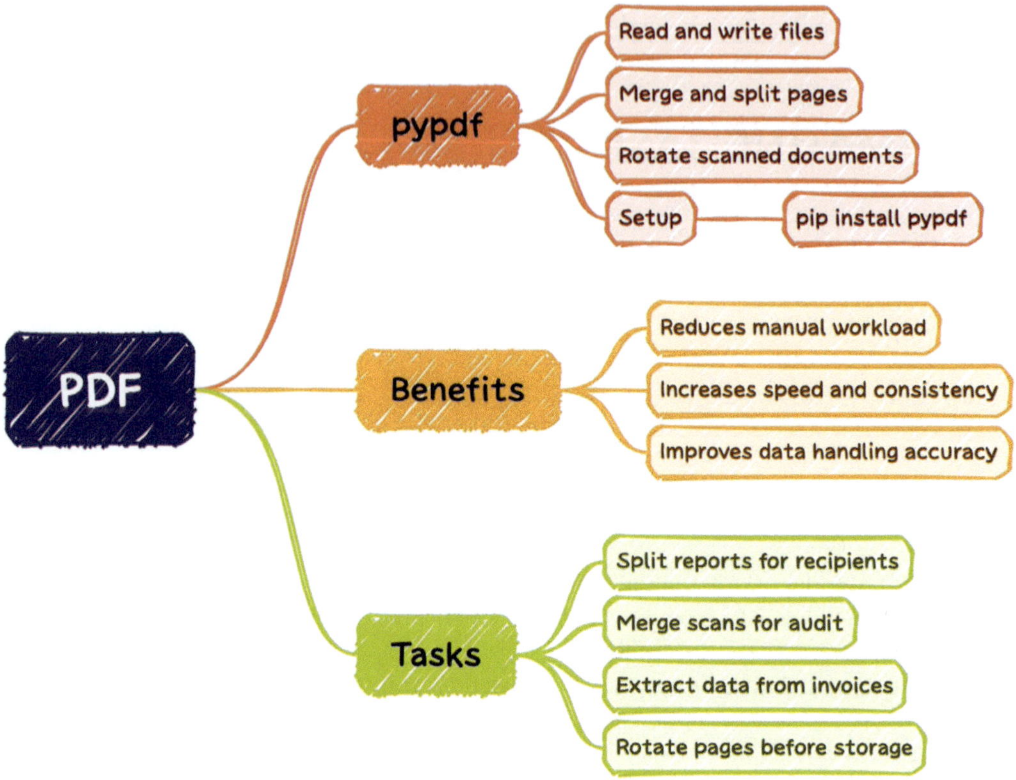

FIGURE 9.2 PDF

9.1.1.2 pypdf

pypdf is a Python library for handling PDF files. It supports reading, writing, merging, splitting, and rotating pages. It is not pre-installed in Google Colab and must be installed using the following command:

```
!pip install pypdf
```

9.1.1.3 Applications in Accounting and Finance

Examples of PDF manipulation tasks include:

- Splitting reports or invoices for distribution to different recipients.
- Merging scanned documents for audit submissions.
- Extracting invoice content for data processing.
- Adjusting page orientation of scanned documents before storage.

9.1.2 Follow-Along Activity

This activity shows a series of tasks to read, rotate, split, and merge PDF files using the pypdf library in Python (see Figure 9.3).

The activity uses an example PDF file named 9_example.pdf, available at the following site:

https://github.com/DrMichaelGuo/PFAAFAMMA

The file 9_example.pdf contains three pages. Each page displays an invoice with an invoice number, total amount, customer name, and invoice date. Page 3 is rotated upside down (180 degrees); this will be corrected by applying a 180-degree rotation in this activity.

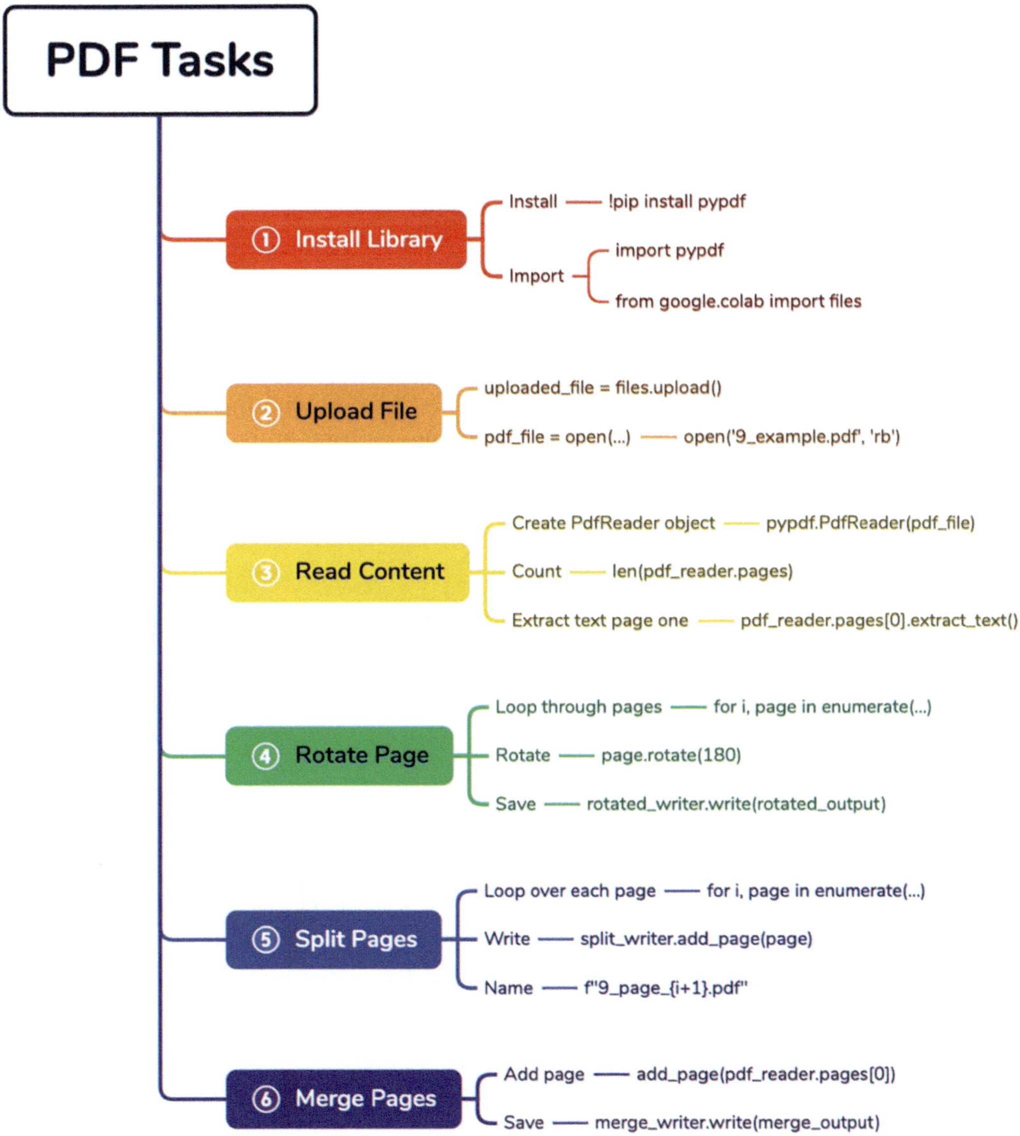

FIGURE 9.3 PDF Tasks

Step 1: Install and Import Libraries

As pypdf is not included in Google Colab by default, let's install the library using the following code. Then import the required libraries for PDF processing and file upload.

```
# Install the pypdf library
!pip install pypdf

# Import the required libraries
import pypdf
from google.colab import files
```

Output:

```
Collecting pypdf
  Downloading pypdf-6.1.3-py3-none-any.whl.metadata (7.1 kB)
Downloading pypdf-6.1.3-py3-none-any.whl (323 kB)
   ────────────────────────────────────────
323.9/323.9 kB 6.9 MB/s eta 0:00:00
Installing collected packages: pypdf
Successfully installed pypdf-6.1.3
```

Explanation

- !pip install pypdf: installs the pypdf library in the Colab environment.
- import pypdf: imports functions to read, write, merge, split, and rotate PDF files.
- from google.colab import files: imports tools to upload PDF files from a local machine.

Step 2: Upload and Open the PDF File

Let's upload the file and open it in the binary read mode.

```
# Upload the pdf file
uploaded_file = files.upload()

# Open the uploaded PDF file in binary read mode
pdf_file = open('9_example.pdf', 'rb')
```

Explanation

- files.upload(): allows selection and upload of the PDF file 9_example.pdf to the Colab environment.
- open('9_example.pdf', 'rb'): opens the uploaded file in the binary mode for pypdf to read it.
  - 'r' stands for read and 'b' stands for binary.
  - PDF files must be read in a binary format to avoid processing errors.

Step 3: Read and Extract PDF Content

Let's read the PDF file, count the number of pages, and extract text from the first page.

```
# Create a PdfReader object to read the PDF
pdf_reader = pypdf.PdfReader(pdf_file)

# Print the total number of pages in the PDF
print("Number of pages:", len(pdf_reader.pages))

# Extract and print text from the first page
print(pdf_reader.pages[0].extract_text())
```

Output

```
Number of pages: 3
Example PDF - Page 1
Invoice Number: 1001
Total Amount: $150.00
Customer: ABC Ltd.
Date: 2025-02-16
Thank you for your business!
```

Explanation

- pdf_reader = pypdf.PdfReader(pdf_file): creates an object for accessing PDF content.
- print("Number of pages:", len(pdf_reader.pages)): prints the total number of pages in the PDF.
    - len(pdf_reader.pages): counts the number of pages.
- print(pdf_reader.pages[0].extract_text()): extracts and prints text from the first page.
    - pdf_reader.pages[0]: accesses the first page of the PDF (indexing starts at 0).
    - .extract_text(): extracts all text from that page.
    - print(...): displays the extracted text.

Try it yourself: replace 0 with 1 to display the second page of the PDF.

Note: The .extract_text() method retrieves text only from digital PDFs that contain selectable text. Scanned or image-based PDFs require optical character recognition tools such as Tesseract to extract text.

Step 4: Rotate Page 3 and Save to a New File

Let's rotate the third page by 180 degrees, save the updated PDF as a new file, and download the file.

```
# Rotate page 3 and save to a new file
rotated_writer = pypdf.PdfWriter()

for i, page in enumerate(pdf_reader.pages):
    if i == 2:
        rotated_page = page.rotate(180)
        rotated_writer.add_page(rotated_page)
    else:
        rotated_writer.add_page(page)

# Save to a new file
rotated_path = "9_rotated.pdf"
rotated_output = open(rotated_path, "wb")
rotated_writer.write(rotated_output)
rotated_output.close()

# Download the file to local machine
files.download(rotated_path)
```

Explanation

- rotated_writer = pypdf.PdfWriter(): creates a new object to store the modified pages.
- The for loop: loops through each page in the original PDF.
    - i: is the page index (starting at 0).
    - page: is the actual page content.
    - enumerate(pdf_reader.pages): returns both the index and the page content during iteration.
    - if i == 2: identifies the third page (index 2).
    - page.rotate(180): rotates the page by 180 degrees.
    - rotated_writer.add_page(...): adds each page (rotated or not) to the object.
- rotated_path = "9_rotated.pdf": defines the path for the new file.
- open(rotated_path, "wb"): opens the file in write-binary mode.
    - "w" creates a new file or overwrites an existing one. "b" sets the binary mode, allowing Python to write the file as binary data.
- write() and close(): write the new file and close it.
- files.download(rotated_path): downloads the new file to the local machine.

Open the downloaded file to confirm that page 3 has been rotated.

Step 5: Split the PDF into Three Separate Files (One Page per File)

Let's split each page of the original PDF into a separate PDF file. Each file is then downloaded.

```
# Split each page into a separate file and download
for i, page in enumerate(pdf_reader.pages):
    split_writer = pypdf.PdfWriter()
    split_writer.add_page(page)

    split_filename = f"9_page_{i+1}.pdf"
    split_output = open(split_filename, "wb")
    split_writer.write(split_output)
    split_output.close()

    # Download each split file
    files.download(split_filename)
```

Explanation

- The for loop: loops through all pages in the original PDF.
    - enumerate(...): returns the page index and content.
    - split_writer = pypdf.PdfWriter(): creates a new object for each page.
    - split_writer.add_page(page): adds the current page to the object.
    - split_filename = f"9_page_{i+1}.pdf": sets the file name for the single-page PDF using an f-string. The page number starts from 1.
    - split_output = open(split_filename, "wb"): opens a new file in write-binary mode.
    - split_writer.write(split_output): writes the single page into the file.
    - split_output.close(): closes the file.
    - files.download(split_filename): downloads each page as a separate PDF.

Open each downloaded file to check that it contains one page only.

Step 6: Merge Page 1 and Page 3 into a New PDF

Let's merge the first and third pages into a new PDF file and download it.

```
# Merge page 1 and page 3 into a new PDF
merge_writer = pypdf.PdfWriter()
merge_writer.add_page(pdf_reader.pages[0])  # Page 1
merge_writer.add_page(pdf_reader.pages[2])  # Page 3

merge_path = "9_merge_1_3.pdf"
merge_output = open(merge_path, "wb")
merge_writer.write(merge_output)
merge_output.close()

# Download the merged file
files.download(merge_path)
```

Explanation

- merge_writer = pypdf.PdfWriter(): creates a new PdfWriter object to hold selected pages.
- merge_writer.add_page(pdf_reader.pages[0]): adds page 1 (index 0) to the new PDF.
- merge_writer.add_page(pdf_reader.pages[2]): adds page 3 (index 2) to the new PDF.
- merge_path = "9_merge_1_3.pdf": sets the name of the new file.
- merge_output = open(merge_path, "wb"): opens the file in write-binary mode.
- merge_writer.write(merge_output): writes the selected pages to the file.
- merge_output.close(): closes the file.
- files.download(merge_path): downloads the merged PDF.

Open the downloaded file to confirm it contains only page 1 and page 3.

9.1.3 *Your Project*

This project uses a PDF file named 9_project.pdf. The file is available at:
https://github.com/DrMichaelGuo/PFAAFAMMA

The file contains 10 pages. Each page presents an invoice with the invoice number, total amount, customer name, and invoice date. Page 10 is rotated upside down.

9.1.3.1 Tasks

- Install and import the required libraries.
- Upload and open the PDF file.
- Read and extract PDF content and display page 1.
- Rotate page 10 by 180 degrees, save the result as a new file, and download it.
- Split the PDF into 10 separate files (one page per file) and download the files.
- Merge page 1 and page 10 into a new PDF and download the file.

Tip: Place each step in a separate code cell when running the project.

9.1.3.2 Example Code

```
# Install the pypdf library
!pip install pypdf
# Import the required libraries
import pypdf
from google.colab import files
```

```
# Upload the PDF file
uploaded_file = files.upload()
# Open the uploaded file in binary read mode
pdf_file = open('9_project.pdf', 'rb')
```

```
# Create a PdfReader object to read the PDF
pdf_reader = pypdf.PdfReader(pdf_file)
```

```
# Print the total number of pages in the PDF
print("Number of pages:", len(pdf_reader.pages))

# Extract and print text from the first page
print(pdf_reader.pages[0].extract_text())
```

```
# Rotate page 10 and save to a new file
rotated_writer = pypdf.PdfWriter()

for i, page in enumerate(pdf_reader.pages):
    if i == 9:
        rotated_page = page.rotate(180)
        rotated_writer.add_page(rotated_page)
    else:
        rotated_writer.add_page(page)

# Save to a new file
rotated_path = "9_rotated.pdf"
rotated_output = open(rotated_path, "wb")
rotated_writer.write(rotated_output)
rotated_output.close()

# Download the file to local machine
files.download(rotated_path)
```

```
# Split each page into a separate file and download
for i, page in enumerate(pdf_reader.pages):
    split_writer = pypdf.PdfWriter()
    split_writer.add_page(page)

    split_filename = f"9_page_{i+1}.pdf"
    split_output = open(split_filename, "wb")
    split_writer.write(split_output)
    split_output.close()

    # Download each split file
    files.download(split_filename)
```

```
# Merge page 1 and page 10 into a new PDF
merge_writer = pypdf.PdfWriter()
merge_writer.add_page(pdf_reader.pages[0])  # Page 1
merge_writer.add_page(pdf_reader.pages[9])  # Page 10

merge_path = "9_merge_1_10.pdf"
merge_output = open(merge_path, "wb")
merge_writer.write(merge_output)
merge_output.close()

# Download the merged file
files.download(merge_path)
```

Scan the QR code to access the code and output (see 9.1.ipynb).

https://github.com/DrMichaelGuo/PFAAFAMMA

9.2 Automating Word File Management Using os and python-docx

This section explores how to use Python to create, rename, and update Word files using the os module and the python-docx library. These tasks are relevant to accounting and finance when managing batches of reports, letters, minutes, summaries, schedules, or documents (see Figure 9.4).

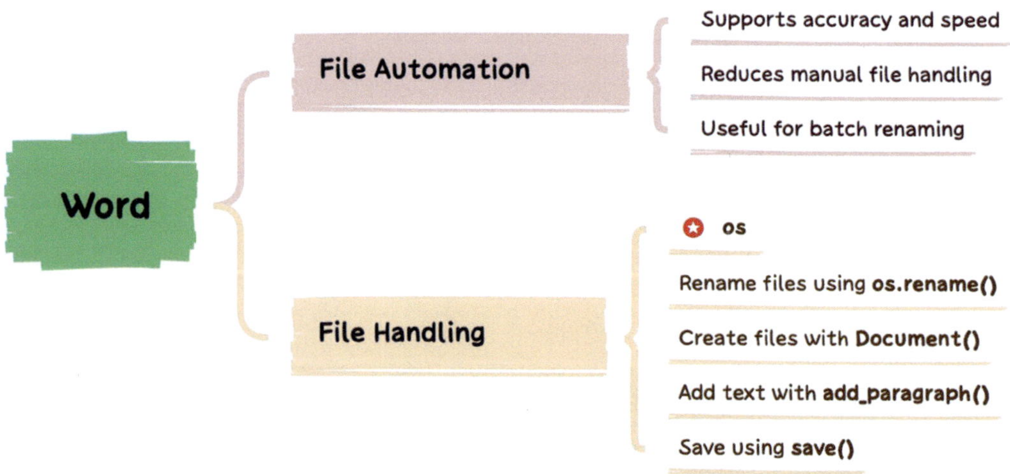

FIGURE 9.4 Word

9.2.1 Key Concepts

9.2.1.1 File Automation

Automating file management supports accuracy, reduces processing time, and limits manual handling. Python can generate files, rename them, and update their content in Word (.docx) format.

9.2.1.2 File Handling Using os

The os module provides functions to interact with the file system. For example, os.rename() changes file names and supports batch processing.

9.2.1.3 *Working with Word Documents Using python-docx*

The python-docx library supports the creation and editing of Word documents. Common functions include:

- Document(): creates a new Word document.
- add_paragraph(): writes text into the document.
- save(): saves the document to a .docx file.

9.2.2 *Follow-Along Activity*

This activity shows how to create, rename, and update Word files using Python (see Figure 9.5).

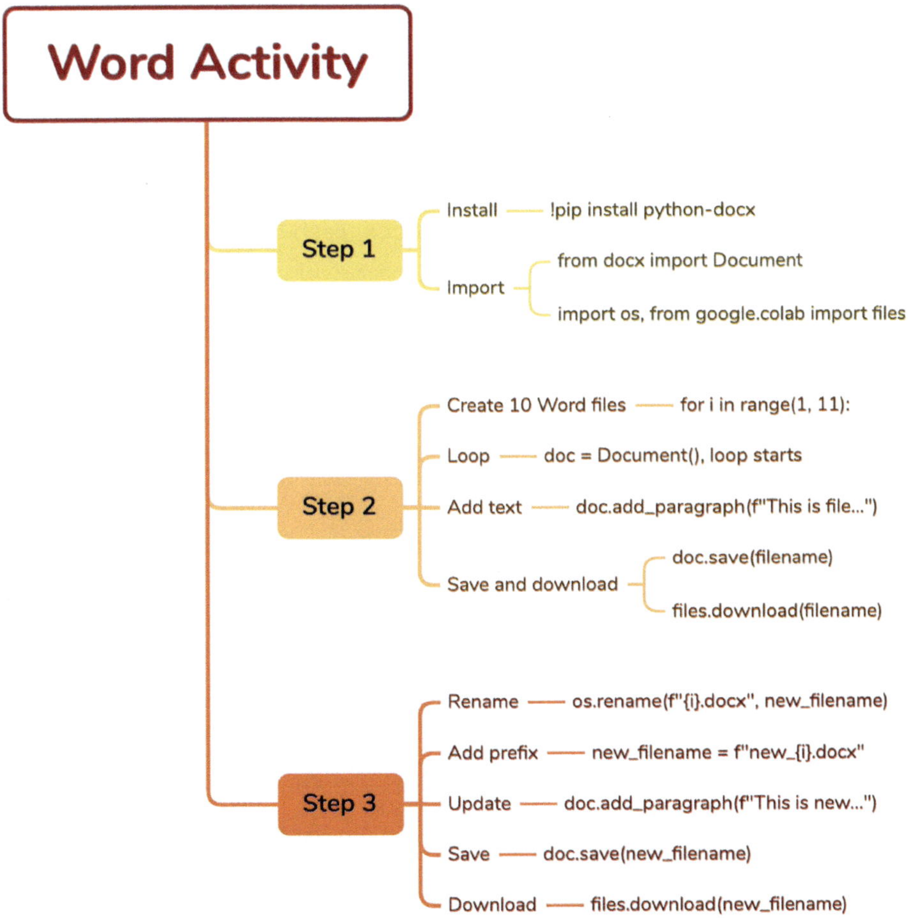

FIGURE 9.5 Word Activity

Step 1: Install and Import Libraries

Let's begin by installing the python-docx library and importing the required tools.

```
!pip install python-docx

from docx import Document
import os
from google.colab import files
```

Explanation

- !pip install python-docx: installs the python-docx library for use in Google Colab.
- from docx import Document: imports in the Document tool to create or edit Word files.
  - The library is called docx, even though it is installed using python-docx.
- import os: imports the os module for file operations. This module is built in Python and does not require installation.
- from google.colab import files: imports the files tool to enable file downloads from Colab to the local machine.

Step 2: Generate 10 Word Files

Let's create 10 Word files named 1.docx to 10.docx. Each file contains a paragraph with the text 'This is file number i'.

```
for i in range(1, 11):
    doc = Document()
    doc.add_paragraph(f"This is file number {i}")
    filename = f"{i}.docx"
    doc.save(filename)
    files.download(filename)

print("10 .docx files generated and downloaded.")
```

Output

```
10 .docx files generated and downloaded.
```

Explanation

- for i in range(1, 11): starts a loop that runs from 1 to 10.
  - Use a colon at the end of the line and indent the block inside the loop.
  - range(1, 11): stops before 11.
- doc = Document(): initialises a new Word document.
- doc.add_paragraph(f"This is file number {i}"): adds a paragraph with the text 'This is file number ' to the document.

- filename = f"{i}.docx": sets the filename by converting the loop index i into a string and appending .docx.
- doc.save(filename): saves the document to a .docx file using the defined filename.
- files.download(filename): downloads the file to the local machine.
- print("10 .docx files generated and downloaded."): prints a message to confirm completion.

Open the downloaded Word files and check the content. For example, 1.docx should contain the paragraph: This is file number 1.

Extra: When the code runs in Google Colab, it creates the files in a temporary folder within the Colab environment. Use the Files panel on the left-hand side of the interface to view them. Click the folder icon to expand the panel to view the files.

We can also run the following code to view the content of any of the generated files:

```
# Open the document
doc = Document("3.docx")

# Read and print all paragraphs in the document
for para in doc.paragraphs:
    print(para.text)
```

Output

```
This is file number 3
```

Explanation

- doc = Document("3.docx"): opens the Word document named 3.docx and stores it in the variable doc.
- for para in doc.paragraphs: creates a loop that goes through each paragraph in the document.
- print(para.text): prints the text content of the current paragraph.

Step 3: Rename Each File and Update Its Content

Let's rename each file by adding the prefix 'new_' and add content to reflect the new filename. For example 1.docx becomes new_1.docx and the content includes the sentence 'This is new file number 1'.

```
for i in range(1, 11):
    new_filename = f"new_{i}.docx"
    os.rename(f"{i}.docx", new_filename)
    doc = Document(new_filename)
    doc.add_paragraph(f"This is new file number {i}")
    doc.save(new_filename)

    files.download(new_filename)

print("10 files have been renamed, updated, and downloaded.")
```

Explanation

- for i in range(1, 11): creates a loop that runs from 1 to 10.
- new_filename = f"new_{i}.docx": sets the new filename by adding the prefix 'new_' to the current number.
- os.rename(f"{i}.docx", new_filename): renames the original file (e.g. 1.docx) to the new filename (e.g. new_1.docx).
- doc = Document(new_filename): opens the renamed Word file.
- doc.add_paragraph(f "This is new file number {i}"): adds a paragraph to the document with updated text.
- doc.save(new_filename): saves the changes to the renamed file.
- files.download(new_filename): downloads the updated file to the local machine.
- print("10 files have been renamed, updated, and downloaded."): prints a message confirming that the task is complete.

Open the downloaded Word files and check the content. For example, new_1.docx should contain the paragraph: This is new file number 1.

Extra: We can also view the updated files in the Files panel on the left-hand side of the Google Colab interface. Click the folder icon to expand the panel and view the files.

We can also run the following code to view the content of any of the renamed files:

```
doc = Document("new_3.docx")

for para in doc.paragraphs:
    print(para.text)
```

Output

```
This is file number 3
This is new file number 3
```

Explanation

- doc = Document("new_3.docx"): opens the Word document named new_3.docx and stores it in the variable doc.
- for para in doc.paragraphs: creates a loop that processes each paragraph in the document.
- print(para.text): prints the text of the current paragraph.

9.2.3 *Your Project*

Continue the above activity by renaming each file again and updating its content.

9.2.3.1 Tasks

- Rename each file (e.g. new_1.docx to new_1_updated.docx).
- Add the text 'This is the updated new file number X' to each file.
- Print the content of new_3_updated.docx.

9.2.3.2 Example Code

```
# Loop through files new_1.docx to new_10.docx
for i in range(1, 11):
    original_filename = f"new_{i}.docx"
    updated_filename = f"new_{i}_updated.docx"

    # Rename the file
    os.rename(original_filename, updated_filename)

    # Open the renamed file and update content
    doc = Document(updated_filename)
    doc.add_paragraph(f"This is the updated new file number {i}")
    doc.save(updated_filename)

    # Download the updated file
    files.download(updated_filename)

print("10 files have been renamed again, updated, and downloaded.")
```

```
# Open the document
doc = Document("new_3_updated.docx")

# Print all paragraphs
for para in doc.paragraphs:
    print(para.text)
```

Scan the QR code to access the code and output (see 9.2.ipynb). The file also contains additional functions and methods for working with the os module and the python-docx library.

https://github.com/DrMichaelGuo/PFAAFAMMA

9.3 Automating Excel Tasks Using openpyxl and pandas

This section explains how to use Python to automate Excel tasks in accounting and finance. It covers how to read, write, and modify Excel files using the openpyxl and pandas libraries. These techniques support the automation of spreadsheets used for budgeting, financial reporting, reconciliations, and data analysis (see Figure 9.6).

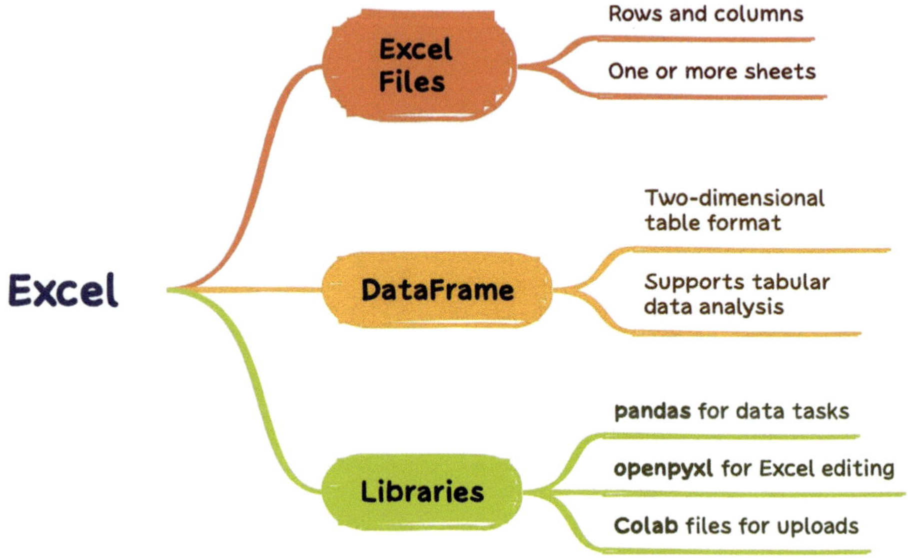

FIGURE 9.6 Excel

9.3.1 Key Concepts

9.3.1.1 Excel Files

An Excel file consists of one or more sheets. Each sheet contains rows and columns that store data. In Python, these sheets can be read, written, and modified using libraries such as pandas and openpyxl.

9.3.1.2 DataFrame

A DataFrame is a two-dimensional data structure used by pandas. It resembles a table in an Excel sheet and allows users to load, organise, and analyse tabular data.

9.3.1.3 Python Libraries

This section uses three Python libraries:

- pandas: provides tools to read, manipulate, and write data.
- openpyxl: enables editing of Excel files.
- google.colab.files: supports file upload and download within the Colab environment.

These libraries are imported using the following code:

```
import pandas as pd
from openpyxl import load_workbook
from google.colab import files
```

9.3.2 *Follow-Along Activity*

This activity shows how to read data from an Excel file, perform a summary calculation, update specific cell values, and write the results to another sheet using Python (see Figure 9.7).

The activity uses a file named 9_excel_example.xlsx, available at:
https://github.com/DrMichaelGuo/PFAAFAMMA
The file contains two sheets:

- Sheet1: contains invoice data including invoice number, amount, customer, and date.
- Summary: is initially empty and will be populated using Python.

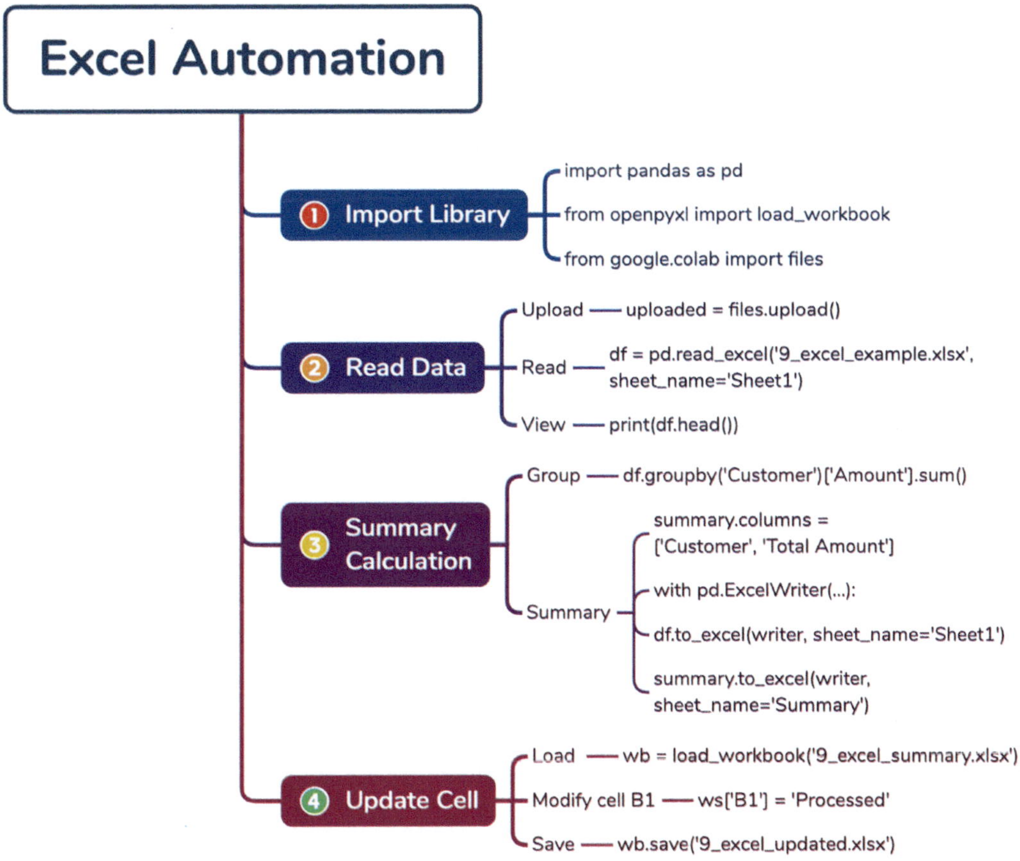

FIGURE 9.7 Excel Automation

Step 1: Import Libraries

Let's import the required libraries for data handling and Excel file processing.

```
import pandas as pd
from openpyxl import load_workbook
from google.colab import files
```

Explanation

- import pandas as pd: imports pandas using the standard alias pd.
- from openpyxl import load_workbook: imports the function for working with Excel files.
- from google.colab import files: provides functions for uploading and downloading files in the Colab environment.

Step 2: Upload and Read the Excel File

Let's upload the Excel file and read the contents of Sheet1 into a DataFrame.

```
uploaded = files.upload()
df = pd.read_excel('9_excel_example.xlsx', sheet_name='Sheet1')
print(df.head())
```

Output

```
 Invoice Number  Amount         Customer        Date
0       INV-1000     152         ABC Ltd.  2024-01-01
1       INV-1001     485  QuickBooks Ltd.  2024-01-02
2       INV-1002     910  QuickBooks Ltd.  2024-01-03
3       INV-1003     320        XYZ Corp.  2024-01-04
4       INV-1004     156  QuickBooks Ltd.  2024-01-05
```

Explanation

- uploaded = files.upload(): allows upload of the Excel file from the local machine to the Colab environment.
- df = pd.read_excel('9_excel_example.xlsx', sheet_name='Sheet1'): reads data from Sheet1 into a DataFrame.
- df.head(): prints the first five rows of the DataFrame.

Step 3: Calculate a Summary and Write to a New Sheet

Let's group the invoice data by customer, calculate the total amount for each customer, and write both the original and summary data to a new Excel file.

```
summary = df.groupby('Customer')['Amount'].sum().reset_index()
summary.columns = ['Customer', 'Total Amount']

with pd.ExcelWriter('9_excel_summary.xlsx', engine='openpyxl',
mode='w') as writer:
    df.to_excel(writer, sheet_name='Sheet1', index=False)
    summary.to_excel(writer, sheet_name='Summary', index=False)

files.download('9_excel_summary.xlsx')
```

Output

- This code creates a file named 9_excel_summary.xlsx and downloads it to the local machine. The file contains two sheets. Sheet1 holds the original invoice data. Summary includes the total amount for each customer.

Explanation

- df.groupby('Customer')['Amount'].sum(): groups the data by the Customer column and calculates the sum of Amount for each group.
  - .reset_index(): converts the grouped result into a new DataFrame by moving the group labels into a column.
  - summary.columns = ['Customer', 'Total Amount']: assigns new column names to the summary table.
- with pd.ExcelWriter('9_excel_summary.xlsx', engine='openpyxl', mode='w') as writer: uses a with statement and pandas.ExcelWriter to control the process of writing to an Excel file.
  - The with statement manages the opening and closing of resources.
  - pd.ExcelWriter(...): creates a context for writing data to an Excel file named 9_excel_summary.xlsx.
  - engine='openpyxl': specifies the engine for handling Excel .xlsx files.
  - mode='w': sets the file mode to write, which creates a new file or replaces an existing one.
  - df.to_excel(...): writes the original DataFrame to a sheet named Sheet1.
  - index=False: excludes the DataFrame index from the Excel file.
  - summary.to_excel(...): writes the summary DataFrame to the sheet named Summary.
- files.download('9_excel_summary.xlsx'): downloads the newly created Excel file to the local machine.

Step 4: Update Specific Cell Values Programmatically

Let's update a single cell within Sheet1 to indicate processing status. For example, set cell B1 to 'Processed'. This replaces the existing header 'Amount' with 'Processed' to show how to overwrite a specific cell value in an Excel worksheet.

```
wb = load_workbook('9_excel_summary.xlsx')
ws = wb['Sheet1']
ws['B1'] = 'Processed'
wb.save('9_excel_updated.xlsx')
files.download('9_excel_updated.xlsx')
```

Output

- This code creates a file named 9_excel_updated.xlsx and downloads it to the local machine. The file contains two sheets: Sheet1 holds the original invoice data with cell B1 updated to 'Processed'. Summary includes the total amount for each customer.

Explanation

- load_workbook(...): loads the Excel file for editing.
- wb['Sheet1']: selects Sheet1.
- ws['B1'] = 'Processed': assigns the value 'Processed' to cell B1. This replaces the existing header 'Amount' with 'Processed'.
- wb.save('9_excel_updated.xlsx'): saves the updated workbook under a new file name 9_excel_updated.xlsx.
- files.download('9_excel_updated.xlsx'): downloads the updated file 9_excel_updated.xlsx to the local machine.

This activity demonstrates how Python can read Excel data, compute summaries, update cell values, and save results. While this example uses a single file, the same process can be applied to multiple files (e.g. 20 or 50 Excel files) by placing the operations inside a loop. Manual updates across many files increase processing time and the risk of error. By contrast, Python provides a consistent and repeatable approach to file management, which is relevant in accounting and finance tasks involving large sets of documents.

9.3.3 *Your Project*

This project builds on the above activity. It applies the same steps to a different Excel file, involving reading sales data, generating a summary, updating a specific cell, and saving the final output. This project uses a file named 9_excel_project.xlsx, available at:

https://github.com/DrMichaelGuo/PFAAFAMMA

The file contains two sheets:

- Data: includes sales transactions for multiple customers.
- Summary: is initially empty and will be populated using Python.

9.3.3.1 Tasks

- Install and import the required libraries.
- Upload and read the file 9_excel_project.xlsx into a DataFrame.
- Calculate total sales per customer.
- Write both the raw data and the summary to a new file named 9_excel_project_output.xlsx, and download the file.
- Update cell A1 in the Summary sheet to 'Sales Summary', and save the file as 9_excel_project_final.xlsx.
- Download the final Excel file named 9_excel_project_final.xlsx.

9.3.3.2 *Example Code*

```
# Import libraries
import pandas as pd
from openpyxl import load_workbook
from google.colab import files

# Upload and read the Excel file
uploaded = files.upload()
df = pd.read_excel('9_excel_project.xlsx', sheet_name='Data')
print(df.head())

# Calculate total sales per customer
summary = df.groupby('Customer')['Sales'].sum().reset_index()
summary.columns = ['Customer', 'Total Sales']

# Write both raw data and summary to a new Excel file
with pd.ExcelWriter('9_excel_project_output.xlsx', engine='openpyxl',
mode='w') as writer:
    df.to_excel(writer, sheet_name='Data', index=False)
    summary.to_excel(writer, sheet_name='Summary', index=False)

files.download('9_excel_project_output.xlsx')

# Update cell A1 in the Summary sheet
wb = load_workbook('9_excel_project_output.xlsx')
ws = wb['Summary']
ws['A1'] = 'Sales Summary'
wb.save('9_excel_project_final.xlsx')

# Download the updated file
files.download('9_excel_project_final.xlsx')
```

Scan the QR code to access the code and output (see 9.3.ipynb).

https://github.com/DrMichaelGuo/PFAAFAMMA

9.3.3.3 *Important Consideration: Data Privacy in Your Future Projects*

Google Colab is used for learning Python in this textbook. For your future projects involving sensitive or proprietary data, a local coding environment is recommended. Local tools run on the user's machine and reduce the risk of storing data on external servers. This approach supports compliance with data protection requirements.

Summary of Chapter 9: Automating Tasks

In this chapter, we have covered the following concepts:

PDF Automation with pypdf

- pypdf is used to read, write, merge, rotate, and split PDF files.
- Tasks include extracting invoice data, correcting page orientation, and dividing multi-page reports.
- Automation improves consistency in managing financial documents.

Word File Automation with os and python-docx

- The os module supports batch file renaming and file system operations.
- The python-docx library enables creation and editing of Word documents.
- Applications include report generation, file renaming, and content updating.

Excel Automation with pandas and openpyxl

- The pandas module reads and summarises Excel data using DataFrames.
- The openpyxl module updates cells and manages worksheets in .xlsx files.
- Tasks include generating summaries, updating status fields, and saving results into structured reports.

File Handling in Google Colab

- The google.colab.files module is used to upload and download files.

Applications in Accounting and Finance

- Automating tasks such as invoice handling, report production, and data consolidation.
- Increasing accuracy and reducing manual input.
- Supporting processes such as audit preparation, period-end reporting, and analysis of large datasets.

Quiz Questions

Scan the QR code below to access the quiz questions for this chapter (see 9.md).

https://github.com/DrMichaelGuo/QuizPFAAFAMMA

Further Reading and Resources

Canny, S. (2013) *python-docx documentation (Version 1.2.0)*. https://python-docx.readthedocs.io/en/latest/ (Accessed 29 July 2025).

Fenniak, M. and pypdf contributors (2006–2025) *Welcome to pypdf*. https://pypdf.readthedocs.io/en/stable/ (Accessed 30 October 2025).

Gazoni, E. and Clark, C. (2024) *openpyxl - A Python library to read/write Excel 2010 xlsx/xlsm files (Version 3.1.3)*. https://openpyxl.readthedocs.io/en/stable/ (Accessed 29 July 2025).

pandas development team (2025) *pandas documentation (Version 2.3.1)*. https://pandas.pydata.org/docs/ (Accessed 29 July 2025).

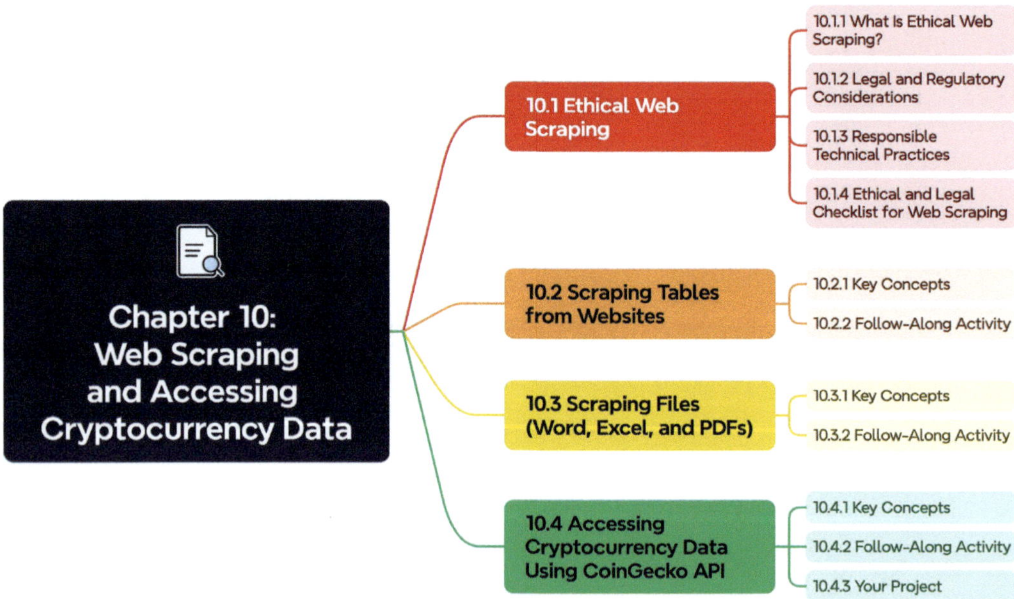

FIGURE 10.1 Structure of Chapter 10

10

WEB SCRAPING AND ACCESSING CRYPTOCURRENCY DATA

This chapter introduces the techniques and responsibilities involved in web scraping using Python. It explains how to extract structured data, such as financial tables and downloadable files, from webpages using libraries such as requests, BeautifulSoup, and pandas. The chapter focuses on legal and ethical compliance, including the use of robots.txt, General Data Protection Regulation (GDPR) requirements, and responsible scripting practices. Activities use demonstration websites created for educational purposes, allowing students to apply data collection and automation techniques in a controlled environment. The chapter also introduces access to cryptocurrency market data through application programming interfaces (APIs) such as CoinGecko (Figure 10.1).

Learning Objectives

By the end of this chapter, you will be able to

- Use Python libraries to retrieve, parse, and extract data from HyperText Markup Language (HTML) tables and downloadable files on the web.
- Apply legal and ethical principles when scraping, including checking robots.txt, reviewing terms of service, and complying with UK GDPR.
- Design and run scraping scripts that incorporate request headers, error handling, logging, and rate limiting.
- Access and analyse cryptocurrency price data using public APIs.

Disclaimer

- The web scraping examples in this chapter use demonstration websites created and owned by the author:
    - https://drmichaelguo.github.io/web-scraping-demo-PFAAFAMMA/
    - https://drmichaelguo.github.io/demo-web-scraping-files/

DOI: 10.4324/9781003656968-10

- These sites were developed for this textbook. The author grants permission for readers to scrape and download content from them solely for educational and non-commercial purposes.
- These examples are designed to demonstrate technical methods in a controlled and lawful environment. These methods must not be applied to third-party websites without proper authorisation.
- Before scraping any other website, readers should review the site's robots.txt file, its terms of service, and any applicable copyright or data protection regulations. Unauthorised scraping may breach legal duties or professional codes of conduct.
- This chapter does not provide legal advice. Readers are responsible for conducting their own legal and ethical assessments when applying these techniques beyond the scope of the textbook (see Figure 10.2).

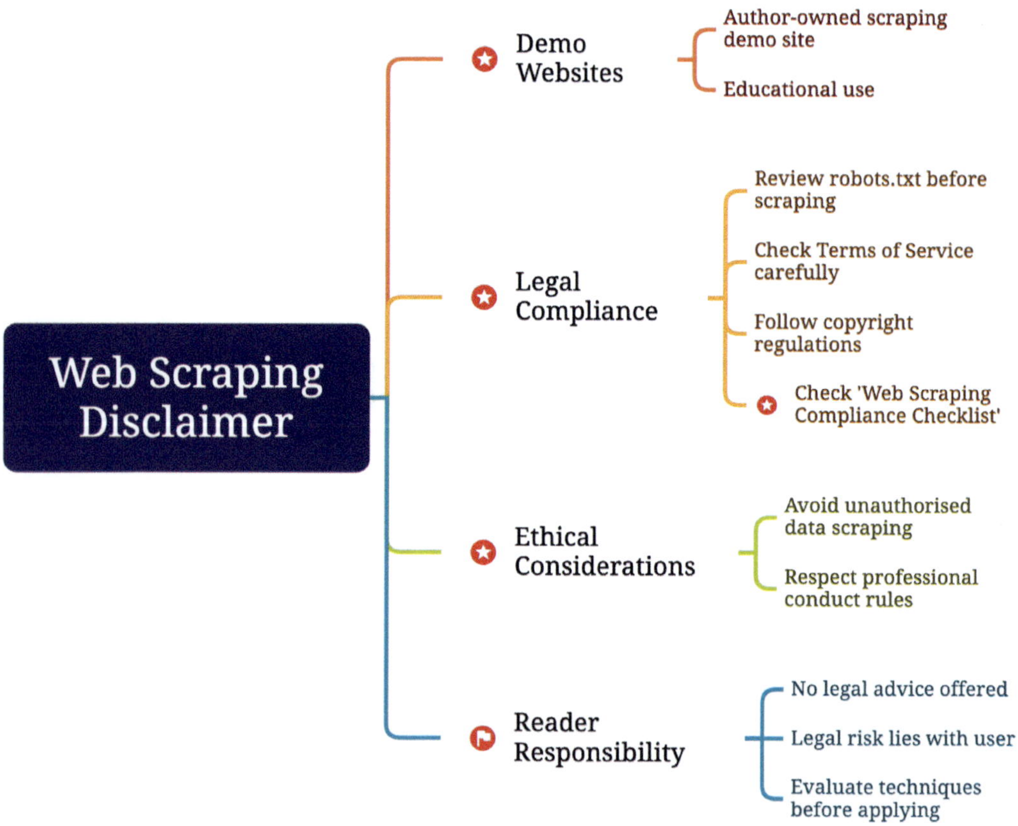

FIGURE 10.2 Web Scraping Disclaimer

10.1 Ethical Web Scraping

10.1.1 What Is Ethical Web Scraping?

Web scraping refers to the automated extraction of data from websites using Python scripts or other tools. It supports data collection from online sources. In accounting and finance, web scraping enables users to collect market data, economic indicators, and financial reports for research and analysis.

Ethical web scraping means carrying out this process in line with legal requirements and professional duties. It requires compliance with rules on data ownership, privacy, intellectual property, and the integrity of data collection. Understanding these rules is necessary to prevent misuse and supports the responsible use of online data (see Figure 10.3).

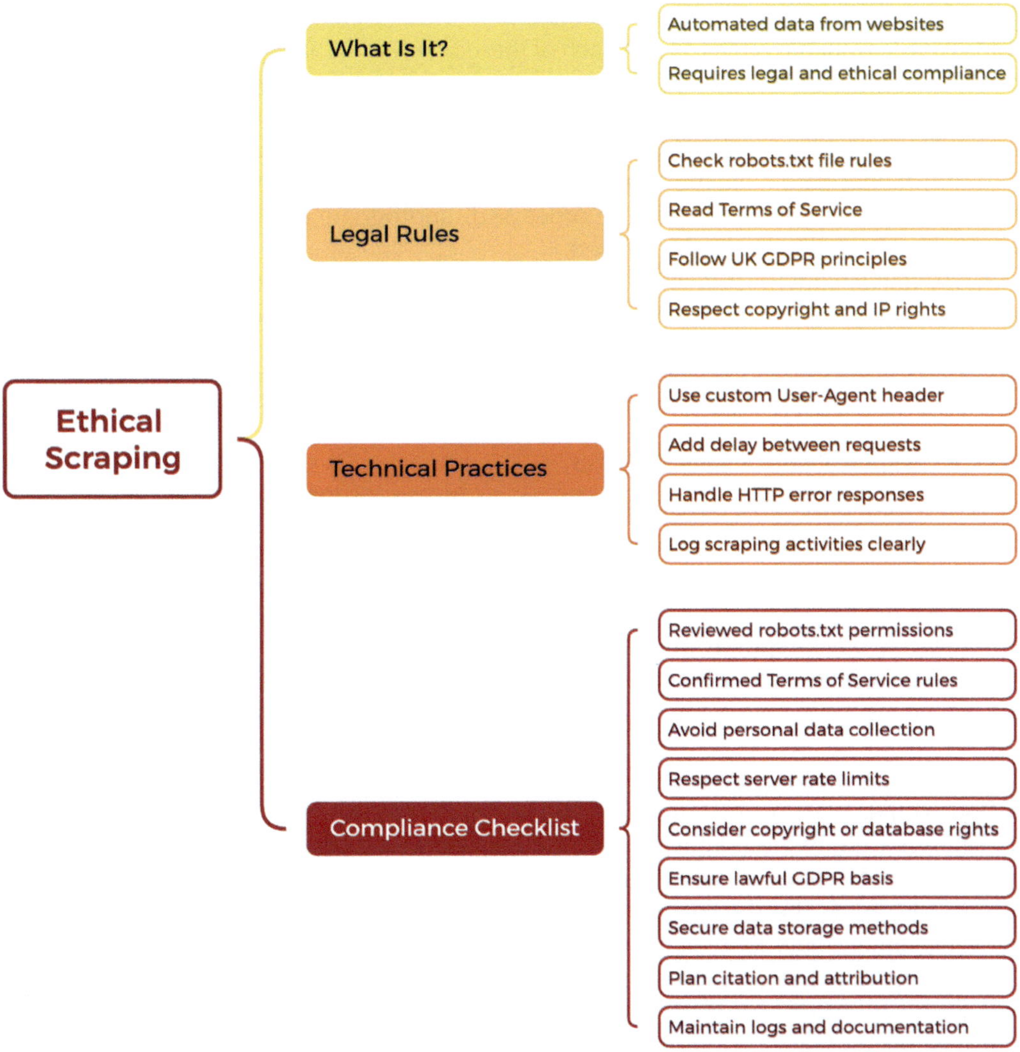

FIGURE 10.3 Ethical Scraping

10.1.2 Legal and Regulatory Considerations

Understanding the legal framework is essential for ethical web scraping. Key areas include (i) robots.txt, (ii) terms of service, (iii) UK GDPR compliance, and (iv) copyright and intellectual property.

The robots.txt file is a plain text document hosted on a website that specifies which sections of the site automated tools should or should not access. These rules are advisory and intended to guide crawler behaviour. The file itself does not provide legal permission to access the site. Users must still comply with the website's terms of service, copyright and database rights, and computer misuse law. Before starting any scraping task, examine the robots.txt file to confirm access rights.

Terms of service refer to the conditions established by a website that govern the use of its content and data. These conditions define the rules for access, use, and sharing of information available on the site. Breach of these conditions may result in a contract violation. Scraping must only proceed after reviewing and understanding the terms of service.

The UK GDPR governs the collection and use of personal data. Public availability does not make processing lawful. You must identify a lawful basis, such as legitimate interests, and ensure that data collection follows the principles of data minimisation and purpose limitation. Where personal data are processed, appropriate transparency, security, and retention controls must also be applied.

Copyright and intellectual property law protect original works, including financial documents, news articles, and market commentary. Scraping a full document or a substantial portion of copyrighted material may breach copyright, regardless of public availability. Scraping must stay within the limits of fair dealing or rely on permission when required.

10.1.3 Responsible Technical Practices

Ethical scraping requires the use of appropriate and controlled methods for data collection. The following practices are recommended:

Scrapers should be identified. This can be done by setting a custom User-Agent header that states the purpose of the scraper. Some websites allow access when the tool is identified but may block requests from anonymous or undeclared tools.

Scrapers should include a delay between requests. High-frequency or repeated requests can reduce website performance, interfere with other users, or activate automated blocking mechanisms. Delays can be added using functions such as time.sleep() in Python. Where specified, the scraping script should follow the crawl-delay setting in the site's robots.txt file.

Scraping scripts should handle errors. Common status codes such as 403 (Forbidden) and 404 (Not Found) should be managed to prevent repeated requests to unavailable pages. Managing these errors helps maintain the stability of the scraping process and prevents unnecessary load on the server.

Scraping activities should be logged. Logs can include timestamps, requested pages, volume of retrieved data, and any errors encountered. Keeping such records supports transparency, allows for internal checks, and helps ensure compliance with legal and institutional requirements.

10.1.4 Ethical and Legal Checklist for Web Scraping

Before starting any web scraping project, it is necessary to confirm that the activity complies with legal, ethical, and technical requirements. The questions below help assess whether a scraping task has been planned and executed responsibly.

Web Scraping Compliance Checklist

1. **Robots.txt and access control:** Have you checked the website's robots.txt file to confirm which sections are accessible to automated tools?
2. **Terms of service and permissions**: Does the website allow this type of data collection? Have you checked the terms of service to confirm whether scraping is permitted?
3. **Personal and identifiable data**: Are you collecting any personal or identifiable data without consent or a valid legal basis?
4. **Request frequency and server load**: Are your requests paced to avoid excessive load on the server? Are you complying with any rate limits?
5. **Intellectual property rights**: Have you considered any copyright or database rights that apply to the content being collected?
6. **Legal justification under UK GDPR**: Have you established a lawful justification for collecting and using any personal data?
7. **Data storage and management**: Do you have secure methods for storing, managing, and deleting scraped data?
8. **Attribution and citation**: Have you planned how to cite the data in publications or outputs, with appropriate acknowledgement where required?
9. **Documentation and logs**: Are you prepared to keep clear records of your scraping process? Are you prepared to explain your activity if asked by the website owner, a regulator, or an academic reviewer?

10.2 Scraping Tables from Websites

This section explains how to extract structured data, including tables, from websites using Python. It covers compliance checks, automated extraction, and conversion of web content into a pandas DataFrame (see Figure 10.4).

10.2.1 Key Concepts

10.2.1.1 Web Scraping

Web scraping is the process of using a program to extract data from websites. It involves sending requests to web pages, retrieving their content, and converting the information (often in HTML format) into a structured form such as a table. Web scraping is used to collect data for analysis, reporting, or automation and must follow legal and ethical rules.

10.2.1.2 HTML

HTML is the format used to structure content on webpages. It defines elements such as headings, paragraphs, and links. These elements can be located and extracted using Python tools.

In HTML, a heading is created using the <h1> tag. For example <h1>Financial Report Summary</h1> defines a main heading that appears at the top of a webpage or section.

A paragraph uses the <p> tag, for example, <p>This report presents the revenue data for the last financial year.</p>, which displays a block of text.

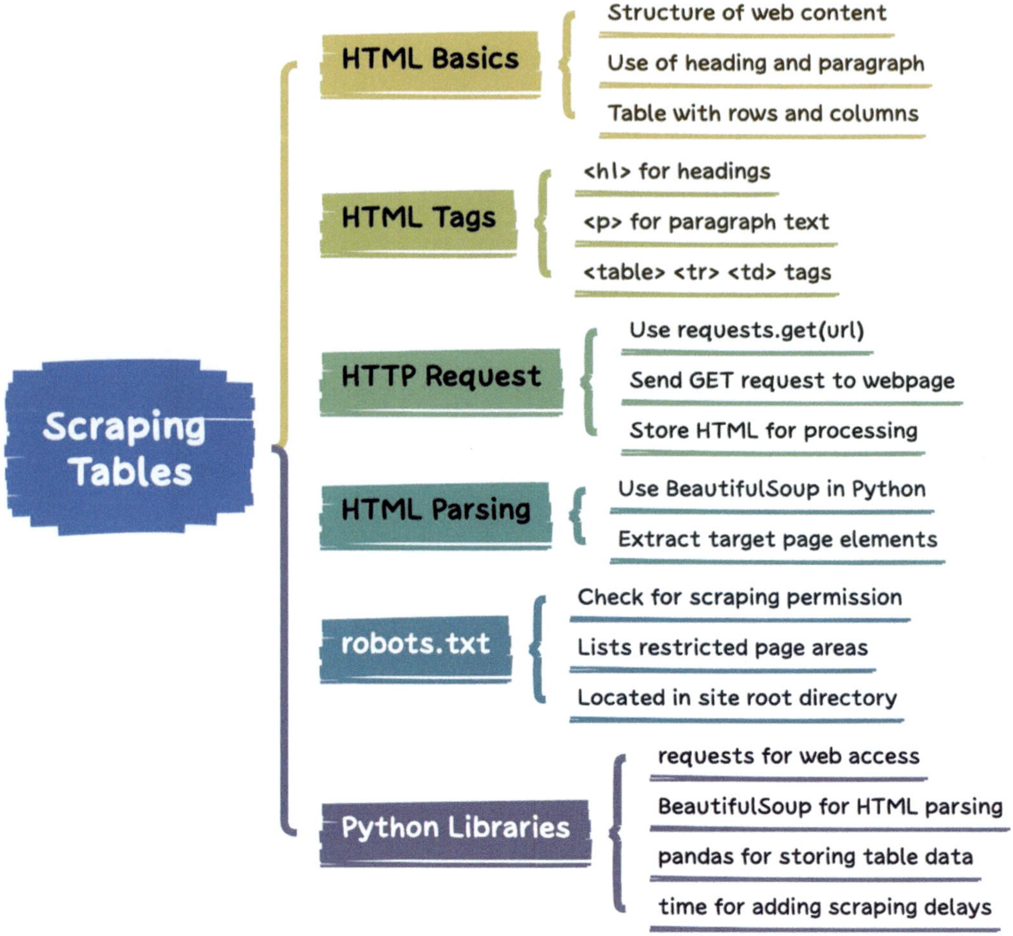

FIGURE 10.4 Scraping Tables

Tables are built using <table>, <tr>, <th>, and <td> tags. The <tr> tag defines a row within an HTML table. Each <tr> element contains one horizontal row of table cells. These cells are defined using <th> for header values and <td> for data values. For example,

```
<table>
 <tr>
   <th>Year</th>
   <th>Revenue</th>
   <th>Cost</th>
 </tr>
 <tr>
   <td>2023</td>
   <td>1500</td>
   <td>900</td>
 </tr>
</table>
```

In this example, the first row contains three header cells, and the second row contains three data cells, such as year, revenue, and cost of sales.

10.2.1.3 HTTP Requests and requests.get(url)

Web scraping begins by sending an HTTP request to a webpage. The requests library in Python performs this task. The function requests.get(url) sends a GET request to the given Uniform Resource Locator (URL) and stores the response for further processing.

10.2.1.4 HTML Parsing

HTML parsing is the process of reading and navigating HTML content using code. In Python-based web scraping, tools such as BeautifulSoup parse the HTML and extract specific elements.

10.2.1.5 robots.txt

The robots.txt file is a public document on a website that states which parts of the site automated tools may or may not access. Users of automated tools should check this file before collecting any data.

10.2.1.6 Python Libraries

Several Python libraries are used in web scraping:

- requests: sends HTTP requests and retrieves webpage content.
- BeautifulSoup: parses HTML and extracts specific elements such as tables.
- pandas: stores and presents extracted data in a table structure.
- time: adds delays between requests to control access frequency.

These libraries are imported as follows:

```
from bs4 import BeautifulSoup
import pandas as pd
import requests
import time
```

10.2.2 Follow-Along Activity

This activity demonstrates how to extract structured financial data from a company web-page developed for educational use in this textbook (see Figure 10.5).

The demonstration website used for this activity is
https://drmichaelguo.github.io/web-scraping-demo-PFAAFAMMA/

The webpage simulates a consolidated income statement for a fictional company. The table presents annual financial data across seven columns: Year, Revenue, Cost of Sales, Gross Profit, Operating Profit, Net Profit, and Earnings Per Share (EPS). Each row shows 1 year of data. Values use commas as thousand separators, brackets to indicate negative amounts, and decimal points for EPS.

FIGURE 10.5 Table Scraping Activity

Step 0: Check the robots.txt File and Complete the Scraping Checklist

Before scraping any website, check its robots.txt file and complete a compliance checklist. The robots.txt file indicates which parts of the site are accessible by automated tools.

Let's check the robots.txt file of the demonstration website:

https://drmichaelguo.github.io/web-scraping-demo-PFAAFAMMA/robots.txt

The robots.txt file contains

```
User-agent: *
Disallow:
```

Explanation

- User-agent: *: applies to all automated agents. The asterisk * means it includes any type of automated access tool.
- Disallow: states which parts of the site the automated tool must avoid. When no path is given after the colon, there are no restrictions. The automated tool may access the entire site.

This means the entire site is accessible to automated tools. The site permits scraping for educational purposes.

10.2.2.2 Real-World Application: Ethics and Compliance Checklist

When scraping real websites, check the robots.txt file but also review legal, ethical, and technical factors. Use the following checklist before any data collection:

Web Scraping Compliance Checklist

1. robots.txt and access control: Have you checked the website's robots.txt file to confirm which parts are accessible to automated tools?
2. Terms of service and permissions: Does the website allow this form of data collection? Have you checked the terms of service to determine whether scraping is permitted?
3. Personal and identifiable data: Are you collecting any personal or identifiable data without consent or a lawful basis?
4. Request frequency and server load: Are your requests spaced adequately to avoid overloading the server and stay within any rate limits?
5. Intellectual property rights: Have you considered any copyright or database rights that apply to the content being collected?
6. Legal justification under UK GDPR: Have you established a lawful justification for collecting and processing any personal data?
7. Data storage and management: Do you have secure methods for storing, managing, and deleting the collected data?
8. Attribution and citation: Have you planned how to cite the data in any publication or output, including appropriate acknowledgement where required?
9. Documentation and transparency: Are you prepared to document and explain your scraping activity if asked by the website owner, a regulator, or an academic reviewer?

Note: The demonstration website used in this textbook has been created for educational use. It allows scraping of all pages and contains no personal data. When working with real websites, you must conduct your own legal and ethical assessment.

Step 1: Import Libraries and Retrieve HTML

Let's begin by importing the necessary libraries and retrieving the HTML content.

```
from bs4 import BeautifulSoup
import pandas as pd
import requests
import time

url = "https://drmichaelguo.github.io/web-scraping-demo-PFAAFAMMA/"
headers = {'User-Agent': 'Mozilla/5.0 (compatible; WebScrapingTuto-
rial/1.0)'}  # identify scraper
response = requests.get(url, headers=headers)

# Handle request errors
if response.status_code != 200:
    print(f"Request failed with status code: {response.status_code}")
    exit()

# Rate limiting
time.sleep(1)  # pause before next request

html_content = response.text
```

Explanation

- from bs4 import BeautifulSoup: imports the BeautifulSoup library for parsing HTML content.
- import pandas as pd: imports the pandas library.
- import requests: imports the requests library for sending HTTP requests.
- import time: imports the time library to control the request rate.
- url = ...: sets the web address of the page to be scrapped.
- headers = {...}: creates a dictionary with a custom User-Agent string. The User-Agent identifies the scraping script when sending a request to the website. Using a User-Agent header to identify the scraper respects website ownership and supports ethical data collection.
- response = requests.get(url): sends a GET request to the URL and stores the server's response.
- if response.status_code != 200: checks whether the request was successful. A status code of 200 means the server returned the content as expected. Other codes, such as 403 (Forbidden) or 404 (Not Found), indicate blocked or missing resources. This check prevents the script from continuing with invalid or incomplete content.
- time.sleep(1): pauses the execution of the script for 1 second. This delay reduces server load and lowers the risk of access being blocked. This approach helps maintain responsible use of automated access tools.
- html_content = response.text: extracts the HTML content from the response.

Note: In practice, additional steps such as setting timeouts, checking response status with raise_for_status(), and handling rate limits (HTTP 429 errors) are recommended to make scripts more reliable. These have been omitted here to keep the example simple for learning purposes.

Step 2: Parse HTML

Let's parse the HTML and extract the table rows.

```
soup = BeautifulSoup(html_content, "html.parser")
rows = soup.find_all("tr")
```

Explanation

- soup = BeautifulSoup(html_content, "html.parser"): parses the HTML content using Python's built-in HTML parser. This enables searching and navigating within the HTML structure.
  - "html.parser": specifies the parser to use. It comes with Python and handles standard HTML.
- rows = soup.find_all("tr"): retrieves all the table row elements (<tr>) from the HTML.
  - tr: represents a table row in HTML. Each <tr> tag contains one row of table data.

Note: This example extracts all table rows on the page because the demonstration site contains only one table. In practice, you should locate the specific table by its identifier (e.g. using soup.find("table", {"id": "financials"})) to avoid collecting unrelated data.

Step 3: Convert Text to Numbers

Let's define a function to convert text values to numeric form.

```
def parse_number(text):
    text = text.strip().replace(",", "")
    if "(" in text and ")" in text:
        return -int(text.replace("(", "").replace(")", ""))
    try:
        return float(text) if "." in text else int(text)
    except ValueError:
        return None
```

Explanation

- def parse_number(text): defines a function to convert a text input into a numeric value.
- text.strip().replace(",", ""): removes spaces at the start and end of the text, and removes commas used as thousands separators.

- if "(" in text and ")" in text: checks whether the text uses brackets to represent a negative value.
- return -int(...): converts bracketed values to negative integers.
- return float(...) if "." in text else int(...): returns a float if the text contains a decimal point; otherwise, returns an integer.
- except ValueError: handles conversion errors and returns None when the input cannot be interpreted as a number.

Note: This demonstration uses simplified data for learning purposes. Negative values appear in brackets for whole numbers only. The parsing function in this example is designed for this format and may require modification if decimal values are also enclosed in brackets in real-world datasets.

Step 4: Extract the Data

Let's loop through the rows and extract each data point into a structured format.

```
data = []
for row in rows[1:]:
   cells = row.find_all("td")
   if len(cells) == 7:
       data.append({
           "Year": int(cells[0].text.strip()),
           "Revenue (£m)": parse_number(cells[1].text),
           "Cost of Sales (£m)": parse_number(cells[2].text),
           "Gross Profit (£m)": parse_number(cells[3].text),
           "Operating Profit (£m)": parse_number(cells[4].text),
           "Net Profit (£m)": parse_number(cells[5].text),
           "EPS (p)": parse_number(cells[6].text),
       })
```

Explanation

- data = [ ]: creates an empty list to store extracted data.
- for row in rows[1:]: loops through the table rows, starting from the second row to exclude the header.
- cells = row.find_all("td"): extracts all table data cells (<td>) in the row.
- if len(cells) == 7: checks that the row contains exactly seven data cells, matching the expected columns: Year, Revenue, Cost of Sales, Gross Profit, Operating Profit, Net Profit, and EPS.
- data.append({...}): adds a dictionary with values for each column to the list. Each dictionary corresponds to one row of financial data.

Step 5: Create a DataFrame

Let's convert the data list into a pandas DataFrame.

```
df = pd.DataFrame(data)
print(df)
```

Output

```
   Year  Revenue (£m)  Cost of Sales (£m)  Gross Profit (£m)  \
0  2021          1245                -757                488
1  2022          1398                -832                566
2  2023          1561                -903                658

   Operating Profit (£m)  Net Profit (£m)  EPS (p)
0                    312              215     35.2
1                    358              249     40.7
2                    421              297     48.3
```

Explanation

- df = pd.DataFrame(data): creates a DataFrame from the list of dictionaries.
- print(df): prints the contents of the DataFrame in tabular format.

Step 6: Logging Reminder

Let's record a log entry to document the scraping activity. It is good practice to keep a log of scraping tasks. The log may include the date and time of access, the target URL, the number of records retrieved, and any errors encountered. Logging supports transparency and accountability, especially when scraping is used in reporting or analysis.

```
print(f"Scraped {len(data)} records from {url} on {pd.Timestamp.
now()}")
```

Output

```
Scraped 3 records from https://drmichaelguo.github.io/web-scraping-
demo-PFAAFAMMA/ on 2025-06-16 08:59:10.659225
```

Explanation

- len(data): counts the number of records extracted from the webpage.
- url: displays the source of the scraped data.
- pd.Timestamp.now(): returns the current date and time.

The log confirms that three records were scraped from the specified URL and records the exact date and time of the scraping activity.

Scan the QR code to access the Python code and output (see 10.2.ipynb).

https://github.com/DrMichaelGuo/PFAAFAMMA

10.3 Scraping Files (Word, Excel, and PDFs)

This section explains how to locate and download Word, Excel, and PDF files from a webpage using Python. The section includes a follow-along activity based on a demonstration site (see Figure 10.6).

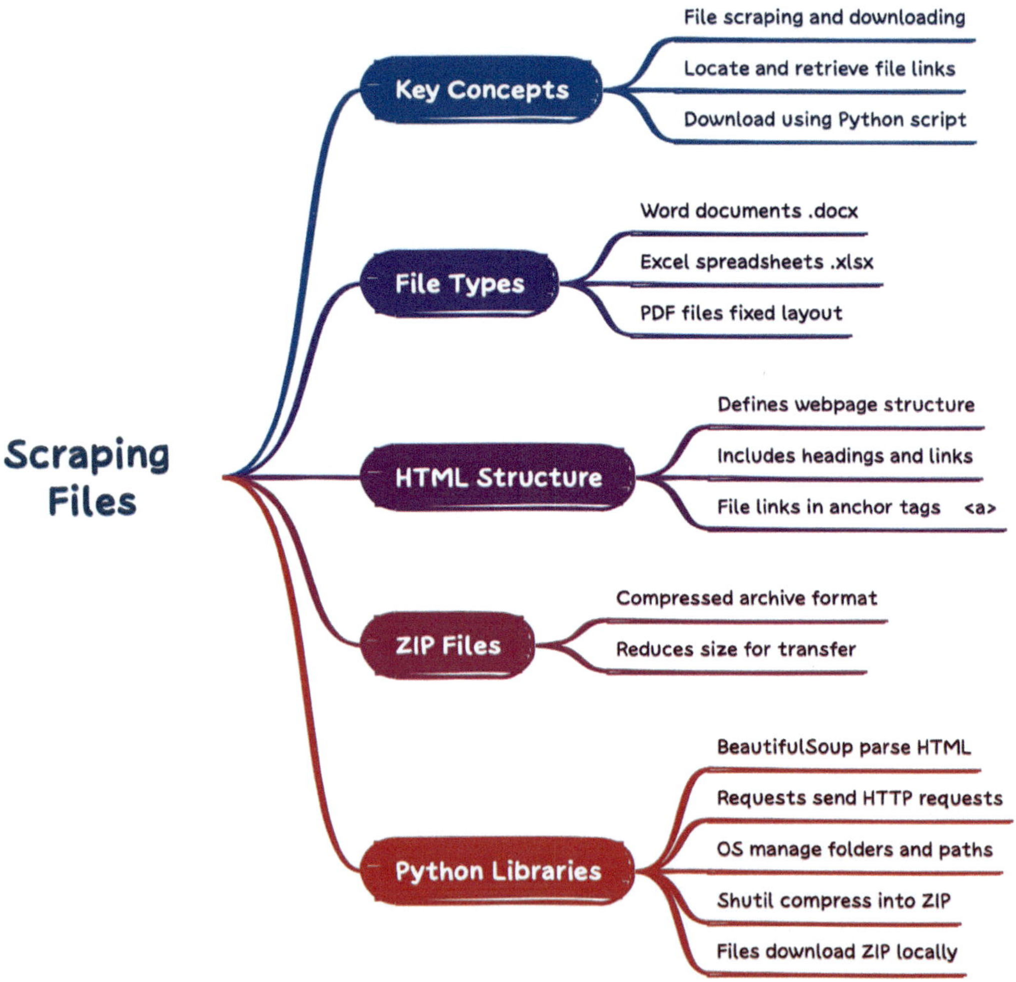

FIGURE 10.6 Scraping Files

10.3.1 Key Concepts

10.3.1.1 File Scraping and Downloading

Some websites host downloadable files such as Word documents, Excel spreadsheets, or PDFs. In this context, scraping refers to locating links to these files and downloading them through a script.

10.3.1.2 File Types

This section covers three file formats

- Word documents (.docx)
- Excel spreadsheets (.xlsx)
- PDF files (.pdf), used to maintain a fixed layout for viewing, sharing, or printing.

10.3.1.3 HTML Structure

HTML (HyperText Markup Language) defines the structure of a webpage. It includes elements such as headings, paragraphs, and links. These elements can be located and processed using Python.

File links are often embedded in <a> tags. For example,

```
<a href="report.pdf">Download the PDF report</a>
```

provides a link to a file named report.pdf.

10.3.1.4 zip

A zip file is a compressed archive that contains one or more files. It reduces file size and simplifies file transfer.

10.3.1.5 Python Libraries

This section uses several Python libraries to support web scraping and file handling.

- BeautifulSoup (from bs4): parses HTML and locates file links.
- requests: sends HTTP requests to retrieve webpages and files.
- os: handles folder creation and file paths.
- shutil: compresses downloaded files into a zip archive.
- files (from google.colab): enables downloading the zip archive to the local system.

These libraries are imported as follows:

```
from bs4 import BeautifulSoup
import requests
import os
import shutil
from google.colab import files
```

10.3.2 Follow-Along Activity

This activity shows how to locate and download files from a webpage developed for educational use in this textbook (see Figure 10.7).

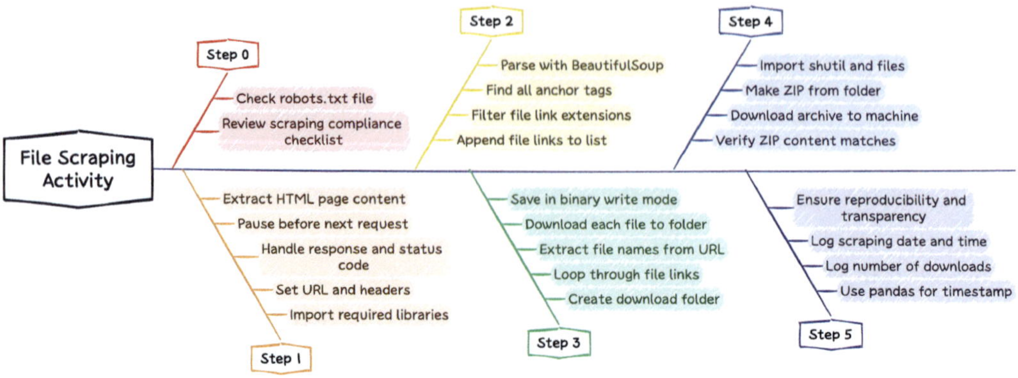

FIGURE 10.7 File Scraping Activity

The demonstration site includes links to 10 Word files, 10 Excel files, and 10 PDF files. The site is:

https://drmichaelguo.github.io/demo-web-scraping-files/

Step 0: Check the robots.txt File and Complete the Scraping Checklist

Before scraping any website, check its robots.txt file and complete a compliance checklist. The robots.txt file indicates which parts of the site are accessible by automated tools.

Let's access the following robots.txt file:

https://drmichaelguo.github.io/demo-web-scraping-files/robots.txt

Content:

```
User-agent: *
Allow: /
Allow: /*.docx
Allow: /*.xlsx
Allow: /*.pdf
```

Explanation

- User-agent: *: applies the rules to all automated tools.
- Allow: /: permits access to all areas of the site.
- Allow: /*.docx: permits access to Word documents.
- Allow: /*.xlsx: permits access to Excel files.
- Allow: /*.pdf: permits access to PDF files.

No paths are disallowed. Automated tools may access all areas of the site and download the listed file types.

10.3.2.2 Real-World Application: Ethics and Compliance Checklist

When scraping real websites, check the robots.txt file but also review legal, ethical, and technical factors. Use the following checklist before any data collection:

Web Scraping Compliance Checklist

1. Robots.txt and access control: Have you checked the website's robots.txt file to confirm which parts are accessible to automated tools?
2. Terms of service and permissions: Does the website allow this form of data collection? Have you checked the terms of service to determine whether scraping is permitted?
3. Personal and identifiable data: Are you collecting any personal or identifiable data without consent or a lawful basis?
4. Request frequency and server load: Are your requests spaced adequately to avoid overloading the server and stay within any rate limits?
5. Intellectual property rights: Have you considered any copyright or database rights that apply to the content being collected?
6. Legal justification under UK GDPR: Have you established a lawful justification for collecting and processing any personal data?
7. Data storage and management: Do you have secure methods for storing, managing, and deleting the collected data?
8. Attribution and citation: Have you planned how to cite the data in any publication or output, including appropriate acknowledgement where required?
9. Documentation and transparency: Are you prepared to document and explain your scraping activity if asked by the website owner, a regulator, or an academic reviewer?

Note: The demonstration website used in this textbook has been created for educational use. It allows scraping of all pages and contains no personal data. When working with real websites, you must conduct your own legal and ethical assessment.

Step 1: Import Libraries and Get HTML

Let's import the required libraries and retrieve the HTML content from the target webpage.

```
from bs4 import BeautifulSoup
import requests
import time

url = "https://drmichaelguo.github.io/demo-web-scraping-files/"
headers = {'User-Agent': 'Mozilla/5.0 (compatible; WebScrapingTuto-
rial/1.0)'}  # identify scraper
response = requests.get(url, headers=headers)

# Handle request errors
if response.status_code != 200:
  print(f"Request failed with status code: {response.status_code}")
  exit()

# Rate limiting
time.sleep(1)  # pause before next request

html_content = response.text
```

Explanation

- from bs4 import BeautifulSoup: imports BeautifulSoup from the bs4 module for parsing HTML content.
- import requests: imports the requests library to send HTTP requests.
- url = "https://drmichaelguo.github.io/demo-web-scraping-files/": stores the URL of the target webpage as a string.
- headers = {...}: defines a dictionary with a custom User-Agent string. The User-Agent identifies the scraping script when sending a request to the website. Using a User-Agent header to identify the scraper respects website ownership and supports ethical data collection.
- response = requests.get(url): sends a GET request to the URL and stores the response.
- if response.status_code != 200:: checks whether the request was successful. A status code of 200 means the server returned the content as expected. Other codes, such as 403 (Forbidden) or 404 (Not Found), indicate blocked or missing resources. This check prevents the script from continuing with invalid or incomplete content.
- time.sleep(1): pauses the execution of the script for 1 second. This delay reduces server load and lowers the risk of access being blocked. This approach helps maintain responsible use of automated access tools.
- html_content = response.text: extracts the HTML content from the response.

Note: In practice, additional steps such as setting timeouts, checking response status with raise_for_status(), and handling rate limits (HTTP 429 errors) are recommended to make scripts more reliable. These have been omitted here to keep the example simple for learning purposes.

Step 2: Parse HTML and Find File Links

Let's parse the HTML content and identify links to Word, Excel, and PDF files.

```
soup = BeautifulSoup(html_content, "html.parser")
links = soup.find_all("a")

file_links = []
for link in links:
    href = link.get("href")
    if href and (
        href.endswith(".docx") or
        href.endswith(".xlsx") or
        href.endswith(".pdf")
    ):
        file_links.append(url + href)
```

Explanation

- soup = BeautifulSoup(html_content, "html.parser"): creates a parser object from the HTML.
- links = soup.find_all("a"): retrieves all (<a>) tags from the HTML and stores them in a list.

- file_links = [ ]: creates an empty list to store file links.
- for link in links:: loops through each anchor tag.
    - href = link.get("href"): retrieves the value of the href attribute from the anchor tag. This value contains the linked URL or file path.
    - if href and (...):: checks if href exists and ends with one of the required file extensions.
    - file_links.append(url + href): adds the full URL of each file to the list.

Note: This example combines the base URL and file path using url + href. This works correctly for the demonstration website, where all links use relative paths. In real-world applications, file links may begin with a slash or include a full domain name. In such cases, the urljoin() function from the urllib.parse module should be used to combine links safely.

Step 3: Download Files

Let's create a folder and download each file to that location.

```
import os
os.makedirs("downloaded_files", exist_ok=True)

for file_url in file_links:
   filename = file_url.split("/")[-1]
   response = requests.get(file_url)
   f = open(os.path.join("downloaded_files", filename), "wb")
   f.write(response.content)
   f.close()
```

Explanation

- import os: imports the os module for file operations.
- os.makedirs("downloaded_files", exist_ok=True): creates a folder named downloaded_files.
    - exist_ok=True: allows folder creation without raising an error if the folder already exists. If set to False, an error is raised when the folder exists.
- for file_url in file_links:: loops through each file URL.
- filename = file_url.split("/")[−1]: extracts the file name from the URL.
    - file_url.split("/"): splits the string file_url into parts using the forward slash / as the separator.
    - [−1]: selects the last element of the list, which is the file name.
- response = requests.get(file_url): sends a GET request to download the file.
- f = open(os.path.join("downloaded_files", filename), "wb"): opens a file with the given name in the downloaded_files folder in binary write mode ("wb").
- f.write(response.content): writes the content of the response to the file.
- f.close(): closes the file after writing.

All files are saved to the downloaded_files folder within the Google Colab environment. To view them, click the folder icon on the left-hand side of the Colab interface. The folder should contain 10 Word files, 10 Excel files, and 10 PDF files.

To download all files to a local machine, it is more efficient to compress them into a zip file. The next step shows how to compress the files into a single zip file and download it.

Step 4: Download as zip File

Let's compress the downloaded files into a zip archive and download it to the local machine.

```
import shutil
from google.colab import files

shutil.make_archive("all_downloads", 'zip', "downloaded_files")
files.download("all_downloads.zip")
```

Explanation

- import shutil: imports the shutil module for file compression.
- from google.colab import files: imports the files module to enable file download in Colab.
- shutil.make_archive("all_downloads", 'zip', "downloaded_files"): compresses the downloaded_files folder into a zip file named all_downloads.zip.
- files.download("all_downloads.zip"): downloads the zip file.

After running this step, check the default download folder on the local machine. The zip file should contain all 10 Word files, 10 Excel files, and 10 PDF files.

Step 5: Logging Reminder

Let's record a log entry to document the scraping activity. It is good practice to keep a log of scraping tasks. Logging supports transparency and accountability, especially when scraping is used for reporting and analysis.

```
import pandas as pd
print(f"Downloaded {len(file_links)} files from {url} on {pd.Times-
tamp.now()}")
```

Output

```
Downloaded 30 files from https://drmichaelguo.github.io/demo-web-
scraping-files/ on 2025-06-16 09:27:06.459668
```

Explanation

- import pandas as pd: imports the pandas library to use the timestamp function.
- len(data): counts the number of records extracted from the webpage.

- url: specifies the data source.
- pd.Timestamp.now(): returns the current date and time.

The log confirms that 30 files were downloaded from the specified URL and records the date and time of the scraping activity. This log supports reproducibility and allows others to verify the collection process.

Scan the QR code to access the Python code and output (see 10.3.ipynb).

https://github.com/DrMichaelGuo/PFAAFAMMA

10.4 Accessing Cryptocurrency Data Using CoinGecko API

This section introduces how to retrieve and analyse cryptocurrency price data using the CoinGecko API. The section focuses on downloading Bitcoin price data from a public API, converting the response into a DataFrame, and visualising the price movement over time (see Figure 10.8).

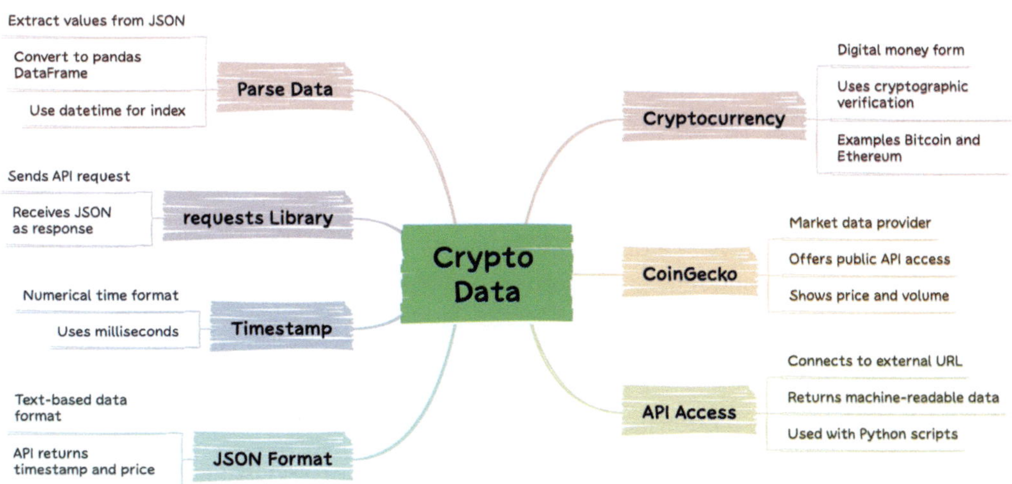

FIGURE 10.8 Crypto Data

10.4.1 Key Concepts

10.4.1.1 Cryptocurrency

Cryptocurrency is a form of digital money. It relies on cryptographic methods to record and verify transactions. Examples include Bitcoin and Ethereum.

10.4.1.2 CoinGecko

CoinGecko is a platform that provides cryptocurrency market data, including price, trading volume, and market capitalisation. It offers a public API that allows users to access cryptocurrency data.

10.4.1.3 API (Application Programming Interface)

An API allows Python to request data from an external service by connecting to a specified URL. The API returns data in a machine-readable format. The CoinGecko API returns data in JSON format.

10.4.1.4 JSON (JavaScript Object Notation)

JSON is a text-based format used for data exchange between systems. The CoinGecko API provides data in this format. A typical structure for price data is

```
{ "prices": [[timestamp, price], [timestamp, price], ...] }
```

Each pair in the square brackets contains two values: (i) a timestamp (in milliseconds) and (ii) a price value. For example,

```
{ "prices": [ [1640995200000, 37240.52], [1641081600000, 37495.68] ] }
```

10.4.1.5 Timestamp

A timestamp is a numerical value that represents a specific point in time. The format used in the above example records time in milliseconds.

10.4.1.6 Requests

The requests library allows Python to communicate with websites and APIs. It is used to send requests to URLs and receive responses. A standard call to retrieve data is

```
requests.get(url, params)
```

10.4.1.7 Parsing JSON to a DataFrame

Parsing is the process of extracting structured data from a response. In this section, the JSON data returned by the CoinGecko API includes timestamp and price pairs. These can be converted into a pandas DataFrame. A common approach is to use pd.to_datetime() to convert timestamp into datetime format. This datetime column can then be set as the index of the DataFrame for data analysis and visualisation.

10.4.2 Follow-Along Activity

This activity demonstrates how to retrieve Bitcoin price data from the CoinGecko API, convert the data into a pandas DataFrame, and visualise the price trend with a moving average (see Figure 10.9).

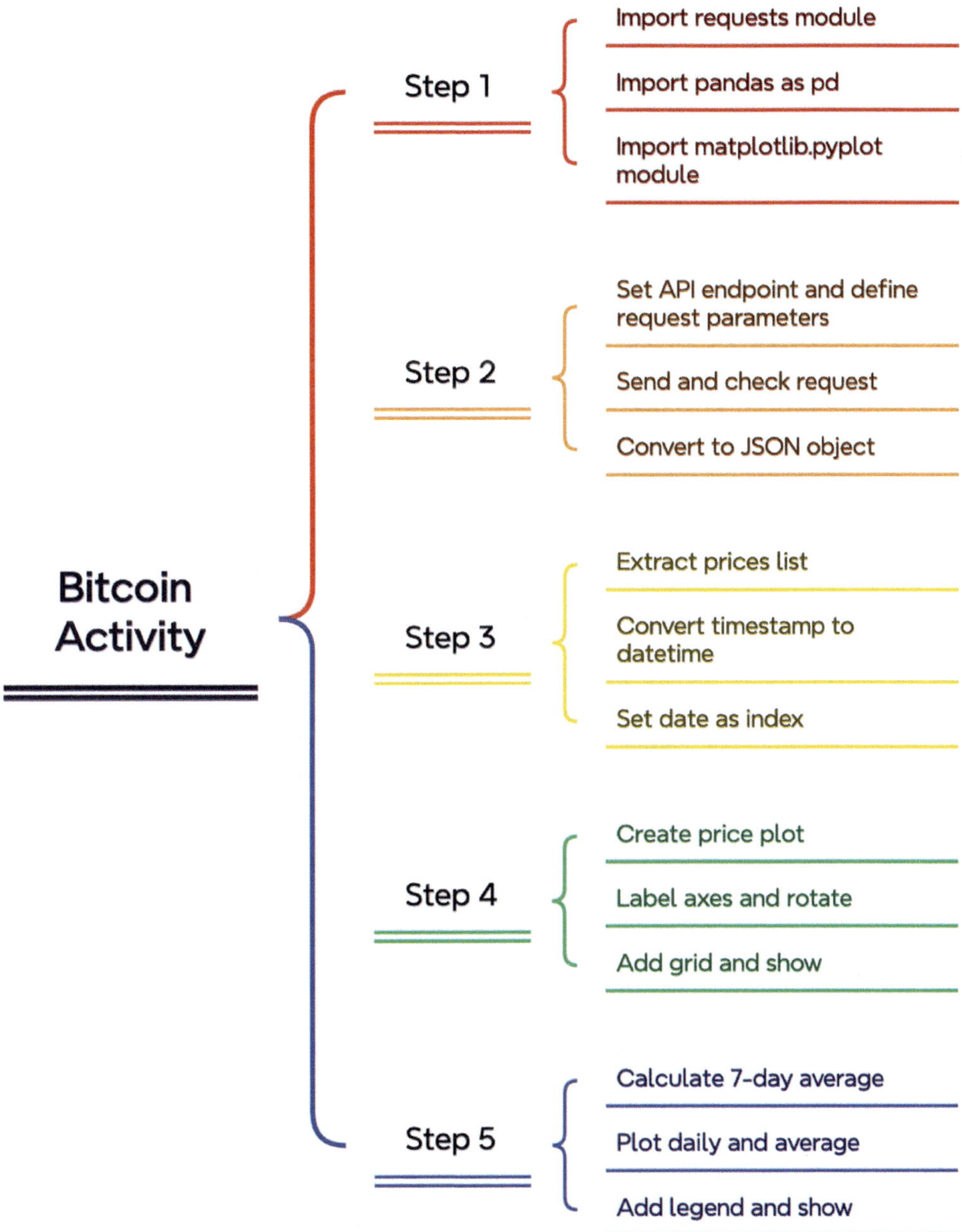

FIGURE 10.9 Bitcoin Activity

Step 1: Install and Import Libraries

Let's begin by importing the required libraries to handle the API request, process the data, and create visualisations.

```
import requests
import pandas as pd
import matplotlib.pyplot as plt
```

Explanation

- import requests: allows Python to send requests to web servers.
- import pandas as pd: imports the pandas library.
- import matplotlib.pyplot as plt: imports the plotting module from Matplotlib.

Step 2: Send Request to Retrieve Data

Let's define API URL, set parameters, and send a request to receive price data. We also check whether the request succeeds before using the data.

```
# Define the API endpoint and parameters
api_url = "https://api.coingecko.com/api/v3/coins/bitcoin/market_chart"
params = {
   "vs_currency": "usd",
   "days": "30",
   "interval": "daily"
}

# Send a request
response = requests.get(api_url, params=params)

# Check response status
if response.status_code == 200:
   data = response.json()
   print("Data successfully retrieved!")
else:
   print("Failed to retrieve data:", response.status_code)
```

Output

```
Data successfully retrieved!
```

Explanation

- api_url = …: assigns the CoinGecko API address to the variable api_url.
- params = {…}: defines a dictionary of request settings.
    - "vs_currency": "usd": sets the price currency to US dollars.
    - "days": "30": requests data for the past 30 days.
    - "interval": "daily": specifies daily price data.

- requests.get(...): sends a request to the API using the URL and parameters and receives a response.
- The if statement checks the response status before using the data.
    - response.status_code == 200: confirms the request succeeded.
    - response.json(): converts the response into a JSON object for use in Python.

Note: The response.status_code returns a number that indicates the result of the request. Common status codes include

- 200: success – data returned.
- 404: not found – the URL may be incorrect.
- 401: unauthorised – access is denied.
- 500: server error – problem on the server side.

Step 3: Convert JSON to DataFrame

Let's extract price data, convert timestamps, and view summary statistics.

```
# Extract 'prices' list
prices = data['prices']

# Create DataFrame and convert timestamps
df = pd.DataFrame(prices, columns=["timestamp", "price"])
df['date'] = pd.to_datetime(df['timestamp'], unit='ms')
df.set_index('date', inplace=True)
df.drop('timestamp', axis=1, inplace=True)

print(df.head())
print(df.describe())
```

Output

```
                    price
date
2025-07-07  109215.197718
2025-07-08  108300.716758
2025-07-09  108953.191877
2025-07-10  111327.530542
2025-07-11  115879.650301
               price
count      31.000000
mean   116287.974950
std      3263.925910
min    108300.716758
25%    114785.506496
50%    117571.025100
75%    118178.868595
max    119955.795706
```

Explanation

- data['prices']: accesses the prices list, which contains timestamp and price pairs.
- pd.DataFrame(...): creates a DataFrame and labels the columns as timestamp and price.
- df['date'] = pd.to_datetime(df['timestamp'], unit='ms'): creates a new date column by converting timestamps from milliseconds to datetime objects.
    - df['timestamp']: refers to the original timestamp column in milliseconds.
    - Unit='ms': tells pandas to interpret the numeric values as milliseconds.
- df.set_index('date', inplace=True): sets the date column as the index of the DataFrame.
    - Inplace=True: applies the change directly to the DataFrame without creating a new object.
- df.drop('timestamp', axis=1, inplace=True): removes the timestamp column from the DataFrame.
    - inplace=True: removes the column in the existing DataFrame.
- print(df.head()): prints the first five rows to confirm the structure and content of the DataFrame.
- df.describe(): provides summary statistics for the price column, including count, mean, standard deviation, minimum, and maximum values.

Note: The output shown here is based on the data retrieved at the time the code was run. When this activity is run again, the data may differ as cryptocurrency prices change over time.

Step 4: Visualise Bitcoin Price

Let's create a line chart to show the daily price of Bitcoin over the past 30 days.

```
plt.figure(figsize=(10, 5))
plt.plot(df.index, df['price'], marker='o', linestyle='-')
plt.title("Bitcoin Price Over the Past 30 Days")
plt.xlabel("Date")
plt.ylabel("Price (USD)")
plt.xticks(rotation=45)
plt.grid(True)
plt.show()
```

Output: see Figure 10.10.

Explanation

- plt.figure(figsize=(10, 5)): sets the plot size to 10 inches wide and 5 inches high.
- plt.plot(df.index, df['price'], marker='o', linestyle='-'): plots the price data using dates on the x-axis and prices on the y-axis.
    - df.index: provides the x-axis values (dates).
    - df['price']: provides the y-axis values (daily Bitcoin prices).

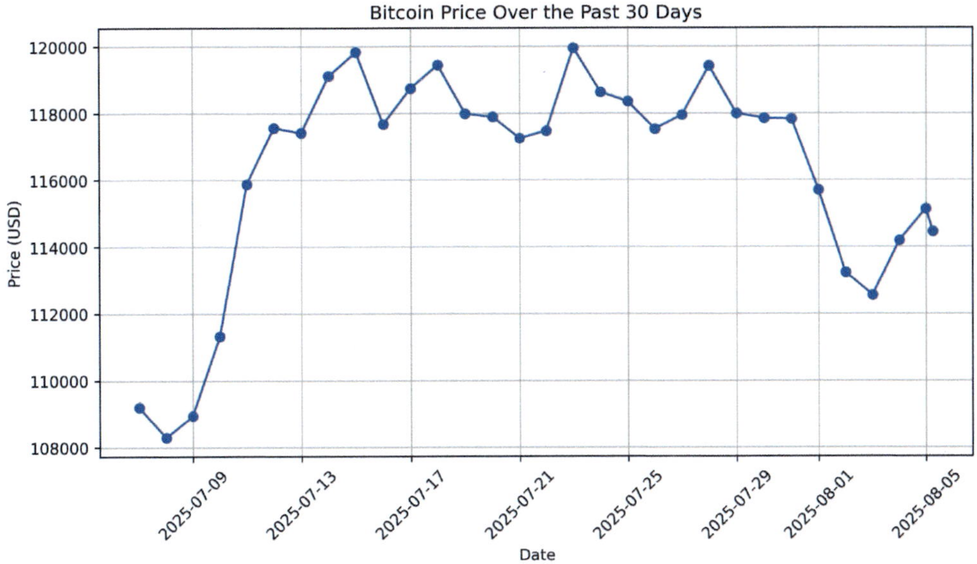

FIGURE 10.10 Bitcoin Price Over the Past 30 Days

- Marker='o': places a circular marker at each data point.
- linestyle='-': connects the data points with a straight line.

- plt.title("Bitcoin Price Over the Past 30 Days"): sets the chart title.
- plt.xlabel("Date"): labels the x-axis as 'Date'.
- plt.ylabel("Price (USD)"): labels the y-axis as 'Price (USD)'.
- plt.xticks(rotation=45): rotates the x-axis labels by 45 degrees for better spacing.
- plt.grid(True): adds a grid to the chart.
- plt.show(): displays the chart.

Step 5: Calculate Moving Average and Visualise

Let's calculate a 7-day moving average and visualise the result to observe the trend in price movement.

```
# Calculate moving average
df['7_day_MA'] = df['price'].rolling(window=7).mean()

# Plot original and moving average
plt.figure(figsize=(10, 5))
plt.plot(df.index, df['price'], label="Daily Price")
plt.plot(df.index, df['7_day_MA'], label="7-Day Moving Average",
linewidth=2)
plt.title("Bitcoin Price with 7-Day Moving Average")
plt.xlabel("Date")
plt.ylabel("Price (USD)")
plt.xticks(rotation=45)
plt.legend()
plt.grid(True)
plt.show()
```

Output: see Figure 10.11.

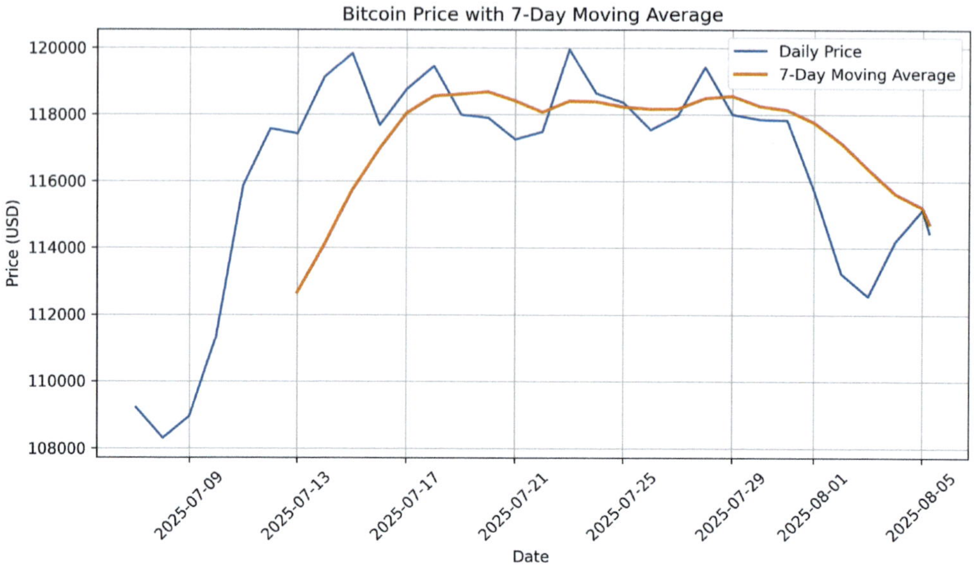

FIGURE 10.11 Bitcoin Price with 7-Day Moving Average

Explanation

- df['7_day_MA'] = df['price'].rolling(window=7).mean(): calculates the 7-day moving average and assigns the result to a new column.
    - df['price'].rolling(window=7).mean(): applies a rolling window of seven rows to the price column and calculates the mean for each group of seven consecutive values.
    - df['7_day_MA']: creates a new column in the DataFrame to store the calculated 7-day moving average values.
- plt.plot(df.index, df['7_day_MA'], label="7-Day Moving Average", linewidth=2): plots the 7-day moving average using dates on the x-axis and the moving average values on the y-axis. Adds a label for the legend and sets the line width to 2.
- plt.legend(): displays a legend that identifies the plotted lines, including daily prices and the 7-day moving average.
- plt.show(): displays the chart.

10.4.3 Your Project

Write Python code to retrieve Ethereum price data and analyse the trend using the following URL:

```
api_url = "https://api.coingecko.com/api/v3/coins/ethereum/
market_chart"
```

10.4.3.1 *Tasks*

- Install and import the required libraries.
- Send a request to retrieve price data for the past 90 days using the above URL and check whether the request is successful.
- Convert the JSON data into a pandas DataFrame and provide summary statistics using describe().
- Visualise the Ethereum price using a plot with dimensions 12 inches wide and 6 inches high.
- Calculate and plot a 14-day moving average.

10.4.3.2 *Example Code*

```
# Import the necessary libraries
import requests
import pandas as pd
import matplotlib.pyplot as plt
```

```
# Retrieve Ethereum Data for 90 days

# Define the API endpoint and parameters
api_url = "https://api.coingecko.com/api/v3/coins/ethereum/
market_chart"
params = {
    "vs_currency": "usd",
    "days": "90",
    "interval": "daily"
}

# Send a request to the API
response = requests.get(api_url, params=params)
# Check if the request was successful and retrieve the JSON data
if response.status_code == 200:
    data = response.json()
    print("Data successfully retrieved!")
else:
    print("Failed to retrieve data:", response.status_code)
```

```
# Convert the JSON Data to a pandas DataFrame

# Extract the 'prices' data from the JSON response
prices = data['prices']

# Create a DataFrame with 'timestamp' and 'price' columns
df = pd.DataFrame(prices, columns=["timestamp", "price"])

# Convert timestamp from milliseconds to datetime
df['date'] = pd.to_datetime(df['timestamp'], unit='ms')
```

```
# Set the date as the DataFrame index
df.set_index('date', inplace=True)

# Drop the 'timestamp' column
df.drop('timestamp', axis=1, inplace=True)

# Display the first few rows to confirm
print(df.head())

print(df.describe())
```

```
# Plot the Ethereum Price

plt.figure(figsize=(12, 6))
plt.plot(df.index, df['price'], color='blue', label='Daily Price')
plt.title("Ethereum Daily Price")
plt.xlabel("Date")
plt.ylabel("Price (USD)")
plt.grid(True)
plt.xticks(rotation=45)
plt.legend()
plt.show()

# Calculate the 14-day moving average
df['14_day_MA'] = df['price'].rolling(window=14).mean()

# Plot the daily price and the 14-day moving average
plt.figure(figsize=(12, 6))
plt.plot(df.index, df['price'], label="Daily Price")
plt.plot(df.index, df['14_day_MA'], label="14-Day Moving Average",
linewidth=2)
plt.title("Ethereum Price with 14-Day Moving Average")
plt.xlabel("Date")
plt.ylabel("Price (USD)")
plt.xticks(rotation=45)
plt.legend()
plt.grid(True)
plt.show()
```

Scan the QR code to access the Python code and output (see 10.4.ipynb).

https://github.com/DrMichaelGuo/PFAAFAMMA

Chapter 10: Web Scraping and Accessing Cryptocurrency Data

In this chapter, we have covered the following concepts:

Web Scraping Basics

- Web scraping refers to the extraction of data from websites using automated tools.
- Python libraries support scraping and data processing, including requests, BeautifulSoup, and pandas.

Legal and Ethical Considerations

- Check the website's robots.txt file to confirm permissions before scraping.
- Review the terms of service to ensure compliance.
- UK GDPR prohibits the scraping of personal data without a lawful basis.
- Copyright law applies to publicly accessible content.
- Ethical scraping involves transparency, respect for data ownership, and minimal server impact.

Responsible Technical Practices

- Use a custom User-Agent header to identify the scraper.
- Insert delays between requests using time.sleep() to prevent server overload.
- Keep a log of scraping activities to support documentation and reproducibility.

Scraping HTML Tables

- Use requests.get() to retrieve the HTML content of a webpage.
- Use BeautifulSoup to parse and extract table rows with find_all("tr").
- Convert text values to numeric data using a parsing function.
- Create a structured dataset using pandas DataFrame.

Downloading Files (Word, Excel, PDFs)

- Locate downloadable file links in HTML using anchor tags (<a href="...">).
- Download files using requests and save them with the os module.
- Combine files into a zip archive using shutil.make_archive() for download.
- Download the archive to a local machine using google.colab.files.

Logging and Documentation

- Record the number of records or files retrieved, the source URL, and the timestamp.
- Logging supports ethical practice, accountability, and academic reproducibility.

Web Scraping Compliance Checklist

1. **Robots.txt and access control:** Have you checked the website's robots.txt file to confirm which sections are accessible to automated tools?
2. **Terms of service and permissions**: Does the website allow this type of data collection? Have you checked the terms of service to confirm whether scraping is permitted?
3. **Personal and identifiable data**: Are you collecting any personal or identifiable data without consent or a valid legal basis?
4. **Request frequency and server load**: Are your requests paced to avoid excessive load on the server? Are you complying with any rate limits?
5. **Intellectual property rights**: Have you considered any copyright or database rights that apply to the content being collected?
6. **Legal justification under UK GDPR**: Have you established a lawful justification for collecting and using any personal data?
7. **Data storage and management**: Do you have secure methods for storing, managing, and deleting scraped data?
8. **Attribution and citation**: Have you planned how to cite the data in publications or outputs, with appropriate acknowledgement where required?
9. **Documentation and logs**: Are you prepared to keep clear records of your scraping process? Are you prepared to explain your activity if asked by the website owner, a regulator, or an academic reviewer?

APIs and Data Access

- APIs allow Python to request data from external sources.
- CoinGecko API is used to access cryptocurrency data.
- API responses are returned in JSON format and processed in Python.

CoinGecko API

- The CoinGecko API provides cryptocurrency price data.
- The API returns price and timestamp pairs in JSON format.
- The requests library sends API requests and retrieves responses.

Data Processing and Analysis

- JSON data are converted into pandas DataFrames.
- Timestamps are converted to datetime format using pd.to_datetime().
- Daily returns are calculated using pct_change() to measure price changes.

Data Visualisation

- Line plots display price trends over time using Matplotlib.
- Daily returns are visualised to show volatility.
- Moving averages are used to smooth data and identify trends.

Quiz Questions

Scan the QR code below to access the quiz questions for this chapter (see 10.md).

https://github.com/DrMichaelGuo/QuizPFAAFAMMA

Further Reading and Resources

CoinGecko (no date) *CoinGecko API Introduction*. https://docs.coingecko.com/v3.0.1/reference/introduction (Accessed 4 August 2025).

Information Commissioner's Office (n.d.) *UK GDPR Guidance and Resources*. https://ico.org.uk/for-organisations/uk-gdpr-guidance-and-resources/ (Accessed 1 August 2025).

pandas (n.d.) *Pandas Documentation (Version 2.3.1)*. https://pandas.pydata.org/docs/ (Accessed 1 August 2025).

Reitz, K. (n.d.) *Requests: HTTP for Humans™ (Version 2.32.4)*. https://requests.readthedocs.io/ (Accessed 1 August 2025).

Richardson, L. (2004–2025). *Beautiful soup documentation*. https://www.crummy.com/software/BeautifulSoup/bs4/doc/ (Accessed 1 August 2025).

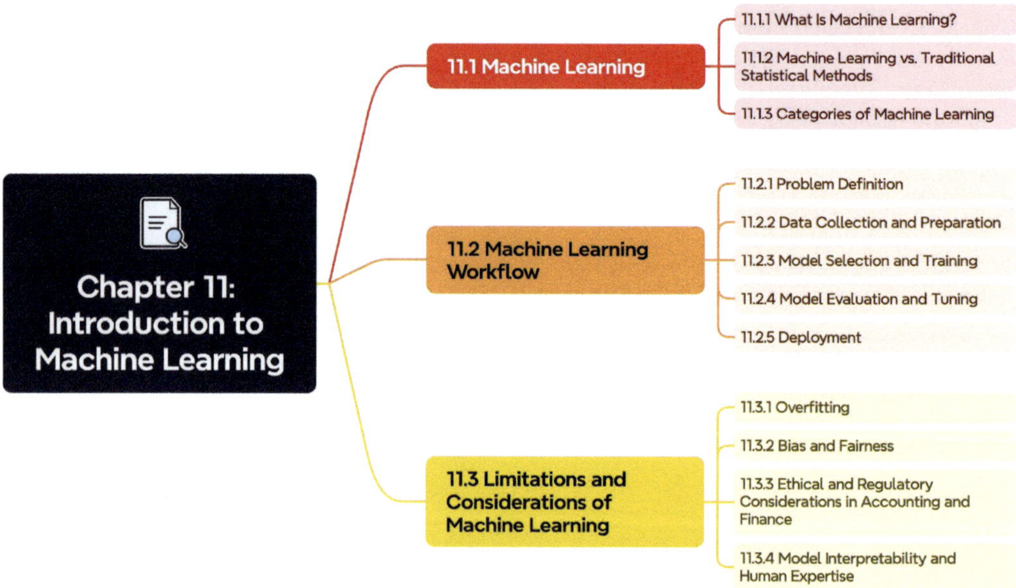

FIGURE 11.1 Structure of Chapter 11

11

INTRODUCTION TO MACHINE LEARNING

This chapter introduces core concepts of machine learning with a focus on how they apply to accounting and finance. It explains the differences between machine learning and traditional statistical methods; explores key categories such as supervised, unsupervised, and reinforcement learning; and describes the workflow from data preparation to deployment. The chapter also presents the potential uses and limitations of machine learning in accounting and financial contexts (Figure 11.1).

Learning Objectives

By the end of this chapter, you will be able to

- Distinguish between supervised, unsupervised, and reinforcement learning, and identify use cases in accounting and finance.
- Describe the stages of a standard machine learning workflow.
- Identify challenges in machine learning and explain methods for addressing them.

11.1 Machine Learning

Machine learning is a method by which computers learn from data to make decisions or predictions. This section introduces key concepts and categories, and compares machine learning with traditional statistical methods (see Figure 11.2).

11.1.1 What Is Machine Learning?

Machine learning involves developing algorithms that learn patterns from data to make predictions or decisions without explicit programming (Samuel, 1959). Rather than following instructions for each possible scenario, the computer identifies patterns in data and uses them to make decisions or predictions.

DOI: 10.4324/9781003656968-11

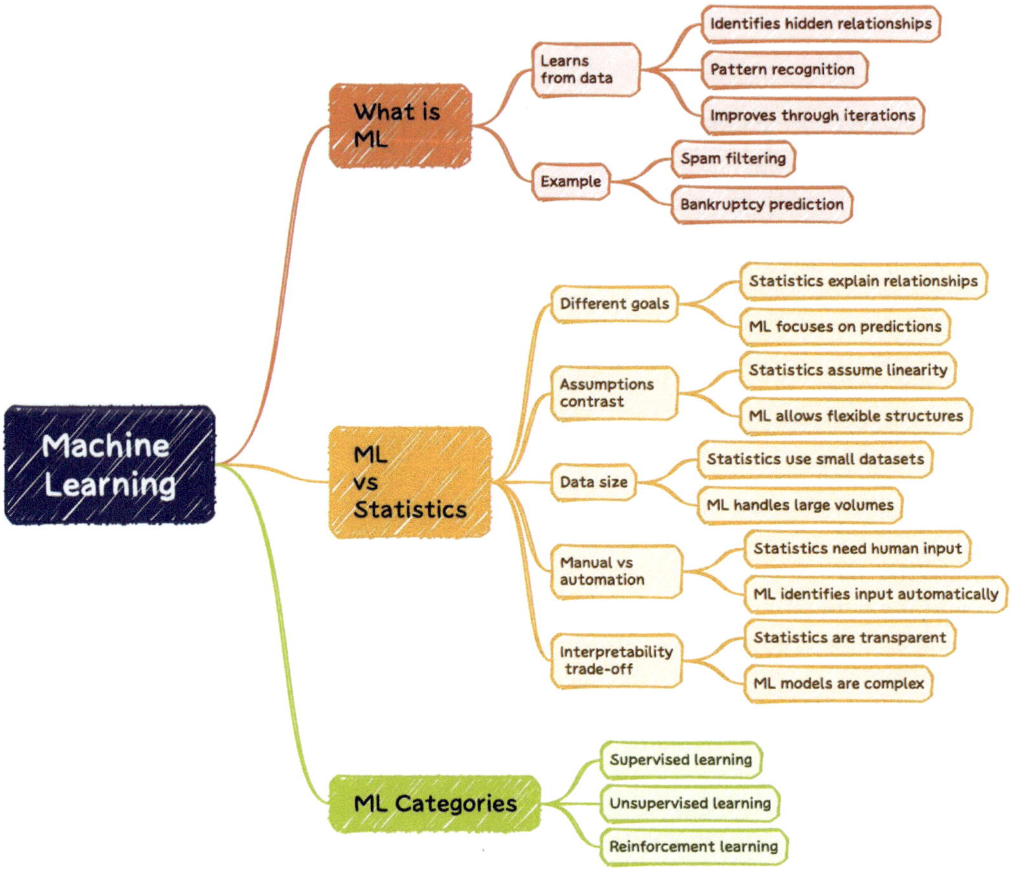

FIGURE 11.2 Machine Learning

For example an email spam filter is trained on a large set of emails labelled as 'spam' or 'not spam'. The algorithm learns which words, phrases, sender details, or patterns tend to appear in spam emails. Based on these features, it builds a model that predicts whether a new email is likely to be spam.

In accounting and finance, machine learning can be applied to historical financial statements to identify patterns that predict bankruptcy. A model trained on such data may detect that companies with certain financial ratios or trends are more likely to go bankrupt. It can then use these patterns to evaluate new cases and predict bankruptcy risk.

Machine learning is a subset of artificial intelligence (AI). AI refers to systems designed to perform tasks that require human intelligence, such as recognition, reasoning, and decision-making. Machine learning contributes to AI by providing algorithms that enable computers to learn from data and adjust based on new input and outcomes. Through this process, performance improves over time on specific tasks.

11.1.2 Machine Learning vs. Traditional Statistical Methods

Many machine learning concepts are grounded in statistics (Rashidi et al., 2023). However, differences exist between machine learning and traditional statistical methods in terms of (i) objectives, (ii) assumptions, (iii) data requirements, (iv) model flexibility, and (v) interpretability.

Firstly, traditional statistical models focus on explaining relationships between variables and testing hypotheses. For example linear regression is used to estimate coefficients and assess whether a change in one variable affects another. In accounting and finance, this might involve testing whether debt levels affect stock returns. Machine learning, on the other hand, is designed for prediction. It focuses on identifying patterns in data without predefining the relationships. A machine learning model might use multiple financial indicators to forecast stock performance by detecting patterns, rather than testing specified links between variables.

Secondly, statistical models rely on assumptions about the data, such as linearity or normality. They are often parametric, with a fixed model structure and a set of parameters to estimate. Machine learning models, by contrast, typically avoid such assumptions. Many are non-parametric and allow the data to determine the structure of the model. For example a traditional credit risk model may assume a linear relationship between risk factors and default probability. A machine learning model, such as a decision tree, does not impose a fixed model structure and can capture non-linear and complex interactions.

Thirdly, traditional statistical models work best with smaller, structured datasets and a limited number of variables. They often struggle with high-dimensional or unstructured data. Machine learning, by contrast, can handle large-scale, high-dimensional data. Machine learning methods can include dozens of variables and train on millions of data points. They use computational power to identify patterns that would exceed the capacity of traditional approaches. For example a machine learning algorithm can analyse all entries in a company's ledger to flag unusual transactions, whereas a traditional audit method might examine only a sample.

Fourthly, building a statistical model often requires manual input, for example selecting variables, choosing functional forms, and performing diagnostic checks. Machine learning automates much of this work. Algorithms can identify relevant inputs and their relationships with outputs, reducing the need for manual specification. However, human expertise remains necessary, especially in data preparation and interpretation. The focus shifts from manual modelling to computational processes, which can shorten research or development time.

Finally, a trade-off is that machine learning models are often complex and less transparent than traditional statistical models. A linear regression provides coefficients that can be explained directly. For example if the dependent variable is earnings per share and one independent variable is the debt ratio, a coefficient of –0.8 indicates that holding other factors constant, a one percentage-point increase in the debt ratio is associated with a £0.80 reduction in earnings per share. In contrast, a machine learning model may combine multiple decision trees or neural network layers; it can be difficult to trace how a particular prediction is formed. In practice, machine learning often exchanges transparency for improved predictive performance (Luo et al., 2019).

11.1.3 Categories of Machine Learning

Machine learning algorithms fall into several categories. The three major ones are (i) supervised learning, (ii) unsupervised learning, and (iii) reinforcement learning.

11.1.3.1 Supervised Learning

In supervised learning, the algorithm is trained on data with known outputs. Each input is paired with its corresponding outcome, forming labelled data (Jiang et al., 2020). The model learns to map inputs to outputs and applies this mapping to predict outputs for new inputs (see Figure 11.3).

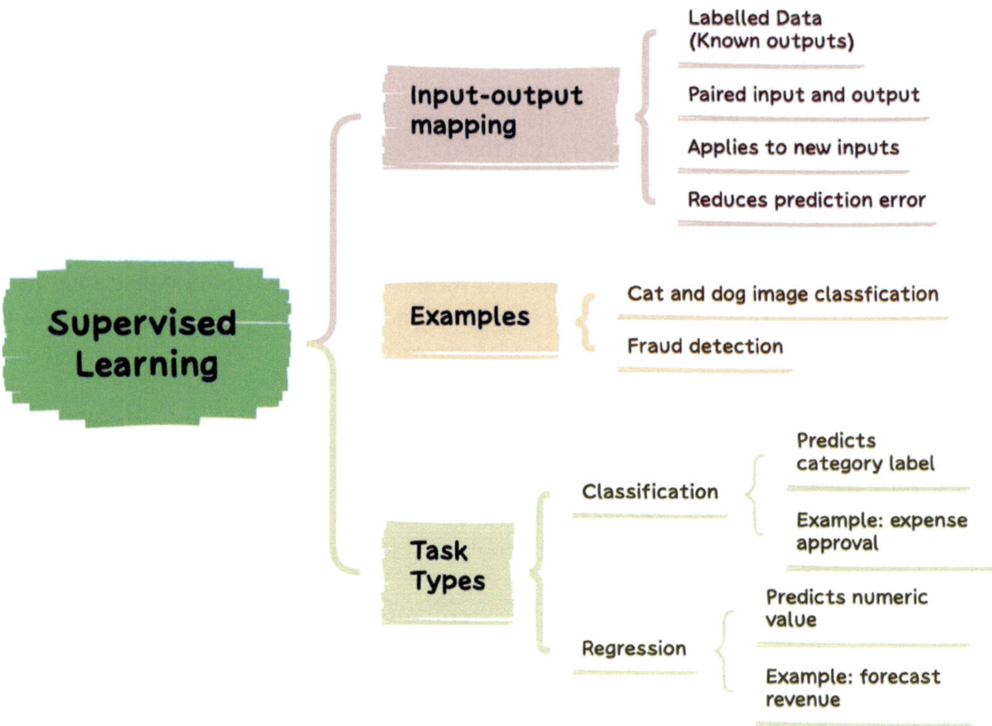

FIGURE 11.3 Supervised Learning

For example consider a dataset of images of cats and dogs, each labelled as either 'cat' or 'dog'. During training, the model uses each image as an input and the corresponding label as the output. The model compares its predictions with the known labels and adjusts its parameters to reduce error.

In accounting and finance, a model can be trained to detect fraud using a dataset of past transactions. Each transaction is labelled as 'fraudulent' or 'legitimate'. The model uses these labels to evaluate its predictions and adjusts its parameters to reduce error.

Supervised learning includes two main types of tasks: classification and regression.

- Classification refers to tasks where the output is a category. For example a model may classify an expense as either allowed or disallowed under a company's policy. In credit scoring, a model may assign borrowers to categories such as low, medium, or high risk based on historical data.

- Regression refers to tasks where the output is a continuous number. A model may estimate a company's future stock price or predict revenue for the next quarter. The model is trained on historical data with continuous outcomes and learns to predict numerical values for new cases.

11.1.3.2 Unsupervised Learning

Unsupervised learning uses unlabelled data. The algorithm is not provided with outputs or correct answers and must identify patterns or structures in the data (see Figure 11.4).

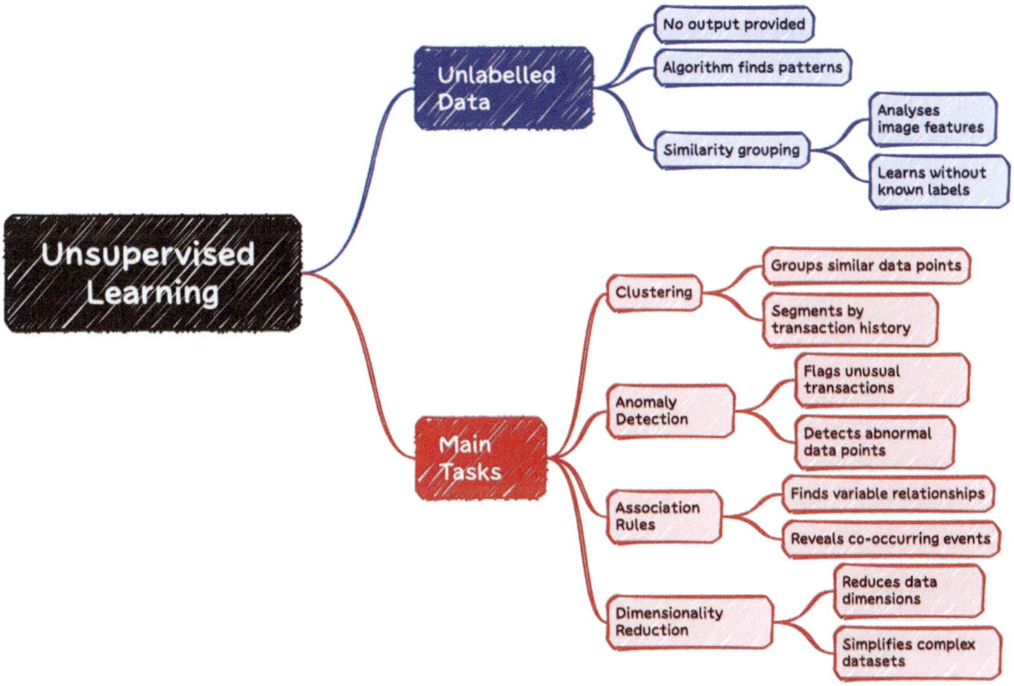

FIGURE 11.4 Unsupervised Learning

For example consider a dataset of images of cats and dogs without any labels. The algorithm does not know which image shows a cat or a dog. It analyses features in the images and groups them by similarity.

Unsupervised learning involves several types of tasks. The main tasks include clustering, anomaly detection, association rule learning, and dimensionality reduction.

- Clustering involves grouping data points with similar characteristics into clusters. In accounting and finance, clustering can be used to segment customers based on transaction histories. For example the algorithm may identify groups such as high-frequency traders or passive investors, without relying on prior labels.
- Anomaly detection focuses on identifying data points that differ from the rest. A model may learn the characteristics of normal transactions and flag those that deviate from these patterns.

- Association rules identify relationships between variables in a dataset. In accounting and finance, this method can uncover links between financial indicators or events. For example, it may show that a sudden increase in a particular expense account is often followed by a revenue restatement in the next quarter.
- Dimensionality reduction reduces the number of variables in the dataset while retaining key information. In accounting and finance, this method can summarise large datasets by reducing dozens of economic indicators to a smaller set of latent factors.

11.1.3.3 Reinforcement Learning

Reinforcement learning involves an agent that interacts with an environment, takes actions, and receives feedback in the form of rewards or penalties (Sutton & Barto, 2018). The agent learns through trial and error to improve future decisions and maximise outcomes (see Figure 11.5).

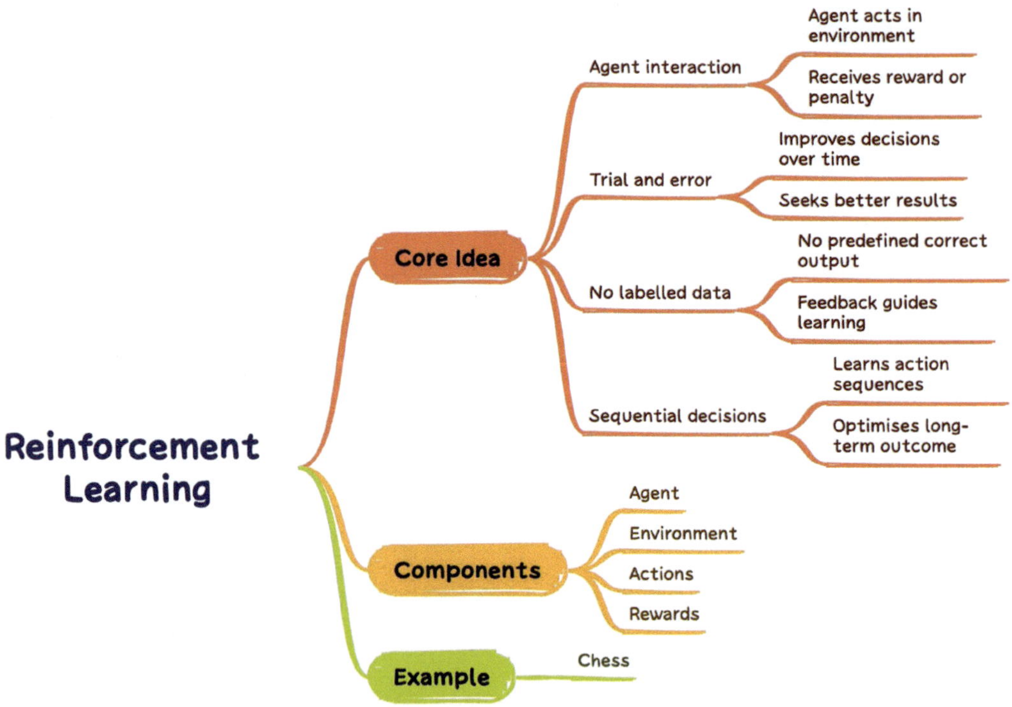

FIGURE 11.5 Reinforcement Learning

Reinforcement learning differs from supervised and unsupervised learning. Reinforcement learning does not rely on labelled data, so it does not follow the structure of supervised learning. It also does not focus on identifying structure in static data, which is typical of unsupervised learning. Instead, reinforcement learning focuses on sequential decision-making. The agent adjusts its actions based on past outcomes to improve performance over time.

Reinforcement learning includes four components: the agent, which makes decisions; the environment, which interacts with the agent; actions, which are the choices available to the agent; and rewards, which provide numerical feedback from the environment. The agent's objective is to learn a strategy that increases the total reward over time.

For example, reinforcement learning can train an algorithm to play chess. The algorithm does not receive labelled data showing the best move in each position. Instead, it plays many games against itself, receives rewards for winning and penalties for losing, and updates its strategy based on the outcomes. Over time, it identifies which sequences of moves lead to better results.

11.2 Machine Learning Workflow

Machine learning follows a sequence of steps that connect a business problem to a deployed model that generates outputs. This sequence, known as the machine learning workflow, is adapted from the CRISP-DM framework (Shearer, 2000). The main stages are problem definition, data collection and preparation, model selection and training, model evaluation and tuning, and deployment (see Figure 11.6).

FIGURE 11.6 ML Workflow

11.2.1 Problem Definition

A machine learning project begins with a defined problem statement. This involves translating a business or research question into a machine learning task and identifying the context in which the model will operate. Problem definition includes three components: business objectives, data requirements, and project constraints and risks.

Business Objectives: What outcome is required from a business perspective? In fraud detection, for example is the aim to reduce financial loss, meet compliance requirements, or increase audit coverage? Which stakeholders need to be involved to ensure the machine learning project addresses a specific purpose and supports decision-making?

Data Requirements: What data is required to train and assess the model? Is there access to historical invoice data with fraud labels? What other sources could provide relevant input? Where will the data come from, and what restrictions apply due to privacy laws, regulations, or internal policy? If the data includes employee communication records, how does this align with General Data Protection Regulation (GDPR) and organisational consent procedures?

Project Constraints and Risks: What risks need to be considered at the outset? Could changes in fraud patterns reduce model accuracy? What are the effects of false negatives, where the model fails to identify fraudulent cases, and false positives, where the model incorrectly flags legitimate cases as fraudulent? How would the organisation manage the costs of missed fraud versus unnecessary investigations or reputational harm? Should one type of error be prioritised, and how would that affect model design and evaluation?

11.2.2 Data Collection and Preparation

The next stage is to collect and prepare the data. The performance of the model depends on the quality of the input data.

Data Collection: Data collection begins with the identification of all sources that contain information relevant to the task. In the case of analysing supplier payment performance, potential sources include the purchase ledger, which contains invoice records such as amounts, dates, supplier details, and authoriser information. External sources may also be relevant, such as credit ratings or industry benchmarks. If data is stored across multiple systems, integration is required to produce a unified dataset.

Data Cleaning: Real-world data often contain missing values, duplicates, and inconsistencies (Rahm & Do, 2000). For example the same supplier may be recorded under different names, or invoice records may be duplicated or contain invalid entries. Data cleaning involves identifying and correcting these issues. When values are missing, a decision is required to impute them or to remove the affected records. Outliers or invalid entries, such as negative invoice amounts, must be examined and addressed. This process ensures that the dataset used is accurate and consistent for modelling.

Exploratory Data Analysis (EDA): Before model training, EDA is used to examine distributions, relationships, and anomalies in the data. This includes plotting variables, calculating correlations, and summarising key statistics (Mukhiya & Ahmed, 2020). EDA can also identify issues such as imbalance, where only a small number of records fall into a specific category (Chawla, 2002). This may require resampling or the use of algorithms that handle imbalance. If the data include a time dimension, it may be necessary to split the data chronologically to examine whether patterns change over time, especially in forecasting tasks.

11.2.3 Model Selection and Training

This stage involves selecting a machine learning algorithm and training a model.

Selecting an Algorithm: The selection of the algorithm depends on several factors. These include the nature of the task, such as classification, regression, or clustering. The selection also depends on the size of the dataset and the number of features, as some algorithms are more effective with high-dimensional data or larger datasets. Computational capacity and time constraints also influence the selection, as some algorithms require more processing time and resources.

Training the Model: Model training involves feeding the prepared data into the algorithm so that it can learn the relationship between the inputs and the target output. Most algorithms require the selection of hyperparameters (i.e. settings that guide the learning process). Examples include the number of trees, the maximum depth of each tree, or the learning rate in a neural network. The training process depends on the algorithm but follows a general structure. The model generates predictions using the training data, compares these predictions with the actual outcomes, and calculates the error. Based on this error, it then adjusts its internal parameters to improve accuracy. This process repeats until the model meets a stopping condition, such as a fixed number of iterations or a plateau in performance improvement.

11.2.4 Model Evaluation and Tuning

This stage assesses whether the model meets defined success criteria and whether it is likely to perform well on new data. Model tuning may also be required to improve performance or to prioritise certain outcomes, such as reducing false negatives or false positives, depending on the context.

Evaluation Metrics: The choice of evaluation metrics depends on the task. In classification, common metrics include accuracy, precision, recall, and the F1 score. Accuracy measures the proportion of correct predictions among all predictions. Precision measures the proportion of predicted fraud cases that are actual fraud. Recall measures the proportion of actual fraud cases that are correctly identified. The F1 score, calculated as the harmonic mean of precision and recall, combines both into a single measure.

In regression tasks, common metrics include root mean square error (RMSE) and mean absolute error (MAE). RMSE calculates the square root of the average squared differences between predicted and actual values, which gives greater weight to larger errors. MAE calculates the average of the absolute differences between predicted and actual values, providing a direct measure of prediction error.

Tuning: If model performance does not meet expectations, several tuning strategies can be applied. Hyperparameter tuning involves adjusting settings such as learning rate, number of trees, or maximum tree depth. Search methods can help identify combinations that improve validation performance.

If many false negatives come from a specific group, a new variable representing group classification or associated risk can be added. A different algorithm may be tested if the current one fails to capture relevant patterns.

Overfitting occurs when a model performs well on training data but poorly on validation data. This can be addressed by simplifying the model or increasing the size of the training set. Classification thresholds may also be adjusted. A higher threshold can improve precision, while a lower threshold can increase recall.

11.2.5 Deployment

Deployment involves placing the machine learning model into use so it can support real tasks. This can take different forms. For example the model may run once a week to process new invoices and flag potential cases for review or it may operate in real time, checking each invoice as it is entered. Some organisations use an application programming interface, which allows other systems to send data to the model and receive results.

Key technical considerations include selecting the platform on which the model will run (e.g. a cloud service or local server) and ensuring the system can process the expected volume of data. After deployment, the model's performance must be monitored. This includes checking whether the model continues to detect relevant cases, such as fraud. If the characteristics of the data change, model accuracy may decline. Regular performance checks are thus required.

Models often require updates based on new data to remain effective. There should be assigned responsibilities for managing the model and procedures for periodic review. Regulatory requirements may also apply. Organisations are expected to provide explanations of how their models function and to maintain human oversight throughout the model lifecycle.

11.3 Limitations and Considerations of Machine Learning

When machine learning models are used to support decisions, users must identify and address issues that can lead to errors or unintended outcomes. This section examines four concerns: overfitting, bias, ethical and regulatory constraints, and model interpretability (see Figure 11.7).

11.3.1 Overfitting

Overfitting is a common issue in machine learning. Overfitting occurs when a model learns patterns in the training data that are either random or specific to that dataset (Montesinos López, 2022). As a result, the model performs well on the training data but fails to generalise to new data.

Overfitting is more likely when the model is too complex in relation to the size or quality of the data. For example, if we build a model to predict bankruptcy based on data from only 100 companies using 50 variables, the model may detect patterns that reflect coincidence rather than useful relationships, such as links between CEO names or auditor choices and bankruptcy. These patterns may not apply to new companies. This issue is common in accounting and finance, where data is often limited or may change over time.

There are several ways to reduce the risk of overfitting. One approach is to split the data into training, validation, and test sets. If the model performs much better on the training set than on the validation or test sets, this may indicate overfitting. Cross-validation,

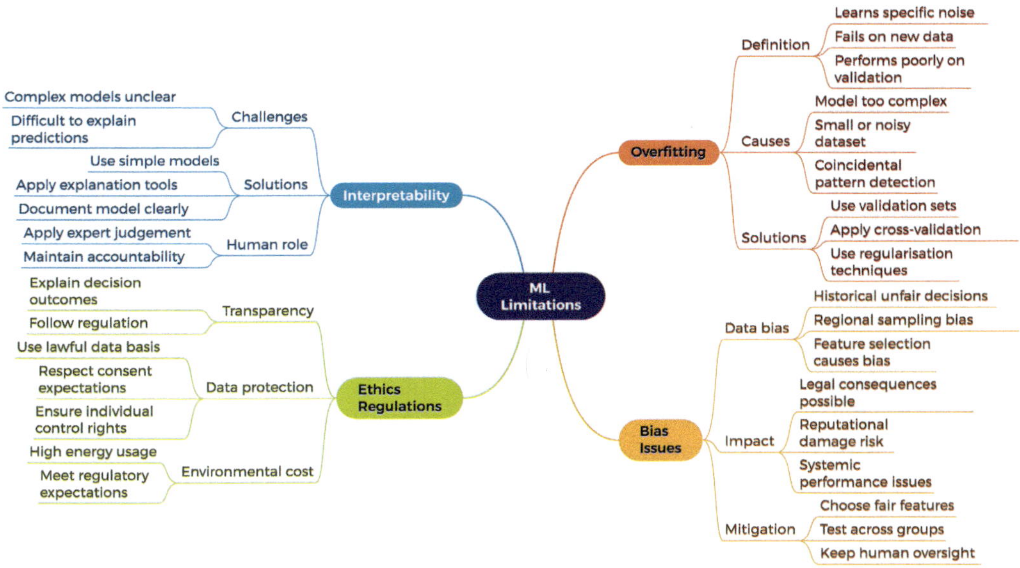

FIGURE 11.7 ML Limitations

which tests the model on different subsets of the data, provides further evidence of performance consistency. Another method is regularisation, which applies constraints to limit model complexity. In some cases, applying domain knowledge can also prevent the model from learning patterns that lack practical meaning.

11.3.2 Bias and Fairness

Machine learning models can produce unfair outcomes as they learn from historical data, which may reflect existing bias (Barocas & Selbst, 2016). For example if a bank has historically approved fewer loans for certain groups, a machine learning model may reproduce that pattern. This can lead to decisions that disadvantage certain communities, even if the model is not explicitly designed to discriminate. This is of importance in accounting and finance, as such models influence access to credit, insurance, and investment.

Bias can arise at different stages of the machine learning process. In some cases, the training data reflects past practices that were unfair, causing the model to reproduce those patterns. In other cases, the method of data collection introduces bias. For example if a model is trained only on data from one region, it may not apply well in another. The selection of features can also introduce bias. For example, using a person's postcode may indirectly reveal income level, which can lead to unfair results.

Bias in machine learning is not only a technical issue but can also lead to legal, ethical, and reputational consequences. Financial institutions in the UK must comply with legislation such as the Equality Act 2010, which aims to prevent individuals from unlawful discrimination. A model that provides more accurate investment advice to men than to women, for example, would likely breach these expectations. Biased models can damage a company's reputation and introduce systemic risks if they fail to perform adequately for underrepresented groups.

There are several ways to reduce bias in machine learning models. It is important to select features carefully and avoid those that may act as proxies for protected characteristics such as gender or race. After training a model, the model's performance should be tested across different groups to assess fairness. Where possible, critical decisions should involve human review to identify issues the model may not detect. It is also necessary, legally or ethically, to provide explanations of how decisions are made and to maintain transparency throughout the process.

11.3.3 Ethical and Regulatory Considerations in Accounting and Finance

When machine learning is applied in accounting and finance, the concern extends beyond model performance. Financial decisions, such as loan approval or fraud detection, affect individuals and carry legal and ethical responsibilities.

One key issue is transparency. If a model influences or determines a decision, the firm must provide a clear explanation. UK regulations, including the Consumer Duty and the GDPR, require firms to explain automated decisions (FCA, 2022; Leslie, 2020). For example if a model rejects a loan application, the reason should be stated clearly, such as income being below the required threshold. Even when using complex models, firms are expected to apply tools that produce appropriate explanations for customers and regulators.

Machine learning models often use personal data, which is protected under data protection laws. Firms must have a lawful basis for using customer data and must avoid using it in ways the customer would not reasonably expect. Another concern is consent and individual control. Customers have the right to request human review of fully automated decisions, especially when those decisions involve significant consequences (Leslie, 2020). As a result, many firms use machine learning to support human decisions rather than replace them.

The development and use of large-scale machine learning models can require high levels of computing power and energy consumption (Strubell et al., 2020). Financial institutions are now expected to assess the environmental impact of their systems. Regulatory bodies in the UK and internationally are increasing oversight of how machine learning is used in financial services and are likely to introduce further requirements to ensure safety, fairness, and accountability.

11.3.4 Model Interpretability and Human Expertise

In accounting and finance, it is necessary to make accurate predictions and also to understand the basis for those predictions. Some models such as linear regression allow users to identify which factors influence the output. However, some models are more difficult to interpret. This lack of transparency can reduce trust.

There are several ways to make complex models easier to understand. One approach is to use simple models, such as decision trees or linear models, when possible. Another approach is to apply explanation tools that describe which input variables had the greatest influence on the model's prediction. Breaking large problems into smaller steps can also help, for example by grouping data first and then applying simpler models to each group. Clear documentation is also necessary. This includes explaining what data is used, what the model does, and any known limitations. These practices help others understand the model and improve trust in the model's application.

Human expertise remains necessary even when machine learning models are available (ACCA, 2019). Financial professionals must understand how tools support their work and continue to apply professional judgement. Relying solely on model results without review can lead to poor decisions. For example if a model suggests approving a loan but the officer identifies a concern, further assessment should be carried out. Legal and professional responsibilities remain with the individual. Those using a model are accountable for how its outputs are used. For this reason, firms often implement review and approval procedures before adopting new models.

Summary of Chapter 11: Introduction to Machine Learning

In this chapter, we have covered the following key concepts:

What Is Machine Learning?

- Machine learning enables computers to learn patterns from data to support decisions or predictions.
- Unlike traditional programming, machine learning does not require explicit rules for each task.
- Machine learning is a subset of AI that focuses on learning from data.

Machine Learning vs. Traditional Statistical Methods

- Machine learning prioritises prediction; statistical methods focus on inference and hypothesis testing.
- Machine learning models are often non-parametric and require fewer assumptions.
- Machine learning processes large, complex, and high-dimensional datasets effectively.
- Machine learning supports automation in model selection and tuning but may reduce interpretability.
- Statistical models provide transparency; machine learning models often involve a trade-off between performance and interpretability.

Categories of Machine Learning

- Supervised Learning: uses labelled data to train models for classification or regression tasks.
- Unsupervised Learning: identifies structure in unlabelled data through clustering, anomaly detection, or association rules.
- Reinforcement Learning: trains agents through trial and error to maximise rewards over time.

Machine Learning Workflow

- Problem Definition: identify business objectives, data requirements, and project constraints.
- Data Collection and Preparation: gather, clean, and explore data to ensure quality and relevance.
- Model Selection and Training: select algorithms, set hyperparameters, and train the model.
- Model Evaluation and Tuning: evaluate performance using metrics and adjust for improvement.
- Deployment: integrate models into systems and monitor performance over time.

Model Evaluation Metrics

- Classification: accuracy, precision, recall, and F1 score.
- Regression: RMSE and MAE.
- Metric selection depends on business requirements and the decision context.

Common Challenges and Considerations

- Overfitting: the model captures noise rather than signal, reducing generalisability.
- Bias and Fairness: historical data can introduce or reinforce bias.
- Ethical and Regulatory Compliance: legal requirements include transparency, data protection (e.g. GDPR), and equal treatment.
- Interpretability: simpler models or explanation tools support user understanding.
- Human Expertise: necessary for oversight, judgement, and accountability in financial decision-making.

Quiz Questions

Scan the QR code below to access the quiz questions for this chapter (see 11.md).

https://github.com/DrMichaelGuo/QuizPFAAFAMMA

References

Association of Chartered Certified Accountants (ACCA) (2019) *Machine learning: More science than fiction*. London: ACCA. Available at: https://www.accaglobal.com/uk/en/professional-insights/technology/machine-learning.html (Accessed 5 August 2025).

Barocas, S. and Selbst, A.D. (2016) 'Big data's disparate impact', *California Law Review*, 104(3), pp. 671–732.

Chawla, N.V., Bowyer, K.W., Hall, L.O. and Kegelmeyer, W.P. (2002) 'SMOTE: Synthetic minority over-sampling technique', *Journal of Artificial Intelligence Research*, 16, pp. 321–357.

Financial Conduct Authority (FCA) (2022) *Policy statement PS22/9: A new consumer duty*. London: FCA. Available at: https://www.fca.org.uk/publications/policy-statements/ps22-9-new-consumer-duty (Accessed 5 August 2025).

Jiang, T., Gradus, J.L. and Rosellini, A.J. (2020) 'Supervised machine learning: A brief primer', *Behavior Therapy*, 51(5), pp. 675–687.

Leslie, D. (2020) *Explaining decisions made with AI*. Available at SSRN: http://dx.doi.org/10.2139/ssrn.4033308 (Accessed 5 August 2025).

Luo, Y., Tseng, H.H., Cui, S., Wei, L., Ten Haken, R.K. and El Naqa, I. (2019) 'Balancing accuracy and interpretability of machine learning approaches for radiation treatment outcomes modelling', *BJR Open*, 1(1), p. 20190021.

Montesinos López, O.A., Montesinos López, A. and Crossa, J. (2022) 'Overfitting, model tuning, and evaluation of prediction performance', in Montesinos López, O. A., Montesinos López, A., & Crossa, J. (eds.) *Multivariate statistical machine learning methods for genomic prediction*. Cham: Springer International Publishing, pp. 109–139.

Mukhiya, S.K. and Ahmed, U. (2020) *Hands-on exploratory data analysis with Python: Perform EDA techniques to understand, summarise, and investigate your data*. Birmingham: Packt Publishing.

Rahm, E. and Do, H.H. (2000) 'Data cleaning: Problems and current approaches', *IEEE Data Engineering Bulletin*, 23(4), pp. 3–13.

Rajula, H.S.R., Verlato, G., Manchia, M., Antonucci, N. and Fanos, V. (2020) 'Comparison of conventional statistical methods with machine learning in medicine: Diagnosis, drug development, and treatment', *Medicina*, 56(9), p. 455.

Rashidi, H.H., Albahra, S., Robertson, S., Tran, N.K. and Hu, B. (2023) 'Common statistical concepts in the supervised machine learning arena', *Frontiers in Oncology*, 13, p. 1130229.

Samuel, A.L. (1959) 'Some studies in machine learning using the game of checkers', *IBM Journal of Research and Development*, 3(3), 210–229.

Shearer, C. (2000) 'The CRISP-DM model: the new blueprint for data mining', *Journal of Data Warehousing*, 5(4), pp. 13–22.

Strubell, E., Ganesh, A. and McCallum, A. (2020) 'Energy and policy considerations for modern deep learning research', in *Proceedings of the AAAI Conference on Artificial Intelligence*, New York, 34(9), pp. 13693–13696.

Sutton, R.S. and Barto, A.G. (2018) *Reinforcement learning: An introduction*. 2nd edn. Cambridge: MIT Press.

FIGURE 12.1 Structure of Chapter 12

12

SUPERVISED LEARNING

This chapter introduces supervised machine learning methods and their application in accounting and finance. Students use Python and the scikit-learn library to apply decision trees, random forests, and logistic regression. Students will build, train, and evaluate predictive models for financial forecasting, credit risk assessment, and audit risk classification (Figure 12.1).

Learning Objectives

By the end of this chapter, you will be able to

- Build and evaluate supervised machine learning models, including decision trees, random forests, and logistic regression.
- Apply classification techniques to accounting and financial tasks.
- Interpret model performance using evaluation metrics.

12.1 Decision Trees

This section introduces decision trees, a method used in supervised machine learning. The section explains how to train and test a decision tree model and how to make predictions in an accounting and finance context (see Figure 12.2).

12.1.1 Key Concepts

12.1.1.1 Decision Tree

A decision tree is a model that splits the dataset based on feature values to make predictions. It is used for classification tasks.

DOI: 10.4324/9781003656968-12

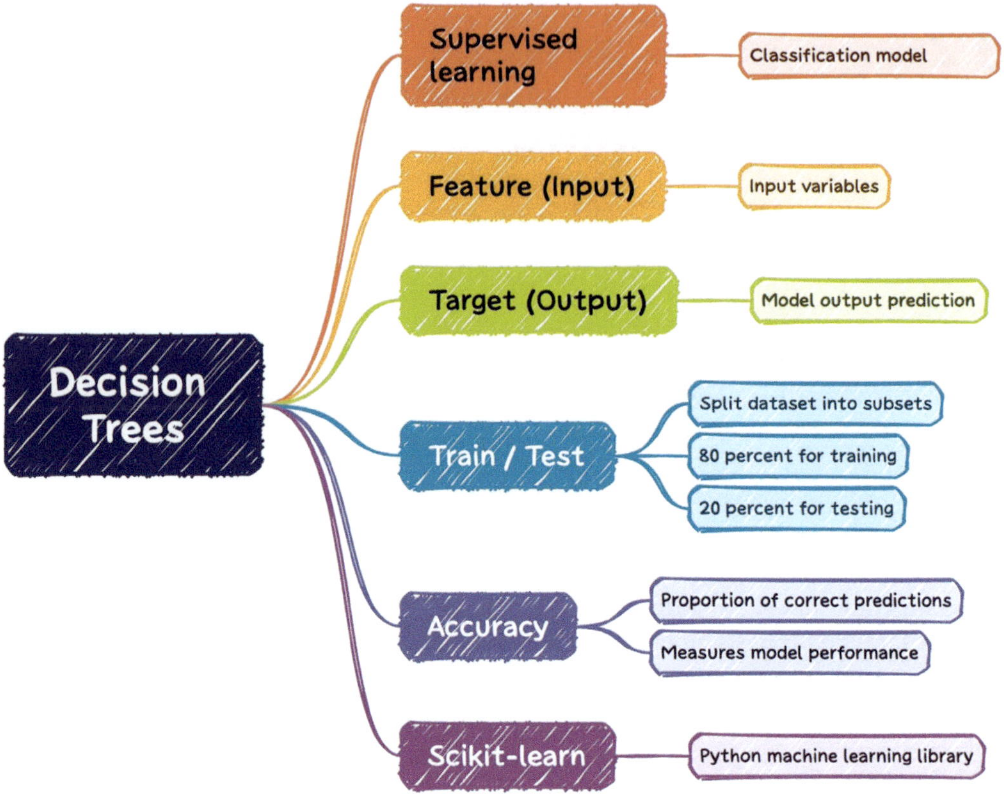

FIGURE 12.2 Decision Trees

For example, a decision tree model can predict a company's financial health category based on variables such as current ratio and debt-to-equity ratio.

12.1.1.2 Feature (Input)

Features are measurable input variables used to make a prediction such as current ratio and debt-to-equity ratio in the above example.

12.1.1.3 Target (Output)

The target is the output the model tries to predict, such as financial health in the above example.

12.1.1.4 Train–Test Split

Train–test split refers to dividing the dataset into two subsets: one for training the model and one for testing it. The training subset is used to learn patterns, while the testing subset is used to evaluate performance. A common split ratio is 80% for training and 20% for testing.

12.1.1.5 Accuracy

Accuracy is the proportion of correct predictions made by the model. It is calculated as the number of correct predictions divided by the total number of predictions.

12.1.1.6 Scikit-learn

Scikit-learn is a Python library for machine learning. It provides tools for data preparation, model building, and performance evaluation.

12.1.2 Follow-Along Activity

This activity shows how to build and evaluate a decision tree model using a small dataset for financial health classification (see Figure 12.3).

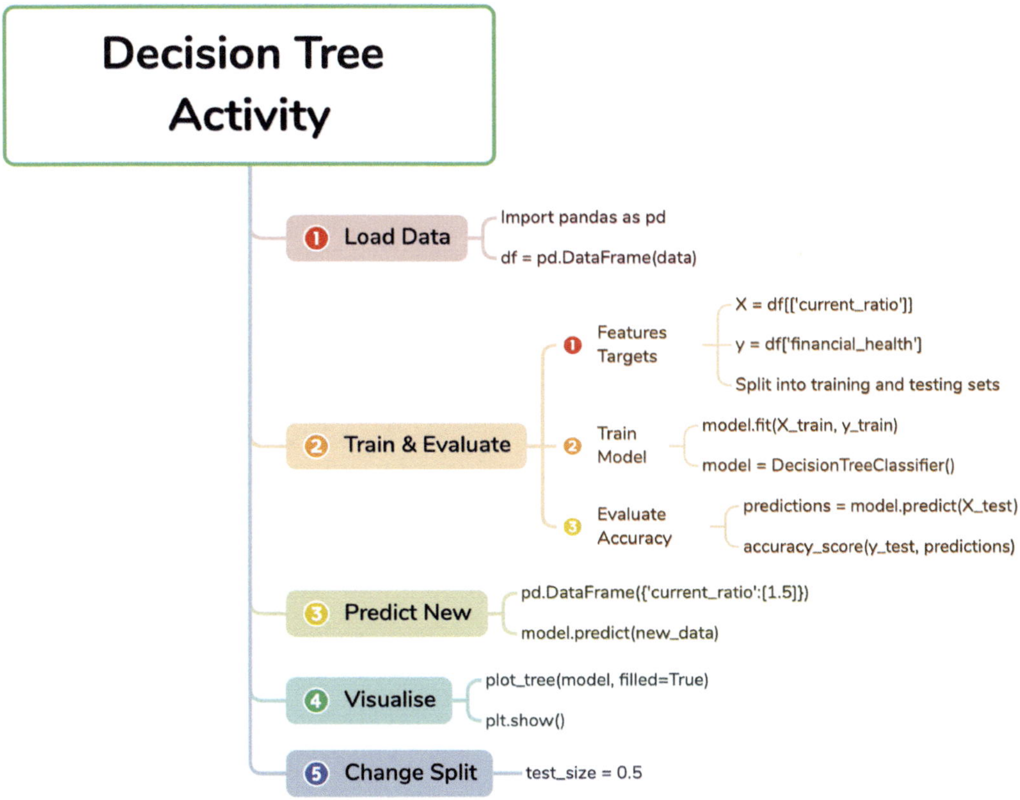

FIGURE 12.3 Decision Tree Activity

Step 1: Load the Dataset

Let's begin by loading the data and printing the first few rows of the dataset. The dataset contains three attributes: current_ratio, debt_to_equity_ratio, and financial_health.

```
import pandas as pd

data = {
    'current_ratio': [
        1.8, 2.5, 1.2, 0.9, 1.4,
        1.1, 3.2, 2.8, 0.7, 1.9,
        2.0, 2.4, 1.6, 2.7, 1.3,
        1.5, 3.1, 0.8, 1.0, 2.2
    ],
    'debt_to_equity_ratio': [
        0.5, 0.3, 1.8, 2.2, 1.2,
        2.5, 0.4, 0.6, 2.8, 0.7,
        0.9, 0.5, 1.3, 0.6, 1.7,
        1.1, 0.3, 2.6, 2.0, 0.8
    ],
    'financial_health': [
        "Healthy", "Healthy", "At Risk",
        "Critical", "At Risk", "Critical",
        "Healthy", "Healthy", "Critical",
        "Healthy", "At Risk", "Healthy",
        "At Risk", "Critical", "At Risk",
        "Critical", "Healthy", "Critical",
        "Critical", "Healthy"
    ]
}

df = pd.DataFrame(data)
print(df.head())
```

The dataset (12.1.ipynb; see 'Follow-Along Activity' section) is available at https://github.com/DrMichaelGuo/PFAAFAMMA

Output:

```
  current_ratio  debt_to_equity_ratio financial_health
0           1.8                   0.5          Healthy
1           2.5                   0.3          Healthy
2           1.2                   1.8          At Risk
3           0.9                   2.2         Critical
4           1.4                   1.2          At Risk
```

Explanation

- import pandas as pd: imports the pandas library and assigns the alias pd.
- The data block: defines a dictionary with three keys: 'current_ratio', 'debt_to_equity_ratio', and 'financial_health'. Each key maps to a list of 20 values.
- pd.DataFrame(data): converts the dictionary into a pandas DataFrame.
- print(df.head()): prints the first five rows of the DataFrame.

Step 2: Train and Evaluate the Decision Tree Model

Let's train and evaluate a decision tree model using the dataset. We train the model by separating variables into

- Features (inputs): current_ratio, debt_to_equity_ratio
- Target (output): financial_health

```
from sklearn.tree import DecisionTreeClassifier
from sklearn.model_selection import train_test_split
from sklearn.metrics import accuracy_score

# Define input features and target variable
X = df[['current_ratio', 'debt_to_equity_ratio']]
y = df['financial_health']

# Split into training and testing sets
X_train, X_test, y_train, y_test = train_test_split(X, y, test_
size=0.2, random_state=42)

# Train the Decision Tree model
model = DecisionTreeClassifier(random_state=42)
model.fit(X_train, y_train)

# Make predictions and evaluate the model
predictions = model.predict(X_test)
accuracy = accuracy_score(y_test, predictions)
print("Decision Tree Model Accuracy:", accuracy)
```

Output

```
Decision Tree Model Accuracy: 0.75
```

Explanation

- from sklearn.tree import DecisionTreeClassifier: imports the DecisionTreeClassifier tool from the sklearn.tree module. This provides the method for building and using a decision tree model.
- from sklearn.model_selection import train_test_split: imports the train_test_split function from the sklearn.model_selection module. This function is used to split the dataset into training and testing sets.
- from sklearn.metrics import accuracy_score: imports the accuracy_score function from the sklearn.metrics module. This function is used to calculate the proportion of correct predictions.
- X = df[['current_ratio', 'debt_to_equity_ratio']]: selects the input features from the DataFrame and assigns them to the variable X. Capital X is conventionally used to represent features in machine learning.
- y = df['financial_health']: selects the target variable financial_health from the DataFrame and assigns it to the variable y.

- X_train, X_test, y_train, y_test = train_test_split(X, y, test_size=0.2, random_state=42): splits the features (X) and the target (y) into training and testing sets.
  - 80% of the data is used for training.
  - 20% of the data is used for testing.
  - random_state=42: ensures that the split is reproducible.
- model = DecisionTreeClassifier(random_state=42): creates a decision tree model and assigns it to model. Setting random_state=42 ensures consistent results.
- model.fit(X_train, y_train): trains the decision tree model using the training data (X_train and y_train).
- predictions = model.predict(X_test): applies the trained model to the test features and stores the results in predictions.
- accuracy = accuracy_score(y_test, predictions): compares the predicted values (predictions) with the actual values (y_test) and stores the proportion of correct predictions in accuracy.
- The output 'Decision Tree Model Accuracy: 0.75' means that the decision tree model correctly predicted the financial health category for 75% of the test data.
  - The model was evaluated using 20% of the original dataset.
  - Out of all the predictions made on the test set, 75% matched the actual values.

Step 3: Predict on New Data

Let's use the trained model to predict the financial health for new input values.

```
# Create a new DataFrame for the sample input
new_data = pd.DataFrame({'current_ratio': [1.5],
'debt_to_equity_ratio': [1.2]})

# Predict the financial health using the trained model
predicted_health = model.predict(new_data)
print("Predicted financial health for new data:")
print(predicted_health)
```

Output:

```
Predicted financial health for new data:
['At Risk']
```

Explanation

- new_data = pd.DataFrame({'current_ratio': [1.5], 'debt_to_equity_ratio': [1.2]}): creates a new pandas DataFrame named new_data. It contains one row with values for current_ratio and debt_to_equity_ratio. These values will be used as input to the trained model.
- model.predict(new_data): applies the trained decision tree model to the values in new_data and generates a prediction. The result is stored in the variable predicted_health.
- print(...): prints the prediction result.

Try yourself: Change the input values and observe the result. For example

- current_ratio = 0.9 and debt_to_equity_ratio = 2.4
- current_ratio = 2.8 or debt_to_equity_ratio = 0.4

Step 4: Visualise the Decision Tree

Let's visualise how the decision tree model makes decisions based on the features.

```
import matplotlib.pyplot as plt
from sklearn.tree import plot_tree

# Visualise the decision tree
plt.figure(figsize=(20, 10))
plot_tree(
    model,
    filled=True,
    feature_names=['current_ratio', 'debt_to_equity_ratio'],
    class_names=model.classes_,
    rounded=True,
    fontsize=12
)
plt.title("Decision Tree: Financial Health of SMEs")
plt.show()
```

Output: see Figure 12.4.

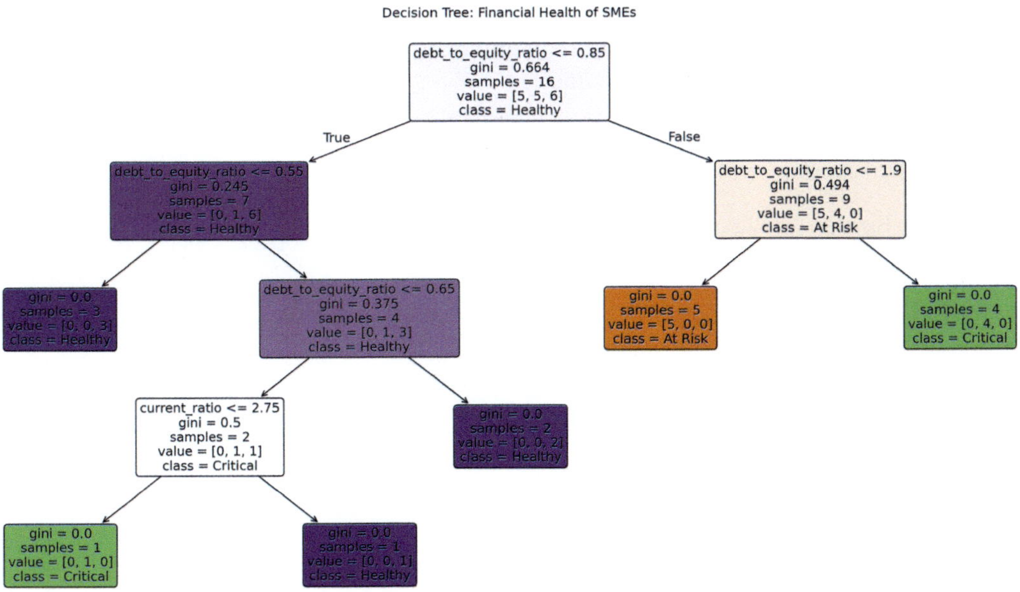

FIGURE 12.4 Decision Tree – Financial Health of SMEs

Explanation

- import matplotlib.pyplot as plt: imports the pyplot module from the Matplotlib library and assigns it the alias plt. This module is used for creating visualisations.
- from sklearn.tree import plot_tree: imports the plot_tree function from sklearn.tree. This function is used to draw a decision tree diagram.
- plt.figure(...): sets the figure size to 20 inches wide and 10 inches high.
- plot_tree(...): draws the structure of the decision tree using the following parameters:
  - model: the trained decision tree classifier.
  - filled=True: fills the nodes with colours based on the predicted class.
  - feature_names: specifies the names of the input features used in the model.
  - class_names: specifies the names of the target classes based on the training data.
  - rounded=True: rounds the corners of the boxes in the plot.
  - fontsize=12: sets the font size for the text in the plot.
- plt.show(): displays the plot.
- This decision tree shows how the model predicts financial health using two input ratios: debt_to_equity_ratio and current_ratio. The model begins at the top and follows branches based on threshold values. Each node shows how many training samples belong to each category: 'At Risk', 'Critical', or 'Healthy'. The Gini value measures how mixed the node is; a value of 0.0 means all samples in the node belong to one category. The model continues to split the data until it reaches a node with a clear classification. The coloured leaf nodes represent the final prediction for each combination of input values.

Step 5: Change the Test Size

We have trained the model using an 80/20 split. Now let's change the test size to 0.5, so that 50% of the data is used for training and 50% for testing. This change allows us to observe how the test size affects accuracy.

```
X_train, X_test, y_train, y_test = train_test_split(X, y, test_
size=0.5, random_state=42) # Change test_size to 0.5

model = DecisionTreeClassifier(random_state=42)
model.fit(X_train, y_train)

predictions = model.predict(X_test)
accuracy = accuracy_score(y_test, predictions)
print("Decision Tree Model Accuracy:", accuracy)
```

Output

```
Decision Tree Model Accuracy: 0.1
```

Explanation

- With a test size of 0.5, the model is trained on only half of the dataset. The accuracy drops to 0.1, meaning the model correctly predicted 10% of the test labels.

- This result suggests that with fewer training samples, the model was unable to learn enough patterns. As a result, its predictions on the test data were mostly incorrect. The accuracy is much lower than in the 80/20 split, where more data is available for training.

12.1.3 *Your Project*

Write Python code to build a decision tree model to predict mental health risk using the following dataset. The dataset contains 20 records, with three variables: stress level, coping ability, and mental health risk. Each record includes values for stress level and coping ability (both measured on a scale from 1 to 10) and a corresponding risk category: low, moderate, or high.

```
# Dataset
data = {
    "stress_level": [
        2, 4, 6, 8, 9,
        3, 5, 7, 10, 1,
        8, 6, 4, 7, 9,
        5, 3, 10, 2, 7
    ],
    "coping_ability": [
        9, 8, 7, 5, 3,
        8, 7, 6, 2, 10,
        4, 7, 8, 5, 3,
        7, 9, 2, 10, 5
    ],
    "mental_health_risk": [
        "Low", "Low", "Moderate",
        "Moderate", "High", "Low",
        "Moderate", "Moderate", "High",
        "Low", "High", "Moderate",
        "Low", "Moderate", "High",
        "Moderate", "Low", "High",
        "Low", "Moderate"
    ]
}
```

The dataset (12.1.ipynb; see 'Your Project' section) is available at
https://github.com/DrMichaelGuo/PFAAFAMMA
Note: This dataset is for coding practice only and does not represent clinical guidance.

12.1.3.1 *Tasks*

- Load the dataset.
- Train and evaluate a decision tree model using stress level and coping ability as features (input), and mental health risk as the target (output) variable.
- Predict the output for new input (e.g. stress_level: 1, coping_ability: 9).
- Visualise the decision tree.

12.1.3.2 Example Code

```
import pandas as pd

# Define the Mental Health Risk dataset
data = {
    "stress_level": [
        2, 4, 6, 8, 9,
        3, 5, 7, 10, 1,
        8, 6, 4, 7, 9,
        5, 3, 10, 2, 7
    ],
    "coping_ability": [
        9, 8, 7, 5, 3,
        8, 7, 6, 2, 10,
        4, 7, 8, 5, 3,
        7, 9, 2, 10, 5
    ],
    "mental_health_risk": [
        "Low", "Low", "Moderate",
        "Moderate", "High", "Low",
        "Moderate", "Moderate", "High",
        "Low", "High", "Moderate",
        "Low", "Moderate", "High",
        "Moderate", "Low", "High",
        "Low", "Moderate"
    ]
}

# Convert the dictionary into a DataFrame
df = pd.DataFrame(data)

# Display the first few rows of the dataset
print(df.head())
```

```
from sklearn.tree import DecisionTreeClassifier
from sklearn.model_selection import train_test_split
from sklearn.metrics import accuracy_score

# Define input features and the target variable
X = df[['stress_level', 'coping_ability']]
y = df['mental_health_risk']

# Split the data into training and testing sets (80% training, 20%
testing)
X_train, X_test, y_train, y_test = train_test_split(X, y, test_
size=0.2, random_state=42)

# Initialise and train the Decision Tree model
model = DecisionTreeClassifier()
model.fit(X_train, y_train)
```

```
# Make predictions on the test set and evaluate the model
predictions = model.predict(X_test)
accuracy = accuracy_score(y_test, predictions)
print("Decision Tree Model Accuracy:", accuracy)
```

```
# Create a new DataFrame for the sample input
new_data = pd.DataFrame({'stress_level': [1], 'coping_ability': [9]})

# Predict the mental health risk using the trained model
predicted_risk = model.predict(new_data)
print("Predicted Mental Health Risk for new data:")
print(predicted_risk)
```

```
# Visualising the Decision Tree
import matplotlib.pyplot as plt
from sklearn.tree import plot_tree

plt.figure(figsize=(20, 10))
plot_tree(
    model,
    filled=True,
    feature_names=['stress_level', 'coping_ability'],
    class_names=model.classes_,
    rounded=True,
    fontsize=12
)
plt.title("Decision Tree Visualisation")
plt.show()
```

Scan the QR code to access the Python code and output (see 12.1.ipynb). The notebook also shows how to save the model, reload it, and make a new prediction.

https://github.com/DrMichaelGuo/PFAAFAMMA

12.2 Random Forest

This section introduces random forests, a supervised machine learning algorithm. The section explains how to train a random forest model, assess its performance, and use it to make predictions in the context of credit risk assessment (see Figure 12.5).

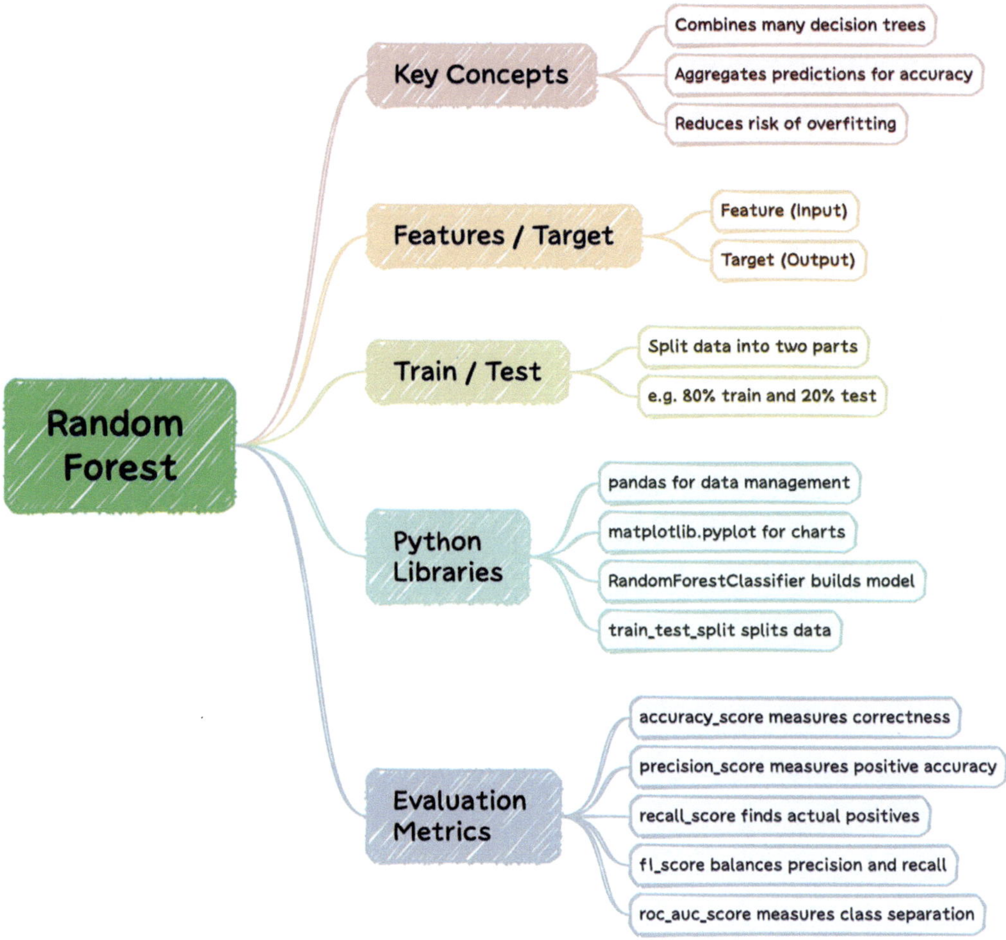

FIGURE 12.5 Random Forest

12.2.1 Key Concepts

12.2.1.1 Random Forest

A random forest is a machine learning method that combines the predictions of multiple decision trees. Instead of relying on a single tree, it builds many trees and aggregates their outputs. This approach increases accuracy and reduces the risk of overfitting.

For example, a random forest model can be used to predict credit risk based on features such as loan amount, annual income, debt-to-income ratio, and credit history.

12.2.1.2 Feature (Input) and Target (Output)

Features are input variables used by the model to make predictions. In the above example, these include loan amount, annual income, debt-to-income ratio, and credit history. The target is the output the model predicts, such as credit risk.

12.2.1.3 Train–Test Split

Train–test split refers to dividing the dataset into training and test subsets: one for training the model, used to learn patterns, and one for testing it, used to evaluate performance. A common split ratio is 80% training and 20% testing.

12.2.1.4 Python Libraries

- pandas: loads, manages, and analyses data with DataFrames.
- matplotlib.pyplot: creates visualisations.
- RandomForestClassifier from sklearn.ensemble: builds a classification model by combining multiple decision trees.
- train_test_split from sklearn.model_selection: divides the dataset into training and testing sets.

12.2.1.5 Evaluation Metrics from sklearn.metrics

- accuracy_score: calculates the proportion of correct predictions.
- precision_score: measures the proportion of predicted positives that are correct.
- recall_score: calculates the proportion of actual positives that are correctly predicted.
- f1_score: measures the harmonic mean of precision and recall.
- roc_auc_score: measures the area under the receiver operating characteristic (ROC) curve to evaluate class separation. The area under the curve (AUC) is calculated using the model's predicted probabilities or scores.

12.2.2 Follow-Along Activity

This activity demonstrates how to train a random forest model to predict credit risk using features such as loan amount, annual income, debt-to-income ratio, and credit history (see Figure 12.6).

Step 1: Import Libraries

Let's start by importing the required libraries for data manipulation, model training, and evaluation.

```
import pandas as pd
import matplotlib.pyplot as plt
from sklearn.ensemble import RandomForestClassifier
from sklearn.model_selection import train_test_split
from sklearn.metrics import (
    accuracy_score, precision_score, recall_score,
    f1_score, roc_auc_score
)
```

Explanation

- import pandas as pd: imports the pandas library and assigns it the alias pd for working with data frames.
- import matplotlib.pyplot as plt: imports the plotting module to generate visualisations.

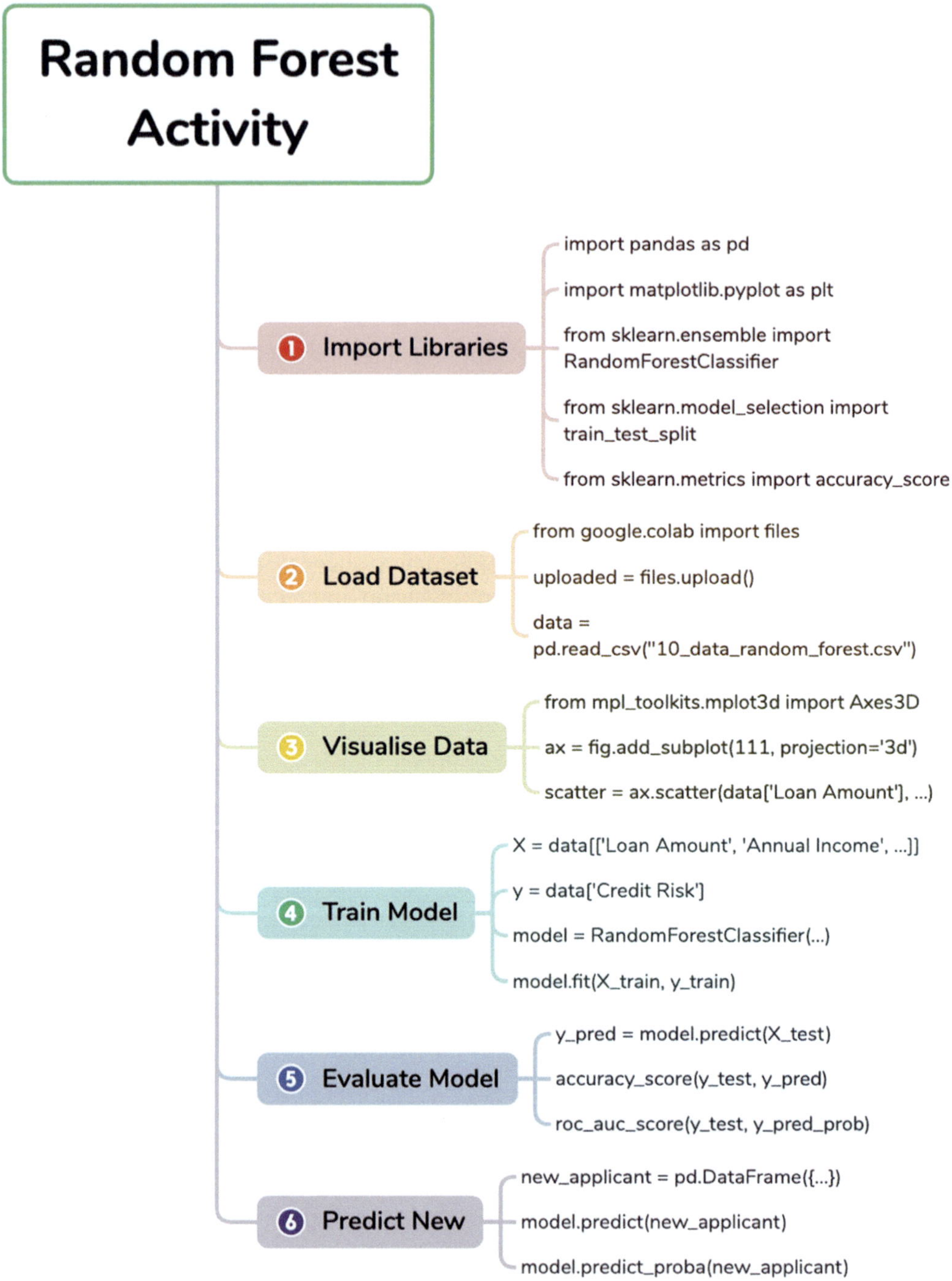

FIGURE 12.6 Random Forest Activity

- from sklearn.ensemble import RandomForestClassifier: imports the random forest classifier model.
- from sklearn.model_selection import train_test_split: imports a method to split data into training and testing sets.
- from sklearn.metrics: imports functions to calculate accuracy, precision, recall, F1 score, and AUC score.

Step 2: Load the Dataset

Let's load the dataset: 12_data_random_forest.csv. The dataset is available at:

https://github.com/DrMichaelGuo/PFAAFAMMA

The dataset contains 500 records on loan applicants, including loan amount, annual income, debt-to-income ratio, and encoded credit history. The target variable, credit risk, indicates whether each applicant is classified as high risk (1) or low risk (0).

```
from google.colab import files
uploaded = files.upload()

# Load data from CSV
data = pd.read_csv("12_data_random_forest.csv")
```

Explanation

- from google.colab import files: imports tools for uploading files in Google Colab.
- uploaded = files.upload(): prompts the user to upload a file.
- data = pd.read_csv("12_data_random_forest.csv"): loads the uploaded CSV file into a data frame named data.

Step 3: Visualise the Data

Let's create a 3D scatter plot of three input features.

```
# Importing the 3D Plotting Module
from mpl_toolkits.mplot3d import Axes3D

# Creating a Figure and 3D Axis
fig = plt.figure(figsize=(11, 7))
ax = fig.add_subplot(111, projection='3d')

# Plot points
scatter = ax.scatter(data['Loan Amount'], data['Debt-to-Income
Ratio'], data['Annual Income'],
                    c=data['Credit Risk'], cmap='coolwarm')

# Labels and color bar
ax.set_xlabel('Loan Amount')
ax.set_ylabel('Debt-to-Income Ratio')
ax.set_zlabel('Annual Income')
plt.colorbar(scatter, label='Credit Risk')
```

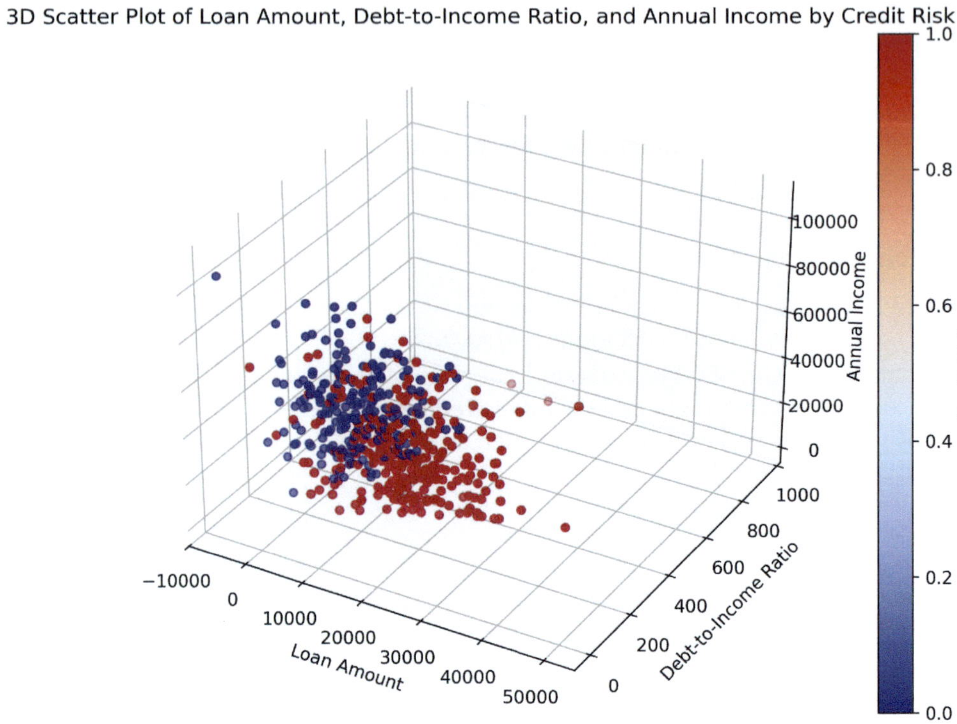

FIGURE 12.7 3D Scatter Plot

```
plt.title("3D Scatter Plot of Loan Amount, Debt-to-Income Ratio, and
Annual Income by Credit Risk")
plt.show()
```

Output: see Figure 12.7.

Explanation

- from mpl_toolkits.mplot3d import Axes3D: imports the module needed for 3D plotting.
- fig = plt.figure(...): creates a figure.
- ax = fig.add_subplot(...): adds a 3D subplot.
- ax.scatter(...): plots a 3D scatter plot using three features.
- ax.set_xlabel(...): sets the label for the x-axis.
- ax.set_ylabel(...): sets the label for the y-axis.
- ax.set_zlabel(...): sets the label for the z-axis.
- plt.colorbar(...): displays a colour bar to indicate the credit risk values.
- plt.title(...): sets the title of the plot.
- plt.show(): displays the final plot.
- The output is a 3D scatter plot that shows the relationship between loan amount, debt-to-income ratio, and annual income. Each point is coloured according to the associated credit risk.

Step 4: Train the Random Forest Model

Let's define the features and train a random forest model to predict credit risk.

```
# Define features and target variables
X = data[['Loan Amount', 'Annual Income', 'Debt-to-Income Ratio',
'Credit History Encoded']]
y = data['Credit Risk']

# Split the data into training and testing sets
X_train, X_test, y_train, y_test = train_test_split(X, y, test_
size=0.2, random_state=42)

# Create and train the random forest classifier
model = RandomForestClassifier(n_estimators=100, max_depth=5,
random_state=42)
model.fit(X_train, y_train)
```

Explanation

- X = data[...]: selects input features from the dataset.
- y = data[...]: selects the target variable.
- train_test_split(...): splits the dataset into training and testing sets.
    - test_size=0.2: allocates 20% of the data for testing and 80% for training.
    - random_state=42: fixes the random seed to ensure reproducibility.
- RandomForestClassifier(...): creates a random forest model with specified parameters.
    - n_estimators=100: specifies the number of trees in the forest.
    - max_depth=5: limits the depth of each decision tree to control overfitting.
    - random_state=42: ensures consistent model behaviour by setting the random seed.
- model.fit(X_train, y_train): trains the model using the training data.

Step 5: Evaluate the Model

Let's evaluate the model using the test dataset. The dataset has been split into training and testing sets. The trained model is assessed on its ability to predict credit risk for the test data.

```
# Predict credit risk on the test set
y_pred = model.predict(X_test)
y_pred_prob = model.predict_proba(X_test)[:, 1]

# Calculate evaluation metrics
accuracy = accuracy_score(y_test, y_pred)
precision = precision_score(y_test, y_pred)
recall = recall_score(y_test, y_pred)
f1 = f1_score(y_test, y_pred)
auc = roc_auc_score(y_test, y_pred_prob)
```

```
print(f"Accuracy: {accuracy}")
print(f"Precision: {precision}")
print(f"Recall: {recall}")
print(f"F1 Score: {f1}")
print(f"AUC: {auc}")
```

Output

```
Accuracy: 0.85
Precision: 0.8823529411764706
Recall: 0.8333333333333334
F1 Score: 0.8571428571428571
AUC: 0.9363929146537842
```

Explanation

- model.predict(X_test): generates predicted credit risk labels (0 or 1) for the test dataset.
- model.predict_proba(X_test)[:, 1]: returns the predicted probability of being high risk (class 1).
- accuracy_score(...): calculates the proportion of correct predictions.
- precision_score(...): calculates the proportion of predicted high-risk cases that are actually high risk.
- recall_score(...): calculates the proportion of actual high-risk cases correctly identified by the model.
- f1_score(...): calculates the harmonic mean of precision and recall.
- roc_auc_score(...): evaluates the model's ability to distinguish between high-risk and low-risk cases using probabilities.
- print(...): prints the evaluation results.
- The model achieved an accuracy of 0.85, meaning it correctly predicted 85% of all cases. The precision score was 0.88, indicating that 88% of applicants predicted as high-risk cases were actually high-risk cases. The recall score was 0.83, showing that the model identified 83% of actual high-risk cases. Some high-risk cases were not identified, which resulted in false negatives. The F1 score was 0.86, representing the harmonic mean of precision and recall. The AUC (ROC AUC score) was 0.94, showing the model's ability to separate low-risk and high-risk cases. A value close to 1 indicates strong separation.

Step 6: Predict Risk for a New Applicant

Let's use the trained model to predict the credit risk of a new loan applicant.

```
# Define a new loan applicant (Modify these values)
new_applicant = pd.DataFrame({
    "Loan Amount": [200000],
    "Annual Income": [60000],
    "Debt-to-Income Ratio": [200000 / 60000 * 100],
    "Credit History Encoded": [1]  # 0 = Good, 1 = Average, 2 = Poor
})
```

```
# Predict risk for new applicant
risk_prediction = model.predict(new_applicant)
risk_probability = model.predict_proba(new_applicant)[:, 1]

print(f"Predicted Credit Risk: {risk_prediction[0]} (1 = High Risk,
0 = Low Risk)")
print(f"Probability of High Risk: {risk_probability[0]:.2f}")
```

Output:

```
Predicted Credit Risk: 1 (1 = High Risk, 0 = Low Risk)
Probability of High Risk: 0.99
```

Explanation

- pd.DataFrame({...}): creates a new data frame representing the financial profile of a loan applicant.
    - "Loan Amount": specifies the amount the applicant wants to borrow.
    - "Annual Income": specifies the applicant's yearly income.
    - "Debt-to-Income Ratio": is calculated as the loan amount divided by annual income, then multiplied by 100.
    - "Credit History Encoded": represents credit history quality as a numerical value.
- model.predict(new_applicant): returns the predicted class label (0 = low risk, 1 = high risk) for the applicant.
- model.predict_proba(new_applicant)[:, 1]: returns the predicted probability that the applicant is a high-risk case.
- print(...): displays the predicted risk label and probability.
- The output shows Predicted Credit Risk: 1, meaning the applicant is classified as high risk. Probability of High Risk: 0.99 indicates a 99% chance of the applicant being high risk according to the model.

12.2.3 Your Project

You continue building on the above trained random forest model by allowing user input. The objective is to collect the user's financial information and predict credit risk. Use exception handling, as introduced in Chapter 3, to manage invalid input.

12.2.3.1 Tasks

- Prompt the user to enter values for loan amount and annual income.
- Calculate the debt-to-income ratio as: debt_to_income_ratio = (loan_amount / annual_income) * 100.
- Prompt the user to enter credit history as a number: 0 = Good, 1 = Average, and 2 = Poor. Validate the input to ensure it is correct.
- Create a DataFrame for the new applicant.
- Use the trained model to make a prediction.
- Print the predicted credit risk and the associated probability.

12.2.3.2 Example Code

```
try:
    # Get user input
    loan_amount = float(input("Enter Loan Amount (£): "))
    annual_income = float(input("Enter Annual Income (£): "))

    # Compute Debt-to-Income Ratio
    debt_to_income_ratio = (loan_amount / annual_income) * 100

    # Get Credit History input as a number
    print("\nCredit History Options: 0 = Good, 1 = Average, 2 = Poor")
    credit_history_encoded = int(input("Enter Credit History (0, 1,
or 2): "))

    # Validate credit history input
    if credit_history_encoded not in [0, 1, 2]:
        print("Invalid input! Please enter 0 for Good, 1 for Average,
or 2 for Poor.")
    else:
        # Create a DataFrame for prediction
        new_applicant = pd.DataFrame({
            "Loan Amount": [loan_amount],
            "Annual Income": [annual_income],
            "Debt-to-Income Ratio": [debt_to_income_ratio],
            "Credit History Encoded": [credit_history_encoded]
        })

        # Make predictions
        risk_prediction = model.predict(new_applicant)
        risk_probability = model.predict_proba(new_applicant)[:, 1]

        # Display results
        print("\nCredit Risk Prediction")
        print(f"Predicted Credit Risk: {risk_prediction[0]} (1 = High
Risk, 0 = Low Risk)")
        print(f"Probability of High Risk: {risk_probability[0]:.2f}")

except ValueError:
    print("Invalid input! Please enter numeric values for Loan
Amount, Annual Income, and Credit History.")
```

Scan the QR code to access the Python code and output (see 12.2.ipynb).

https://github.com/DrMichaelGuo/PFAAFAMMA

12.3 Logistic Regression

This section introduces logistic regression, a supervised learning method for binary classification. The section explains how to train and evaluate a logistic regression model and how to interpret the results in a finance context (see Figure 12.8).

12.3.1 Key Concepts

12.3.1.1 Logistic Regression

Logistic regression is a machine learning model that estimates the probability of a binary outcome (e.g. 0 or 1). It classifies data into two categories.

For example a logistic regression model can use income and credit score to predict whether a loan will default (1) or not default (0).

12.3.1.2 Scikit-learn

Scikit-learn is a Python library that provides tools for logistic regression and other classification methods. It includes functions to train models, assess performance, and produce visual output.

12.3.1.3 Feature (Input) and Target (Output)

Features are input variables used by the model to generate predictions, such as income and credit score in the above example. The target is the variable the model predicts, such as loan default status (1 = default, 0 = no default).

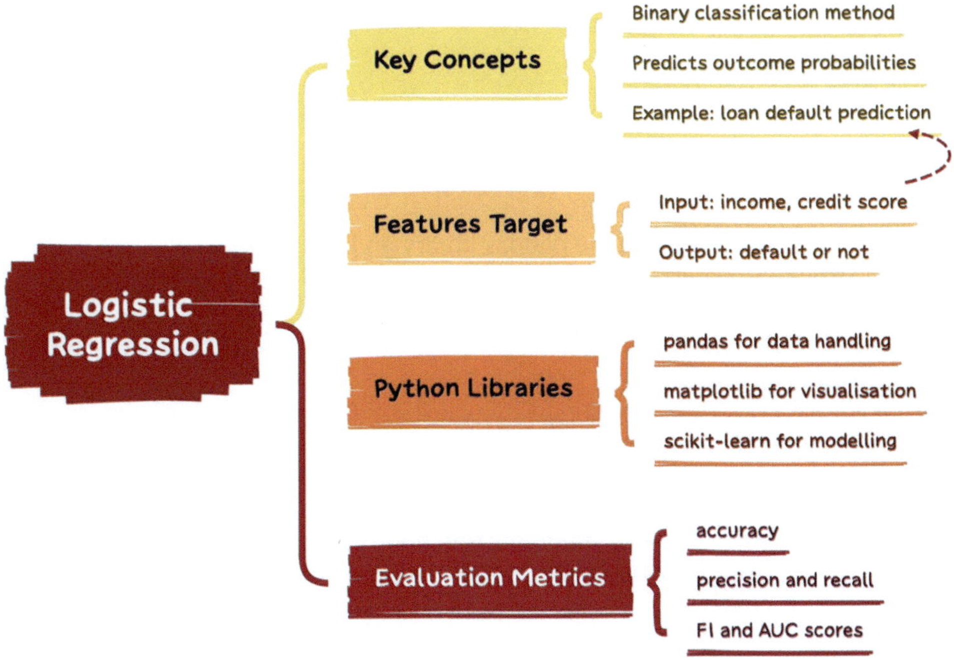

FIGURE 12.8 Logistic Regression

12.3.1.4 Python Libraries

Libraries such as pandas, Matplotlib, and scikit-learn are used for data handling, visualisation, and machine learning.

12.3.1.5 Measurement Metrics

Accuracy, precision, recall, F1 score, and AUC are used to evaluate model performance.

12.3.2 Follow-Along Activity

This activity shows how to build and evaluate a logistic regression model for predicting loan default based on income and credit score (see Figure 12.9).

Step 1: Import Libraries

Let's begin by importing the required Python libraries for data handling, visualisation, and logistic regression.

```
import pandas as pd
import matplotlib.pyplot as plt
from sklearn.linear_model import LogisticRegression
from sklearn.model_selection import train_test_split
from sklearn.preprocessing import StandardScaler
from sklearn.metrics import (
    accuracy_score,
    precision_score,
    recall_score,
    f1_score,
    roc_auc_score,
    roc_curve
)
```

Explanation

- import pandas as pd: imports the pandas library and assigns it the alias pd.
- import matplotlib.pyplot as plt: imports the pyplot module from Matplotlib and assigns it the alias plt.
- from sklearn.linear_model import LogisticRegression: imports the logistic regression model from scikit-learn.
- from sklearn.model_selection import train_test_split: imports the function for splitting data into training and test sets.
- from sklearn.preprocessing import StandardScaler: imports the standardisation class used to scale features before training the model.
- from sklearn.metrics import (...): imports functions to calculate model evaluation metrics such as accuracy, precision, recall, F1 score, and AUC.

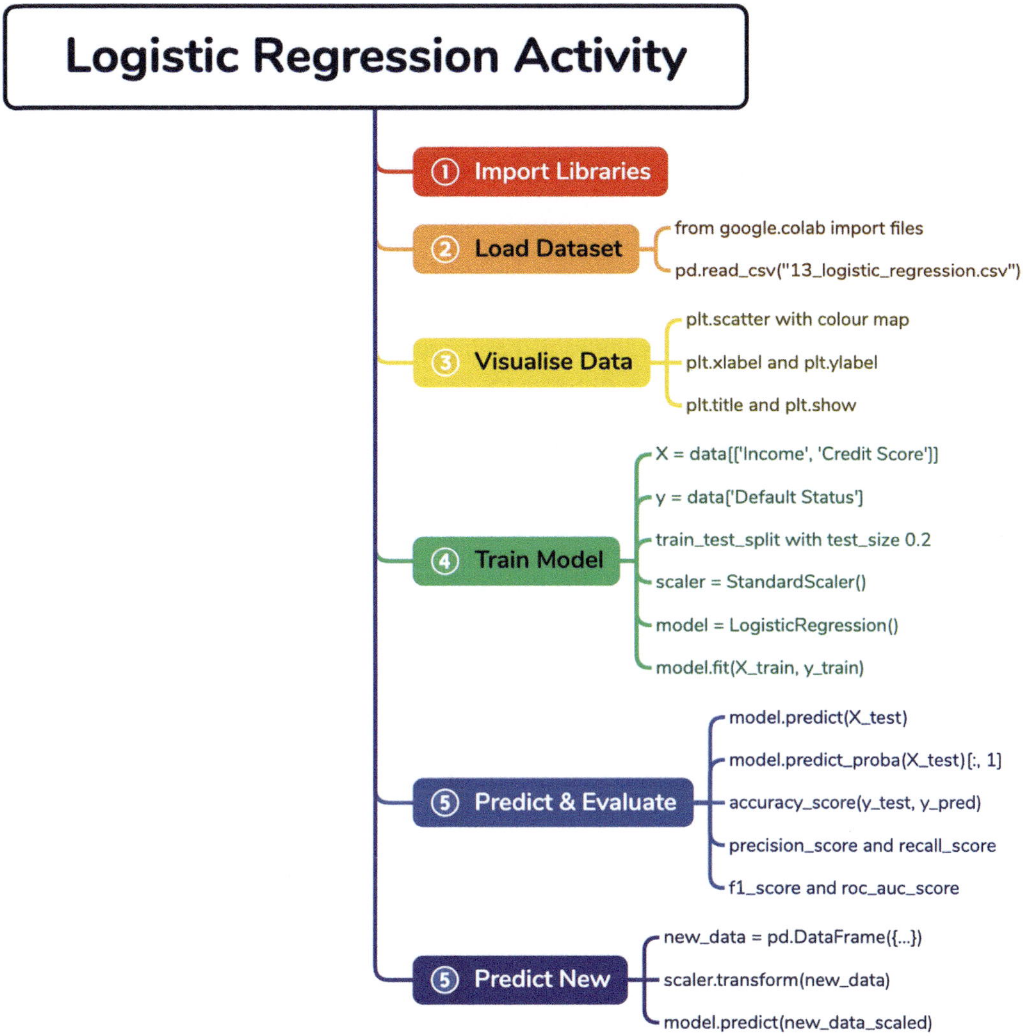

FIGURE 12.9 Logistic Regression Activity

Step 2: Load the Dataset

Let's upload and read the dataset (12_logistic_regression.csv) into a DataFrame. The dataset is available at:

https://github.com/DrMichaelGuo/PFAAFAMMA

```
from google.colab import files
upload = files.upload()

# Load data from CSV
data = pd.read_csv("12_logistic_regression.csv")
print(data.head())
```

Output

```
     Income  Credit Score  Default Status
0  67640.52        794.16               0
1  54001.57        632.61               1
2  59787.38        636.48               1
3  72408.93        748.47               0
4  68675.58        641.34               1
```

Explanation

- from google.colab import files: imports the file upload tool in Google Colab.
- upload = files.upload(): opens a file selector to upload the dataset.
- pd.read_csv(...): reads the CSV file and stores the result in the data DataFrame.
- print(data.head()): prints the first five rows of the DataFrame.

Step 3: Visualise the Data

Let's create a scatter plot to visualise the relationship between income, credit score, and default status.

```
plt.figure(figsize=(10, 6))
plt.scatter(data['Income'], data['Credit Score'], c=data['Default Status'], cmap='coolwarm', marker='o')
plt.xlabel('Income (£)')
plt.ylabel('Credit Score')
plt.title('Income vs Credit Score with Default Status')
plt.colorbar(label='Default Status')
plt.show()
```

Output: see Figure 12.10.

Explanation

- plt.figure(figsize=(10, 6)): sets the figure size to 10 inches wide and 6 inches high.
- plt.scatter(...): creates a scatter plot where each point is coloured based on default status.
- plt.xlabel('Income (£)'): labels the x-axis.
- plt.ylabel('Credit Score'): labels the y-axis.
- plt.title('Income vs Credit Score with Default Status'): adds a title to the plot.
- plt.colorbar(...): displays a colour bar indicating the default status.
- plt.show(): displays the plot.
- The output shows that each point represents an individual. Colour indicates default status: red for default, blue for no default. Low income and low credit score are linked to a higher chance of default.

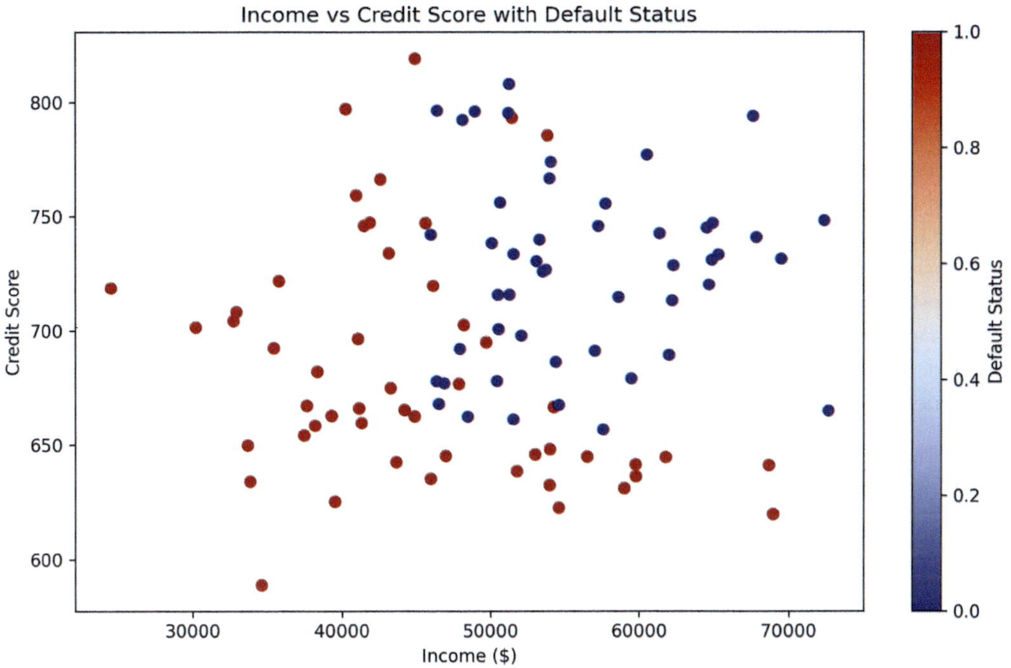

FIGURE 12.10 Income vs Credit Score with Default Status

Step 4: Train the Logistic Regression Model

Let's define the features and the target variable and then train the logistic regression model.

```
# Define features and target
X = data[['Income', 'Credit Score']]
y = data['Default Status']

# Split the data into training and testing sets
X_train, X_test, y_train, y_test = train_test_split(X, y, test_
size=0.2, random_state=42)

# Standardise the features
scaler = StandardScaler()
X_train = scaler.fit_transform(X_train)
X_test = scaler.transform(X_test)

# Train the model
model = LogisticRegression()
model.fit(X_train, y_train)
```

Explanation

- X = data[['Income', 'Credit Score']]: selects income and credit score as input features.
- y = data['Default Status']: selects default status as the output variable.
- train_test_split(...): splits the data into training (80%) and testing (20%) sets.
- scaler = StandardScaler(): creates an object to calculate the scaling parameters based on the training data.
- X_train = scaler.fit_transform(X_train): fits the scaler to the training data and applies the transformation.
- X_test = scaler.transform(X_test): transforms the test data using the same parameters. This ensures consistency between training and prediction.
- model = LogisticRegression(): creates a logistic regression model.
- model.fit(X_train, y_train): trains the model using the training data.

Step 5: Make Predictions and Evaluate the Model

Let's use the trained model to make predictions and evaluate performance.

```
# Predict default status on the test set
y_pred = model.predict(X_test)
y_pred_prob = model.predict_proba(X_test)[:, 1]

# Calculate evaluation metrics
accuracy = accuracy_score(y_test, y_pred)
precision = precision_score(y_test, y_pred)
recall = recall_score(y_test, y_pred)
f1 = f1_score(y_test, y_pred)
auc = roc_auc_score(y_test, y_pred_prob)

# Display evaluation results
print("Model Evaluation Metrics:")
print(f"Accuracy: {accuracy:.2f}")
print(f"Precision: {precision:.2f}")
print(f"Recall: {recall:.2f}")
print(f"F1 Score: {f1:.2f}")
print(f"AUC: {auc:.2f}")
```

Output:

```
Model Evaluation Metrics:
Accuracy: 0.70
Precision: 0.82
Recall: 0.69
F1 Score: 0.75
AUC: 0.81
```

Explanation

- y_pred = model.predict(X_test): generates predicted class labels (0 = no default, 1 = default) for each observation in the test set.
- y_pred_prob = model.predict_proba(X_test)[:, 1]: returns predicted probabilities for both classes. [:, 1] selects the probability of class 1 (default). These probabilities are used in evaluation metrics that require score-based inputs, such as AUC.
- accuracy_score(y_test, y_pred): calculates the proportion of correct predictions.
- precision_score(y_test, y_pred): measures the proportion of predicted defaults that are actual defaults.
- recall_score(y_test, y_pred): calculates the proportion of actual defaults that were correctly predicted.
- f1_score(y_test, y_pred): computes the harmonic mean of precision and recall.
- roc_auc_score(y_test, y_pred_prob): calculates the area under the ROC curve using predicted probabilities.
- print(...): displays the evaluation metrics, rounded to two decimal places.
- The model achieved an accuracy of 0.70, meaning 70% of predictions match actual outcomes. A precision of 0.82 indicates that most predicted defaults were correct. A recall of 0.69 shows that the model identified just over two-thirds of actual defaults. The F1 score of 0.75 reflects a balance between precision and recall. The AUC of 0.81 indicates good ability to distinguish between default and non-default cases.

Step 6: Make a Prediction on New Data

Let's use the trained model to make a prediction for a new individual based on income and credit score.

```
new_data = pd.DataFrame({'Income': [48000], 'Credit Score': [670]})
new_data_scaled = scaler.transform(new_data)
predicted = model.predict(new_data_scaled)
print("Predicted Default Status for new data:", predicted)
```

Output:

```
Predicted Default Status for new data: [1]
```

Explanation

- new_data = pd.DataFrame({'Income': [48000], 'Credit Score': [670]}): creates a new DataFrame with one record.
- new_data_scaled = scaler.transform(new_data): applies the same scaling used on the training data.
- model.predict(new_data_scaled): uses the trained model to generate a prediction.
- print(...): prints the predicted class label (0 = no default, 1 = default).
- The model predicts that the individual will default.

12.3.3 *Your Project*

Build a logistic regression model to classify companies as either low audit risk or high audit risk based on financial indicators.

The dataset 12_logistic_regression_your_project.csv contains 1,000 company records and includes three variables: Gross Profit Margin (Gross Profit divided by Revenue), Inventory Turnover (Cost of Sales divided by Average Inventory), and Audit Risk (0 for low risk, 1 for high risk).

The dataset 12_logistic_regression_your_project.csv can be downloaded from: https://github.com/DrMichaelGuo/PFAAFAMMA

Tasks

- Import the required libraries: pandas, Matplotlib, and relevant modules from scikit-learn.
- Use files.upload() to upload the dataset into a DataFrame.
- Create a scatter plot of gross profit margin against inventory turnover using Matplotlib.
- Train the logistic regression model.
    - Define the feature variables: gross_profit_margin and inventory_turnover.
    - Define the target variable: audit_risk.
    - Split the dataset into training and testing sets (80% training, 20% testing).
    - Train a logistic regression model using the training data.
- Use the test set to generate predictions and evaluate model performance using accuracy, precision, recall, F1 score, and AUC.
- Use the trained model to predict audit risk for a new company with input: {'gross_profit_margin': [0.25], 'inventory_turnover': [4.2]}.

12.3.3.1 *Example Code*

```
# Import libraries
import pandas as pd
import matplotlib.pyplot as plt
from sklearn.linear_model import LogisticRegression
from sklearn.model_selection import train_test_split
from sklearn.metrics import (
    accuracy_score,
    precision_score,
    recall_score,
    f1_score,
    roc_auc_score,
    roc_curve
)

# Load the dataset
from google.colab import files
upload = files.upload()
df = pd.read_csv("12_logistic_regression_your_project.csv")
print(df.head())
```

```
# Visualise the Data
plt.figure(figsize=(10, 6))
plt.scatter(
    df['gross_profit_margin'],
    df['inventory_turnover'],
    c=df['audit_risk'],
    cmap='coolwarm',
    marker='o'
)
plt.xlabel("Gross Profit Margin")
plt.ylabel("Inventory Turnover")
plt.title("Audit Risk: Gross Profit Margin vs Inventory Turnover")
plt.colorbar(label="Audit Risk (1 = High)")
plt.show()

# Train the Logistic Regression Model
X = df[['gross_profit_margin', 'inventory_turnover']]
y = df['audit_risk']
X_train, X_test, y_train, y_test = train_test_split(X, y, test_
size=0.2, random_state=42)
model = LogisticRegression()
model.fit(X_train, y_train)

# Evaluate Model Performance
y_pred = model.predict(X_test)
y_pred_prob = model.predict_proba(X_test)[:, 1]

# Probability of class 1 (high risk)
accuracy = accuracy_score(y_test, y_pred)
precision = precision_score(y_test, y_pred)
recall = recall_score(y_test, y_pred)
f1 = f1_score(y_test, y_pred)
auc = roc_auc_score(y_test, y_pred_prob)

print("\nModel Evaluation Metrics:")
print(f"Accuracy: {accuracy:.2f}")
print(f"Precision: {precision:.2f}")
print(f"Recall: {recall:.2f}")
print(f"F1 Score: {f1:.2f}")
print(f"AUC: {auc:.2f}")

# Make a Prediction for a New Client
new_data = pd.DataFrame({'gross_profit_margin': [0.25],
'inventory_turnover': [4.2]})
predicted_risk = model.predict(new_data)

print("\nPredicted Audit Risk for New Client:")
print(predicted_risk)  # 0 = Low Risk, 1 = High Risk
```

Scan the QR code to access the Python code and output (see 12.3.ipynb).

https://github.com/DrMichaelGuo/PFAAFAMMA

Summary of Chapter 12: Supervised Learning

In this chapter, we have covered the following concepts:

Supervised Learning Overview

- Supervised learning trains a model using labelled data.
- Common applications include classification and prediction in finance and accounting.

Decision Trees

- A decision tree splits data based on feature values to make predictions.
- Used for classification tasks such as predicting financial health.
- Key terms: features (inputs), target (output), train–test split, and accuracy.
- Visualisation with plot_tree() helps interpret decision logic.

Random Forests

- An ensemble method that combines multiple decision trees.
- Improves accuracy and reduces overfitting.
- Applied in credit risk prediction using variables such as loan amount and income.
- Evaluation metrics include accuracy, precision, recall, F1 score, and AUC.

Logistic Regression

- A statistical model used for binary classification (e.g. default vs no default).
- Outputs probabilities and class labels (0 or 1).
- Commonly used for predicting audit risk and loan default.
- Standardisation of input features is performed using StandardScaler.

Model Evaluation

- Accuracy: proportion of correct predictions.
- Precision: proportion of predicted positives that are correct.
- Recall: proportion of actual positives identified.

- F1 score: harmonic mean of precision and recall.
- AUC: area under the ROC curve, measuring classification performance.

Python Tools and Libraries

- pandas: data management and preparation.
- scikit-learn: model building and evaluation.
- Matplotlib: data and model visualisation.
- Core supervised learning tools: train_test_split, DecisionTreeClassifier, RandomForestClassifier, and LogisticRegression.

Quiz Questions

Scan the QR code below to access the quiz questions for this chapter (see 12.md).

https://github.com/DrMichaelGuo/QuizPFAAFAMMA

Further Reading and Resources

Hunter, J., Dale, D., Firing, E., Droettboom, M. and The Matplotlib Development Team (2025) *Matplotlib 3.10.5 documentation*. Available at: https://matplotlib.org/stable/index.html (Accessed 7 August 2025).

Pandas Development Team (2025) *pandas documentation (version 2.3.1)*. Available at: https://pandas.pydata.org/docs/ (Accessed 7 August 2025).

scikit-learn (2024) *scikit-learn: Machine Learning in Python*. Available at: https://scikit-learn.org/stable/documentation.html (Accessed 7 August 2025).

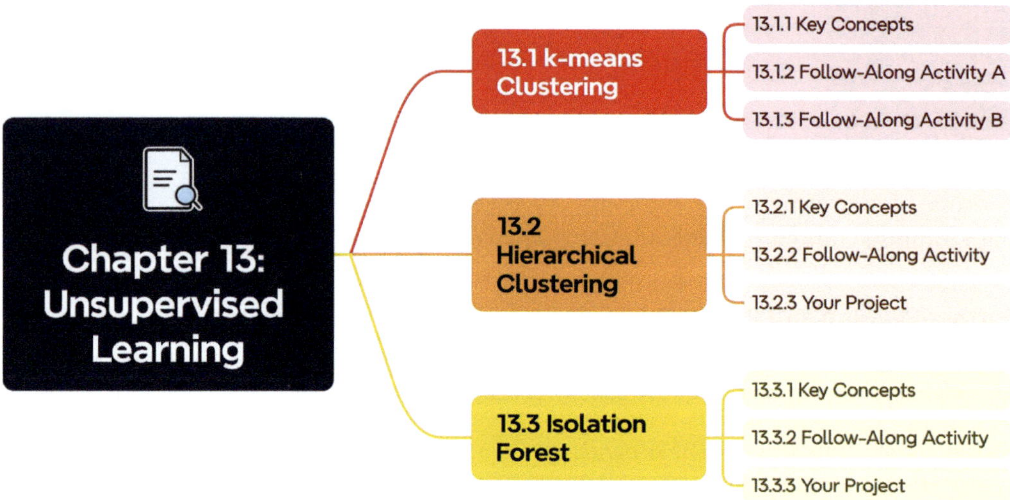

FIGURE 13.1 Structure of Chapter 13

13

UNSUPERVISED LEARNING

This chapter introduces the principles and techniques of unsupervised learning, with a focus on identifying structure and patterns in unlabelled data. It presents three methods: k-means clustering for grouping data into clusters, hierarchical clustering for building clusters, and Isolation Forest for detecting anomalies in datasets. Step-by-step activities support your development of skills for applying these techniques to data analysis tasks in accounting and finance contexts (Figure 13.1).

Learning Objectives

By the end of this chapter, you will be able to:

- Apply the k-means clustering algorithm to group unlabelled data using feature similarity.
- Construct and interpret dendrograms from hierarchical clustering to identify relationships among financial indicators.
- Use the Isolation Forest algorithm to detect and review anomalous transactions in financial datasets.

13.1 k-means Clustering

This section introduces k-means clustering, a method in unsupervised machine learning. The section explains how to segment data based on patterns without labelled output and how to apply this method in accounting and finance (see Figure 13.2).

13.1.1 Key Concepts

13.1.1.1 Unsupervised Learning

Unsupervised learning is a type of machine learning that uses unlabelled data. Unlike supervised learning, which relies on datasets containing both input and output variables,

DOI: 10.4324/9781003656968-13

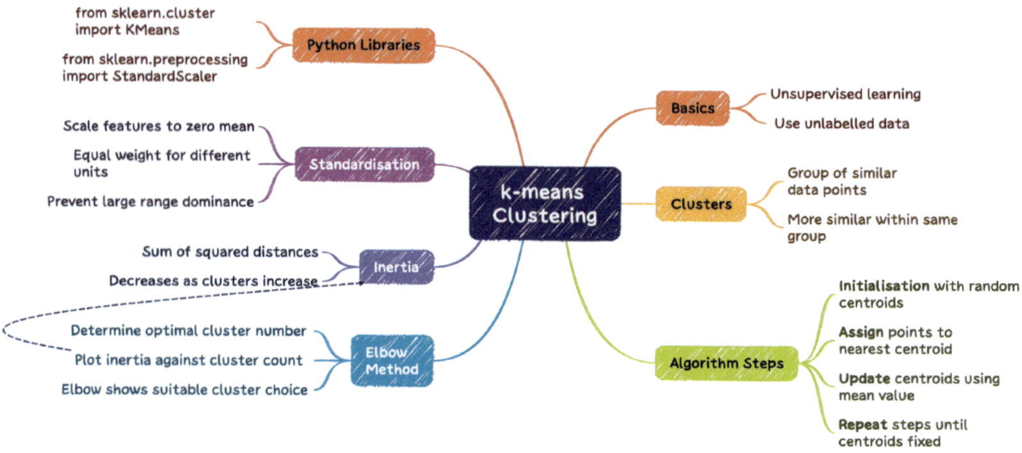

FIGURE 13.2 k-means Clustering

unsupervised learning uses input data only. The objective is not to predict outcomes but to identify patterns or clusters based on similarity or structure.

13.1.1.2 Clusters

A cluster is a group of data points that share similarity in selected features. Clustering aims to organise data into such groups so that points in the same group are more similar to each other than to those in other groups.

13.1.1.3 k-means Clustering

k-means clustering is an unsupervised learning algorithm that divides a dataset into K distinct clusters. The aim is to group data points so that those in the same cluster are closer to each other than to those in other clusters. The algorithm minimises the distance between each data point and the centroid of its assigned cluster.

k-means clustering involves four steps: initialisation, assignment, update, and iteration. The process begins with initialisation, where K centroids are randomly selected. Each centroid marks the starting point of a cluster. In the assignment step, each data point is assigned to the cluster with the nearest centroid. In the update step, the centroid of each cluster is recalculated as the mean of the data points assigned to it, and the old centroid is replaced with this new value. The iteration step repeats the assignment and update steps until the centroids remain unchanged between iterations. When this condition is met, the algorithm has converged and the clustering process ends.

13.1.1.4 Elbow Method

The elbow method is used to determine the optimal number of clusters (K) in k-means clustering. It involves plotting inertia (the sum of squared distances between data points and their assigned centroids) against different values of K. The point where the rate of decrease in inertia slows is the 'elbow'. This point indicates a suitable number of clusters, as increasing K further produces limited improvement.

13.1.1.5 Inertia

Inertia measures the sum of squared distances between each data point and the centroid of its assigned cluster. As the number of clusters increases, inertia decreases. Inertia is used with the elbow method to help identify a suitable number of clusters.

13.1.1.6 Standardisation

Standardisation is the process of scaling features to have a mean of 0 and a standard deviation of 1. This ensures that features with different units or scales contribute equally to the k-means clustering. Without standardisation, variables with larger numerical ranges could dominate the clustering process.

13.1.1.7 Python Libraries

```
from sklearn.cluster import KMeans
```

This line imports KMeans from the sklearn.cluster module. KMeans is a clustering algorithm that groups data into a specified number of clusters based on similarity in the feature space.

```
from sklearn.preprocessing import StandardScaler
```

This line imports StandardScaler from the sklearn.preprocessing module. StandardScaler is used to standardise features by removing the mean and scaling to unit variance. This ensures that all features contribute equally to clustering.

13.1.2 Follow-Along Activity A

This activity demonstrates k-means clustering. It involves loading data for 30 clients, visualising the data, and applying k-means to identify patterns (see Figure 13.3). In this introductory example, the data is analysed in their original units to help you focus on understanding how clustering works. The process of standardisation is introduced in Section 13.1.3, Follow-Along Activity B.

Step 1: Load the Dataset

Let's create a dataset of 30 clients with their annual revenue (in thousands) and risk score using the following code. You can type the code in your notebook or copy and paste it from the file 13.1.ipynb available at the following site:

https://github.com/DrMichaelGuo/PFAAFAMMA

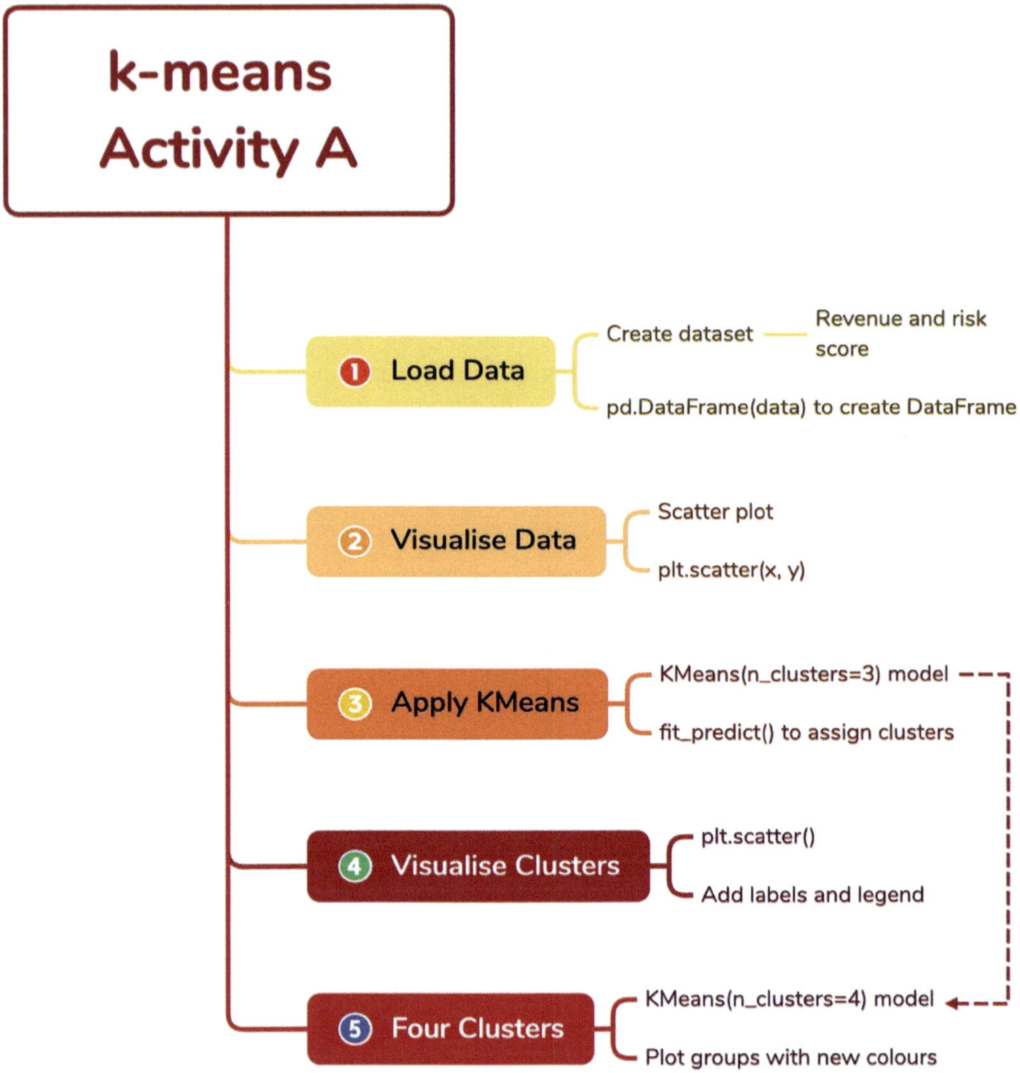

FIGURE 13.3 k-means Activity A

```
import pandas as pd

data = {
    'Client': [
        'CL1', 'CL2', 'CL3', 'CL4', 'CL5',
        'CL6', 'CL7', 'CL8', 'CL9', 'CL10',
        'CL11', 'CL12', 'CL13', 'CL14', 'CL15',
        'CL16', 'CL17', 'CL18', 'CL19', 'CL20',
        'CL21', 'CL22', 'CL23', 'CL24', 'CL25',
        'CL26', 'CL27', 'CL28', 'CL29', 'CL30'
    ],
```

```
    'Annual_Revenue': [
        100, 150, 200, 250, 300,
        350, 400, 420, 430, 450,
        520, 550, 580, 600, 620,
        630, 650, 670, 680, 700,
        720, 740, 750, 780, 800,
        820, 850, 880, 900, 950
    ],
    'Risk_Score': [
        39, 81, 6, 77, 40,
        50, 60, 20, 30, 55,
        25, 35, 45, 50, 60,
        55, 47, 65, 70, 75,
        40, 35, 85, 15, 80,
        90, 10, 25, 95, 5
    ]
}

# Create a DataFrame
df = pd.DataFrame(data)

# Show the first few rows
print(df.head())
```

Output

```
  Client  Annual_Revenue  Risk_Score
0    CL1             100          39
1    CL2             150          81
2    CL3             200           6
3    CL4             250          77
4    CL5             300          40
```

Explanation

- import pandas as pd: imports the pandas library for data handling.
- data = {...}: defines a dictionary with client identifiers, annual revenue (in thousands), and risk scores.
- pd.DataFrame(data): converts the dictionary to a DataFrame.
- print(df.head()): prints the first five rows of the DataFrame.

Step 2: Visualise the Data

Let's create a scatter plot to show the relationship between revenue and risk score.

```
import matplotlib.pyplot as plt

# Scatter plot of the clients
plt.figure(figsize=(10, 6))
plt.scatter(df['Annual_Revenue'], df['Risk_Score'])
```

```
plt.xlabel('Annual Revenue (£000s)')
plt.ylabel('Risk Score (1 - 100)')
plt.title('Client Data: Annual Revenue vs Risk Score')
plt.show()
```

Output: see Figure 13.4.

FIGURE 13.4 Client Data

Explanation

- import matplotlib.pyplot as plt: imports the plotting library.
- plt.figure(figsize = (10, 6)): defines the figure size.
- plt.scatter(df['Annual_Revenue'], df['Risk_Score']): plots annual revenue against risk score.
- plt.xlabel('Annual Revenue (£000s)'): labels the x-axis.
- plt.ylabel('Risk Score (1 - 100)'): labels the y-axis.
- plt.title('Client Data: Annual Revenue vs Risk Score'): sets the title.
- plt.show(): displays the plot.

Step 3: Apply k-means Clustering (3 Clusters)

Let's apply the k-means algorithm to classify the clients into three groups.

```
from sklearn.cluster import KMeans

# Select features
features = df[['Annual_Revenue', 'Risk_Score']]

# Create the KMeans model with 3 clusters
kmeans = KMeans(n_clusters=3, random_state=42)

# Fit the model and predict clusters
df['Cluster'] = kmeans.fit_predict(features)

print(df)
```

Output

```
 Client  Annual_Revenue  Risk_Score  Cluster
0     CL1             100          39        2
1     CL2             150          81        2
2     CL3             200           6        2
3     CL4             250          77        2
4     CL5             300          40        2
5     CL6             350          50        2
6     CL7             400          60        0
7     CL8             420          20        0
8     CL9             430          30        0
9    CL10             450          55        0
10   CL11             520          25        0
11   CL12             550          35        0
12   CL13             580          45        0
13   CL14             600          50        0
14   CL15             620          60        0
15   CL16             630          55        0
16   CL17             650          47        0
17   CL18             670          65        1
18   CL19             680          70        1
19   CL20             700          75        1
20   CL21             720          40        1
21   CL22             740          35        1
22   CL23             750          85        1
23   CL24             780          15        1
24   CL25             800          80        1
25   CL26             820          90        1
26   CL27             850          10        1
27   CL28             880          25        1
28   CL29             900          95        1
29   CL30             950           5        1
```

Explanation

- from sklearn.cluster import KMeans: imports the KMeans algorithm from the sklearn library.
- features = df[['Annual_Revenue', 'Risk_Score']]: selects the features (columns) for clustering.
- kmeans = KMeans(n_clusters=3, random_state=42): creates a KMeans model with three clusters and sets a random seed for reproducibility.
- df['Cluster'] = kmeans.fit_predict(features): fits the model to the data and assigns a cluster label to each observation.
- print(df): prints the updated DataFrame.
- The output includes a new column, Cluster, which shows the group assigned to each client.

Note: Without standardisation, features with larger numeric ranges may dominate distance calculations. This example prioritises intuition; we standardise in Section 13.1.3.

Step 4: Visualise the Clusters

Let's plot the clustered data to see how the clients are grouped.

```
# Plot clustered data points
plt.figure(figsize=(10, 6))

# Custom colour scheme
colors = ['red', 'blue', 'green']

# Loop through each cluster
for cluster in range(3):
    cluster_data = df[df['Cluster'] == cluster]
    plt.scatter(
        cluster_data['Annual_Revenue'],
        cluster_data['Risk_Score'],
        color=colors[cluster],
        label=f'Cluster {cluster}'
    )

plt.xlabel('Annual Revenue (£000s)')
plt.ylabel('Risk Score (1 - 100)')
plt.title('Client Segments (3 Clusters)')
plt.legend()

plt.show()
```

Output: see Figure 13.5.

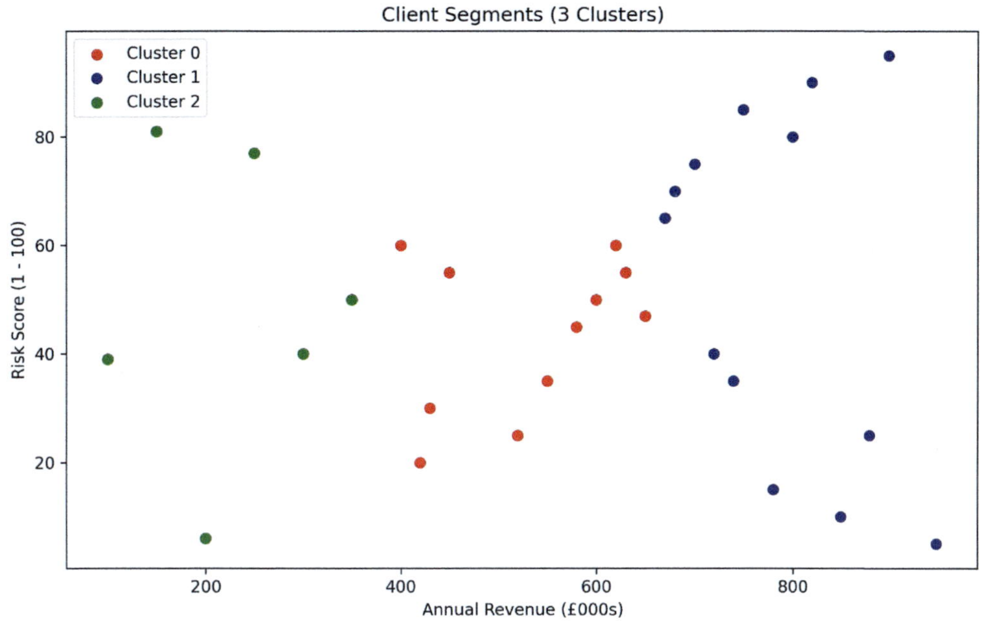

FIGURE 13.5 Client Data (3 Clusters)

Explanation

- plt.figure(figsize=(10, 6)): sets the figure size.
- colors = ['red', 'blue', 'green']: defines a list of colours for each cluster.
- for cluster in range(3): iterates through the cluster labels.
    - df[df['Cluster'] == cluster]: filters the data for the current cluster.
    - plt.scatter(...): plots the points for the current cluster.
- plt.xlabel(...), plt.ylabel(...), plt.title(...): set axis labels and the chart title.
- plt.legend(): adds a legend to identify clusters.
- plt.show(): displays the chart.

Step 5: Apply k-means Clustering (4 Clusters) and Visualise

Let's increase the number of clusters to four and plot the new grouping.

```
# 4 Clusters
kmeans = KMeans(n_clusters=4, random_state=42)
df['Cluster'] = kmeans.fit_predict(features)

plt.figure(figsize=(10, 6))
colors = ['red', 'blue', 'green', 'orange']
```

```
for cluster in range(4):
    cluster_data = df[df['Cluster'] == cluster]
    plt.scatter(
        cluster_data['Annual_Revenue'],
        cluster_data['Risk_Score'],
        color=colors[cluster],
        label=f'Cluster {cluster}'
    )

plt.xlabel('Annual Revenue (£000s)')
plt.ylabel('Risk Score (1 - 100)')
plt.title('Client Segments (4 Clusters)')
plt.legend()
plt.show()
```

Output: see Figure 13.6.

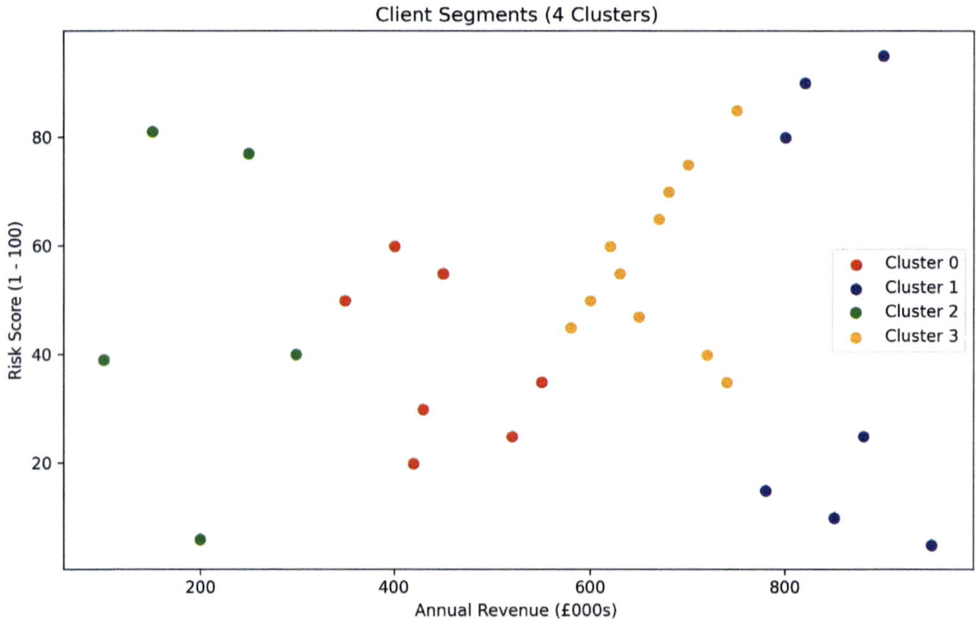

FIGURE 13.6 Client Data (4 Clusters)

Explanation

- features = df[['Annual_Revenue', 'Risk_Score']]: selects the columns used for clustering.
- kmeans = KMeans(n_clusters=4, random_state=42): creates a KMeans model with four clusters and sets the random seed for reproducibility.
- df['Cluster'] = kmeans.fit_predict(features): fits the model to the data and assigns a cluster label to each observation.
- plt.scatter(...): plots each group with a different colour.
- plt.show(): displays the chart.

Scan the QR code to access the code and output (see 13.1.ipynb).

https://github.com/DrMichaelGuo/PFAAFAMMA

13.1.3 Follow-Along Activity B

This activity applies k-means clustering to a dataset of 2,000 synthetic clients. It includes data preprocessing through standardisation, determining the number of clusters, and visualising the resulting client groups (see Figure 13.7).

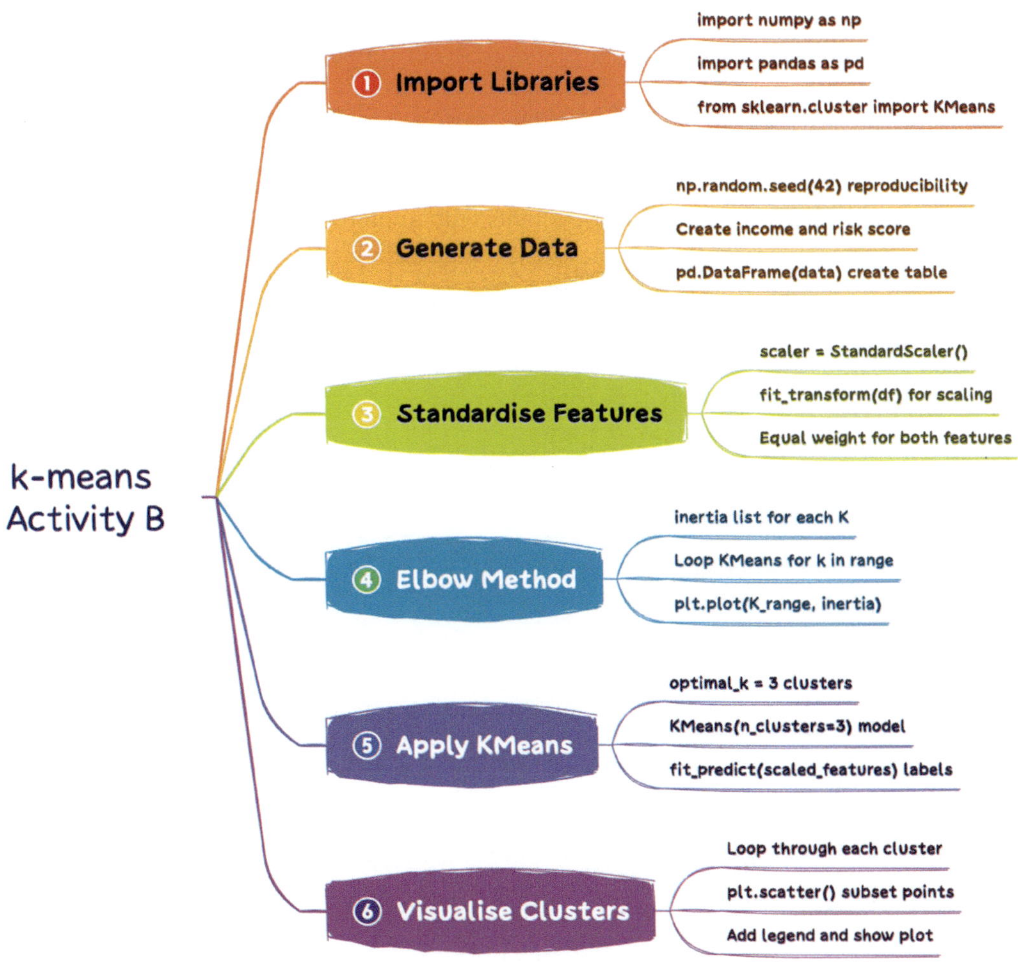

FIGURE 13.7 k-means Activity B

Step 1: Import Libraries

Let's import the required Python libraries for data handling, visualisation, and clustering.

```
import numpy as np
import pandas as pd
import matplotlib.pyplot as plt
from sklearn.cluster import KMeans
from sklearn.preprocessing import StandardScaler
```

Explanation

- import numpy as np: imports the NumPy library and assigns it the alias np.
- import pandas as pd: imports the pandas library for data manipulation and assigns it the alias pd.
- import matplotlib.pyplot as plt: imports the plotting module from matplotlib and assigns it the alias plt.
- from sklearn.cluster import KMeans: imports the KMeans algorithm from the scikit-learn clustering module.
- from sklearn.preprocessing import StandardScaler: imports the scaler used to standardise features.

Step 2: Generate Synthetic Dataset

Let's create a synthetic dataset of 2,000 clients with annual income and risk score data.

```
# Generate a simple synthetic dataset for client segmentation
np.random.seed(42) # Ensures reproducibility
data = {
    'Annual_Income': np.round(np.random.normal(50000, 15000, 2000), 2),
    'Risk_Score': np.round(np.random.normal(50, 10, 2000)).astype(int)
}

# Create a DataFrame
df = pd.DataFrame(data)

# Show the first few rows
print(df.head())
```

Output:

```
   Annual_Income  Risk_Score
0       57450.71          43
1       47926.04          49
2       59715.33          42
3       72845.45          47
4       46487.70          31
```

Explanation

- np.random.seed(42): sets the random seed to ensure reproducibility of the generated data.
- data = {...}: creates a dictionary with synthetic values for annual income and risk score.
    - np.round(np.random.normal(50000, 15000, 2000), 2): generates 2,000 values from a normal distribution with a mean of 50,000 and a standard deviation of 15,000. These values simulate annual income. The function rounds each value to two decimal places.
    - np.round(np.random.normal(50, 10, 2000)).astype(int): generates 2,000 values from a normal distribution with a mean of 50 and a standard deviation of 10. These values simulate risk scores. The function rounds each score to the nearest whole number and converts the result to integer type.
- pd.DataFrame(data): converts the dictionary into a DataFrame.
- print(df.head()): prints the first five rows of the DataFrame.

Step 3: Standardise Features for Clustering

Let's scale the features so they have equal weight during distance-based clustering.

```
scaler = StandardScaler()
scaled_features = scaler.fit_transform(df)
```

Explanation

- scaler = StandardScaler(): creates an instance of the StandardScaler class from sklearn.preprocessing. This object is used to standardise numeric features by adjusting each feature to have a mean of 0 and a standard deviation of 1. This standardisation process is important before applying machine learning algorithms such as KMeans, which are sensitive to differences in feature scale.
- scaler.fit_transform(df): computes the mean and standard deviation of each column in the DataFrame df, and then applies standardisation using these values. Both 'Annual_Income' and 'Risk_Score' are transformed to have a mean of 0 and a standard deviation of 1.
- Without standardisation, one feature with a larger range of values (e.g. Annual_Income) could dominate the distance calculation and bias the clustering results.

Step 4: Determine Optimal Number of Clusters (Elbow Method)

Let's identify how many clusters best represent the data by plotting inertia values.

```
# Create an empty list to store inertia values for each K
inertia = []

# Define a range of K values to test (from 1 to 9 clusters)
K_range = range(1, 10)
```

```
# Loop through each K value to fit a KMeans model and calculate
inertia
for k in K_range:
    kmeans = KMeans(n_clusters=k, random_state=42)
    kmeans.fit(scaled_features)
    inertia.append(kmeans.inertia_)

# Create a figure with specified size for the plot
plt.figure(figsize=(8, 4))
plt.plot(K_range, inertia, marker='o')
plt.xlabel('Number of clusters (K)')
plt.ylabel('Inertia')
plt.title('Elbow Method For Optimal K')

# Display the plot
plt.show()
```

Output: see Figure 13.8.

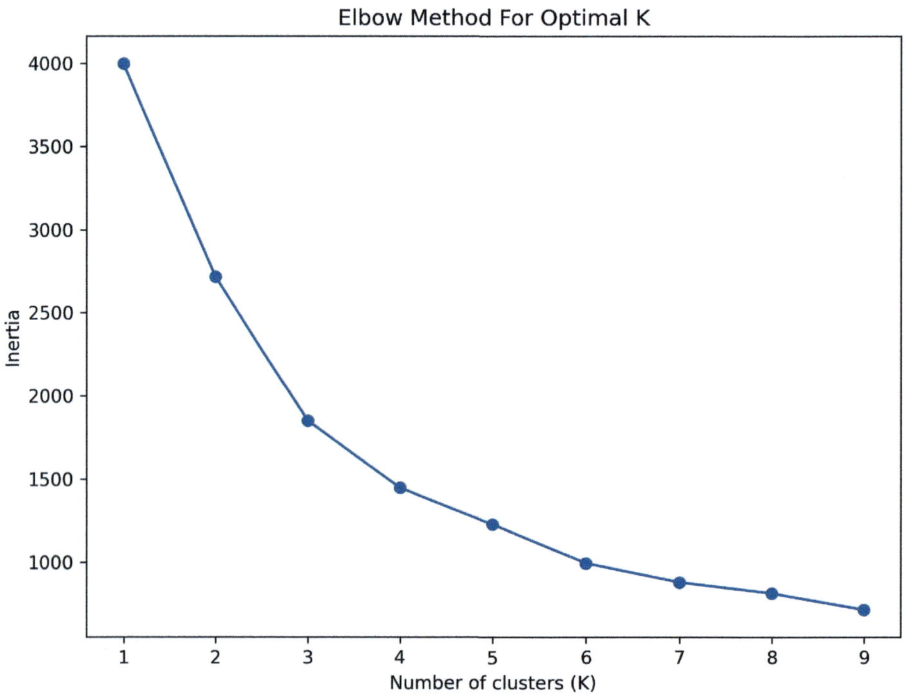

FIGURE 13.8 Elbow Method for Optimal K

Explanation

- inertia = [ ]: creates an empty list to store inertia values. Inertia refers to the sum of squared distances between data points and their assigned cluster centroids.
- range(1, 10): specifies the number of clusters (K) to test, from 1 to 9.

- KMeans(n_clusters=k, random_state=42): creates a k-means model for each value of K with a fixed random seed for reproducibility.
- kmeans.fit(scaled_features): fits the model to the standardised data.
- inertia.append(kmeans.inertia_): records the inertia value for the fitted model.
- plt.figure(figsize=(8, 4)): sets the figure size.
- plt.plot(K_range, inertia, marker='o'): plots the number of clusters against the inertia values.
- plt.xlabel(...), plt.ylabel(...), plt.title(...): labels the axes and sets the title.
- plt.show(): displays the plot.
- The output graph shows how inertia decreases as the number of clusters increases. The point where the reduction slows, often called the 'elbow', occurs at K = 3. This indicates that three clusters is the suitable number for this dataset.

Step 5: Apply k-means Clustering (K=3)

Let's use K = 3 based on the elbow method and apply k-means clustering.

```
optimal_k = 3
kmeans = KMeans(n_clusters=optimal_k, random_state=42)
df['Cluster'] = kmeans.fit_predict(scaled_features)
print(df.head(10))
```

Output

```
   Annual_Income  Risk_Score  Cluster
0       57450.71          43        1
1       47926.04          49        0
2       59715.33          42        1
3       72845.45          47        1
4       46487.70          31        1
5       46487.95          52        0
6       73688.19          50        1
7       61511.52          42        1
8       42957.88          57        2
9       58138.40          59        2
```

Explanation

- optimal_k = 3: sets the number of clusters to three.
- kmeans = KMeans(n_clusters=optimal_k, random_state=42): creates a KMeans clustering model.
- df['Cluster'] = kmeans.fit_predict(scaled_features): fits the model and assigns a cluster label to each observation.
- print(df.head(10)): displays the first ten rows with the cluster labels.
- The output shows the annual income, risk score, and assigned cluster for the first ten records in the dataset. Each record is assigned to one of three clusters (0, 1, or 2) based on patterns in the scaled data.

Step 6: Visualise the Clusters

Let's visualise the client segments using a scatter plot.

```
plt.figure(figsize=(8, 6))

for cluster in range(optimal_k):
    subset = df[df['Cluster'] == cluster]
    plt.scatter(subset['Annual_Income'], subset['Risk_Score'],
label=f'Cluster {cluster}')

plt.xlabel('Annual Income')
plt.ylabel('Risk Score (1 - 100)')
plt.title('Client Segmentation using k-means Clustering')
plt.legend()
plt.show()
```

Output: see Figure 13.9.

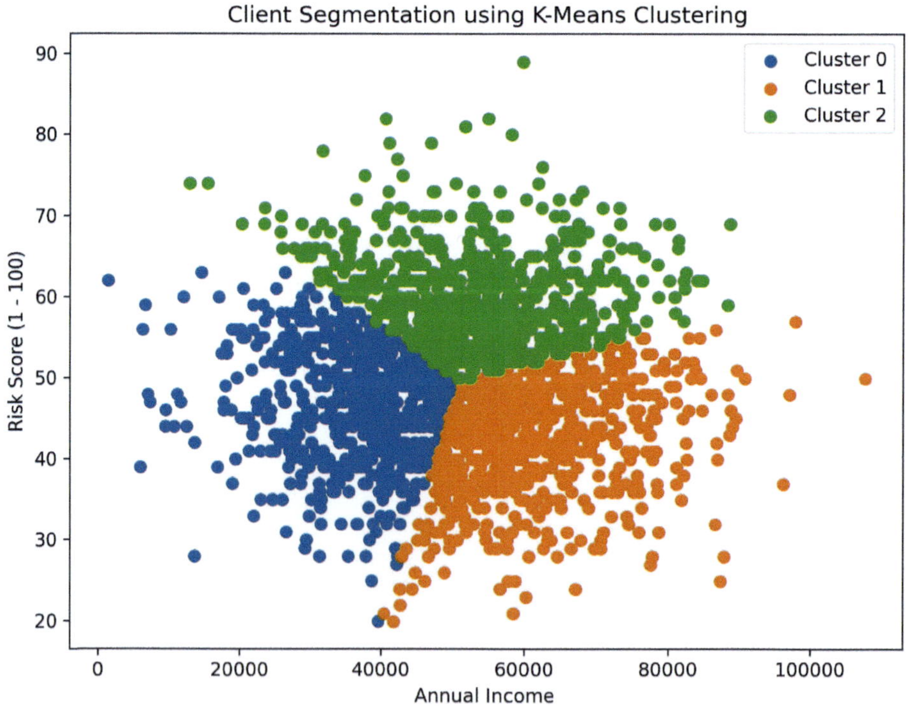

FIGURE 13.9 Client Segmentation

Explanation

- plt.figure(figsize=(8, 6)): creates a figure with a width of 8 inches and a height of 6 inches.
- for cluster in range(...): loops through each cluster label.
    - df[df['Cluster'] == cluster]: filters the data for each cluster.
    - plt.scatter(...): plots points for each cluster.
- plt.xlabel(...), plt.ylabel(...), plt.title(...): labels the axes and sets the title.
- plt.legend(): adds a legend.
- plt.show(): displays the scatter plot.

The scatter plot shows three client segments based on annual income and risk score. Cluster 0 (blue) includes clients with income below approximately £50,000 and risk scores between 30 and 60. Cluster 1 (orange) includes clients with income above £50,000 and risk scores between 20 and 50. Cluster 2 (green) includes clients with a broad income range and risk scores above 50.

These segments provide insights for decision-making. High-risk clients in Cluster 2 can be prioritised for monitoring and review. Cluster 1 clients, with high income and relatively low risk, can be targeted for premium services or tailored engagement strategies.

Scan the QR code to access the code and output (see 13.1.ipynb).

https://github.com/DrMichaelGuo/PFAAFAMMA

13.2 Hierarchical Clustering

Hierarchical clustering is a method of grouping data based on the similarity between observations. It uses a step-by-step merging or splitting process to build a tree-like structure. This section explains how to apply hierarchical clustering to financial data, interpret a dendrogram, and determine the number of clusters (see Figure 13.10).

13.2.1 Key Concepts

13.2.1.1 Clustering

Clustering is the process of grouping data points so that points in the same group are more similar to each other than to those in other groups.

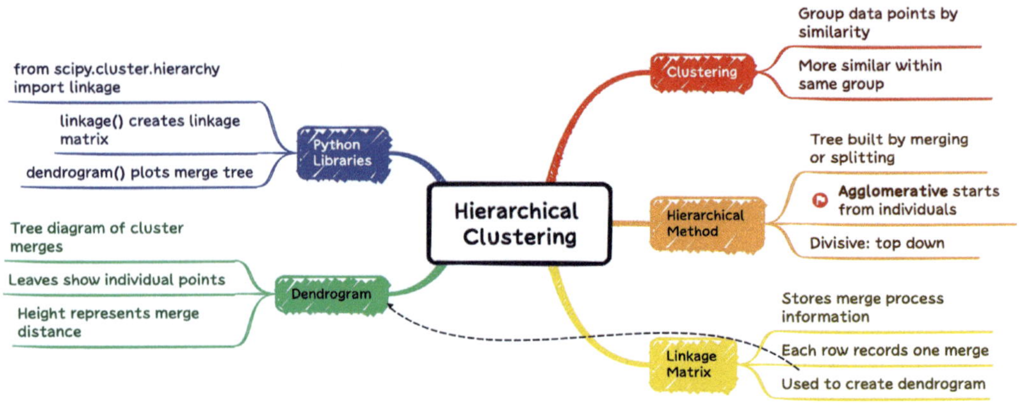

FIGURE 13.10 Hierarchical Clustering

13.2.1.2 Hierarchical Clustering

Hierarchical clustering builds a tree of clusters either from the bottom up (agglomerative) or top down (divisive). This section focuses on agglomerative clustering, which starts with individual data points and merges them into clusters step by step.

13.2.1.3 Linkage Matrix

The linkage matrix stores information about the steps in the hierarchical clustering process. Each row records one merge. This matrix is used to create the dendrogram and to identify how the data form clusters.

13.2.1.4 Dendrogram

A dendrogram is a tree diagram that records the sequence of merges in hierarchical clustering. It shows the relationships between data points and clusters.

In a dendrogram, the leaves represent individual data points and appear along the x-axis. The branches indicate merges between clusters. The height of each merge, shown on the y-axis, represents the distance between the two clusters at the time they are joined. This structure helps to assess the similarity between data points. Drawing a horizontal line across the dendrogram can help determine the number of clusters.

13.2.1.5 Python Libraries

Hierarchical clustering in Python can be performed using functions from the scipy.cluster.hierarchy module. The linkage function computes the linkage matrix, which stores the information needed to build the clustering hierarchy. The dendrogram function uses this matrix to produce a visual representation of the clustering process. These functions are imported using

```
from scipy.cluster.hierarchy import dendrogram, linkage
```

13.2.2 Follow-Along Activity

This activity shows how to apply hierarchical clustering to synthetic financial data, construct a dendrogram, and choose the number of clusters (see Figure 13.11).

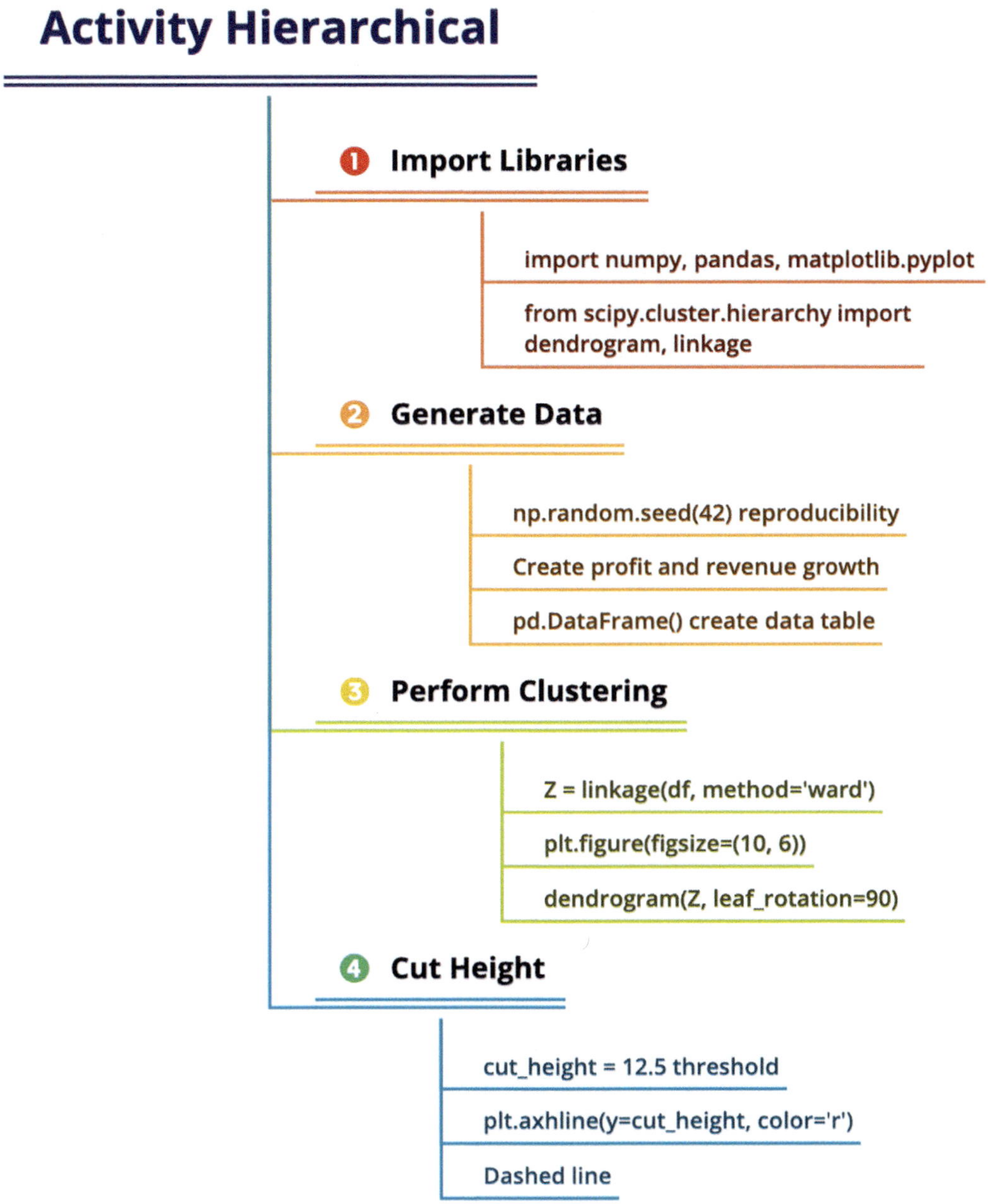

FIGURE 13.11 Activity Hierarchical

Step 1: Import Libraries

Let's import the required libraries.

```
import numpy as np
import pandas as pd
import matplotlib.pyplot as plt
from scipy.cluster.hierarchy import dendrogram, linkage
```

Explanation

- import numpy as np: imports the NumPy library and assigns it the alias np.
- import pandas as pd: imports the pandas library and assigns it the alias pd.
- import matplotlib.pyplot as plt: imports the pyplot module from the Matplotlib library and assigns it the alias plt.
- from scipy.cluster.hierarchy import dendrogram, linkage: imports the dendrogram and linkage functions from the scipy.cluster.hierarchy module. These functions perform hierarchical clustering and visualise them using dendrograms.

Step 2: Generate Data

Let's generate synthetic financial data as follows:

```
# Set random seed for reproducibility
np.random.seed(42)

# Generate synthetic financial data (rounded to 2 decimal places)
profit_margin = np.round(np.random.normal(loc=5, scale=2, size=50), 2)
revenue_growth = np.round(np.random.normal(loc=10, scale=3,
size=50), 2)

# Create a DataFrame
df = pd.DataFrame({'Profit_Margin': profit_margin, 'Revenue_Growth':
revenue_growth})

print(df.head())
```

Output

```
   Profit_Margin  Revenue_Growth
0           5.99           10.97
1           4.72            8.84
2           6.30            7.97
3           8.05           11.84
4           4.53           13.09
```

Explanation

- np.random.seed(42): sets the seed for the random number generator to ensure reproducibility.

- profit_margin = np.round(np.random.normal(loc=5, scale=2, size=50), 2): generates 50 values from a normal distribution with a mean of 5 and a standard deviation of 2, then rounds to two decimal places.
- revenue_growth = np.round(np.random.normal(loc=10, scale=3, size=50), 2): generates 50 values from a normal distribution with a mean of 10 and a standard deviation of 3, then rounds to two decimal places.
- df = pd.DataFrame(...): creates a DataFrame using the generated profit margin and revenue growth values.
- print(df.head()): prints the first five rows of the DataFrame.

Step 3: Perform Hierarchical Clustering

Let's perform hierarchical clustering by computing the linkage matrix and plotting the dendrogram.

```
Z = linkage(df, method='ward')

plt.figure(figsize=(10, 6))
dendrogram(Z, leaf_rotation=90)
plt.title('Hierarchical Clustering Dendrogram')
plt.xlabel('Sample index')
plt.ylabel('Distance')
plt.show()
```

Output: see Figure 13.12.

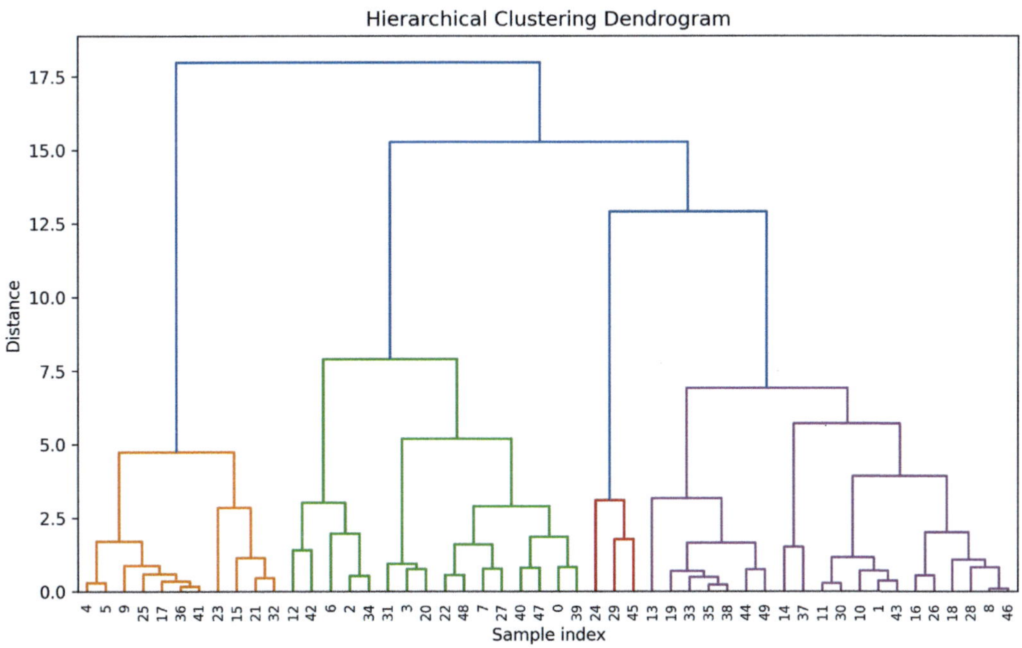

FIGURE 13.12 Hierarchical Clustering Dendrogram

Explanation

- Z = linkage(df, method='ward'): computes the linkage matrix using Ward's method. This method forms clusters by minimising the total within-cluster variance. At each step, it merges the pair of clusters that results in the smallest increase in total within-cluster variance.
- plt.figure(figsize=(10, 6)): sets the figure size.
- dendrogram(Z, leaf_rotation=90): plots the dendrogram from the linkage matrix.
  - leaf_rotation=90: rotates the leaf labels by 90 degrees for readability.
- plt.title(...), plt.xlabel(...), plt.ylabel(...): label the axes and provide a title.
- plt.show(): displays the dendrogram.

The dendrogram presents the hierarchical clustering of 50 observations. Each leaf at the bottom represents a data point. Branches show how clusters are merged step by step. The height of each merge indicates the distance between the clusters at that step.

Step 4: Determine Clusters by Applying a Cut Height

Let's define a cut height and display it on the dendrogram to identify the clusters.

```
# Define the height at which to cut the dendrogram
cut_height = 12.5

# Plot the dendrogram
plt.figure(figsize=(10, 6))
dendrogram(Z, leaf_rotation=90)

# Add the cut line to the dendrogram
plt.axhline(y=cut_height, color='r', linestyle='--')

plt.title('Hierarchical Clustering Dendrogram with Cut Line')
plt.xlabel('Sample index')
plt.ylabel('Distance')

# Show the plot
plt.show()
```

Output: see Figure 13.13.

Explanation

- cut_height = 12.5: sets the height at which the dendrogram will be cut. All branches below this height are treated as separate clusters.
- plt.figure(figsize=(10, 6)): sets the figure size.
- dendrogram(Z, leaf_rotation=90): draws the dendrogram from the linkage matrix with leaf labels rotated for readability.

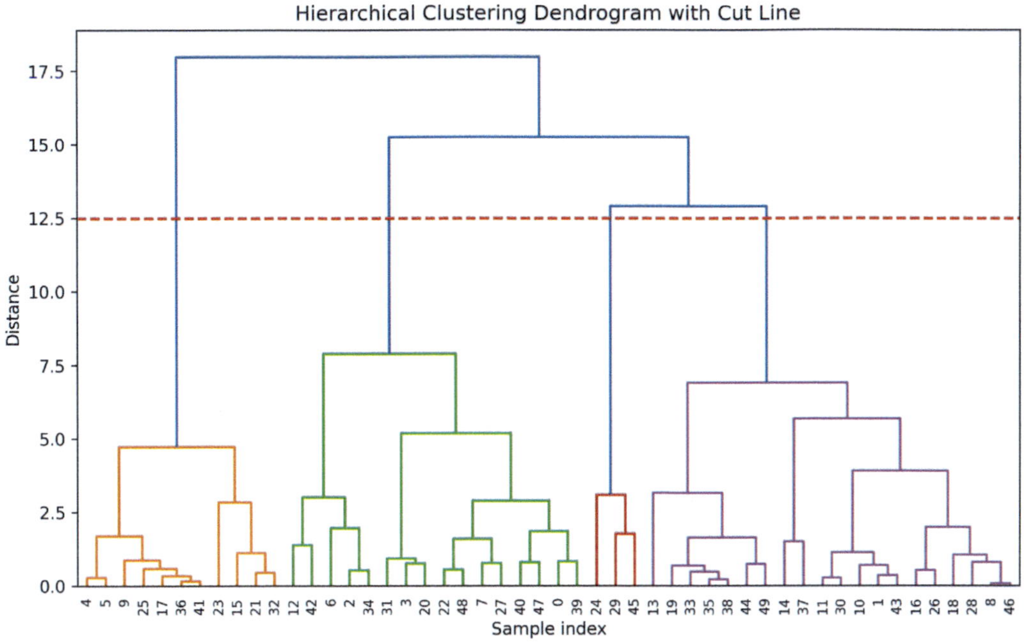

FIGURE 13.13 Hierarchical Clustering Dendrogram with Cut Line

- plt.axhline(y=cut_height, color ='r', linestyle='--'): draws a horizontal dashed red line across the plot at the cut height.
  - Color='r': sets the colour of the line to red. 'r' is the shorthand notation for red in Matplotlib.
  - Linestyle='--': specifies the style of the line. '--' indicates a dashed line.
- plt.title(...), plt.xlabel(...), plt.ylabel(...): label the axes and provide a title.
- plt.show(): displays the dendrogram.

A dendrogram in hierarchical clustering shows how data points are grouped through successive merges. Drawing a horizontal line at a chosen height sets the clustering threshold. Each vertical branch crossed by this line represents a separate cluster. This method provides a visual method to decide how many clusters to retain.

Note: To select a suitable cut height, examine the dendrogram for the largest vertical gap between horizontal merge lines. This gap often marks a potential division between groups. One approach is to scan from the bottom to the top, locate the widest gap, and draw a horizontal line just below it. The number of vertical branches crossed by this line gives the number of clusters. In this example, a large gap in linkage distance appears between heights 8 and 13 units. Cutting at height 12.5, just below 13, results in four clusters.

13.2.3 *Your Project*

Write Python code to perform hierarchical clustering using the dataset *13_your_project_hierarchical_clustering.csv*. The dataset includes two indicators:

- ROA: Return on Assets, a measure of financial performance.
- Debt_to_Equity: Debt-to-Equity Ratio, a measure of financial leverage.

The dataset is available from:
https://github.com/DrMichaelGuo/PFAAFAMMA

13.2.3.1 *Tasks*

- Upload the dataset 13_your_project_hierarchical_clustering.csv to your Google Colab environment.
- Read the uploaded CSV file into a pandas DataFrame.
- Perform hierarchical clustering by computing the linkage matrix using the 'ward' method. Then plot the dendrogram.
- Observe the dendrogram, consider possible clusters, and add a horizontal cut line to determine the number of clusters.

13.2.3.2 *Example Code*

```
# Step 1: Upload the dataset
from google.colab import files
uploaded = files.upload()

# Step 2: Read the uploaded CSV file
import pandas as pd
df = pd.read_csv('13_your_project_hierarchical_clustering.csv')

# Step 3: Perform hierarchical clustering
import matplotlib.pyplot as plt
from scipy.cluster.hierarchy import dendrogram, linkage

# Compute the linkage matrix using the 'ward' method
Z = linkage(df, method='ward')

# Plot the dendrogram
plt.figure(figsize=(10, 6))
dendrogram(Z, leaf_rotation=90)
plt.title('Hierarchical Clustering Dendrogram')
plt.xlabel('Sample index')
plt.ylabel('Distance')
plt.show()

# Step 4: Define cut height and plot dendrogram with cut line
cut_height = 300  # Adjust this value to experiment with the cut

plt.figure(figsize=(10, 6))
dendrogram(Z, leaf_rotation=90)
```

```
plt.axhline(y=cut_height, color='r', linestyle='--')
plt.title('Hierarchical Clustering Dendrogram with Cut Line')
plt.xlabel('Sample index')
plt.ylabel('Distance')
plt.show()
```

Scan the QR code to access the code and output (see 13.2.ipynb).

https://github.com/DrMichaelGuo/PFAAFAMMA

13.3 Isolation Forest

Isolation Forest is an unsupervised machine learning method for detecting anomalies in large datasets. This section explains how to simulate financial transactions, introduce anomalies, and apply the Isolation Forest algorithm (see Figure 13.14).

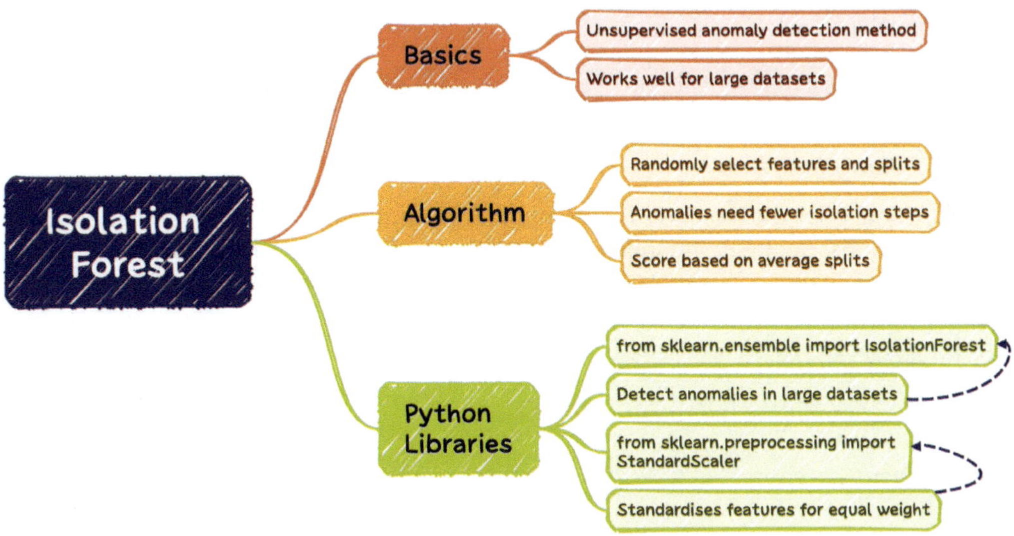

FIGURE 13.14 Isolation Forest

13.3.1 Key Concepts

13.3.1.1 Isolation Forest

Isolation Forest is an unsupervised learning model that detects anomalies by isolating observations through random decision trees. Anomalies, which differ from most observations, require fewer splits to isolate. This method is suitable for large datasets and can support auditors and risk analysts in identifying unusual transactions.

13.3.1.2 Isolation Forest Algorithm

The algorithm works by randomly selecting features and split values to isolate data points. Anomalies are isolated faster as they occur infrequently and deviate from common patterns. The model assigns scores based on the average number of splits needed to isolate each point.

13.3.1.3 Python Libraries

To apply the Isolation Forest model, import it from scikit-learn using

```
from sklearn.ensemble import IsolationForest
```

Feature scaling is used to ensure that variables with different units or ranges contribute proportionately to the model. StandardScaler from scikit-learn standardises features so that each has a mean of 0 and a standard deviation of 1. The following code imports StandardScaler:

```
from sklearn.preprocessing import StandardScaler
```

13.3.2 Follow-Along Activity

This activity applies the Isolation Forest method to identify unusual or potentially fraudulent transactions. Synthetic financial data is used for illustration. The objective is to flag unusually large transactions that occur at uncommon times (see Figure 13.15).

Step 1: Import Libraries

Let's begin by importing the required libraries.

```
import numpy as np
import pandas as pd
from sklearn.ensemble import IsolationForest
import matplotlib.pyplot as plt
```

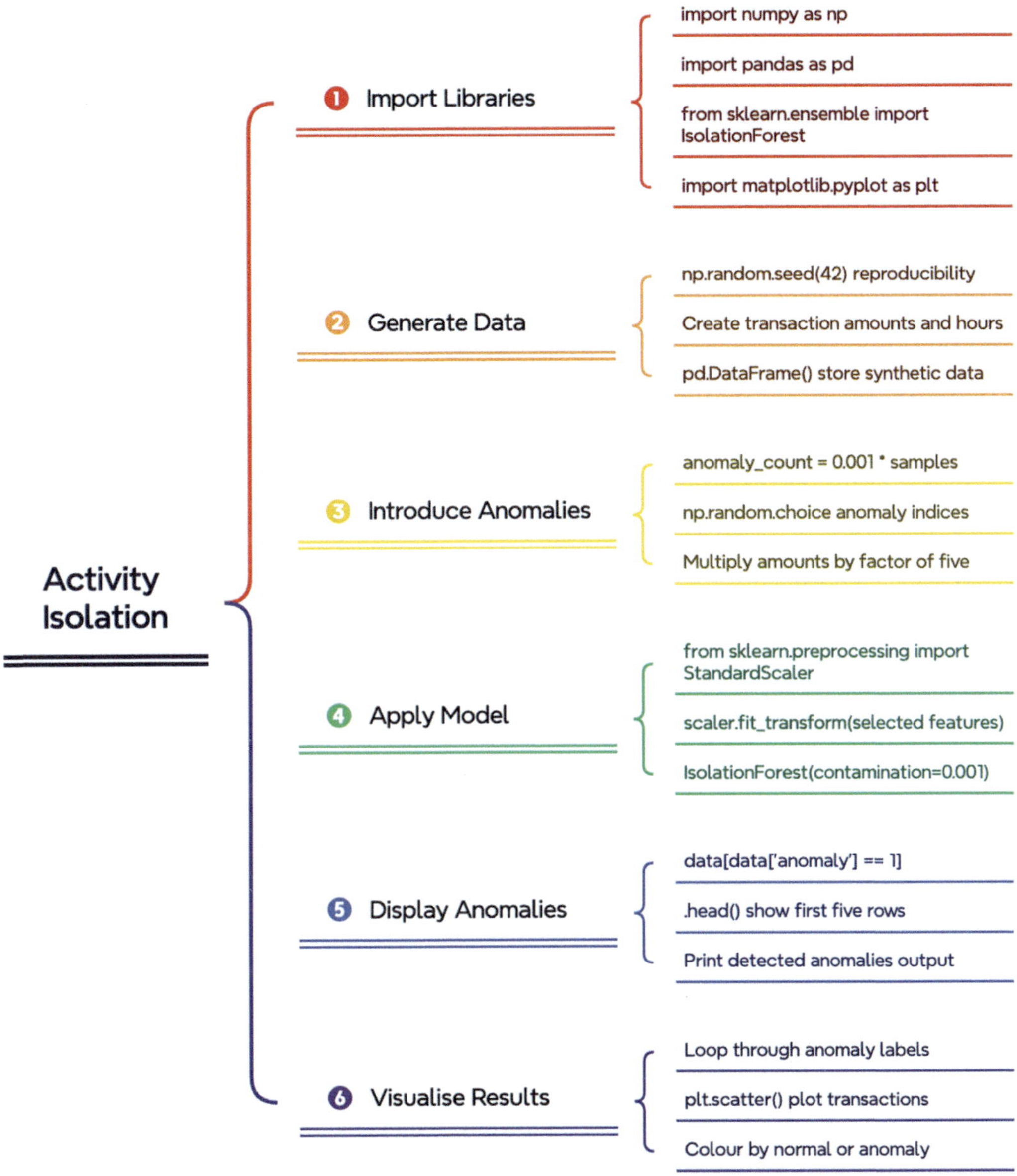

FIGURE 13.15 Activity Isolation

Explanation

- import numpy as np: imports the NumPy library and assigns it the alias np.
- import pandas as pd: imports the pandas library and assigns it the alias pd.
- from sklearn.ensemble import IsolationForest: imports the Isolation Forest Model from scikit-learn. Note that IsolationForest uses capital letters I and F.
- import matplotlib.pyplot as plt: imports the plotting module from Matplotlib and assigns it the alias plt.

Step 2: Generate Synthetic Data

Let's generate 100,000 synthetic financial transactions for analysis.

```
np.random.seed(42)
n_samples = 100_000

transaction_amounts = np.round(np.random.normal(loc=100, scale=20,
size=n_samples),2)
transaction_hours = np.round(np.random.normal(loc=13, scale=4,
size=n_samples)).astype(int)
transaction_hours = np.clip(transaction_hours, 0, 23)

data = pd.DataFrame({
    'transaction_id': range(1, n_samples + 1),
    'transaction_amount': transaction_amounts,
    'transaction_hour': transaction_hours
})

print(data.head())
```

Output

```
   transaction_id  transaction_amount  transaction_hour
0               1              109.93                17
1               2               97.23                 8
2               3              112.95                15
3               4              130.46                11
4               5               95.32                12
```

Explanation

- np.random.seed(42): sets the random seed to 42 to ensure that results are reproducible each time the code runs.
- n_samples = 100_000: assigns the number of transactions to generate. The underscore in 100_000 is a visual separator used to improve readability.
- transaction_amounts = np.round(np.random.normal(loc=100, scale=20, size=n_samples),2): generates transaction amounts from a normal distribution with a mean of 100 and a standard deviation of 20, rounded to two decimal places.
- transaction_hours = np.round(np.random.normal(loc=13, scale=4, size=n_samples)).astype(int): generates transaction hours from a normal distribution with a mean of 13 and a standard deviation of 4, rounds to the nearest whole number, and converts to integers.
- transaction_hours = np.clip(transaction_hours, 0, 23): restricts transaction hours to the valid range of 0 to 23.
- pd.DataFrame({...}): creates a DataFrame that stores three columns.
  - 'transaction_id': assigns a unique identifier to each transaction.
  - 'transaction_amount': stores the simulated transaction amounts.
  - 'transaction_hour': stores the assigned transaction hours.
- print(data.head()): prints the first five rows of the DataFrame.

Step 3: Introduce Anomalies

Let's simulate anomalies by inflating the transaction amounts for 0.1% of the data. This reflects a contamination level of 0.001, which specifies the expected proportion of anomalies in the dataset.

```
anomaly_count = int(0.001 * n_samples)
anomaly_indices = np.random.choice(n_samples, size=anomaly_count,
replace=False)
data.loc[anomaly_indices, 'transaction_amount'] =
data.loc[anomaly_indices, 'transaction_amount'] * 5
```

Explanation

- anomaly_count = int(0.001 * n_samples): calculates the number of anomalies as 0.1% of the total sample size. With n_samples = 100_000, this gives 100 anomalies.
- np.random.choice(n_samples, size=anomaly_count, replace=False): selects anomaly_count unique indices from the dataset. replace=False: ensures that no index is selected more than once. This simulates the random selection of transactions to label as anomalous.
- data.loc[anomaly_indices, 'transaction_amount'] = data.loc[anomaly_indices, 'transaction_amount'] * 5: multiplies the transaction amounts at the selected indices by 5 to create unusually high values.
    - data.loc[anomaly_indices, 'transaction_amount']: accesses the transaction_amount column for the rows identified as anomalies.
    - * 5: multiplies the selected values by five to create unusually high amounts.

Step 4: Apply Isolation Forest

Let's apply the Isolation Forest model to detect anomalies in the dataset.

```
from sklearn.preprocessing import StandardScaler
scaler = StandardScaler()
scaled = scaler.fit_transform(data[['transaction_amount',
'transaction_hour']])

model = IsolationForest(contamination=0.001, random_state=42,
verbose=1)
model.fit(scaled)
data['anomaly'] = model.predict(scaled)
```

Output

```
[Parallel(n_jobs=1)]: Done   1 out of   1 | elapsed:    0.3s finished
[Parallel(n_jobs=1)]: Done  49 tasks      | elapsed:    0.3s
[Parallel(n_jobs=1)]: Done 100 out of 100 | elapsed:    0.5s finished
[Parallel(n_jobs=1)]: Done  49 tasks      | elapsed:    0.2s
[Parallel(n_jobs=1)]: Done 100 out of 100 | elapsed:    0.5s finished
```

Explanation

- from sklearn.preprocessing import StandardScaler: imports the scaler used to standardise the features.
- scaler = StandardScaler(): creates an instance of the scaler.
- scaler.fit_transform(data[['transaction_amount', 'transaction_hour']]): fits the scaler to the selected features and transforms them into standardised values with a mean of 0 and a standard deviation of 1.
- model = IsolationForest(contamination=0.001, random_state=42, verbose=1): creates an Isolation Forest model.
    - contamination=0.001: sets the expected proportion of anomalies in the data to 0.1%.
    - random_state=42: ensures reproducibility.
    - verbose=1: prints progress messages during model training.
- model.fit(scaled): trains the model on the scaled data.
- data['anomaly'] = model.predict(scaled): assigns the model's predictions to a new column in the DataFrame.
    - The predict() method in sklearn.ensemble.IsolationForest returns 1 for normal observations and –1 for anomalies.
- The output messages confirm that the model has completed training.

Step 5: Display Anomalies

Let's print the first few records identified as anomalies (–1) by the model.

```
# Display detected anomalies
print("\nDetected Anomalies:\n")
print(data[data['anomaly'] == -1].head())
```

Output

```
Detected Anomalies:

      transaction_id  transaction_amount  transaction_hour  anomaly
1464            1465              441.95                11       -1
2429            2430              466.60                 5       -1
3713            3714               57.35                 0       -1
4725            4726               36.59                23       -1
5535            5536              150.02                 1       -1
```

Explanation

- print("\nDetected Anomalies:\n"): prints a label to indicate the output contains anomalies.
    - \n: inserts blank lines before and after the label for spacing.

- print(data[data['anomaly'] == −1].head()): displays the selected rows.
  - data[data['anomaly'] == −1]: filters the DataFrame to include only rows where the 'Anomaly' column equals −1.
  - .head(): selects the first five rows from the filtered DataFrame.

Step 6: Visualise the Results

Let's create a scatter plot to compare normal and anomalous transactions by transaction amount and hour.

```
plt.figure(figsize=(10, 6))

for label, colour in [(1, 'blue'), (-1, 'red')]:
    subset = data[data['anomaly'] == label]
    plt.scatter(subset['transaction_amount'],
                subset['transaction_hour'],
                c=colour,
                label='Normal' if label == 1 else 'Anomaly')

plt.xlabel('Transaction Amount')
plt.ylabel('Transaction Hour')
plt.title('Isolation Forest: Anomaly Detection on Transactions')
plt.legend()
plt.show()
```

Output: see Figure 13.16.

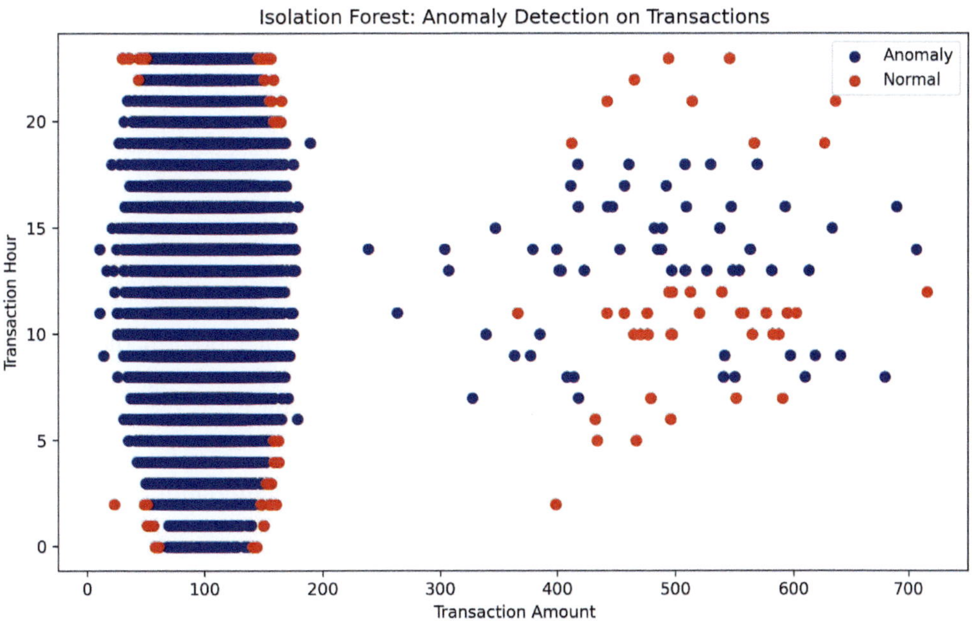

FIGURE 13.16 Isolation Forest Results

Explanation

- plt.figure(figsize=(10, 6)): sets the figure size to 10 units wide and 6 units high.
- for label, colour in [(1, 'blue'), (–1, 'red')]: loops through the anomaly labels, with 1 for normal and –1 for anomalies, and assigns a colour to each group.
    - subset = data[data['anomaly'] == label]: filters the dataset for rows with the current label.
    - plt.scatter(...): creates a scatter plot using the filtered data.
    - c=colour: sets the colour of the data points according to the current label in the loop. When label is 1, the colour is 'blue'; when label is –1, the colour is 'red'.
    - label='Normal' if label == 1 else 'Anomaly': sets the label for the legend. If the label is 1, the label is 'Normal'; otherwise, it is set to 'Anomaly'.
- plt.xlabel('Transaction Amount'): labels the x-axis.
- plt.ylabel('Transaction Hour'): labels the y-axis.
- plt.title('Isolation Forest: Anomaly Detection on Transactions'): adds a title to the chart.
- plt.legend(): displays the legend to identify normal and anomalous transactions.
- plt.show(): displays the plot.

13.3.3 Your Project

Write a Python code to apply the Isolation Forest method to support accounts payable staff in reviewing supplier invoices for a large company. Unusually large invoices that are paid almost immediately may indicate control failures, duplicate payments, or fraud.

The dataset contains 8,000 records and includes the following fields:

- supplier_id
- invoice_amount
- days_to_pay

The dataset is provided in the file *13_your_project_isolation_forest.csv*, available at: https://github.com/DrMichaelGuo/PFAAFAMMA

13.3.3.1 Tasks

- Import the required libraries, including files from google.colab.
- Upload the file *13_your_project_isolation_forest.csv* to your Google Colab environment and load it into a pandas DataFrame.
- Standardise the features and apply the Isolation Forest model.
    - Standardise the invoice_amount and days_to_pay columns using StandardScaler.
    - Fit an Isolation Forest model to the scaled data with contamination=0.001 to indicate the expected proportion of anomalies.
    - Add the model predictions to the DataFrame.
- Print five rows identified as anomalies (–1).

- Create a scatter plot to visualise the normal and anomalous records.
  - Plot invoice_amount against days_to_pay.
  - Use blue to represent normal records and red to represent anomalies.
  - Add axis labels, a title, and a legend.

13.3.3.2 Example Code

```
# Step 1: Import libraries
import pandas as pd
import matplotlib.pyplot as plt
from sklearn.preprocessing import StandardScaler
from sklearn.ensemble import IsolationForest
from google.colab import files

# Step 2: Upload the CSV file and load the uploaded file
uploaded = files.upload()
df = pd.read_csv("13_your_project_isolation_forest.csv")

# Step 3: Scale the features and perform analysis
scaler = StandardScaler()
scaled = scaler.fit_transform(df[['invoice_amount', 'days_to_pay']])
model = IsolationForest(contamination=0.001)
model.fit(scaled)
df['anomaly'] = model.predict(scaled)  # 1 = normal, -1 = anomaly

# Step 4: Display sample anomalies
print("\nSample Detected Anomalies:\n")
print(df[df['anomaly'] == -1].head())

# Step 5: Plot results
plt.figure(figsize=(10, 6))
for label, colour in [(1, 'blue'), (-1, 'red')]:
   subset = df[df['anomaly'] == label]
   plt.scatter(subset['invoice_amount'],
               subset['days_to_pay'],
               c=colour,
               label='Normal' if label == 1 else 'Anomaly')

plt.xlabel('Invoice Amount')
plt.ylabel('Days to Pay')
plt.title('Isolation Forest: Anomaly Detection on Supplier Invoices')
plt.legend()
plt.show()
```

Scan the QR code to access the code and output (see 13.3.ipynb).

https://github.com/DrMichaelGuo/PFAAFAMMA

Summary of Chapter 13: Unsupervised Learning

In this chapter, we have covered the following concepts:

Unsupervised Learning

- Uses unlabelled data without predefined outputs.
- Identifies patterns, groupings, and anomalies in datasets.
- Applied in segmentation, fraud detection, and exploratory analysis.

k-means Clustering

- Groups data into *K* clusters based on feature similarity.
- Main steps: initialisation, assignment, update, and iteration.
- The elbow method is used to determine the number of clusters by plotting inertia.
- Standardisation ensures all features contribute equally to clustering.

Hierarchical Clustering

- Groups data using a tree structure (dendrogram).
- Focuses on agglomerative clustering (bottom-up method).
- The linkage matrix records how clusters are merged.
- A cut height defines the number of final groups.

Isolation Forest

- Detects unusual data points without labelled outcomes.
- Identifies outliers by isolating observations with fewer splits in random trees.
- StandardScaler is used to scale features before model application.
- Applied to large datasets such as financial transactions and supplier invoices.

Quiz Questions

Scan the QR code below to access the quiz questions for this chapter (see 13.md).

https://github.com/DrMichaelGuo/QuizPFAAFAMMA

Further Reading and Resources

Hunter, J., Dale, D., Firing, E., Droettboom, M. and The Matplotlib Development Team (2025) *Matplotlib 3.10.5 documentation*. Available at: https://matplotlib.org/stable/index.html (Accessed 7 August 2025).

Pandas Development Team (2025) *pandas documentation (version 2.3.1)*. Available at: https://pandas.pydata.org/docs/ (Accessed 7 August 2025).

scikit-learn (2024) *scikit-learn: Machine Learning in Python*. Available at: https://scikit-learn.org/stable/documentation.html (Accessed 7 August 2025).

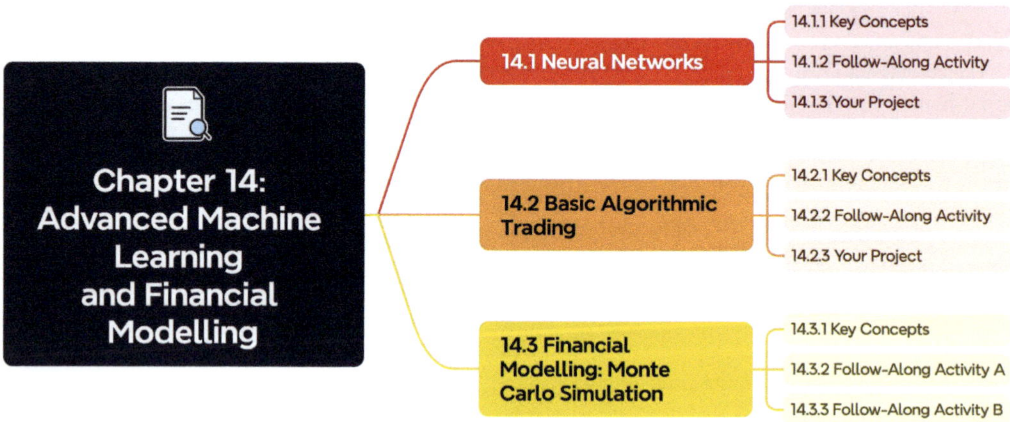

FIGURE 14.1 Structure of Chapter 14

14

ADVANCED MACHINE LEARNING AND FINANCIAL MODELLING

This chapter explores applications of machine learning in finance, including predictive modelling, trading strategy design, and risk simulation. It covers building and training neural networks to classify creditworthiness, developing and backtesting algorithmic trading strategies using logistic regression and technical indicators, and applying Monte Carlo simulations to assess investment risk and option pricing (Figure 14.1).

Learning Objectives

By the end of this chapter, you will be able to

- Construct, train, and evaluate a neural network model to classify financial outcomes.
- Develop and test a basic algorithmic trading strategy using logistic regression.
- Apply Monte Carlo simulations to model investment uncertainty, forecast returns, and estimate option prices.

14.1 Neural Networks

Neural networks are machine learning models that use a layered structure to identify patterns in data. This section explains how to build, train, and evaluate a neural network to predict creditworthiness from financial variables (see Figure 14.2).

14.1.1 Key Concepts

14.1.1.1 Neural Network Model

A neural network consists of a sequence of layers containing units called neurons or nodes. Each neuron performs a mathematical operation on its input data and passes the result to the next layer. The final output is produced after the data passes through all layers.

DOI: 10.4324/9781003656968-14

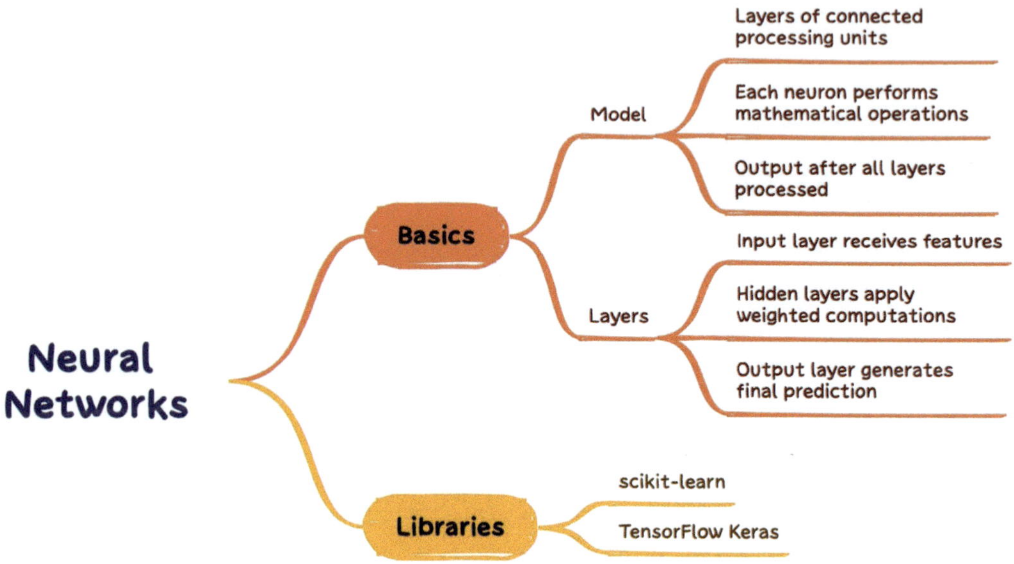

FIGURE 14.2 Neural Networks

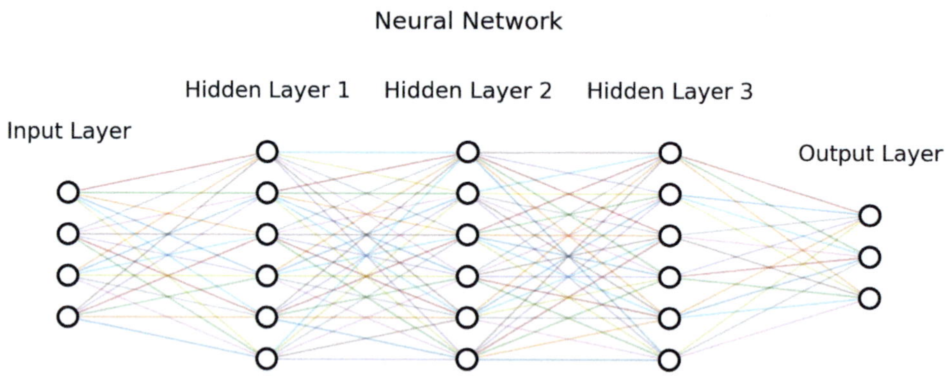

FIGURE 14.3 Multi-Layer Neural Network

14.1.1.2 Layers

A neural network includes three types of layers: (i) the input layer, (ii) the hidden layers, and (iii) the output layer (see Figure 14.3).

The input layer receives the features from the data. The hidden layers process these features by applying weighted computations. The output layer generates the prediction. In classification tasks, the output is a category. In regression tasks, it is a numerical value.

For example the input layer may include features such as annual income, debt-to-income ratio, and credit history. The output layer may represent creditworthiness. During training, the model adjusts the weights in the hidden layers to map the input features to the output.

14.1.1.3 Python Libraries

scikit-learn is a Python library for machine learning that provides functions for data preparation, model training, and model evaluation. The train_test_split function divides a dataset into training and testing sets. StandardScaler standardises numerical features by centring them at zero and scaling them to unit variance.

For classification models, accuracy_score calculates the proportion of correct predictions; classification_report returns precision, recall, and F1-score; and roc_auc_score measures a model's ability to rank positive instances above negative ones. These functions can be imported using

```
from sklearn.model_selection import train_test_split
from sklearn.preprocessing import StandardScaler
from sklearn.metrics import accuracy_score, classification_report,
roc_auc_score
```

TensorFlow Keras is a deep learning library for training neural networks. The sequential model creates a linear stack of layers, where the output of one layer becomes the input to the next. A dense layer connects each neuron to all neurons in the previous layer, allowing the network to combine features during training. The Adam optimiser updates model weights based on the loss function. The input layer specifies the shape of the input data and acts as the model entry point. These modules are imported using

```
from tensorflow.keras.models import Sequential
from tensorflow.keras.layers import Dense
from tensorflow.keras.optimizers import Adam
from tensorflow.keras.layers import Input
```

14.1.2 Follow-Along Activity

This activity demonstrates how to build and evaluate a neural network to predict creditworthiness using income, debt-to-income ratio, and credit history. Synthetic data is used for demonstration purposes to support entry-level students in understanding the basic structure and application of a neural network (see Figure 14.4).

Step 1: Import Libraries

Let's import the required libraries to handle data, build the model, and evaluate performance.

```
import numpy as np
import pandas as pd
import matplotlib.pyplot as plt
from sklearn.model_selection import train_test_split
from sklearn.preprocessing import StandardScaler
from sklearn.metrics import accuracy_score, classification_report,
roc_auc_score
from tensorflow.keras.models import Sequential
from tensorflow.keras.layers import Dense
from tensorflow.keras.optimizers import Adam
from tensorflow.keras.layers import Input
```

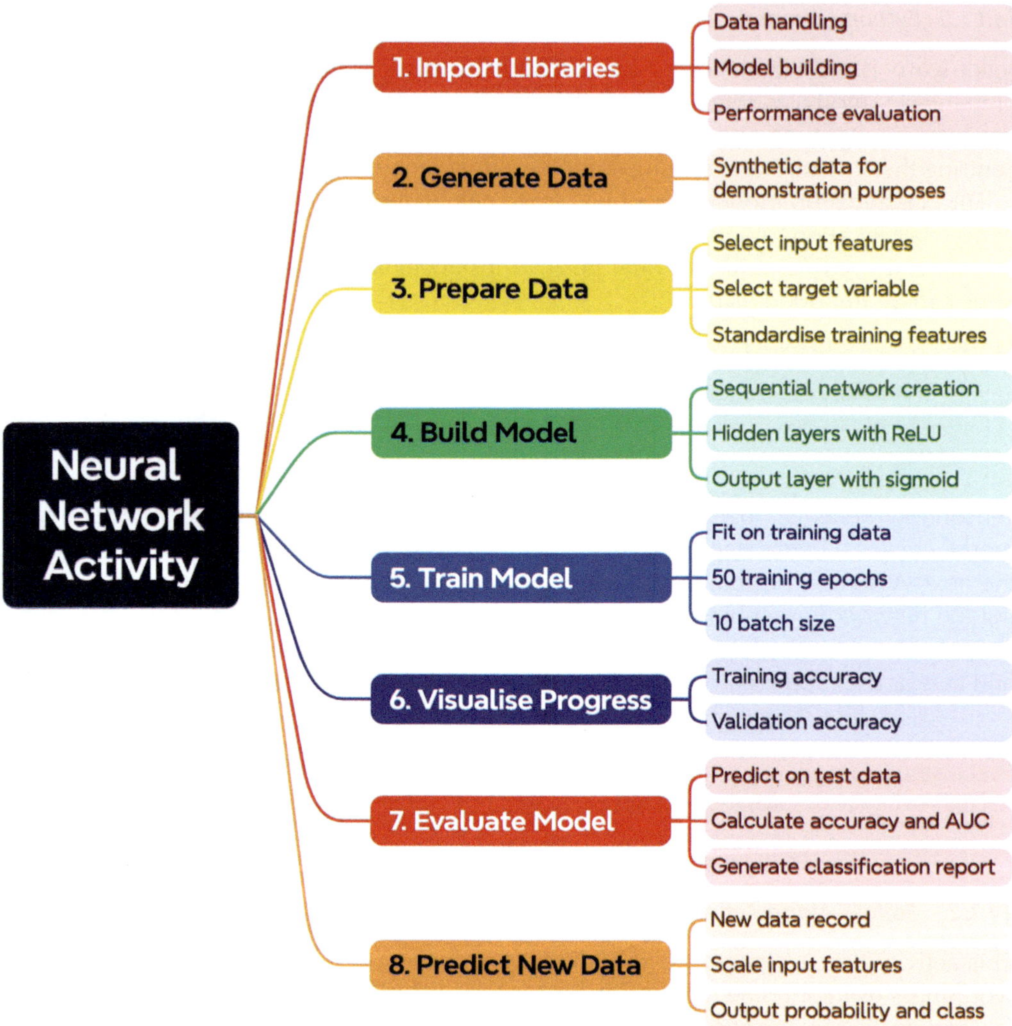

FIGURE 14.4 Neural Network Activity

Explanation

- train_test_split: splits data into training and testing sets.
- StandardScaler: standardises input features.
- accuracy_score, classification_report, roc_auc_score: evaluate model performance.
- Sequential, Dense, Input, Adam: construct and optimise the neural network.

Step 2: Generate Synthetic Financial Data

Let's create synthetic data to represent financial characteristics and corresponding creditworthiness. The dataset is designed as a simple example to help understand the basic structure and logic of a neural network.

```
np.random.seed(42)
num_points = 500

annual_income = np.random.normal(loc=60000, scale=15000,
size=num_points).round(2)

debt_to_income_ratio = np.random.normal(loc=20, scale=10,
size=num_points).round(2)

credit_history = np.random.choice(['Good', 'Average', 'Poor'],
size=num_points)
credit_history_encoded = pd.Series(credit_history).map({'Good': 0,
'Average': 1, 'Poor': 2})

credit_worthiness = ((debt_to_income_ratio < 30) & (credit_history ==
'Good')) | \
                    ((debt_to_income_ratio < 25) & (credit_history ==
'Average'))
credit_worthiness = credit_worthiness.astype(int)

data = pd.DataFrame({
    "Annual Income": annual_income,
    "Debt-to-Income Ratio": debt_to_income_ratio,
    "Credit History": credit_history,
    "Credit History Encoded": credit_history_encoded,
    "Creditworthiness": credit_worthiness
})

print(data.head())
```

Output

```
  Annual Income  Debt-to-Income Ratio Credit History  Credit History Encoded  \
0      67450.71                 29.26           Poor                       2
1      57926.04                 39.09           Good                       0
2      69715.33                  6.01           Poor                       2
3      82845.45                 25.63           Good                       0
4      56487.70                 13.49           Poor                       2

   Creditworthiness
0                 0
1                 0
2                 0
3                 1
4                 0
```

Explanation

- np.random.seed(42): fixes the seed value to ensure reproducible output.
- num_points = 500: defines the number of observations to generate.

- annual_income = np.random.normal(loc=60000, scale=15000, size=num_points).round(2): generates annual income values from a normal distribution with a mean of 60,000 and a standard deviation of 15,000.
- debt_to_income_ratio = np.random.normal(loc=20, scale=10, size=num_points).round(2): generates debt-to-income ratios from a normal distribution with a mean of 20 and a standard deviation of 10.
- credit_history = np.random.choice(['Good', 'Average', 'Poor'], size=num_points): assigns one of three credit history categories to each observation by random selection.
- credit_history_encoded = pd.Series(credit_history).map({'Good': 0, 'Average': 1, 'Poor': 2}): replaces credit history categories with numerical codes for modelling.
- credit_worthiness: is determined by two factors: the debt-to-income ratio and credit history. A value of 1 (creditworthy) is assigned if either of the following conditions is met:
    - The debt-to-income ratio is less than 30 and the credit history is 'Good'.
    - The debt-to-income ratio is less than 25 and the credit history is 'Average'.
    - A value of 0 (not creditworthy) is assigned for all other cases.
- credit_worthiness = credit_worthiness.astype(int): converts the Boolean values produced by the logical conditions into integer values.
- pd.DataFrame(...): combines the variables into a DataFrame.
- print(data.head()): prints the first five rows of the DataFrame.

Step 3: Prepare Data for Training

Let's prepare the input features and labels and standardise the data for training. Neural networks perform better when features are on a similar scale.

```
X = data[['Annual Income', 'Debt-to-Income Ratio', 'Credit History
Encoded']]
y = data['Creditworthiness']

X_train, X_test, y_train, y_test = train_test_split(X, y, test_
size=0.2, random_state=42)

scaler = StandardScaler()
X_train = scaler.fit_transform(X_train)
X_test = scaler.transform(X_test)
```

Explanation

- X = data[['Annual Income', 'Debt-to-Income Ratio', 'Credit History Encoded']]: selects the input features for model training.
- y = data['Creditworthiness']: selects the target variable.
- X_train, X_test, y_train, y_test = train_test_split(X, y, test_size = 0.2, random_state = 42): splits data into training and test sets.

- test_size = 0.2: allocates 20% of the data to the test set and 80% to the training set.
- The function returns four outputs:
    - X_train: input features for model training.
    - X_test: input features for model evaluation.
    - y_train: target values for training.
    - y_test: target values for evaluation.
- scaler = StandardScaler(): creates a scaling object.
- X_train = scaler.fit_transform(X_train): calculates scaling parameters from the training features and applies them.
- X_test = scaler.transform(X_test): applies the same scaling to the test features.

Step 4: Build the Neural Network Model

Let's construct the neural network model by stacking layers in a sequential manner.

```
model = Sequential()
model.add(Input(shape=(X_train.shape[1],)))
model.add(Dense(16, activation='relu'))
model.add(Dense(8, activation='relu'))
model.add(Dense(1, activation='sigmoid'))

model.compile(optimizer=Adam(learning_rate=0.001), loss='binary_
crossentropy', metrics=['accuracy'])
```

Explanation

- model = Sequential(): defines a linear model where each layer passes its output to the next.
- model.add(Input(shape=(X_train.shape[1],))): adds an input layer. X_train.shape[1] sets the number of input features based on the structure of the training data.
- model.add(Dense(16, activation='relu')): adds the first hidden layer with 16 units. Each unit calculates a weighted sum of the inputs and applies the ReLU (Rectified Linear Unit) function. The ReLU function replaces negative values with zero and retains positive values. This introduces non-linearity into the model.
- model.add(Dense(8, activation='relu')): adds a second hidden layer with eight units. This layer also uses the ReLU function and processes the output of the previous layer to extract further structure from the data.
- model.add(Dense(1, activation='sigmoid')): adds the output layer with one unit. The sigmoid function transforms the output into a value between 0 and 1. This value represents the predicted probability that the input belongs to the positive class. The structure is suitable for binary classification.
- model.compile(...): prepares the model for training.
    - optimizer=Adam(learning_rate=0.001): sets the Adam optimiser, which adjusts the learning rate for each parameter during training, based on observed gradient patterns.

- loss='binary_crossentropy': selects binary cross-entropy as the loss function. This measures the difference between predicted probabilities and actual binary labels.
- metrics=['accuracy']: specifies accuracy as the evaluation metric, calculated as the ratio of correct predictions to total predictions.

Step 5: Train the Model

Let's train the model using the training data and monitor its performance.

```
history = model.fit(X_train, y_train, epochs=50, batch_size=10,
validation_split=0.1, verbose=1)
```

Sample Output:

```
Epoch 1/50
36/36 ━━━━━━━━━━━━━━━━━━━━ 2s 9ms/step - accuracy: 0.5663 - loss:
0.6714 - val_accuracy: 0.8250 - val_loss: 0.5806
Epoch 2/50
36/36 ━━━━━━━━━━━━━━━━━━━━ 0s 4ms/step - accuracy: 0.7693 - loss:
0.5779 - val_accuracy: 0.9250 - val_loss: 0.4800
Epoch 3/50
36/36 ━━━━━━━━━━━━━━━━━━━━ 0s 4ms/step - accuracy: 0.8466 - loss:
0.4930 - val_accuracy: 0.9000 - val_loss: 0.3950
Epoch 4/50
36/36 ━━━━━━━━━━━━━━━━━━━━ 0s 4ms/step - accuracy: 0.8692 - loss:
0.4056 - val_accuracy: 0.9000 - val_loss: 0.3331
```

Explanation

- history = model.fit(...): fits the model to the training data. This returns a history object, which records the values of loss and accuracy after each epoch, for both training and validation data.
    - epochs=50: runs 50 complete passes through the training dataset. Each full pass is called an epoch.
    - batch_size=10: updates model weights after processing every 10 samples, rather than after the entire dataset. This is known as mini-batch training.
    - validation_split=0.1: holds back 10% of the training data for validation. This subset is not used for learning but for monitoring performance and detecting overfitting.
    - verbose=1: displays progress after each epoch, including accuracy and loss for training and validation sets.
- Only the first four epochs are shown. Each line presents the number of batches processed, the time taken, and the accuracy and loss for both training and validation data.

Step 6: Visualise Training Progress

Let's plot the model's training and validation accuracy over epochs.

```
plt.plot(history.history['accuracy'], label='Train Accuracy')
plt.plot(history.history['val_accuracy'], label='Validation Accuracy')
plt.xlabel('Epochs')
plt.ylabel('Accuracy')
plt.legend()
plt.title('Training and Validation Accuracy')
plt.show()
```

Output: see Figure 14.5.

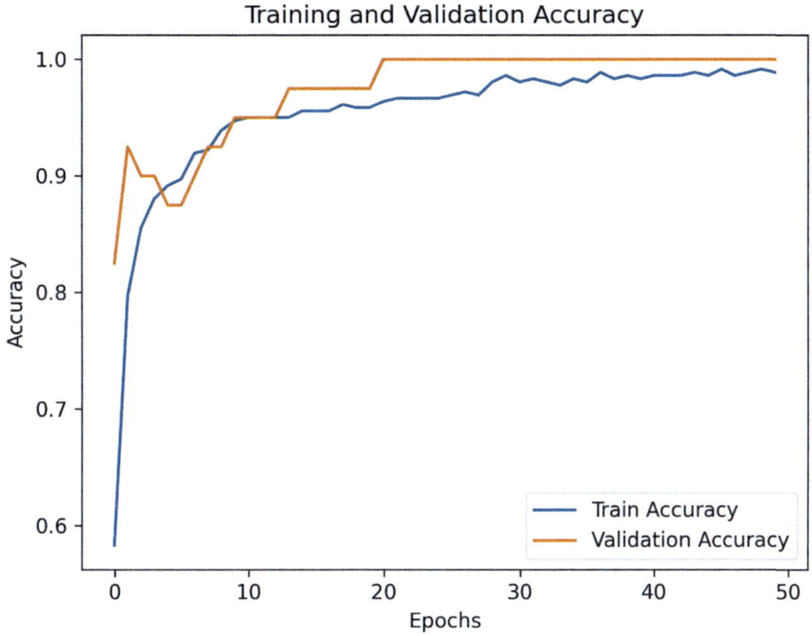

FIGURE 14.5 Training and Validation Accuracy

Explanation

- plt.plot(history.history['accuracy'], label='Train Accuracy'): plots the training accuracy for each epoch. This value comes from the history object returned by model.fit().
- plt.plot(history.history['val_accuracy'], label='Validation Accuracy'): plots the validation accuracy for each epoch for comparison with training accuracy.
- plt.xlabel('Epochs'): labels the x-axis.
- plt.ylabel('Accuracy'): labels the y-axis.
- plt.legend(): adds a legend.
- plt.title('Training and Validation Accuracy'): sets the title.
- plt.show(): displays the plot.

The output shows that the blue line, labelled 'Train Accuracy', represents the model's accuracy on the training data at each epoch. An epoch is a complete pass through the training dataset. During each epoch, the model adjusts its parameters to improve its predictions. The orange line, labelled 'Validation Accuracy', shows the model's accuracy on the validation data. This data is not used for training but is used to measure how well the model generalises to unseen data.

In the first few epochs, both training and validation accuracy increase rapidly, showing that the model learns to classify the data correctly early in training. The validation accuracy soon reaches 1, indicating perfect classification of the validation data. The training accuracy continues to rise but remains slightly below the validation accuracy, suggesting that the model generalises well without clear signs of overfitting.

Step 7: Evaluate the Model on Test Data

Let's assess the model's performance using the test data.

```
y_prob = model.predict(X_test)
y_pred = (y_prob > 0.5).astype(int)

accuracy = accuracy_score(y_test, y_pred)
auc = roc_auc_score(y_test, y_pred)
report = classification_report(y_test, y_pred)

print(f"Accuracy: {accuracy:.2f}")
print(f"AUC: {auc:.2f}")
print("Classification Report:")
print(report)
```

Output

```
Accuracy: 0.99
AUC: 0.99
Classification Report:
              precision    recall  f1-score   support

           0       1.00      0.98      0.99        53
           1       0.98      1.00      0.99        47

    accuracy                           0.99       100
   macro avg       0.99      0.99      0.99       100
weighted avg       0.99      0.99      0.99       100
```

Explanation

- y_prob = model.predict(X_test): generates continuous probability scores between 0 and 1. Each value represents the model's confidence that a case is creditworthy (class 1).
- y_pred = (y_prob > 0.5).astype(int): applies a 0.5 threshold to assign binary class labels.
- accuracy = accuracy_score(y_test, y_pred): calculates the proportion of correct predictions in the test set.
- auc = roc_auc_score(y_test, y_pred): calculates the area under the ROC curve, which quantifies the model's ability to distinguish between the two classes.

- report = classification_report(y_test, y_pred): returns a summary of precision, recall, F1-score, and support for each class.
- print(...): displays the evaluation results.

The model achieves an accuracy of 0.99 and an AUC of 0.99, indicating that it correctly predicts creditworthiness in 99% of the test cases and distinguishes effectively between the two classes. The classification report shows precision, recall, and F1-score values of 0.99 for both classes, confirming balanced and consistent performance. Precision is slightly higher for class 0 (non-creditworthy), while recall is perfect for class 1 (creditworthy).

These results reflect the synthetic and simplified nature of the dataset. Because the relationships in this data are predefined and contain no random noise or missing information, the model can achieve near-perfect accuracy and AUC. In real financial datasets, such as those involving loan defaults or credit risk, performance metrics are much lower due to incomplete records, overlapping class features, and changing economic conditions. The purpose of this example is to demonstrate the process of building, training, and evaluating a neural network, not to represent the performance expected in real-world applications.

Step 8: Make a Prediction on New Data

Let's apply the trained neural network to a new data point to estimate creditworthiness.

```
new_data = pd.DataFrame({
    "Annual Income": [55000],
    "Debt-to-Income Ratio": [18],
    "Credit History Encoded": [1]  # 'Average'
})

new_data_scaled = scaler.transform(new_data)

prediction = model.predict(new_data_scaled)
predicted_class = (prediction > 0.5).astype(int)

print(f"Predicted Probability: {prediction[0][0]:.4f}")
print("Predicted Class:", "Creditworthy" if predicted_class[0][0] ==
1 else "Not Creditworthy")
```

Output

```
Predicted Probability: 0.9961
Predicted Class: Creditworthy
```

Explanation

- new_data = pd.DataFrame(...): creates a DataFrame containing one record.
- new_data_scaled = scaler.transform(new_data): standardises the new input using parameters learned during training.
- prediction = model.predict(new_data_scaled): produces a probability that the observation belongs to class 1 (creditworthy).

- predicted_class = (prediction > 0.5).astype(int): applies a threshold of 0.5 to convert the probability to a binary class label (1 = creditworthy, 0 = not creditworthy).
- print(f"Predicted Probability: {prediction[0][0]:.4f}"): prints the predicted probability rounded to four decimal places.
- print("Predicted Class:", ...): prints the class label based on the thresholded probability.

In binary classification, a neural network outputs a probability between 0 and 1 rather than a class label. A threshold is applied to convert this probability into a label. A threshold of 0.5 is common: values above 0.5 are assigned to class 1, and values of 0.5 or less to class 0.

In this example, the predicted probability is 0.9961. Since this exceeds the 0.5 threshold, the predicted class is creditworthy.

14.1.2.9 Considerations for Practice

Neural networks can learn complex patterns but are not always easy to interpret. In practice, finance professionals must understand which variables influence predictions and ensure compliance with data and regulatory standards. Simpler models such as logistic regression are often preferred when transparency is required.

14.1.3 Your Project

Build a neural network to classify loan applicants as either likely to default or not default on their loan.

The dataset *14_your_project_neural_networks.csv* contains 500 loan application records. Each record includes the following variables:

- Annual Income: the applicant's annual income.
- Loan Amount: the amount of the loan requested.
- Credit Score: a numerical credit score indicating credit history.
- Number of Loans: the number of active loans the applicant holds.
- Employment Encoded: employment status, where 0 indicates employed, 1 indicates self-employed, and 2 indicates unemployed.
- Missed Payments: the number of missed repayments on previous loans.
- Default: the target variable indicating whether the applicant defaulted on their loan (1) or not (0).

The dataset 14_your_project_neural_networks.csv is available at:

https://github.com/DrMichaelGuo/PFAAFAMMA

Note: When you run this project with real or less structured data, expect lower accuracy and AUC values. This variation reflects real-world uncertainty and makes evaluation more meaningful.

14.1.3.1 Tasks

- Import libraries: import the required libraries for CSV file upload, data processing, neural network modelling, and evaluation.
- Load CSV: upload the CSV file and read it into a DataFrame.

- Prepare data: select the following features as input variables: Annual Income, Loan Amount, Credit Score, Number of Loans, Employment Encoded, and Missed Payments. Use Default as the target variable. Standardise numerical features using StandardScaler. Split the dataset into training (80%) and testing (20%) sets.
- Build a neural network model: use a sequential model with an input layer matching the number of input features, two hidden layers (e.g. 16 and 8 units with ReLU activation), and an output layer with one unit and sigmoid activation.
- Train model: train the model using the training set for 50 epochs with a batch size of 10. Use 10% of the training data for validation.
- Visualise accuracy: plot both training and validation accuracy against the number of epochs to show the model's learning progress.
- Evaluate model: evaluate the model's performance using the test set. Report the accuracy and AUC score. Generate a classification report.
- Make predictions on new applicants: use the financial data below of a new sample applicant to predict whether they are likely to default. Display both the predicted probability of default and the final class label.

```
# New Data
new_applicants = pd.DataFrame({
    'Annual Income': [38000, 52000],
    'Loan Amount': [17000, 10000],
    'Credit Score': [580, 690],
    'Number of Loans': [2, 1],
    'Employment Encoded': [2, 0],
    'Missed Payments': [3, 0]
})
```

14.1.3.2 Example Code

```
# Step 1: Import Libraries
import numpy as np
import pandas as pd
import matplotlib.pyplot as plt
from sklearn.model_selection import train_test_split
from sklearn.preprocessing import StandardScaler
from sklearn.metrics import accuracy_score, classification_report,
roc_auc_score
from tensorflow.keras.models import Sequential
from tensorflow.keras.layers import Dense, Input
from tensorflow.keras.optimizers import Adam

# Step 2: Upload CSV
from google.colab import files
uploaded = files.upload()  # Choose the CSV file when prompted

# Read the uploaded file
data = pd.read_csv('14_your_project_neural_networks.csv')  # <-
change filename to match new dataset
```

```
# Step 3: Prepare Data
X = data[['Annual Income', 'Loan Amount', 'Credit Score', 'Number of
Loans', 'Employment Encoded', 'Missed Payments']]
y = data['Default']

X_train, X_test, y_train, y_test = train_test_split(X, y, test_
size=0.2, random_state=42)

scaler = StandardScaler()
X_train = scaler.fit_transform(X_train)
X_test = scaler.transform(X_test)

# Step 4: Build Model
model = Sequential()
model.add(Input(shape=(X_train.shape[1],)))
model.add(Dense(16, activation='relu'))
model.add(Dense(8, activation='relu'))
model.add(Dense(1, activation='sigmoid'))

model.compile(optimizer=Adam(learning_rate=0.001),
loss='binary_crossentropy', metrics=['accuracy'])

# Step 5: Train Model
history = model.fit(X_train, y_train, epochs=50, batch_size=10,
validation_split=0.1, verbose=1)

# Step 6: Visualise Accuracy
plt.plot(history.history['accuracy'], label='Train Accuracy')
plt.plot(history.history['val_accuracy'], label='Validation
Accuracy')
plt.xlabel('Epochs')
plt.ylabel('Accuracy')
plt.title('Training and Validation Accuracy')
plt.legend()
plt.show()

# Step 7: Evaluate Model
y_prob = model.predict(X_test)
y_pred = (y_prob > 0.5).astype(int)

accuracy = accuracy_score(y_test, y_pred)
auc = roc_auc_score(y_test, y_pred)
report = classification_report(y_test, y_pred)

print(f"Accuracy: {accuracy:.2f}")
print(f"AUC: {auc:.2f}")
print("Classification Report:")
print(report)
```

```
# Step 8: Make Predictions on New Data

new_applicants = pd.DataFrame({
    'Annual Income': [38000, 52000],
    'Loan Amount': [17000, 10000],
    'Credit Score': [580, 690],
    'Number of Loans': [2, 1],
    'Employment Encoded': [2, 0],  # 2 = Unemployed, 0 = Employed
    'Missed Payments': [3, 0]
})

# Standardise using the same scaler used for training
new_applicants_scaled = scaler.transform(new_applicants)

# Predict probabilities
predictions = model.predict(new_applicants_scaled)

# Convert probabilities to binary predictions
predicted_classes = (predictions > 0.5).astype(int)

# Display predictions
for i, (prob, pred) in enumerate(zip(predictions,
predicted_classes)):
    print(f"Applicant {i+1}:")
    print(f"  Predicted Probability of Default: {prob[0]:.4f}")
    print(f"  Predicted Class: {'Default' if pred[0] == 1 else 'No
Default'}\n")
```

Scan the QR code to access the Python code and output (see 14.1.ipynb). The notebook also shows how to save and reload a model.

https://github.com/DrMichaelGuo/PFAAFAMMA

14.2 Basic Algorithmic Trading

Algorithmic trading uses computer code to make trading decisions based on fixed rules. This section presents an example that combines the relative strength index (RSI) with logistic regression to generate trading signals and evaluate performance using historical data (see Figure 14.6).

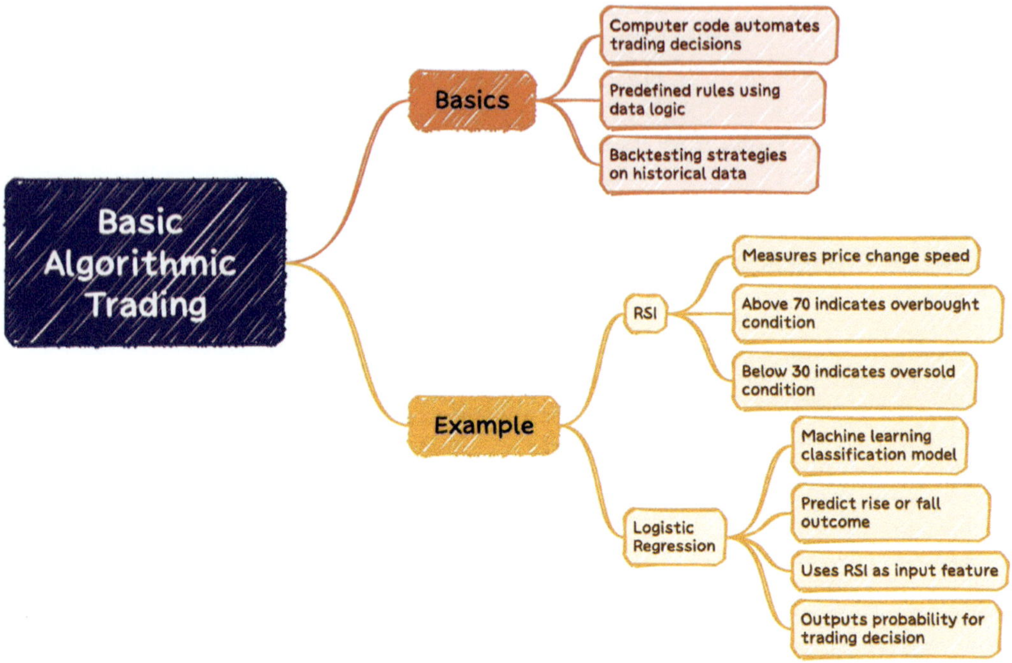

FIGURE 14.6 Basic Algorithmic Trading

14.2.1 Key Concepts

14.2.1.1 Algorithmic Trading

Algorithmic trading uses computer code to automate decisions about buying and selling financial assets. Instead of manual judgement or emotional response, rules are defined in advance using data, logic, or models. These rules are applied to market data to execute trades. Algorithmic trading enables strategies to be tested on historical data before use in live markets and can increase trading speed and consistency.

14.2.1.2 RSI (Relative Strength Index)

The RSI is a technical indicator that measures the speed and size of recent price changes. It produces a value between 0 and 100 to indicate whether an asset may be overbought or oversold. An RSI above 70 may suggest that the asset is overbought and could fall. An RSI below 30 may indicate that the asset is oversold and could rise. RSI is used to identify entry and exit points based on price momentum.

14.2.1.3 Logistic Regression

Logistic regression is a machine learning model used for classification tasks, where the aim is to predict one of two outcomes. In the following activity, it predicts whether the price of a financial asset will rise or fall the next day. The model uses input features such as RSI to produce a probability, which is then converted into a decision on whether to take a trading action.

14.2.2 *Follow-Along Activity*

This activity demonstrates how to build a simple, rule-based trading strategy that combines the RSI with logistic regression to predict whether the price of a financial asset will rise the following day. The strategy is simulated using the model's predictions. A purchase is made only when the model predicts a price increase. If no increase is predicted, no trade is made (see Figure 14.7).

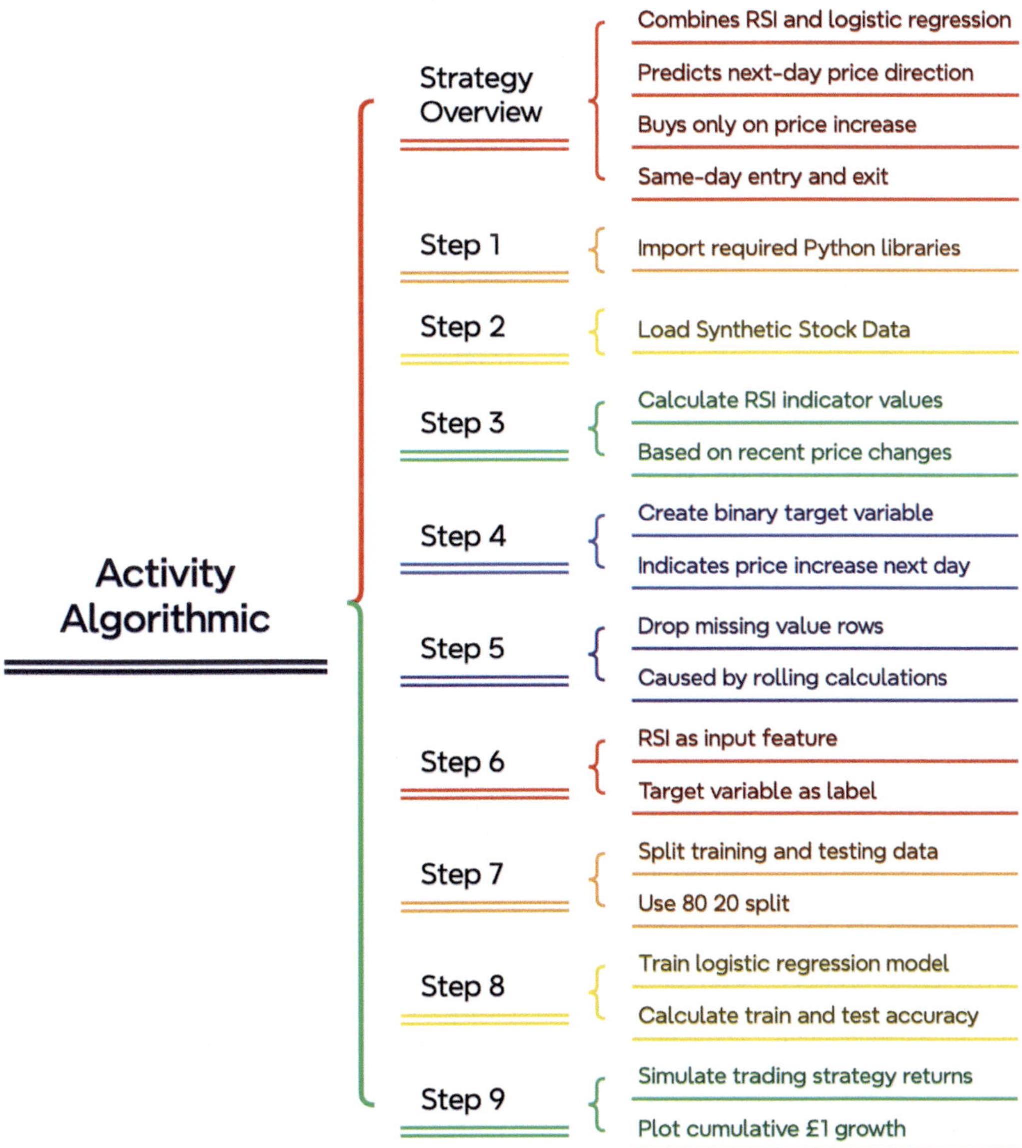

FIGURE 14.7 Activity Algorithmic

This example is for demonstration purposes only and is deliberately simplified. It assumes entry at today's close and exit at tomorrow's close, meaning positions are held overnight. The strategy uses one input variable (RSI) and one modelling technique (logistic regression), which limits its predictive power. The results are specific to the dataset used and should not be assumed to apply to other markets or time periods.

Disclaimer: This material is for educational purposes to illustrate how technical indicators and machine learning models can be applied in financial contexts. It is not financial advice or investment guidance. Readers should seek professional advice before making any financial decisions.

Step 1: Import Libraries

Let's import the libraries required for data analysis and machine learning.

```
import pandas as pd
import numpy as np
import matplotlib.pyplot as plt
from sklearn.model_selection import train_test_split
from sklearn.linear_model import LogisticRegression
```

Explanation

- import pandas as pd: imports the pandas library.
- import numpy as np: imports the NumPy library.
- import matplotlib.pyplot as plt: imports Matplotlib for creating plots.
- from sklearn.model_selection import train_test_split: imports function to split data into training and testing sets.
- from sklearn.linear_model import LogisticRegression: imports the logistic regression model.

Step 2: Load Synthetic Stock Data

This example uses synthetic data representing a fictional market called the Simulated Market Index (SMI). The dataset *14_basic_algorithmic_trading.csv* is available at the following site:

https://github.com/DrMichaelGuo/PFAAFAMMA

```
from google.colab import files
uploaded = files.upload()
data = pd.read_csv("14_basic_algorithmic_trading.csv", parse_
dates=["Date"], index_col="Date")
price_col = "price"
data = data[[price_col]].rename(columns={price_col: "price"})
```

Explanation

- pd.read_csv(...): loads the saved synthetic dataset.
- parse_dates=["Date"]: ensures that dates are recognised as datetime objects.

- index_col="Date": sets the date column as the DataFrame index.
- data = data[[price_col]]: extracts the price column for analysis.
- rename(...): standardises the column name to "price".

Step 3: Calculate RSI

Let's calculate the RSI based on recent price changes. The calculation uses simple rolling averages of gains and losses over a 14-day window to estimate momentum in price movements.

```
def compute_rsi(series, window=14):
    delta = series.diff()
    gain = delta.clip(lower=0)
    loss = -delta.clip(upper=0)
    avg_gain = gain.rolling(window).mean()
    avg_loss = loss.rolling(window).mean()
    rs = avg_gain / avg_loss
    rsi = 100 - (100 / (1 + rs))
    return rsi

data["rsi"] = compute_rsi(data["price"])
```

Explanation

- compute_rsi(...): defines a function to calculate RSI.
- delta = series.diff(): calculates daily changes in price.
- gain = delta.clip(lower=0): captures gains.
- loss = -delta.clip(upper=0): captures losses.
- avg_gain = gain.rolling(...): calculates rolling average of gains.
- avg_loss = loss.rolling(...): calculates rolling average of losses.
- rs = avg_gain/avg_loss: calculates relative strength ratio.
- rsi = 100 - ...: converts the ratio to the RSI value between 0 and 100.
- data["rsi"] = ...: stores RSI values.

Step 4: Create Target Variable

Let's create a binary target variable to indicate whether the price increases the following day.

```
data["return"] = data["price"].pct_change()
data["target"] = (data["return"].shift(-1) > 0).astype(int)
```

Explanation

- data["return"] = ...: calculates daily percentage return.
- data["target"] = ...: sets 1 if the price increases the next day, otherwise 0.

Step 5: Drop Missing Values

Let's remove rows with missing values caused by rolling calculations.

```
data = data.dropna()
```

Explanation

- data.dropna(): removes rows with missing values caused by rolling calculations, percentage change, and shifting. These missing values appear in the first and last rows and must be removed to prepare the dataset for model training.

Step 6: Prepare Features and Labels

Let's separate input features from the target label.

```
X = data[["rsi"]]
y = data["target"]
```

Explanation

- X = data[["rsi"]]: selects RSI as an input feature.
- y = data["target"]: selects the target variable as label.

Step 7: Split into Training and Testing Sets

Let's split the data for model training and testing.

```
X_train, X_test, y_train, y_test = train_test_split(X, y, test_
size=0.2, shuffle=False)
```

Explanation

- test_size=0.2: assigns 20% of the data for testing and 80% for training.
- shuffle=False: preserves chronological order so the model is trained on past prices and tested on future prices.

Step 8: Train Logistic Regression Model

Let's train a logistic regression model to predict whether the price will increase.

```
model = LogisticRegression()
model.fit(X_train, y_train)

train_score = model.score(X_train, y_train)
test_score = model.score(X_test, y_test)

print("Train Accuracy:", round(train_score, 2))
print("Test Accuracy:", round(test_score, 2))
```

Output

```
Train Accuracy: 0.53
Test Accuracy: 0.55
```

Explanation

- model = LogisticRegression(): creates a logistic regression model.
- model.fit(...): trains the model on historical data.
- train_score = model.score(...): calculates accuracy on the training set.
- test_score = model.score(...): calculates accuracy on the test set.
- print(...): displays the accuracy results.
- Train Accuracy: 0.53: the model correctly predicted the next-day direction for 53% of the training data.
- Test Accuracy: 0.55: the model correctly predicted the next-day direction for 55% of the test data.

Step 9: Simulate Trading Strategy

Let's simulate a trading strategy based on the model's prediction. Buy when the model predicts an increase. Exit the position at tomorrow's close. Remain in cash otherwise.

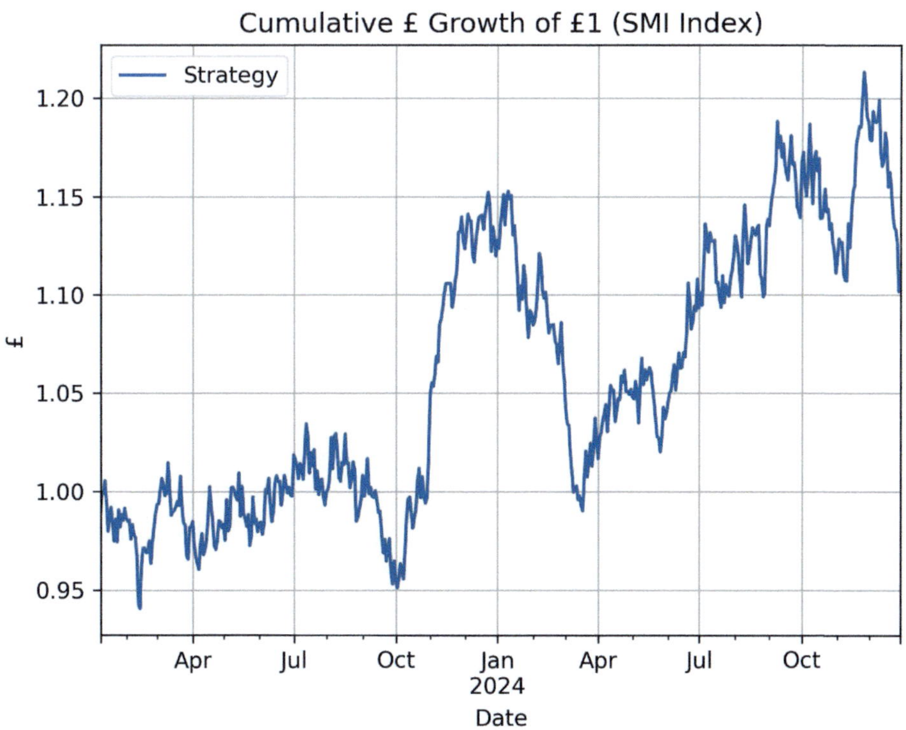

FIGURE 14.8 Cumulative Growth

```
predictions = model.predict(X_test)
signals = pd.Series(predictions, index=X_test.index)

next_day_return = data["return"].shift(-1)
strategy_returns = next_day_return.loc[signals.index] * signals
strategy_returns = strategy_returns.dropna()

(1 + strategy_returns).cumprod().plot(label="Strategy")
plt.title("Cumulative £ Growth of £1")
plt.legend()
plt.grid(True)
plt.ylabel("£")
plt.show()
```

Output: see Figure 14.8.

Explanation

- predictions = model.predict(...): generates binary predictions (1 for increase, 0 otherwise).
- signals = pd.Series(...): stores the trading signals with their corresponding dates.
- strategy_returns = ...: calculates returns only on days when the model signals a position.
- (1 + strategy_returns).cumprod(): calculates cumulative product of returns to simulate growth.
- .plot(label="Strategy"): plots the cumulative growth.
- plt.title(...): sets the chart title.
- plt.legend(): adds a legend.
- plt.grid(True): adds grid lines for readability.
- plt.ylabel("£"): labels the y-axis with the currency symbol.
- plt.show(): displays the chart.

The plot shows the cumulative growth of a £1 investment based on trading signals generated by the logistic regression model for the SMI. The value fluctuates around its initial level during much of 2023, showing alternating gains and losses. An upward trend emerges from late 2023 into early 2024, indicating a period when the strategy captured several profitable movements. Mid-2024 sees temporary pullbacks followed by renewed gains before a decline towards the end of the year. Despite this late-year fall, the strategy finishes above its starting value, showing positive performance overall.

14.2.2.10 Considerations for Practice

Algorithmic trading models are sensitive to market conditions and data quality. Real trading must account for transaction costs, timing differences, and changes in market behaviour that can reduce model performance. Results from simplified examples should not be applied directly to live markets.

14.2.3 Your Project

Continue from the code developed in the follow-along activity. The objective is to examine how changes in model inputs affect performance. For example the RSI indicator used earlier can be replaced with moving average convergence divergence (MACD). MACD is calculated as the difference between two exponential moving averages of the price. The following function performs this calculation:

```
def compute_macd(price, short=12, long=26):
    ema_short = price.ewm(span=short, adjust=False).mean()
    ema_long = price.ewm(span=long, adjust=False).mean()
    return ema_short - ema_long

data["macd"] = compute_macd(data["price"])

X = data[["macd"]]
```

14.2.3.1 *Tasks*

- Load the synthetic dataset created earlier (*14_basic_algorithmic_trading.csv*).
- Compute the MACD indicator using the code provided above.
- Create the target variable by shifting the return series to indicate whether the next day's return is positive.
- Remove rows with missing values caused by percentage change and rolling calculations.
- Define the input feature as MACD and the output label as the target variable.
- Split the data into training and testing sets without shuffling to preserve time order.
- Train a logistic regression model on the training set and evaluate its accuracy on both training and test sets.
- Generate predictions, simulate trading returns from those predictions, and plot the cumulative return of the strategy.

14.2.3.2 *Example Code*

```
import pandas as pd
import numpy as np
import matplotlib.pyplot as plt
from sklearn.model_selection import train_test_split
from sklearn.linear_model import LogisticRegression

# Step 1: Load synthetic stock data for the SMI Index
data = pd.read_csv("14_basic_algorithmic_trading.csv", parse_
dates=["Date"], index_col="Date")
price_col = "price"
data = data[[price_col]].rename(columns={price_col: "price"})

# Step 2: Compute the Relative Strength Index (RSI)
def compute_rsi(series, window=14):
    delta = series.diff()
    gain = delta.clip(lower=0)
    loss = -delta.clip(upper=0)
    avg_gain = gain.rolling(window).mean()
    avg_loss = loss.rolling(window).mean()
    rs = avg_gain / avg_loss
```

```
    rsi = 100 - (100 / (1 + rs))
    return rsi

data["rsi"] = compute_rsi(data["price"])

# Step 3: Create target variable (1 if next day's return is
positive, otherwise 0)
data["return"] = data["price"].pct_change()
data["target"] = (data["return"].shift(-1) > 0).astype(int)

# Step 4: Drop missing values
data = data.dropna()

# Step 5: Prepare features and labels
X = data[["rsi"]]
y = data["target"]

# Step 6: Split into training and testing sets (no shuffle to
preserve time order)
X_train, X_test, y_train, y_test = train_test_split(X, y, test_
size=0.2, shuffle=False)

# Step 7: Train logistic regression model
model = LogisticRegression()
model.fit(X_train, y_train)

train_score = model.score(X_train, y_train)
test_score = model.score(X_test, y_test)

print("Train Accuracy:", round(train_score, 2))
print("Test Accuracy:", round(test_score, 2))

# Step 8: Simulate trading strategy
predictions = model.predict(X_test)
signals = pd.Series(predictions, index=X_test.index)

next_day_return = data["return"].shift(-1)
strategy_returns = next_day_return.loc[signals.index] * signals
strategy_returns = strategy_returns.dropna()

(1 + strategy_returns).cumprod().plot(label="Strategy")
plt.title("Cumulative £ Growth of £1 (SMI Index)")
plt.legend()
plt.grid(True)
plt.ylabel("£")

plt.show()
```

Scan the QR code to access the Python code and output (see 14.2.ipynb).

https://github.com/DrMichaelGuo/PFAAFAMMA

14.3 Financial Modelling: Monte Carlo Simulation

Monte Carlo simulation is a method for financial modelling that applies to investment analysis, risk assessment, and financial planning when outcomes depend on variables that cannot be known in advance. Python can be used to implement Monte Carlo simulation by automating repeated calculations, generating visual outputs, and analysing the distribution of results (see Figure 14.9).

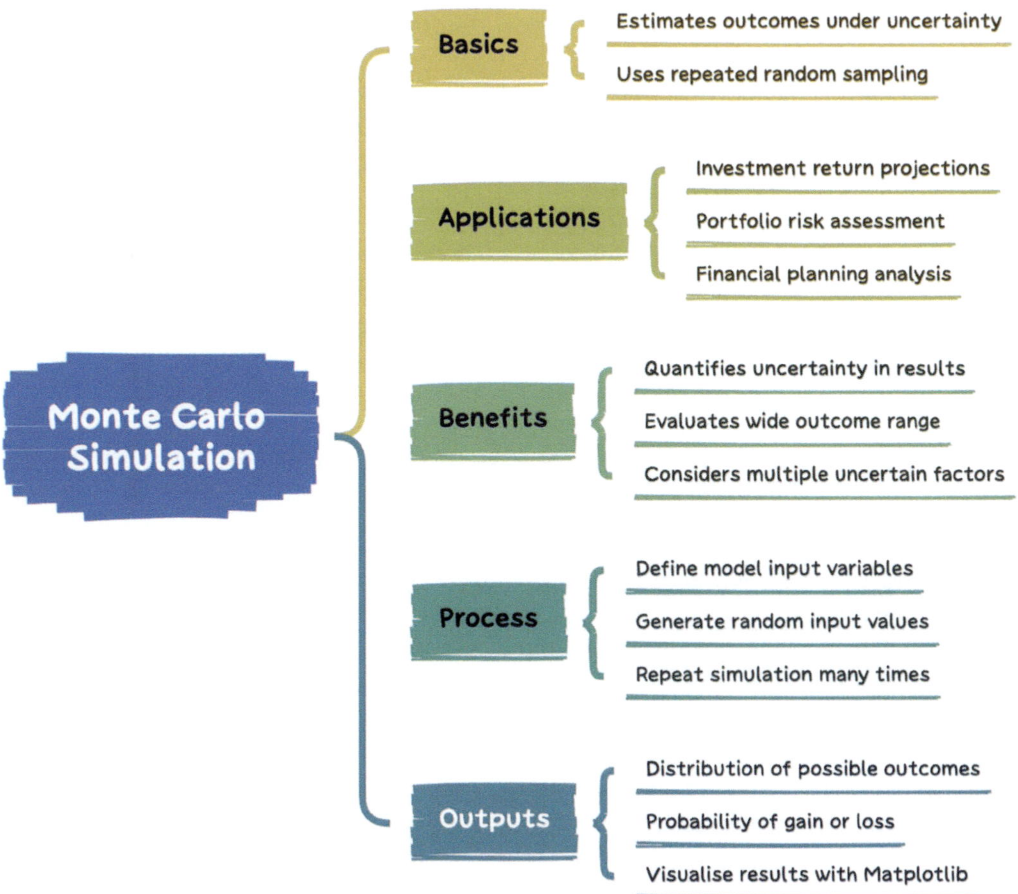

FIGURE 14.9 Monte Carlo Simulation

14.3.1 Key Concepts

14.3.1.1 Monte Carlo Simulation

Monte Carlo simulation is a technique used in financial modelling to estimate the range of possible outcomes under uncertainty. It uses random sampling and repeated calculations to simulate future scenarios. The method is named after the city of Monte Carlo, known for its casinos, to reflect the use of chance in the sampling process.

In portfolio risk analysis, for example Monte Carlo simulation can assess the possible future value of an investment or portfolio. Rather than predicting a single outcome, it generates many possible outcomes based on inputs such as expected return, volatility, and time horizon. This allows for the evaluation of the distribution of returns and the estimation of the probability of specific gains or losses.

14.3.1.2 Benefits of Monte Carlo Simulation

Monte Carlo simulation quantifies uncertainty in financial outcomes by replacing single-point estimates with a range of results generated through many simulated scenarios with random inputs. This helps users examine how results change under different assumptions and conditions.

Monte Carlo simulation applies when variables are uncertain or interact in ways that standard formulas cannot capture, such as investment returns, interest rates, or future cash flows. Through repeated random sampling, the method models systems where outcomes depend on multiple uncertain factors.

Monte Carlo simulation also supports communication of financial risk. For example visual outputs created in Python with Matplotlib show the full distribution of outcomes, enabling the interpretation of probabilities, potential losses, and returns. This helps inform decisions in planning, risk management, and performance evaluation.

14.3.2 Follow-Along Activity A

This activity introduces Monte Carlo simulation by estimating the possible outcomes of a long-term investment. The objective is to simulate different future investment values based on uncertain annual returns (see Figure 14.10).

Let's consider the following context. An investor places £1,000 in an investment for a 10-year period. The investment has an average annual return of 5% and an annual standard deviation of 2%. These returns are assumed to follow a normal distribution. The simulation will run 1,000 scenarios to estimate the distribution of final investment values.

Disclaimer: This content is for educational purposes only. It is intended to demonstrate technical implementation using Python and Monte Carlo simulation. It does not constitute financial, investment, or professional advice, nor should it be relied upon for any financial decision-making. Readers are strongly advised to seek independent professional advice before making any financial or investment decisions.

FIGURE 14.10 Monte Carlo Activity A

Step 1: Import Libraries

Let's import the necessary libraries for numerical calculations and visualisation.

```
import numpy as np
import matplotlib.pyplot as plt
np.random.seed(42)
```

Explanation

- import numpy as np: imports the NumPy library for numerical operations and random number generation.
- import matplotlib.pyplot as plt: imports Matplotlib for plotting.
- np.random.seed(42): sets a fixed seed for random number generation so that the code produces the same results each time it is run.

Step 2: Define Parameters

Let's set the input parameters for the simulation.

```
initial_investment = 1_000
years = 10
mean_return = 0.05
std_deviation = 0.02
simulations = 1_000
```

Explanation

- initial_investment = 1_000: sets the initial investment amount to £1,000.
- years = 10: defines the investment period as 10 years.
- mean_return = 0.05: sets the average annual return to 5%.
- std_deviation = 0.02: sets the annual standard deviation of returns to 2%.
- simulations = 1_000: defines the number of simulation runs.

Step 3: Run Monte Carlo Simulation

Let's simulate the investment value over 10 years for 1,000 different scenarios.

```
final_values = []

for simulation in range(simulations):
    value = initial_investment
    for year in range(years):
        annual_return = np.random.normal(mean_return, std_deviation)
        value = value * (1 + annual_return)
    final_values.append(value)
```

Explanation

- final_values = [ ]: creates an empty list to store the final values.
- for simulation in range(simulations): repeats the simulation for the set number of runs (i.e. 1000).
- value = initial_investment: assigns the starting amount at the beginning of each run.
  - for year in range(years): iterates through each year in the investment period.
  - annual_return = np.random.normal(mean_return, std_deviation): generates a return from a normal distribution.
  - value = value * (1 + annual_return): updates the value by applying the annual return.
- final_values.append(value): records the value at the end of the investment period.

Step 4: Plot the Results

Let's plot a histogram to show the distribution of final investment values after 10 years.

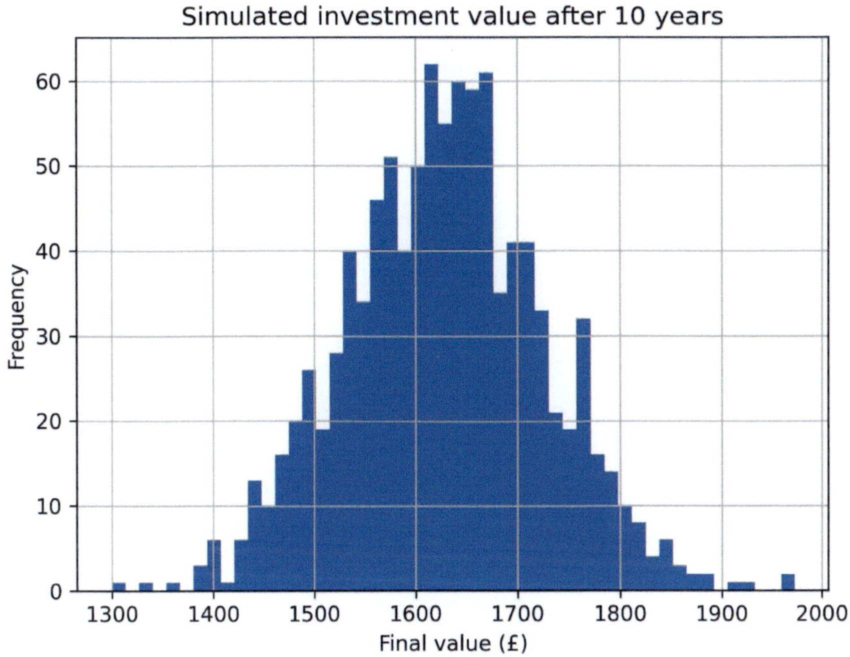

FIGURE 14.11 Simulated Investment Value after 10 Years

```
plt.hist(final_values, bins=50)
plt.title("Simulated investment value after 10 years")
plt.xlabel("Final value (£)")
plt.ylabel("Frequency")
plt.grid(True)
plt.show()
```

Output: see Figure 14.11.

Explanation

- plt.hist(final_values, bins=50): creates a histogram of the final values.
    - bins=50: divides the data into 50 intervals of equal width.
- plt.title("Simulated investment value after 10 years"): sets the title of the chart.
- plt.xlabel("Final value (£)"): labels the x-axis.
- plt.ylabel("Frequency"): labels the y-axis.
- plt.grid(True): displays a grid.
- plt.show(): displays the chart.

The output shows the distribution of final investment values after 10 years across 1,000 simulated scenarios. Most values cluster between £1,600 and £1,700. Values below £1,400 and above £1,850 occur less frequently.

Step 5: Summary Statistics

Let's display key summary statistics from the simulation.

```
mean_value = np.mean(final_values)
percentile_5 = np.percentile(final_values, 5)
percentile_95 = np.percentile(final_values, 95)
loss_probability = np.mean(np.array(final_values) < initial_investment)

print(f"Mean final value: £{mean_value:.2f}")
print(f"5th percentile : £{percentile_5:.2f}")
print(f"95th percentile: £{percentile_95:.2f}")
print(f"Probability of losing money: {loss_probability:.2f}")
```

Output

```
Mean final value: £1628.16
5th percentile : £1471.05
95th percentile: £1785.39
Probability of losing money: 0.000
```

Explanation

- mean_value = np.mean(final_values): calculates the mean of all final investment values.
- percentile_5 = np.percentile(final_values, 5): finds the value below which 5% of the results fall.
- percentile_95 = np.percentile(final_values, 95): finds the value below which 95% of the results fall.
- loss_probability = np.mean(np.array(final_values) < initial_investment): converts the list to a NumPy array, compares each value with the initial investment, and calculates the proportion of results where the final value is lower.
- print(...): prints the results.

The output shows a mean final value of about £1,628 after 10 years, with most values falling between £1,471 (5th percentile) and £1,785 (95th percentile). The distribution is centred above the initial investment of £1,000. The estimated probability of loss is zero under these parameters because the simulation assumes low volatility and normally distributed returns.

In practice, investment returns often show larger fluctuations and heavier tails than a normal distribution. This means real investments carry a non-zero risk of loss even when the long-term expected return is positive.

Step 6: Try It Yourself

Change the input values in Step 2 and observe how the summary statistics and histogram change.

```
# Step 2
initial_investment = 1_000
years = 10
mean_return = 0.05
std_deviation = 0.02
simulations = 1_000
```

Adjust one or more variables and run the simulation. For example increase the number of years, change the mean return, or increase the standard deviation to model greater variability. Compare the updated output with the original results to assess how the changes affect the range, shape, and position of the distribution.

14.3.2.7 Considerations for Practice

Monte Carlo simulation assumes that returns follow stable statistical patterns. In real markets, sudden events and wider return distributions can lead to different results. Always interpret simulated outcomes as estimates rather than guarantees.

14.3.3 Follow-Along Activity B

This activity shows how to estimate the value of a European call option using Monte Carlo simulation. A European call option gives the holder the right, but not the obligation, to purchase an asset at a fixed price (the strike price) on a specified future date. The option has value only if the market price of the asset at expiry exceeds the strike price. If the market price is lower, the option expires with no value. The buyer pays a premium for the potential to gain from a favourable price change, without the obligation to proceed if the outcome is less beneficial (see Figure 14.12).

Let us consider the following scenario: An investor is assessing a European call option on a stock currently priced at £100. The option expires in 1 year and has a strike price of £105. The annual risk-free interest rate is 5%, and the stock's annual volatility is 20%. The simulation will generate 10,000 possible future prices to estimate the option value by averaging the resulting payoffs.

Disclaimer: This content is for educational purposes only. It is intended to demonstrate technical implementation using Python and Monte Carlo simulation. It does not provide financial advice or investment guidance. Readers should seek professional advice before making any financial decisions.

Step 1: Import Libraries

Let's import the necessary libraries for numerical calculations and plotting.

```
import numpy as np
import matplotlib.pyplot as plt
np.random.seed(42)
```

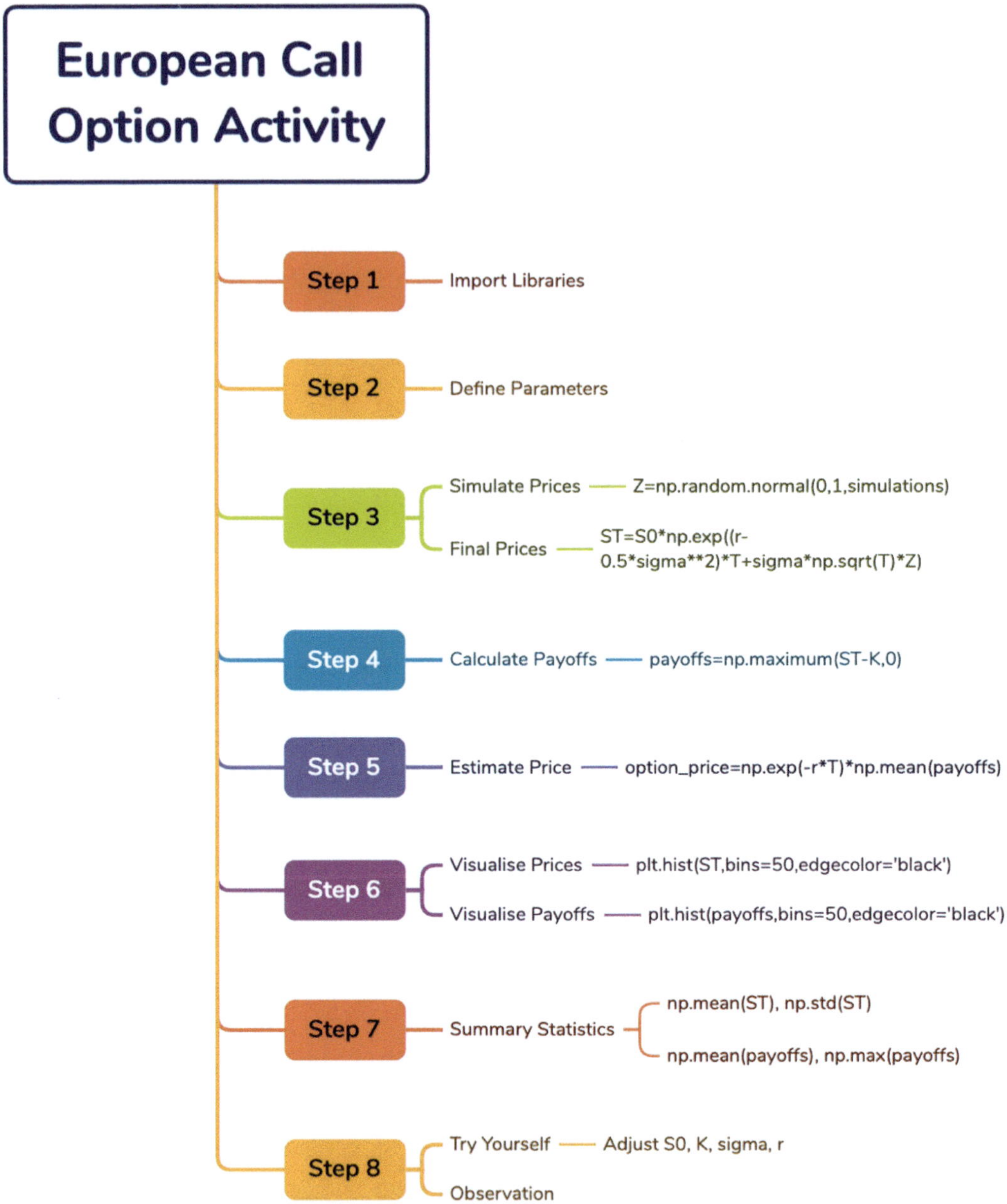

FIGURE 14.12 European Call Option Activity

Explanation

- import numpy as np: imports the NumPy library for numerical operations.
- import matplotlib.pyplot as plt: imports Matplotlib for plotting.
- np.random.seed(42): sets the seed for random number generation to ensure the same results in each run.

Step 2: Define Parameters

Let's define the option and simulation parameters.

```
S0 = 100
K = 105
r = 0.05
sigma = 0.2
T = 1
simulations = 10000
```

Explanation

- S0 = 100: sets the current stock price.
- K = 105: sets the strike price of the option.
- r = 0.05: defines the annual risk-free interest rate.
- sigma = 0.2: sets the annual volatility of the stock.
- T = 1: sets the time to expiry in years.
- simulations = 10000: defines the number of simulation paths.

Step 3: Simulate Final Stock Prices

Let's simulate the stock price at expiry using random sampling under the assumptions of geometric Brownian motion, a model used in financial analysis.

```
Z = np.random.normal(0, 1, simulations)
ST = S0 * np.exp((r - 0.5 * sigma**2) * T + sigma * np.sqrt(T) * Z)
```

Explanation

- Z = np.random.normal(0, 1, simulations): generates random values from a standard normal distribution.
- ST = S0 * np.exp(...): calculates the simulated stock price at expiry for each scenario.

Step 4: Calculate Payoffs

Let's calculate the payoff of the European call option. The payoff is defined as the maximum of zero or the difference between the final stock price and the strike price.

```
payoffs = np.maximum(ST - K, 0)
```

Explanation

- np.maximum(ST - K, 0): calculates the payoff for each simulation. The option is exercised if the stock price at expiry exceeds the strike price.

Step 5: Estimate the Option Price

Let's discount the average payoff to present value using the interest rate (assumed to be risk-free).

```
option_price = np.exp(-r * T) * np.mean(payoffs)
print(f"Estimated European Call Option Price: £{option_price:.2f}")
```

Output

```
Estimated European Call Option Price: £8.02
```

Explanation

- option_price = np.exp(-r * T) * np.mean(payoffs): calculates the present value of the option by applying the discount factor to the average payoff.
  - np.mean(payoffs): calculates the average payoff across all simulations.
- print(...): displays the estimated option price.
- The output shows the estimated price of the European call option based on the simulation. It reflects the average payoff across simulated paths, discounted using the risk-free rate. In this case, the estimated price is £8.02.

Step 6: Visualise the Results

Let's display the distribution of simulated outcomes using two histograms. The first histogram shows the final stock prices at expiry.

```
plt.hist(ST, bins=50, edgecolor='black')
plt.title("Simulated Stock Prices at Expiry")
plt.xlabel("Stock Price (£)")
plt.ylabel("Frequency")
plt.grid(True)
plt.show()
```

Output: see Figure 14.13.

Explanation

- plt.hist(ST, bins=50, edgecolor='black'): plots a histogram of the simulated final stock prices.
- plt.title(...): sets the title of the plot.
- plt.xlabel(...), plt.ylabel(...): label the horizontal and vertical axes.
- plt.grid(True): adds grid lines to the plot.
- plt.show(): displays the plot.

The histogram shows the range of final stock prices from 10,000 simulations. The distribution is right-skewed, with a mean near £105 and a longer right tail.

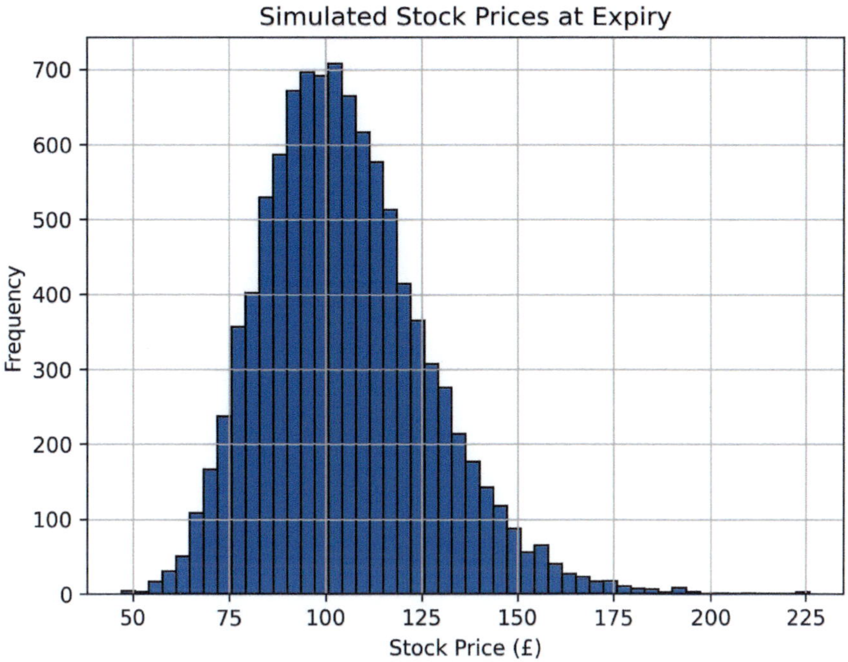

FIGURE 14.13 Simulated Stock Prices at Expiry

The second histogram shows the corresponding option payoffs.

```
plt.hist(payoffs, bins=50, edgecolor='black')
plt.title("Distribution of Option Payoffs")
plt.xlabel("Payoff (£)")
plt.ylabel("Frequency")
plt.grid(True)
plt.show()
```

Output: see Figure 14.14.

Explanation

- plt.hist(ST, bins=50, edgecolor='black'): plots a histogram of the simulated option payoffs.
- The remaining lines follow the same explanation as the previous histogram.

This histogram shows the distribution of payoffs from the European call option. Most simulated payoffs are zero, indicating that in many scenarios, the option expires out of the money. As the payoff amount increases, the frequency declines, resulting in a skewed distribution with a long right tail.

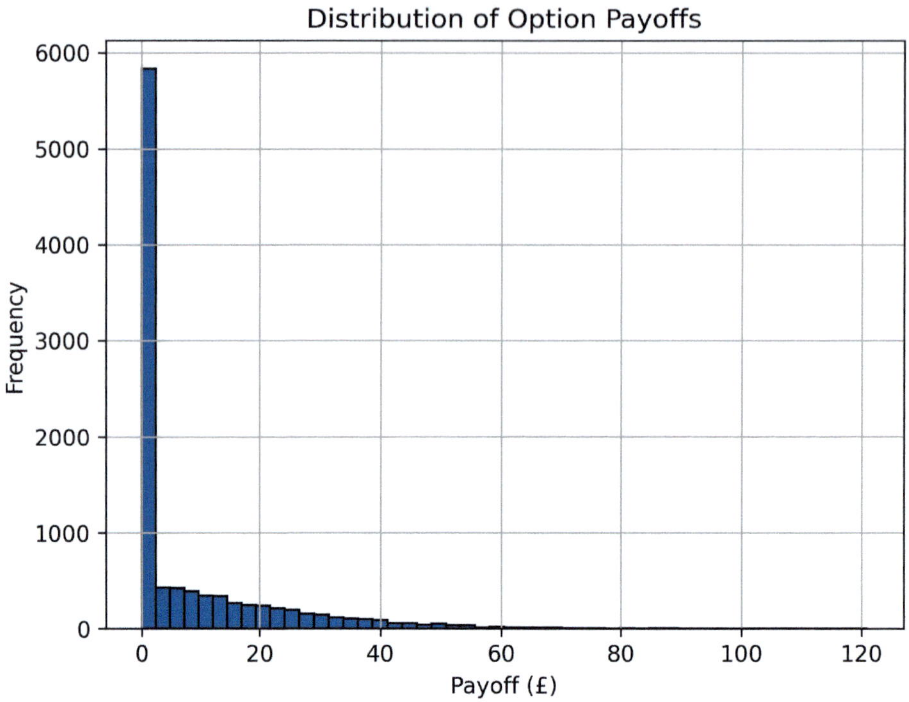

FIGURE 14.14 Distribution of Option Payoffs

Step 7: Summary Statistics

Let's print key statistics from the simulation results.

```
print("----- Summary Statistics -----")
print(f"Mean final stock price: £{np.mean(ST):.2f}")
print(f"Standard deviation of stock prices: £{np.std(ST):.2f}")
print(f"Mean payoff: £{np.mean(payoffs):.2f}")
print(f"Probability of positive payoff: {np.mean(payoffs > 0):.2f}")
print(f"Maximum payoff: £{np.max(payoffs):.2f}")
print(f"Minimum payoff: £{np.min(payoffs):.2f}")
```

Output

```
----- Summary Statistics -----
Mean final stock price: £105.10
Standard deviation of stock prices: £21.32
Mean payoff: £8.44
Probability of positive payoff: 0.46
Maximum payoff: £120.97
Minimum payoff: £0.00
```

Explanation

- np.mean(ST): calculates the average final stock price across simulations.
- np.std(ST): calculates the standard deviation of the final stock prices.
- np.mean(payoffs): calculates the average option payoff.
- np.mean(payoffs > 0): estimates the proportion of simulations with a positive payoff.
- np.max(payoffs): identifies the highest payoff value observed.
- np.min(payoffs): identifies the lowest payoff value observed.

The statistics show that the average final stock price after 1 year is £105.10, with a standard deviation of £21.32. The average payoff from the option is £8.44. A positive payoff occurs in 46% of the simulations, where the stock price exceeds the strike price. The maximum observed payoff is £120.97, and the minimum is £0.00.

Step 8: Try It Yourself

Change the input values in **Step 2** and observe how the summary statistics and histograms change.

```
# Step 2
S0 = 100
K = 105
r = 0.05
sigma = 0.2
T = 1
simulations = 10000
```

Adjust one or more variables and run the simulation. For example change the initial stock price and strike price, or increase the number of simulations. Compare the resulting option price, the distribution of stock prices, and the payoff histogram to the original results.

14.3.3.9 Considerations for Practice

Monte Carlo models for option pricing depend on assumptions about volatility and interest rates. In practice, these factors change over time, and valuation requires calibration to current market data.

Scan the QR code to access the Python code and output (see 14.3.ipynb).

https://github.com/DrMichaelGuo/PFAAFAMMA

Summary of Chapter 14: Advanced Machine Learning and Financial Modelling

In this chapter, we have covered the following concepts:

Neural Networks

- Neural networks are machine learning models used to detect patterns and make predictions.
- Structure consists of input, hidden, and output layers, with weights adjusted during training.
- Key Python libraries include scikit-learn for preprocessing and evaluation and TensorFlow Keras for building and training models.
- The process involves data preparation, scaling, model definition, compilation, training, visualisation, and evaluation.
- An example application is predicting creditworthiness using income, debt-to-income ratio, and credit history.

Algorithmic Trading

- Algorithmic trading automates buy and sell decisions using predefined rules and market data.
- An example uses the RSI and logistic regression to predict next-day price movement.
- The process involves downloading historical data, computing indicators, creating target variables, training the model, and simulating trading performance.

Monte Carlo Simulation

- Monte Carlo simulation models uncertainty through repeated random sampling.
- Applications include forecasting investment values and pricing options.
- The investment example involves simulating long-term returns with varying growth rates and volatility.
- The option pricing example involves simulating future stock prices using geometric Brownian motion and calculating the call option value.
- Summary statistics and histograms are used to interpret probabilities and potential outcomes.

Quiz Questions

Scan the QR code below to access the quiz questions for this chapter (see 14.md).

https://github.com/DrMichaelGuo/QuizPFAAFAMMA

Further Reading and Resources

Hunter, J., Dale, D., Firing, E., Droettboom, M. and The Matplotlib Development Team (2025) *Matplotlib 3.10.5 documentation*. Available at: https://matplotlib.org/stable/index.html (Accessed 7 August 2025).

Pandas Development Team (2025) *pandas documentation (version 2.3.1)*. Available at: https://pandas.pydata.org/docs/ (Accessed 7 August 2025).

scikit-learn (2024) *scikit-learn: Machine Learning in Python*. Available at: https://scikit-learn.org/stable/documentation.html (Accessed 7 August 2025).

TensorFlow (no date) *Keras: The high-level API for TensorFlow*. Available at: https://www.tensorflow.org/guide/keras (Accessed 11 August 2025).

INDEX